GRAMMAR AND

Routledge Applied Linguistics is a series of comprehensive resource books providing students and researchers with the support they need for advanced study in the core areas of English Language and Applied Linguistics.

Each book in the series guides readers through three main sections, enabling them to explore and develop major themes within the discipline:

- Section A, Introduction, establishes the key terms and concepts and extends readers' techniques of analysis through practical application.
- Section B, Extension, brings together influential articles, sets them in context, and discusses their contribution to the field.
- Section C, Exploration, builds on knowledge gained in the first two sections, setting thoughtful tasks around further illustrative material. This enables readers to engage more actively with the subject matter and encourages them to develop their own research responses.

Throughout the book, topics are revisited, extended, interwoven and deconstructed, with the readers' understanding strengthened by tasks and follow-up questions.

*Grammar and Context*:

- considers how grammatical choices influence and are influenced by the context in which communication takes place
- examines the interaction of a wide variety of contexts – including socio-cultural, situational and global influences – with a range of different types of grammar – functional, pedagogic, descriptive and prescriptive
- explores grammatical features in a lively variety of communicative contexts, such as advertising, dinner-table talk, email and political speeches
- gathers together influential readings from key names in the discipline, including David Crystal, M.A.K. Halliday, Joanna Thornborrow, Ken Hyland and Stephen Levey

Written by experienced teachers and researchers in the field, *Grammar and Context* is an essential resource for students and researchers of Applied Linguistics.

**Ann Hewings** is a senior lecturer in the Centre for Language and Communications at the Open University in the UK. **Martin Hewings** is a senior lecturer in the English for the International Students Unit at the University of Birmingham, UK.

# ROUTLEDGE APPLIED LINGUISTICS

## SERIES EDITORS

**Christopher N. Candlin** is Senior Research Professor in the Department of Linguistics at Macquarie University, Australia and Professor of Applied Linguistics at the Open University, UK. At Macquarie, he has been Chair of the Department of Linguistics; established and was Executive Director of the National Centre for English Language Teaching and Research (NCELTR); and was foundation Director of the Centre for Language in Social Life (CLSL). He has written or edited over 150 publications and from 2004 will co-edit the new *Journal of Applied Linguistics*. From 1996 to 2002 he was President of the International Association of Applied Linguistics (AILA). He has acted as a consultant in more than 35 countries and as external faculty assessor in 36 universities worldwide.

**Ronald Carter** is Professor of Modern English Language in the School of English Studies at the University of Nottingham. He has published extensively in applied linguistics, literary studies and language in education, and has written or edited over 40 books and 100 articles in these fields. He has given consultancies in the field of English language education, mainly in conjunction with the British Council, in over 30 countries worldwide, and is editor of the Routledge Interface series and advisory editor to the Routledge English Language Introduction series. He was recently elected a Fellow of the British Academy for Social Sciences and is currently UK Government Advisor for ESOL and Chair of the British Association for Applied Linguistics (BAAL).

## TITLES IN THE SERIES

*Intercultural Communication: An advanced resource book*
Adrian Holliday, Martin Hyde and John Kullman, Canterbury Christ Church University College, UK

*Translation: An advanced resource book*
Basil Hatim, Heriot-Watt University, UK and The American University of Sharjah, UAE and Jeremy Munday, University of Surrey, Guildford, UK

*Grammar and Context: An advanced resource book*
Ann Hewings, Open University, UK and Martin Hewings, University of Birmingham, UK

# Grammar and Context

## An Advanced Resource Book

Ann Hewings and Martin Hewings

Routledge
Taylor & Francis Group

LONDON AND NEW YORK

First published 2005
by Routledge
2 Park Square, Milton Park, Abingdon, Oxon OX14 4RN

Simultaneously published in the USA and Canada
by Routledge
270 Madison Ave, New York, NY 10016

Routledge is an imprint of the Taylor & Francis Group

Designed and typeset in Akzidenz Grotesk, Minion and Novarese
by Keystroke, Jacaranda Lodge, Wolverhampton
Printed and bound in Great Britain
by TJ International Ltd, Padstow, Cornwall

*British Library Cataloguing in Publication Data*
A catalogue record for this book is available from the British Library

*Library of Congress Cataloging in Publication Data*
A catalog record for this book has been requested

ISBN 0–415–31080–6 (hbk)
ISBN 0–415–31081–4 (pbk)

# Contents

Contents

Contents

# Contents cross-referenced

## Section B: Extension

## Section C: Exploration

# Series Editors' Preface

This series provides a comprehensive guide to a number of key areas in the field of applied linguistics. Applied linguistics is a rich, vibrant, diverse and essentially interdisciplinary field. It is now more important than ever that books in the field provide up-to-date maps of ever changing territory.

The books in this series are designed to give key insights into core areas. The design of the books ensures, through key readings, that the history and development of a subject is recognised while, through key questions and tasks, integrating understandings of the topics, concepts and practices that make up its essentially interdisciplinary fabric. The pedagogic structure of each book ensures that readers are given opportunities to think, discuss, engage in tasks, draw on their own experience, reflect, research and to read and critically re-read key documents.

Each book has three main sections, each made up of approximately ten units:

A:  An **Introduction** section: in which the key terms and concepts are introduced, including introductory activities and reflective tasks, designed to establish key understandings, terminology, techniques of analysis and the skills appropriate to the theme and the discipline.

B:  An **Extension** section: in which selected core readings are introduced (usually edited from the original) from existing books and articles, together with annotations and commentary, where appropriate. Each reading is introduced, annotated and commented on in the context of the whole book, and research/follow-up questions and tasks are added to enable fuller understanding of both theory and practice. In some cases, readings are short and synoptic and incorporated within a more general exposition.

C:  An **Exploration** section: in which further samples and illustrative materials are provided with an emphasis, where appropriate, on more open-ended, student-centred activities and tasks, designed to support readers and users in undertaking their own locally relevant research projects. Tasks are designed for work in groups or for individuals working on their own.

The books also contain a glossary or glossarial index and a detailed, thematically organised A–Z guide to the main terms used in the book and which lays the ground for further work in the discipline. There are also annotated guides to further reading and extensive bibliographies.

The target audience for the series is upper undergraduates and postgraduates on language, applied linguistics and communication studies programmes as well as teachers and researchers in professional development and distance learning programmes. High-quality applied research resources are also much needed for teachers of EFL/ESL and foreign language students at higher education colleges and universities worldwide. The books in the Routledge Applied Linguistics series are aimed at the individual reader, the student in a group and at teachers building courses and seminar programmes.

We hope that the books in this series meet these needs and continue to provide support over many years.

## The Editors

Professor Christopher N. Candlin and Professor Ronald Carter are the series editors. Both have extensive experience of publishing titles in the fields relevant to this series. Between them they have written and edited over one hundred books and two hundred academic papers in the broad field of applied linguistics. Chris Candlin was president of AILA (International Association for Applied Linguistics) from 1997–2003 and Ron Carter is Chair of BAAL (British Association for Applied Linguistics) from 2003–2006.

Professor Christopher N. Candlin
Senior Research Professor
Department of Linguistics
Division of Linguistics and Psychology
Macquarie University
Sydney NSW 2109
Australia

and

Professor of Applied Linguistics
Faculty of Education and Language Studies
The Open University
Walton Hall
Milton Keynes MK7 6AA
UK

Professor Ronald Carter
School of English Studies
University of Nottingham
Nottingham NG7 2RD
UK

# Acknowledgements

We begin by thanking our series editors Ron Carter and Chris Candlin for giving us the opportunity to write this book and for their advice and encouragement. At Routledge, thanks to Louisa Semlyen, Christy Kirkpatrick, Ruth Bourne, Kate Parker, Ruth Jeavons and Rosemary Morlin for their support at various stages in the writing process.

A number of people have kindly given us permission to include their research data in Section C. For this we wish to thank Kristie Collins, Jane Cullen, Koo-Cheah Swit Ling, Helen Sauntson, Martin Warren and Steve Thorne. Steve Thorne's transcriptions of speakers from Birmingham came originally from Birmingham-Lives SBC Digbeth (the Carl Chinn Archive), and we wish to thank Carl Chinn for permission to include them here.

Many others have provided original data and other information, or have commented on sections of the book. We wish to thank Hajime Fukuda, Suzanne Hewings, David Hewings, Susan Hunston, Miki Ishitani, Catherine Kay, Chris Kennedy, Tetsuya Ooba, Louise Ravelli, Nick Richens, Taeko Takahashi and Geoff Thompson.

We are grateful to the copyright holders of the following texts for permission to reproduce extracts in Section B:

P. Allison, R. Beard and J. Willcocks, 'Subordination in children's writing', from *Language and Education*, vol. 16, no. 2 (2002), copyright © 2002 P Allison *et al.*, reprinted by permission of Multilingual Matters.

B. Bernstein, *Class, Codes and Control*, vol. 1, *Theoretical Studies Towards a Sociology of Language*, Routledge & Kegan Paul, 1971, reprinted by permission of Taylor & Francis.

D. Biber *et al.*, *The Longman Grammar of Spoken and Written English*, Pearson, 1999, reprinted by permission of Pearson Education Ltd.

R. Carter and M. McCarthy, 'Grammar and the spoken language', from *Applied Linguistics*, vol. 16, no. 2 (June 1995), copyright © Oxford University Press 1995, reprinted by permission of Oxford University Press.

M. Collot and N. Belmore, 'Electronic Language: A new variety of English', from *Computer-Mediated Communication: Linguistic, Social and Cross-Cultural Perspectives* by S. Herring (ed.), copyright © 1996 John Benjamins BV, reprinted by permission of John Benjamins Publishing Company.

D. Crystal, *Language and the Internet*, Cambridge University Press, 2001.

G. Ferguson, 'If you pop over there: a corpus-based study of conditionals in medical discourse' from *English for Specific Purposes*, 20 (2001), copyright © 2001 The American University, published by Elsevier Science Ltd, reprinted with permission from Elsevier.

S. Gramley and K.-M. Pätzold, *A Survey of Modern English*, Routledge, 1992, reprinted by permission of Taylor & Francis.

M.A.K. Halliday, 'Some grammatical problems in scientific English' from *Writing Science: Literacy and Discursive Power*, by M.A.K. Halliday and J. R. Martin (eds.), Falmer Press, 1993, reprinted by permission of Taylor & Francis.

J. Holmes, *An Introduction to Sociolinguistics*, second edition. Longman, 2001, reprinted by permission of Pearson Education Ltd.

K. Hyland, 'Directives: Argument and engagement in academic writing', from *Applied Linguistics*, vol. 23, no. 2 (June 2002), copyright © Oxford University Press 2002, reprinted by permission of Oxford University Press.

S. Levey, 'Relative clauses and register expansion in Tok Pisin', from *World Englishes*, vol. 20, no. 3, copyright © Blackwell Publishers Ltd. 2001.

S. Levey, 'He's like "Do it now!" and I'm like "No!"', from *English Today*, 73, vol. 19, no. 1 (January 2003), copyright © 2003 Cambridge University Press, reprinted with permission.

R. Macaulay, 'Extremely interesting, very interesting, or only quite interesting? Adverbs and social class' from *Journal of Sociolinguistics*, vol. 6, no. 3, copyright © Blackwell Publishers Ltd 2002, reprinted with permission.

C. Marley, 'Popping the question: questions and modality in written dating advertisements' from *Discourse Studies*, vol. 4, no. 1 (February 2002), copyright © 2002 Sage Publications, reprinted by permission of Sage Publications Ltd.

P. Master, 'The effect of systematic instruction on learning the English article system', from *Perspectives on Pedagogical Grammar*, by Odlin, T. (ed.), copyright © 1994 Cambridge University Press.

M. Newbrook, 'Which way? That way? Variation and ongoing changes in the English relative clause' from *World Englishes*, vol. 17, no. 1, copyright © Blackwell Publishers Ltd. 1998.

C. Painter, 'The development of language as a resource for learning', from *Applying English Grammar*, Arnold with Open University Press, 2004.

P. Simpson, *Language, Ideology and Point of View*, Routledge, 1993, copyright © 1993 Paul Simpson, reprinted by permission of Taylor & Francis.

J. Thornborrow, *Power Talk: Language and Interaction in Institutional Discourse*, Longman, 2002.

G. Tottie, *Negation in English Speech and Writing*, pp. 42 to 43, copyright © 1991 by Academic Press Inc., reprinted with permission from Elsevier.

For extracts from The Indian Component of the International Corpus of English, we wish to thank the ICE–IND Corpus, Shivaji University, Kolhapur and the Frei Universität, Berlin.

Examples quoted from The British National Corpus (http://www.natcorp.ox.ac.uk) are the copyright of the original rights holders, and used by permission of the BNC Consortium. Thanks to Lou Burnard for helping us gain access to this material.

For permission to include the figure on page 43, thanks to Catherine Nickerson and Eric van Broekhuizen at Rodopi Publishers.

And a special 'Thank you' to David and Suzanne for their constant good humoured tolerance of 'book talk'.

Every effort has been made to trace the copyright holders, but if any have been inadvertently overlooked the publishers will be pleased to make the necessary arrangement at the first opportunity.

# How to use this book

A commonly held view of grammar is that it is a rather dull topic, something that must be mastered in order to understand better our first language or learn another language. One of the aims of this book is to put the case that grammar is a fascinating area of study and at the heart of our ability to communicate with one another. The ease with which most of us are able to exchange information, social pleasantries and get things done is a reflection of our ability to control grammatical choices in our dealings with people, whether face to face, in writing or on the telephone. The choices we make are influenced not only by the message we want to convey but also by factors such as who we are talking to, the purpose of the communication and the formality of the situation; that is, the context in which we are using the language. Most of us are aware that we use different words in different contexts, but are less sensitised to the differences in how we put the words together – how the grammar of speech and writing is affected by context and how grammar in turn shapes that context as an interaction continues.

*Grammar and Context* is a book designed to illustrate the relationships between grammatical choices and the contexts in which they are made. It is not a book that will teach you how to conduct a detailed grammatical analysis, but it will introduce the growing amount of research that is opening up new views on how grammar functions in communication. You will have the opportunity to read about, reflect on and explore grammar used in a wide range of contexts. So, for example, you will learn about grammar in electronic communication, in workplace and institutional settings, in language acquisition, in different social, cultural, gender and age groups, and also about differences between spoken and written grammar.

Our approach to studying the relationships between grammar and context will be particularly relevant for students of applied linguistics or English language at final year undergraduate or postgraduate level. Students of media or communications will also find much that is of interest. We assume some basic knowledge of grammatical concepts and terminology, but anything beyond this is explained and illustrated so that the material should be easily accessible to most readers. For additional support we have included a glossary of grammatical terms. While our focus is very much on the grammar of English, much of what is included in *Grammar and Context* will have more general relevance to other languages.

The book is divided into three sections. *A: Introduction* consists of nine units dealing with the central concepts of grammar and context. It contains activities for you to carry out alone or with others if you are studying this book as part of a course. *B: Extension* provides a number of extracts from articles and books relating to grammar and context which give you further insights into the concepts introduced in Section A. Each extract in *B: Extension* is preceded and followed by activities to focus your reading and then help you to evaluate critically what you have read and understand how it links to a wider discussion of grammar and context. *C: Exploration* builds on the material you will already have found in the book. In this section you are encouraged to become active researchers of the language. Each unit provides structured opportunities for analysis of authentic data, with feedback, and then additional data is provided for further analysis by individuals or groups. Finally, suggestions are given for research projects including ways of finding and collecting suitable data. You will find more information about how each section is organised in the section introductions.

The organisation of this book means that you can concentrate on particular themes such as *Grammar in conversation* or *Grammar and gender* by reading the relevant units from *B: Extension* and *C: Exploration* consecutively. However, we recommend that you read the whole of *A: Introduction* before embarking on Sections B and C as it provides important foundation material. There is extensive cross-referencing throughout the book to help you to find your way around. At the end of the book there is a *Further reading* section relating to each unit. In addition to the book itself, there is also a website (http://routledge.tandf.co.uk/textbooks/0415310814) in which we will indicate additional reading or other relevant information to keep you up to date on how grammar and context are being researched.

# SECTION A
## Introduction

The view we take in this book is that grammatical choices in speech and writing are made in response to the opportunities and constraints provided by the context in which they occur, and in turn contribute to context. By observing grammatical variations in different contexts we can learn more about those contexts and, conversely, by studying relevant features of context we can learn about their influence on grammar.

Section A is designed to introduce you to the concepts central to an investigation of how grammar and context are interrelated. It is divided into nine units dealing with different aspects of either grammar or context or with the relationship between them. Each unit contains explanations and discussion of important questions such as 'What do we mean by grammar?', 'What is context?' and 'How do transitivity choices influence our view of the world?'. The units also contain activities which we have labelled 'Tasks'. These generally appear at points at which we would like you to stop reading and either consider the points that have been made – whether you agree with them, whether they apply to your own use of English – or to undertake a short task. If you are working with others, some of this material can be used for discussion. A number of these items are also ways of getting you to think about something before we discuss it in the book – they are like mini brainstorming activities to help you bring to mind what you already know about a topic. After a 'Task' there is often a response, but we hope that you will stop and carry out the activity before you read on.

In this section we will refer to some of the people who have been influential in thinking about and researching grammar and context. But there are many other people that we do not have the space to mention by name. Those who have written books or articles that can help you explore issues further will be indicated in the Further reading section at the end of the book.

Section A is designed to set the scene for you to read examples of research into grammar and context in Section B and to undertake your own explorations and analyses in Section C. We have therefore provided a brief 'Looking ahead' paragraph at the end of each unit. This will indicate where the ideas discussed in each unit are explored in more detail later in the book, although many of the ideas will be referred to in passing in other places.

We assume that before working with this book you have already undertaken some study of English grammar, although different readers will have very different experiences. Perhaps you have formally studied a particular way of analysing language, and done a course on, for example, transformational-generative or systemic functional grammar; or you may just have picked up what you know during your study of English as your first or second language. One of the difficulties in talking about grammar is that different approaches have radically different views of what grammar means, and what a grammatical description is designed to uncover, and so they may use very different terminology and methods of analysis. Consequently, the word 'grammar' will have different connotations for different readers. With this in mind, Unit A1 will explore some fundamental ideas about grammar. The aim is to prepare the ground so that all readers, whatever their previous experience, will have sufficient background understanding to make sense of what follows in the discussions in later parts of Section A, the readings in Section B and the analytical activities in Section C.

# Unit A1
# Grammar, grammars and grammaticality

## A1.1  GETTING STARTED

By way of introduction to this unit, look at the following sentences. How many meanings of the word 'grammar' can you identify?

a.  It's a really complicated area of grammar.
b.  Why don't you look it up in a grammar?
c.  Her spelling is good, but her grammar is almost non-existent.
d.  Children don't do enough grammar at school.
e.  We had to do generative grammar on the course.
f.  He needs to work on his grammar and punctuation.
g.  Systemic grammar is generally associated with the work of M.A.K. Halliday.
h.  I've always had problems with German grammar.
i.  It's a grammar for learners of English as a foreign language.
j.  Oh, no, we're doing grammar again today.

While there is clearly overlap in the meanings intended by the word 'grammar', we suggest that:

- In a and h, it refers to the way in which words are organised in a language in order to make correct sentences. We discuss this view of grammar in A1.2 below under the heading 'Grammatical description'.
- In b and i, it refers to a book in which these organising principles are laid out. Sometimes these are given as a set of rules. We discuss 'grammars' in A1.3.
- In c and f, it refers to whether a person follows rules of grammar. We discuss 'Grammaticality' in A1.4.
- In d and j, it refers to the study of these rules. In A1.4 we consider the reasons for undertaking such a study under 'Why study grammar and context?'
- In e and g, it refers to a particular theory of language description. We return to the main theories, focusing especially on how they approach the relationship between grammar and context, in Unit A5.

## A1.2 GRAMMATICAL DESCRIPTION

A description of the grammar of a language gives an account of the sentence structures that are possible in that language. In essence, it will identify certain grammatical units smaller than the sentence and give rules to explain how these are combined to make sentences. The smallest unit of grammar is generally taken to be the word, but we clearly need to categorise words into higher-level units in order to offer a description that is anything other than a (hugely long!) list of possible word combinations. Many grammatical descriptions present a hierarchy of units, in which a **sentence** (at the top of the hierarchy) consists of one or more **clauses**, which consist of one or more **phrases**, which consist of one or more **words**. There are various ways of representing such a hierarchy; for example, in the form of a tree diagram:

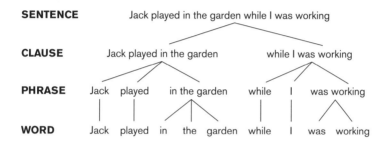

Each type of unit can be categorised and labelled, and the labels tell us something about the potential the units have for appearing in higher-level units. Words are typically grouped using word class labels such as **noun**, **verb**, **adjective**, **adverb**, **preposition**, **determiner** and **conjunction**; phrases can be categorised according to their central component (sometimes referred to as the **head**) into **noun phrases** (e.g. *music, David's guitar*), **verb phrases** (e.g. *has looked, might have been eaten*), **adjective phrases** (e.g. *very angry, too late for dinner*), **adverb phrases** (e.g. *extremely slowly, slowly enough to be seen by the naked eye*), and **prepositional phrases** (e.g. *at midday, outside the house*); and clauses can be divided into **main** (or **independent**) and **subordinate** (or **dependent**). So an analysis of the same sentence, using such labels would be:

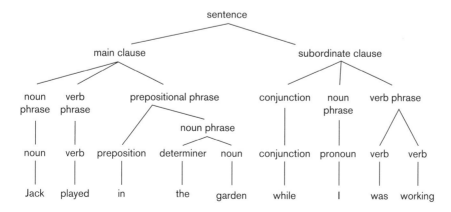

The components of phrases may themselves be phrases or clauses, and the components of clauses may themselves be clauses. This feature of the hierarchical approach is known as **embedding** (or sometimes **nesting**). For example, the prepositional phrase 'at the bottom of the garden' has the prepositional phrase 'of the garden' embedded within it, and 'The boy who was playing football is called Jack' can be said to have the clause 'who was playing football' embedded within it.

The kind of grammatical description presented so far identifies units according to form (for example, a noun phrase is identified on the basis that it has a noun as its central component). Many grammatical descriptions go on to categorise the elements of clauses according to their grammatical function, using labels such as **subject, verb, object, complement** and **adverbial**, as in:

| Subject | Verb | Adverbial | | | [Clause link] | Subject | Verb | |
|---|---|---|---|---|---|---|---|---|
| Jack | played | in | the | garden | while | I | was | working. |

| Adverbial | Subject | Verb | Object | | Complement |
|---|---|---|---|---|---|
| Actually, | I | thought | her | work | remarkable. |

There is often – but not always – a correspondence between certain grammatical units and elements having particular grammatical functions. For example, the verb element is always realised by a verb phrase; the subject element is usually realised by a noun phrase but may be realised by a clause (e.g. *What I want to know* is where he gets his money from); an adverbial is often realised by an adverb phrase but may be realised by a noun phrase (e.g. She slept *all day*), prepositional phrase (e.g. She went out *in the evening*) or clause (e.g. She went to bed *feeling rather ill*).

What we have presented is the barest outline of some principles that underpin most approaches to grammatical description. We will see, however, in Unit A5 that not all approaches adopt these principles, and that there is considerable variety in the grammatical descriptions that are produced and in the terminology used even when such principles are adopted.

 **Task A1.2.1**

➤ Consider what approach or approaches to grammar and associated terminology you are familiar with. Have a look at any grammar books that you use in language study or foreign language learning.

➤ Examine the similarities and differences that exist between the approaches to grammar adopted in them and the approach we have outlined.

We have assumed – along with most grammatical descriptions – that the sentence is the unit we are trying to analyse on the basis that it is the largest unit of grammar. However, there are a number of difficulties with this. One is that in unprepared speech, such as most conversation, we do not speak in well-formed sentences. If we take a transcription of spoken language such as the following extract from a dinner-table conversation, uttered by a single speaker, it would be difficult to consistently insert sentence-final punctuation marks (full stops, question marks, or exclamation marks):

(1) . . . and he set off this chap he was a schoolteacher in I think it was Denver he started from uh he he I don't know whether he got the sack from his job but anyway he's got he decided he he he he'd got a year off and he decided to get his ol– get his old uh he had a an old van that he rigged up with a bed in the back you know . . .

(Cullen 1996: 272)

In conversation, then, the sentence seems to be problematic as the fundamental grammatical unit. In written text, too, there may be difficulties. Electronic texts, such as email and text messages, are often written without the punctuation conventions associated with 'well-formed' writing, including the capital letters and full stops which mark sentence start and finish. Here are two examples to illustrate, the first an email and the second a text message:

(2) yes just to emphasize what [name] said about vacation essays – we missed our deadlines a bit on the last lot (those that didn't I'll buy you a drink! – claims in by Monday pse) so it'd be nice to get this lot in on time

best

(3) yep that will be fine . . . see u there . . . whats ur phone number again and ill mobile u on the way up

In response to difficulties such as these, some grammatical descriptions reject the sentence as the main unit of analysis and focus instead on the clause, usually defined as a group of words having a central (and necessary) verb together with any associated subject, object(s), complement(s) and adverbial(s). Although complications exist (such as the need to recognise 'verbless' clauses [e.g. He lay on his back, *feet in the air*]), definition of the clause certainly seems to be less problematic than definition of the sentence. Clauses are often classified according to **mood** as follows:

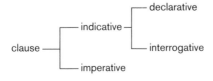

In an **imperative** clause, English uses the base form of the verb, without a subject. Imperatives are typically used to express an instruction or command (e.g. *Wash hands well after use; Turn left*). **Indicative** clauses are used to exchange information in either **declaratives**, typically expressing a statement (e.g. *I'm on my way*), or **interrogatives**, typically expressing a question (e.g. *What do you want?; Are you lost?*).

However, there remains the problem, particularly in conversation, of how to classify material that is not associated with the clause. One solution is offered by the authors of the *Longman Grammar of Spoken and Written English* (Biber *et al.* 1999). They distinguish between **clausal units** and **non-clausal units**. A clausal unit is defined as a structure 'consisting of an independent clause together with any dependent clauses embedded within it' (p. 1069), while a non-clausal unit 'cannot be analysed in terms of clause structure, and . . . is not analysable as part of any neighbouring clause' (p. 224). In the following extract from their conversational data (p. 1070), non-clausal units are indicated in bold and the boundaries of clausal and non-clausal units marked with ||:

(4)  *B:*  ||So this was your mother's? ||
     *A:*  ||**No**, ||**my father's.** ||
     *B:*  ||**Your father's mother?** ||
     *A:*  ||**Yeah.** ||Her name was Martha <name>||
     *B:*  ||**Uh huh.** ||

Non-clausal material is found particularly in conversation (although it is often also found in writing in, for example, newspaper headlines, book titles, lists and advertisements) and its existence is one important reason why traditional grammatical descriptions are now generally considered to be inadequate for spontaneous speech.

Grammatical descriptions vary in how far they attempt to relate grammatical forms to meaning, and a division is sometimes made between **structural** (or **formal**) descriptions and **functional** descriptions. Structural grammatical descriptions are primarily concerned with accounting for all the possible forms of a language, and distinguishing these from forms which are not possible. For example, they might account for the fact that 'He advised me to give up smoking' is correct, but 'He advised me giving up smoking' is not. Functional grammatical descriptions are concerned more with the difference in meaning that is conveyed in using one grammatical form rather than another. For example, they might account for the distinction implied in the use of one verb tense over another, as in 'Jemma is learning to drive' and 'Jemma has learnt to drive.'

Grammatical descriptions also vary in how far they take contextual considerations into account. One of the aims of this book is to demonstrate that in a certain context an utterance may express a meaning that is not contained solely in the sentence itself but derives from the interplay between grammar and context. Depending on context, the sentences 'Jemma is learning to drive' and 'Jemma has learnt to drive' might express warning (she'll be an awful driver!), surprise (she's too old!), admiration (after her long illness . . .), and so on, in addition to the conventional meanings of 'continuation' and 'completion' conveyed by the use of the present continuous and present perfect.

Functional grammatical descriptions often use a set of terminology which focuses less on formal features, and more on the role of grammatical components in communication. Examples from one of the best-known functional descriptions, Systemic Functional Linguistics (see Unit A5), include **actor** ('the constituent of the clause who does the deed or performs the action'), **goal** (the participant 'at whom the process is directed and to whom the action is extended'), **recipient** (the participant 'to whom something is given') and **client** (the participant 'for whom something is done') (Eggins 1994). For example, in the sentence *He made the cakes for his grandchildren*, *He* is actor, *the cakes* goal, and *his grandchildren* client.

We return to a number of the points made here in A5.

## A1.3 GRAMMARS AND GRAMMATICALITY

We began A1.2 by saying that a grammatical description sets out to describe what sentences (or clauses) are possible in a language. This implies that there is a set of criteria against which a judgement of them can be made as either 'possible' or 'impossible' (or even 'perhaps possible'!): 'possible' sentences conform to rules of grammar that are based on a particular grammatical theory. A distinction is sometimes made between **prescriptive** and **descriptive** grammars, which differ in how the judgement of what is possible is made.

The authors of prescriptive grammars generally set themselves as the arbiters of correctness and on the basis of their judgement tell readers how language should be used. For example, the influential *A Short History of English Grammar* by Robert Lowth, first published in 1762, instructs readers as follows (p. 116):

"It is not *me* you are in love with." Spect. No 290

The Preposition *with* should govern the Relative *whom* understood, not the Antecedent *me*; which ought to be *I*."

While some school grammars and grammars written for learners of English as a foreign or second language (often called **pedagogical** grammars) remain prescriptive, information about 'correct' grammar for adult native speakers of English now appears largely in style or usage guides rather than grammars. For example, here is some advice on preposition usage from a guide to writing skills called *Plain English*:

English is particularly rich in prepositions. Judiciously used, they help to give our thoughts precise expression. Make sure you use the correct preposition. Here are some examples of correct and incorrect uses.

> It seemed *like* the whole country was on holiday. (incorrect)
> It seemed *as if* the whole country was on holiday. (correct)
> I am different *than* my sister. (incorrect)
> I am different *from* my sister. (correct)
> I have been suffering *with* bronchitis this winter. (incorrect)
> I have been suffering *from* bronchitis this winter. (correct)
>
> (Collinson, *et al.* 1992: 56)

A major problem in adopting a prescriptive approach to grammar is that the notion of 'correctness' can be hard to pin down: people disagree about what is correct and, because language changes over time, so does grammatical usage.

 **Task A1.3.1**

In the 1960s a survey was conducted in Britain 'to discover the nature and extent of agreement and of disagreement over certain [debatable usages] in English' (Mittins *et al.* 1970). Nearly 500 people were surveyed, mainly teachers, examiners, trainee teachers and lecturers. They were asked to decide whether a particular part of a sentence (italicised in the examples below) was acceptable or not in four contexts: informal speech, informal writing, formal speech and formal writing. Here are ten of the fifty-five items that focused on grammatical usage:

a.  He is older than *me.*
b.  He is in London, but his family *are* in Bournemouth.
c.  The performance ended early, *due to* illness among the players.
d.  There were *less* road accidents this Christmas than last.
e.  Competitors should try *and* arrive in good time.
f.  The process is *very unique.*
g.  We *have got* to finish the job.
h.  He *only had* one chapter to finish.
i.  They would accept this if it *was* offered.
j.  He did it *quicker* than he had ever done it before.

While most respondents considered that these were more acceptable in informal than formal contexts, overall some were judged to be more acceptable than others.

➤ Decide how you would rank these ten sentences, starting from 1 = 'most acceptable' to 10 = 'least acceptable'? (If you are working in a group, you may want to work out an average ranking.)

➤ When you have done this, compare your ranking with that found in the 1960s survey (given in note 1 on p. 319). If there are differences, do you think this reflects changes in views on grammatical acceptability since the 1960s?

➤ Look back at the extract from Collinson, *et al.* on p. 10. Do you agree that the three sentences are incorrect?

It is interesting to consider how notions of 'correct usage' become established. Here is one writer's view on the subject, referring to British English. Niloofar Haeri is professor of anthropology at Johns Hopkins University in Baltimore in the United States, and this is from an article of hers, primarily on the Arabic language, that appeared in the *Guardian* newspaper (14 June 2003).

> In the past few weeks I have been talking to British journalists, subeditors and writers (mostly at the *Guardian*) and I have asked them who or what defines correct usage in English. Who has the authority? Almost invariably they respond that "time" is the ultimate authority. Once a usage becomes prevalent, it must be, and is, accepted as the correct one.
>
> I have also been going through readers' letters . . . and most of them seem to share that view – even when they complain about this or that usage.

She contrasts this with the linguistic situation in the Arab world, giving the example of Egypt, where

> subeditors and writers told me only the Koran provides linguistic authority for classical Arabic. Since many people consider the Koran to be the word of God, the authority that ultimately determines correctness is therefore divine.

More secular arbiters of 'correctness' exist in other countries. In France, for example, the *Académie française* aims to preserve the 'purity' of the French language, protecting it, for example, from the introduction of English loan words (such as *le parking, le debriefing, le happy few, le email*) particularly where equivalent French words exist.

Most influential grammars in recent years have claimed to be descriptive rather than prescriptive. In other words, they present a snapshot of actual patterns of use at a particular time. For example, in perhaps the most definitive grammar of modern English, *A Comprehensive Grammar of the English Language (CGEL)* (Quirk *et al.* 1985) the authors say that their approach is 'to focus on the common core that is shared by standard British English and standard American English', and they leave as unmarked (that is, they take to be fully acceptable) 'any features that the two standard varieties have in common' (p. 33). Another important work, the *Longman Grammar of Spoken and Written English (LGSWE)* (Biber *et al.* 1999), describes grammar in four main **registers** or **varieties** of English (see also Unit A4, p. 37) taken largely from British and North American sources: conversation, written fiction, newspaper, and academic texts. For written English 'the grammatical forms and patterns actually used in published texts' (p. 18) are described, while standard spoken English is taken to be the 'grammatical characteristics shared widely across dialects, excluding those variants restricted to local or limited social/regional varieties'. In other words, the authors deliberately avoid making a subjective judgement as to what is 'standard' and what is 'non-standard' (or 'vernacular').

While such descriptive grammars are unlikely to disagree significantly on whether language is clearly grammatical or ungrammatical, differences do exist in how they deal with language whose acceptability is disputed. The difficulty is clearly illustrated if we look at the coding that these grammars use for language that is somewhere between 'acceptable' and 'unacceptable'. *CGEL* (p. x) uses three categories:

> ?* tending to unacceptability, but not fully unacceptable e.g. *I taught her three years.*

> ? native speakers unsure about acceptability e.g. *She spoke clearly indeed.*

> (*), (?) native speakers differ in their reactions e.g. *I never stayed there last night.*

while *LGSWE* (p. vi) uses two:

> ? marginally unacceptable: *e.g. a most promising pupil of hers*

> ?* on the boundary of unacceptability: e.g. *excuse me a little*

There is clearly a scale from more to less acceptable. There will inevitably be disagreements on where on the scale a particular utterance lies, and therefore into which of the categories it falls. We return to questions of 'standard' grammar and acceptability in Unit A8.

Finally in this section, we consider the sources of information used in producing grammatical description. Three main sources of information are used. One is the intuitions of the writer, sometimes checked against the intuitions of a small number of informants. The second is the use of citations: that is, examples of actual use in spoken or written text. An advantage of this over the use of intuition is that hard evidence is provided from third parties so that there is less danger that the grammar simply describes what an individual believes to be the case. Citations may also give useful information about meaning from the surrounding context. While the use of citations is generally recognised as an improvement over reliance on intuition, the problem remains that there is no indication of how typical is the grammatical feature being exemplified in the citation. In addition, there is no indication of how comprehensive is the grammatical description that is being presented: citations can only be used to exemplify what the grammarian has chosen to include in the grammar.

Recent advances in computational technology have made available a third source of information: a **corpus** (plural **corpora**) of language – that is, a large collection of text stored and accessed electronically. A corpus can be used to check intuitions and provide illustrative examples in context. It allows explorations of language which can help uncover characteristics of grammar in use that we might be hard pressed to come up with from intuition alone.

## Task A1.3.2

> Before reading on, take a few moments to consider how we use the '*get*-passive'. This is formed by *get/gets/got* + a past participle (e.g. He *got arrested*) and has a meaning similar to a normal passive (compare 'He was arrested').

➤ Consider what your intuitions tell you about the contexts in which the *get*-passive is used. For example, is it mainly used in speech or writing, what kinds of verbs usually follow *get*, and is it usually followed by an agent (e.g. *by the police*)?

Even for experienced language users, it can be difficult to come up with answers to questions like these and be confident that they reflect reality. Examining a corpus can be of value in leading us to new insights into the way in which language is used, and helping either to confirm (or counter) our intuitions. If the corpus is large enough, then we can be fairly confident that what we observe is representative of general usage.

So what does a corpus say about the *get*-passive? If we compare corpora of written and spoken English, we see that it is far more common in speech. Michael McCarthy (1998: 82ff.) notes that in the CANCODE corpus of conversational English (for more on this see Unit A9) there are 139 instances of *get*-passives, such as *got flung about in the car, got killed, got locked in/out*. Of these, 89 per cent refer to contexts which are judged by the speaker as in some way 'adversative', defined as 'a state of affairs that is signalled by the conversational participants as manifestly undesirable, or at the very least, problematic' (p. 83). In addition, it was found that 93 per cent lack an explicit agent. This, he suggests, places the emphasis in *get*-passive constructions on the person or thing affected by the process, referred to in the subject, rather than its cause or agent. Findings of this kind clearly allow us to go beyond making statements about grammatical form and to characterise the relationship between grammar and context (in this case, the relevant feature of context is the stance of the speaker, presenting a context as problematic), and also to describe the probability of occurrence of a grammatical form (in this case, that the *get*-passive is predominantly used without an agent). We return to corpus analysis in explorations of grammar and context in Units A5 and A9.

In practice, many grammatical descriptions use a combination of sources of information. The authors of another recent descriptive grammar, *The Cambridge Grammar of the English Language* make their procedures explicit:

> The evidence we use comes from several sources: our own intuitions as native speakers of the language; the reactions of other native speakers we consult when we are in doubt; data from computer corpora . . ., and data presented in dictionaries and other scholarly work on grammar. We alternate between the different sources and cross-check them against each other, since intuitions can be misleading and texts can contain errors.
>
> (Huddleston and Pullum 2002:11)

## A1.4  WHY STUDY GRAMMAR IN CONTEXT?

Most people study grammar either to find out more about how their first language works or during the course of learning a second language. It is generally accepted that an understanding of the grammar of our first language can help in constructing well-formed language when it is important to do so, such as writing done in formal contexts or for a wide audience. Similarly, whether or not we believe that grammar should drive the second-language syllabus, most teachers and students would accept that an understanding of second-language grammar is a necessary part of successful learning at some stage. But explicit knowledge of grammar has other applications too. Here we give four very brief illustrations of how a study of grammar in context is put into practice. You will find other illustrations at various points throughout the book.

 **Task A1.4.1**

➤ Before reading on, list three ways – or more if possible – in which a knowledge of grammar can be applied.

1. Organisations such as the Plain English Campaign have highlighted the need to write public documents in a way that is easy to understand. Here is an illustration of how grammatical knowledge was brought to the texts that accompany exhibits in museums in order to make them more accessible to visitors. The work was a cooperation between a linguist and staff at the Australian Museum in Sydney. The result was improved texts in this museum, and more general guidelines for writers of such texts (Ferguson *et al.* 1995). For example, it was noted that in the following text (pp. 26–27) there was a large gap between the reference items *its* and their referent *Australia*.

> (5) Because of *its* long geographical isolation from other continents and *its* wide range of habitat types, one of the most diverse marine faunas in the world has evolved in *Australia's* waters.

This, it was felt, could be confusing for readers who may have to pause to work out what is being referred to, and that the text would be improved by moving *Australia* close to the reference items. A suggested improvement was:

Because of *its* long geographical isolation from other continents and *its* wide range of habitat types, *Australia's waters* are host to one of the most diverse marine faunas ever to have evolved.

2. A developing area in applied linguistics is that of forensic linguistics in which analysis of written and spoken language is undertaken to inform legal questions; for example, to determine whether an accused person was the speaker in a recorded conversation. Judith Levi (1994) gives an example case in which she was involved where grammatical analysis was important. In the United States a case was brought by the Legal Assistance Foundation of Chicago on behalf of 20,000 recipients of Aid to Families with Dependent Children (AFDC) against the Illinois Department of Public Aid (CITPA) partly on the grounds that a notice sent 'had language which was so inadequate to its task of informing the recipients of their rights as to be unconstitutional'. Here is an example from the notice:

> If your AFDC financial assistance benefits are continued at the present level and the fair hearing decides your AFDC financial assistance reduction was correct, the amount of AFDC assistance received to which you were not entitled will be recouped from future AFDC assistance payment or must be paid back if your AFDC case is cancelled.

Levi's analysis of the notice led her to believe that there were a number of grammatical constructions that would interfere with the reader's understanding. In the sentence above she noted: a complex internal structure of seven clauses, six passive verbs without subjects (a construction which can obscure who is doing what), and a number of complex compound nouns (e.g. *financial assistance reduction*) including nominalised verbs without explicit subjects.

3. A central concern of computational linguistics is to develop machines capable of both understanding naturally produced speech and writing and of communicating with humans. Applications of such machines include: indexing and retrieval in databases of text (for example, to provide access to newspaper archives); machine translation (the texts produced in the European Union, for example, need to be translated into an increasing number of languages); automatically providing summaries of texts (in large institutions, for example, it may be impossible for staff to read the full versions of all the texts that are produced); automatic dialogue and information systems (phone conversations with machines to get information about train timetables and book tickets are now commonplace, and such interactions are likely to become more widespread and to achieve more sophisticated information retrieval). A basic technique in such applications is the automatic recognition and tagging of components of the text, particularly grammatical components. However, in order to achieve success in applications such as those mentioned above, the machine needs to recognise connections in text across sentences (for example, this may be necessary in order to identify what a pronoun refers to), and to recognise what makes a discourse coherent or not. In order to process natural language successfully machines need to be taught to understand and produce language that occurs in context rather than language in discrete sentences.

4. Language analysis is applied in the study of communication disability, such as in language-delayed children. There follow some examples of utterances characteristic of the speech of 24–27-month-old children but here taken from a conversation with a language-delayed four-year-old (Crystal and Varley 1993: 177). The main problem seems to lie in the verb.

the cat had kitten                    Mummy house be in there
it black                              it have a nice bed
mother cat like it                    what it doing now

Undertaking a systematic and comprehensive grammatical analysis assists in making a linguistic assessment of a child's developmental language disorder. Further, providing an indication of the expected sequence of acquisition of grammatical structures and the approximate ages by which these structures are usually acquired, allows us to assess the degree of delay in a child with language disorder and to focus treatment. Of course, for a complete picture, information would need also to be collected on phonological, semantic and pragmatic difficulties.

**Summary**

In this unit we have looked at:

- meanings of the word 'grammar'
- units and hierarchies in grammatical description
- problems with the notion of the 'sentence'
- prescriptive, descriptive and pedagogical grammars
- sources of information in grammatical description: intuition, citations, a corpus
- reasons for studying grammar in context

### LOOKING AHEAD

You will read more about many of the ideas in this unit later in the book. In particular: Unit A5 looks again at different approaches to grammar; Unit A9 examines corpus approaches to grammar in context; Unit B1 exemplifies grammatical analysis of speech using corpora; Units B8 and B9 return to the notions of standard and non-standard language; and Units C1 and C9 provide example analyses of spoken language.

# Unit A2
# Context: Some preliminaries

In this unit we introduce the notion of 'context' and set out some assumptions about it that underpin what follows in this book. In A2.1 we illustrate the relationship between language and context, and much of the rest of the book is concerned with exploring in detail the nature of this relationship. A2.2 and A2.3 highlight the complexity of what we mean by the term 'context'. In A2.2, we present one way of categorising the components of context in order to make it possible to talk about it in a systematic way. In A2.3, we show that the context in which an interaction takes place is constantly changing.

## A2.1  LANGUAGE AND CONTEXT ARE RELATED

The fact that there is a relationship between language and the context in which it occurs can be demonstrated in a number of ways.

First, note that we use different language to achieve similar purposes in different contexts.

### Task A2.1.1

➤ Think about what language you might use in the following contexts:

   a. You haven't got any money on you, but want to buy a newspaper. How might you ask a close friend to lend you a small amount?
   b. You need to borrow a few thousand pounds (euros/ dollars etc.) to buy a new flat. How might you ask your parents to lend you the money?
   c. You would like to go on a world cruise, but need to borrow most of the money for this from your bank. How might you ask your bank manager (who is noted for being particularly unwilling to lend!) for a loan?

Clearly, in each situation many different things could be said or written. What is important to note, however, is that different types of language are likely to be appropriate in different contexts, and our choice of language depends on such things as who is involved in the communication and the relationship between them, and what we hope to achieve through our communication.

Second, the same language can have different meanings in different contexts.

**Task A2.1.2**

➤ Think about what the questions mean in the following situations:

a. A has fallen off his bike and landed awkwardly. B does an initial assessment of his injuries and then says:

'Can you move your legs?'

b. X is sitting with legs outstretched in an armchair in a small sitting room. Y is carrying a tray of glasses past where X is sitting. Y says:

'Can you move your legs?'

While an analysis of linguistic form would suggest that the two utterances are identical, the messages they convey in the invented contexts is different. In the first, B asks about A's physical ability to move his legs in order to assess the seriousness of the injury. In the second, Y makes a request. The same words, then, can convey different messages depending on the context in which they occur.

Third, even when a stretch of language is taken out of context, we can sometimes infer a great deal about the context from which it was taken.

 **Task A2.1.3**

➤ Think about what you can say about the context for each of the following:

a. Fifteen – love.
b. First check the contents to make sure that nothing is missing.
c. This town ain't big enough for the both of us.
d. The hour was late.

The usual context for the first is quite specific: said by an umpire in a tennis match. The second is often the first instruction that comes with a self-assembly item, for example flat-packed furniture. The third is the kind of thing said in old cowboy and western films prior to a (usually violent) confrontation between two characters. The fourth example is perhaps a little more difficult to contextualise. In everyday speech we would be more likely to say 'It was late', and 'The hour . . .' used in this way has a literary feel to it. In fact, we found it used as the first line of a children's story. Of course, there can never be any certainty in relating language to context. Even a highly specialised utterance like 'Fifteen-love' might be said in everyday use in a humorous way to mean that someone had gained an advantage over someone else. It is also true that when language is isolated from its context, it can sometimes be very difficult to understand. Consider the following extract from a speech event:

A:   well – everything I'm hearing says there needs to be some further work on this before we wind up with egg all over our face

*B:* yeah – do you want me to – follow up on that

*A:* OK – well I think I think – we definitely need more information on what the other guys are doing – in order to make – to make any sort of meaningful decision

*B:* we've got to ring up the other guys as well – I mean – what their policy is and what actually happens – probably – two different things

(Rogerson-Revell 1998: 330)

It is possible to infer certain things about the context in which it took place: that the speakers are involved in some decision-making process; that others are involved ('I'm hearing . . .' [from others], 'other guys'); perhaps that A holds some kind of superior status (B offers to 'follow up on that'). However, without additional knowledge of the setting, the participants, the communicative goals of the interaction, and so on, the language makes little sense to an outside observer.

As we gain experience of a variety of contexts, we build up an expertise in language use appropriate to them so that as adults we are usually able rapidly to assess a situation in which we find ourselves and fine-tune our language use so that it is appropriate. Even as skilled language users, however, we occasionally find ourselves in new contexts and may be unsure of what to say and how to say it. For example, in the early days of our university careers both of us faced the difficulty of having to write references (that is, letters of recommendation) to potential employers of our students. However, not having been employers ourselves, we had not read employment references before, so were unsure about the kind of information that goes into a reference, and how this is conventionally expressed.

## Task A2.1.4

➤ Recall any new contexts that you may have faced as an adult in which you did not know what kinds of things to say or write. Remember how you overcame any difficulties, for example by drawing on your knowledge of language use in other contexts.

➤ Think of any knowledge you now have that would enable you to communicate more effectively in the same context.

## A2.2  CONTEXT IS MULTIFACETED

While we are aware of a relationship between language and context, and are able to make remarkably subtle variations in language depending on our assessment of context, it is very hard to say exactly what 'context' is. Of course, we might in a vague way say that the context for any **utterance** (which we take here to mean either a spoken or written contribution to an interaction) is what is going on around it, or take a dictionary definition of context in a more general sense. However, a more technical characterisation of context is problematic. This is both because 'context' acts as an umbrella term for a wide range of elements, and because writers working in different disciplines and different research paradigms may categorise contextual elements in different ways, and focus on different sets of these depending on the goals of the research.

However, there is broad agreement that in grouping elements which together constitute the context of an utterance, it is useful to divide linguistic and non-linguistic elements, and elements which are in the more immediate context and those which provide a broader background against which an utterance is interpreted. No diagram can adequately represent the complexity of the number of relevant contextual factors and the interplay between them and discourse. However, Figure A2.1 represents a preliminary representation of an utterance in its context and we will use it as a way of framing our exploration of context in the remainder of this unit and in Units A3 and A4.

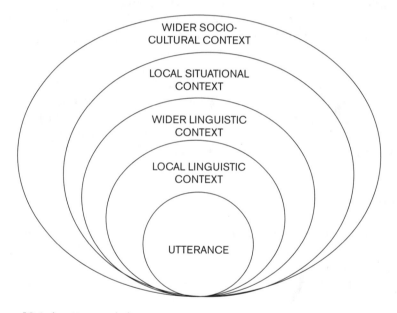

*Figure A2.1* An utterance in its context

The **local linguistic context** is both prior language in a communication (the writing or speech that comes before the utterance in focus) and what follows it. Perhaps the most obvious language elements that may need prior contextual information are deictics (that is, words that 'point to' what they refer to, such as *here, this, these*), pronouns and certain abstract vocabulary. It is impossible to interpret the highlighted words in:

> *This* is explained in Chapter 5.
> *The others* are in the kitchen.
> *The process* is painful, but well worth it.

without previous understanding of what 'this' is, who or what 'the others' are, and what 'process' is being referred to. Other linguistic resources are used to refer forward to what is to follow. In examples such as:

> You might not believe *this*, but. . . .
> In fact, *what I said was*. . . .
> The procedure is explained in section 5 *below.*

a context is created such that there is an expectation that further information will follow to clarify what has been said or written. The term **co-text** is sometimes used to refer to what here we call the local linguistic context, although other writers may use it to mean the linguistic context more generally (here, both the local and wider linguistic context).

The **wider linguistic context** concerns the way in which a particular text relates to other texts, and the way in which our interpretation of a text is influenced by our previous experience of other texts. The term **intertextuality** is often used to refer to the kind of knowledge that we bring to a text from our experience of other texts, particularly other texts of the same type. For example, in an academic context, novice academics writing their first science research article for publication will draw on the knowledge they have gained in reading such articles in organising and phrasing information. They will know that research articles typically organise information in the order 'Introduction – Methods – Results – Discussion', and they will know from experience that Methods are often reported with the passive, and that the Discussion often includes modal verbs and adverbs, intended to present conclusions tentatively. Another type of intertextuality is of course very common in academic texts, where specific reference is made to other texts as in 'Smithers (1978) notes that. . . .'

The linguistic similarities of texts of the same type are not the only aspect of intertextuality that is relevant here. Speakers and writers make presuppositions about the textual experiences of the people with whom they interact. This is clear in a series of works such as the Harry Potter books by J. K. Rowling where events that took place in earlier books may be mentioned in passing, without full explanation, in later books. The expectation is that to understand these events fully readers will have already read (or will need to read) these earlier books.

However, we need to recognise that the term 'intertextuality' is not only used to refer to knowledge of other related texts. Norman Fairclough (2001: 127) gives an example text from the magazine *Woman's Weekly* (9 August 1987) of which the following is the first part. It is taken from a report on the wedding of Sarah Ferguson and Prince Andrew.

> Wasn't it a lovely day?
> The sun came out, the colourful crowds gathered, and at the centre of it all were Sarah and Andrew, spilling their happiness in every direction and making it a day to remember – for them and for us.

Fairclough notes a number of presuppositions made in the text about the knowledge shared by the readers. These include: that they knew it was a lovely day, that the crowds were colourful, and that they are happy. What is presented to readers are parts of preceding 'texts' that the writer assumes the readership will be familiar with. However, in this case, the 'texts' may include television footage, radio reports, and even witnessing the event in person.

### ★ Task A2.2.1

➤ Take a newspaper and look at a number of examples of different text types (e.g. news reports, editorials, letters to the editor, reviews). Consider whether the writers make any assumptions in them that the reader will be familiar with other 'texts' (used in Fairclough's broad sense).

Relevant contextual aspects of the **local situational context** may include the time, the location, the age and gender of participants and their relative status. We look further at the local situational context in Unit A3. The **wider socio-cultural context** is the broader background against which communication is interpreted, and includes social and political aspects of language or national groups as a whole, and features of institutional domains. We will return to this in Unit A4.

While context is multifaceted, not all features of context will be relevant in any given communicative setting. A coffee shop may be in the high street, or it may be within a hospital building, but the language used to order a cup of coffee is likely to be similar. The fact that the coffee shop is within a hospital is clearly part of its context, but this feature of context may have no impact on this communicative act. What counts as relevant depends on what contextual information the participants in the interaction mobilise in order to understand what is said or written. In this view, context can be seen as a resource that can be used by participants in interaction to help interpret what is intended.

A number of challenges face us, then, if we want to describe and analyse context. While certain features of context may be readily observable, such as those in the immediate physical location of the interaction, others which may play a part in interpreting language are not. These might include the participants' cultural assumptions and their previous experiences. How are we to go about gaining information about these? Further, while we may be able to carefully describe certain features of context, how are we to know which of these are relevant to the interaction from the perspective of the participants?

A way forward is to study context through language on the basis that the part of context which is relevant to participants may be reflected in the language which is produced. John Gumperz (1982) has demonstrated that any aspect of linguistic behaviour – lexical, prosodic, phonological, syntactic or stylistic – may function as a **contextualisation cue**, indicating which aspects of the context are relevant in interpreting what a speaker means and allowing participants to infer each other's roles and purposes in the interaction. To illustrate, here are three (constructed) openings to conversations between college students on the day in which an essay is due to be handed in:

> Did you get the thing finished?
> Do you think they'll be happy with three pages?
> I've been up most of the night typing the stuff.

As these are openings, 'the thing', 'they' and 'the stuff' have no explicit referents in the conversations so far. The speakers' use of implicit reference assumes a context in which the other participants in the conversations know what is being referred to without clarification. A consequence is that speaker and hearer are marked as members of the group who have shared the experience of meeting the essay deadline. Through observation of language, then, we can make inferences about what is contextually relevant to the participants.

## A2.3 CONTEXT IS DYNAMIC

One view of context is that it is the pre-existing 'framework' within which interaction and communication take place. Paul Drew and John Heritage (1992: 19) have referred to this as the 'bucket' view of context in that it is thought to contain and constrain what can be said and how. An alternative view, and one that has become much more widely accepted (e.g. Fetzer and Akman 2002), is that context is *dynamic*. Not only are utterances shaped by their context, in that they cannot be properly understood without reference to the context in which they occur, but utterances also shape their context in that they themselves form part of the context in which following utterances are to be understood. In other words, context is constantly being changed by the act of communication itself.

A dynamic approach also assumes that the participants use language to construct social contexts, rather than simply producing language in response to contextual constraints. For example, participants in an interaction construct the social identities of themselves and others in the language they use. Elinor Ochs (2002) illustrates this in an analysis of interaction during a school softball game in which Erin, a young girl with autism, is taking part. To simplify the presentation we have removed most of the transcription conventions that appeared in the original. Her unaffected classmates at various times act as her teammate when she hits a legitimate ball, shouting:

> *Teammates*:   GOOD!
>          GO ERIN!
>          GOooo!
>          RUN ERIN!

as her instructor (constructing Erin as a novice):

> Gary:              Erin. Swing like that okay?
>                    [*swings bat horizontally*]

and as her advocate when there is a disputed hit (constructing Erin as someone who is unable or unwilling to speak in her own support):

> Gary+ teammates:   It hit her on the hand
>                    [*pointing to hand*]
>                    [*Opposite team members shout objections*]

The dynamism of context is also well illustrated in discourse in which participants take on multiple roles. For example, Deborah Tannen and Cynthia Wallat (1987) have shown how a paediatrician adjusts her language in a consultation with a child (Jody) and her parent, which is being video-recorded for training purposes.

 **Task A2.3.1**

➤ Here is a small section of Tannen and Wallat's data. Read it and see what adjustments to the paediatrician's language you observe.

| | | |
|---|---|---|
| 1. | *Paediatrician:* | Let's see. Can you open up like this, Jody. Look. [Paediatrician opens her own mouth] |
| 2. | *Child:* | Aaaaaaaaaaaaah. |
| 3. | *Paediatrician:* | Good. That's good. |
| 4. | *Child:* | Aaaaaaaaaaah. |
| 5. | *Paediatrician:* | /Seeing/ for the palate, she has a high arched palate. |
| 6. | *Child:* | Aaaaaaaaaaaaaaaaaaaaaaaah. |
| 7. | *Paediatrician:* | but there's no cleft, [maneuvers to grasp child's jaw] |
| 8. | *Paediatrician* [to parent]: | what we'd want to look for is to see how she . . . mmoves her palate . . . which may be some of the difficulty with breathing that we're talking about |

Tannen and Wallat argue that when she is talking to the child she uses a 'teasing register' (1 and 3); when she is talking to the mother she uses a 'conversational register' (8); and because the consultation is being video-recorded for training purposes, she uses a 'reporting register' to note her diagnosis, for the benefit of those who might later view the recording (5 and 7).

In this unit we have looked at:

- evidence that language and context are related
- a division of context into:
    - the local linguistic context (or co-text)
    - the wider linguistic context (related to intertextuality)
    - the local situational context
    - the wider socio-cultural context
- problems in determining which aspects of context are relevant in an interaction
- ways in which context is dynamic.


## LOOKING AHEAD

In this unit we have introduced some general ideas about the notion of context. In the next two units you will read about these in more detail. In Unit A3 you will read about aspects of the local situational context in which language is produced and then in Unit A4 about aspects of the wider social and cultural context. Sections B and C go on to introduce you to analysis of the grammatical features of language produced in a variety of contexts, including radio phone-ins, medical consultations and language-learning classrooms, and in the speech and writing of particular groups of people, including writers of academic texts, children carrying out classroom activities and elderly people with dementia.

# Unit A3
# The local situational context

## A3.1  APPROACHES TO THE STUDY OF THE RELATIONSHIP BETWEEN LOCAL SITUATION AND LANGUAGE

What features of context influence the forms of language selected, and how do we interpret the meaning of a particular utterance? This question has exercised linguists and those in related disciplines at least since the work of the anthropologist Bronislaw Malinowski in the early years of the twentieth century. Malinowski conducted ethnographic research among the peoples of Eastern New Guinea, where he noted the difficulty of translating words and ideas from the native languages of the islanders. This led to his expression of the importance of context in communication:

> All words which describe the native social order, all expressions referring to native beliefs, to specific customs, ceremonies, magical rites – all such words are obviously absent from English as from any European language. Such words can only be translated into English, not by giving their imaginary equivalent – a real one obviously cannot be found – but by explaining the meaning of each of them through an exact Ethnographic account of the sociology, culture and tradition of that native community.
>
> (Malinowski 1923/1994: 1)

For Malinowski, then, words took on a particular meaning only by virtue of features of the context in which they occur.

Although Malinowski highlighted the significance of context in communication, he did not set out to describe more precisely either the nature of context, or its impact on language choice, and it has been left to later researchers to explore in more detail the relationship between context and how language is organised to achieve communication. Three in particular – J. R. Firth, Dell Hymes and Michael Halliday – have had a major impact on current thinking, and we will briefly outline their approaches here.

J. R. Firth's concern was to determine which of the many variables in a situation allow us to predict the language to be used. He suggested the following dimensions of situations as being of potential influence:

A. The relevant features of participants: persons, personalities.

  (i) The verbal action of the participants.
  (ii) The non-verbal action of the participants.

B. The relevant objects.
C. The effect of the verbal action.

(Firth 1957: 182)

To illustrate, we might imagine a scene in a theatre box office where a customer is booking a ticket for a future performance. Relevant features of the participants may be that one is a customer who wishes to check seat availability and purchase a ticket, while the other is a booking clerk who has access to information about availability and the means of receiving payment. Verbal actions may involve greeting, checking, requesting, confirming, and so on. Non-verbal actions may include keying in information on the computer, pointing to a seating plan, and handing over a credit card. Relevant objects might include a computer, a seating plan, a credit card, and a machine for transacting credit card payments. The effect of the verbal action is that the customer receives tickets for the performance, and the seats are designated reserved by the booking clerk.

Firth's interest in specifying the features of context which are potentially relevant to the form, appropriacy and meaning of utterances was also pursued by Dell Hymes (e.g. 1962, 1964, 1974). Hymes (1974) provides what is essentially a checklist of contextual factors that could be noted by researchers in investigating communicative events. He usefully organises these using the mnemonic 'SPEAKING':

- S refers to the **setting** and **scene**, including the time, place and concrete physical circumstances in which the event is produced.
- P refers to the **participants** involved. Some events, such as a conversation, may have just two participants who exchange roles between speaker and hearer, while a formal lecture will have many participants but only one who takes on the role of speaker.
- E refers to **ends**, or the purposes or goals of an event. Some events have very clear ends. Announced over the public address system during the interval in a concert, the purpose of the following is very clear: 'Ladies and gentlemen. This evening's performance will recommence in five minutes. Please take your seats in the auditorium now.'
- A refers to **act sequence**, or the form and content of the 'event'. Events such as lecture, chat, shopping list and instruction manual will be associated with different things talked or written about and different kinds of language.
- K refers to **key**, the tone in which a communicative act is done, such as serious or painstaking.
- I refers to **instrumentalities**, including the channel in which communication takes place such as speech, writing or some other mode of communication.
- N refers to **norm of interaction and interpretation**, such as the norms associated with interaction in a church service or speaking to a stranger.
- G refers to **genre**, such as poem, sermon or joke.

Building closely on Firth's work, Michael Halliday explores which aspects of context influence how we use language. For Halliday (1978) the social context:

> consists of those general properties of the situation which collectively function as the determinants of text, in that they specify the semantic configurations that the speaker will typically fashion in contexts of the given type.

He suggests that in any situation these general properties can be organised into three dimensions that have linguistic consequences, which he calls the **field**, **tenor** and **mode**. Field refers to what the language is being used to talk about. Tenor refers to the role relationships between the people involved in the interaction. Significant variables include the relative status of the interactants, how frequently interaction between them occurs, and the extent to which the interactants are involved emotionally in a situation. Mode refers to the way in which language functions in the situation: for example, whether it is spoken or written.

Halliday (1994: 30) provides an illustration characterising field, tenor and mode for a communicative event in which a small child and an adult are playing with toy vehicles:

*Field*
Child at play: manipulating movable objects (wheeled vehicles) with related fixtures, assisted by adult; concurrently associating (i) similar past events, (ii) similar absent objects; also evaluating objects in terms of each other and of processes.

*Tenor*
Small child and parent interacting: child determining course of action, (i) announcing own intentions, (ii) controlling actions of parent; concurrently sharing and seeking corroboration of own experience with parent.

*Mode*
Spoken, alternately monologue and dialogue, task-oriented; pragmatic, (i) referring to processes and objects of situation, (ii) relating to and furthering child's own actions, (iii) demanding other objects; interposed with narrative and exploratory elements.

★ **Task A3.1.1**

➤ Think of a particular communicative event that you have recently been involved in, e.g. buying a train ticket; asking your tutor for advice; texting a friend to arrange a night out. Consider how you would describe the field, tenor and mode in this event.

## A3.2  AN ILLUSTRATION: THE INFLUENCE OF AUDIENCE ON LANGUAGE

Having briefly outlined the approaches taken by influential scholars in the field, we will go on to explore some examples in which grammar reflects the contexts in which it is used. We will focus on just one aspect of context (or, perhaps more accurately, one set of contextual factors): the influence of the audience – the person or group the speech or writing is addressed to – and in particular the relationship between the addressor and the addressee. We will see that language tends to be adapted for different audiences. Firth, Hymes and Halliday all recognise the importance of this feature of context: Firth primarily within his 'relevant features of participants', Hymes primarily under his 'participants' heading, and Halliday primarily within the dimension of 'tenor'.

Our first example concerns that language used by adults to children. The ways in which adults modify their speech when talking to children have been studied extensively, particularly in connection with language acquisition research. The phenomenon is referred to variously as 'baby talk', 'motherese', or more generally, 'care-giver speech' or 'child-directed speech'. While lexical and phonological modifications are clearly part of child-directed speech, we will note here only some of its grammatical features. Charles Ferguson (1977) and Dorothy Willis (1977), for example, observe modifications such as:

(i)   the omission of 'it' and articles, as in 'Too big, won't fit' and 'Orange is all gone.'
(ii)  the use of 'colourless' auxiliaries such as 'make', 'go' and 'give' with 'baby words' to make action phrases, as in 'go sleepy-byes', 'make peepee'.
(iii) the avoidance of first and second person pronouns, as in 'Baby is finished?' (rather than 'Are you finished?') and 'Mommy is coming' (rather than 'I'm coming').

Although these examples are taken from English, Ferguson's work (1977) shows that phenomena such as these occur in a wide variety of languages.

It seems that adults use such features, some of which replicate those of the developing language of the child, in order to simplify their speech and so make what they say more comprehensible. Interestingly, while linguists are primarily concerned with describing such features, in the wider community there is debate about whether they are a positive or negative influence on child language acquisition. For example, there has been a heated argument in the media and elsewhere over the children's TV programme *Teletubbies*. Aimed at pre-school children, the characters speak in a form of 'baby talk' or 'play language': 'Eh-oh' (hello), 'bootiful flaaer' (beautiful flower). This has been criticised by some observers for providing a poor model of language for the young audience. The London *Evening Standard*, for example, labelled the language in the programme as 'regressive for children who are beyond the babbling stage', while a nursery in England banned *Teletubbies* videos because 'the language used by the central characters is unsuitable for educational purposes' (Reported in the *Guardian*, 24 August 1999).

Child-directed speech may of course be transferred to other contexts, with different addressees, and with other communicative purposes and outcomes. In research by Alison Sealey (2000) adult, native English-speaking informants were asked to respond to scenarios in which they had to reflect on what Sealey refers to generally as 'childly language'.

 **Task A3.2.1**

Before reading on, consider what your response would be to the following scenario provided by Sealey (2000: 173):

> Mr and Mrs Taylor attend a parents' evening at their children's primary school. On their way home, they discuss the conversations they have had with the teachers. They agree that one teacher in particular has a way of speaking which 'makes you feel as if you're still at junior school'.

➤ Can you suggest some of the things this teacher says to parents?

One suggested feature from Sealey's informants was that the pronoun 'we' occurred more frequently than others, and also that tag questions were commonly used, as in:

Now, what do we want to talk about?
We don't do that, do we?
Of course, we know that . . . don't we?

Transferring such features of adult-to-child speech to contexts where different age and role relationships occur may have the effect – deliberate or otherwise – of 'talking down to' or patronising the addressee(s). The choice of child-directed speech may, of course, be well intentioned, as in the reassuring language of doctors or the encouraging and sympathetic language used by relatives and other carers to people with a mental or physical disability.

A similar sort of adaptation of language is sometimes found in the language that native speakers use to learners of their language – so-called 'foreigner talk'. In a case study of the interaction between Zoila, a Spanish speaker learning English in the United States, and Rina, her native-speaker friend, Evelyn Hatch and colleagues (1978) noted a number of grammatical (and other) adjustments in Rina's speech, including:

(i)  the deletion of the pronoun 'it', as in
     Z:  Do you think is ready?
     R:  I think is ready.

(ii)  the use of uninflected verb forms for all time references, as in
      R:  Every time she come here./ She need the work. (with present time
          reference)
and   R:  But he go with you, no?/ Who give you the opal? (with past time
          reference)

(iii)  the simplification of negative structures, as in
       R:  I no liking. / Is no old./ No is good for you.

The motivation for such change would seem to be to ease communication, in
some cases (such as 'it' deletion) by mimicking the errors in Zoila's speech. However,
not all of her recurrent errors are copied by Rina. For example, while Zoila had
difficulties with possessives (e.g. 'You look very good in the face and the hair is nice';
' the car de Carlo'), these were always used correctly in Rina's speech.

While changes in speech such as these often seem to be made to ease communication, their motivations may be more complex. For example, changes have been
observed in the speech that people use when talking to elderly people. Howard
Giles and Nikolas Coupland (1984) noted features such as slower and more carefully
articulated speech, less abstract and more familiar vocabulary, and lower grammatical complexity (e.g. with fewer elements in major syntactic constituents).
While the reason might be partly to do with speaking clearly to people who may
display signs of deafness or mental confusion (though this could be simply the
speaker's stereotypical view of elderly people), it may also be the result of an
assumption that elderly people need to be cheered up by light-hearted, cheery
conversation.

It is important to point out that, while the phenomena of child-directed speech,
foreigner talk and 'elderly speech' are well attested, there is considerable individual
variation in their characteristics. For example, native speakers may have different
levels of experience in interacting with non-native speakers, and this may influence
their ability to make allowances for comprehension difficulties. And in our own
experience of parenting, we both avoided substitution of first and second person
pronouns when we spoke to our children. This was not a deliberate decision in order
to make the interaction more 'natural', but rather that we felt uncomfortable with
utterances such as:

Can't David do it?
(When addressing David; we preferred 'Can't you do it?')

and

Mummy/ Daddy will help you.
(When referring to ourselves; we preferred 'I'll help you.')

So far we have focused on face-to-face spoken interaction. However, this kind of linguistic accommodation to audience is also found in written text to an unspecified readership. For example, Allan Bell (1991) has looked at style and the audience of British newspapers, focusing on one linguistic variable, the deletion of the determiner in appositional naming expressions of the form:

[the] Australian entrepreneur Alan Bond
[a] Spanish tourist Josefa Morelli
[his] fellow left-winger Bob Cryer

He found that in the three 'quality' (broadsheet) newspapers, *The Times*, *Guardian* and *Daily Telegraph*, very few determiners were deleted where this was possible. At 12 per cent, the *Telegraph* had the highest number of deletions. In the 'popular' (tabloid) newspapers, in contrast, the majority of determiners were deleted, ranging from 73 per cent in the *Daily Mail* to 89 per cent in the *Sun*. These figures corresponded very closely to the social status of their readership, measured using six socio-economic groups: A, B, C1, C2, D and E. The quality press draws its readership largely from groups A, B and C1 (upper-middle, middle-middle and lower-middle classes), while the readership of the popular press comes mainly from groups C2, D and E (working classes). The *Sun*, for example, draws about 80 per cent of its readership from these groups. Bell (p. 196) argues that determiner deletion has the effect of giving the person more news value, providing the naming expression with a status similar to that of a title such as 'President Bush' or 'Lord Hutton'. This, he claims, is part of a less formal, more popular style, more typical of the North American media, in which determiner deletion is usual even in the 'prestige' media, and now copied by the British mass press.

 **Task A3.2.1**

To round off this consideration of changes in language made in response to audience, here is an extract from a newspaper column written by a medical doctor (Haslam 2003). The article is about the difficulties that doctors and patients have in communicating.

It often seems that doctors and patients use at least three different languages. There are the words doctors use when talking to doctors – the technical jargon that all professions use. There are the words that some doctors use when talking to patients, that they would not use in any other circumstances – curious words such as 'pop', as in 'pop up on the couch', or plurals such as 'we' as in 'We'll just have a look at you.' And then there are the words that patients use about their anatomy, health or bodily function that they would never use when to talking to doctors.

Answer the following questions:

➤ What is your experience of doctors using 'different languages' (or different registers) in their speech?

➤ Do you have experience of other professional groups using different registers in this way?

In this unit we have looked at:

Summary

■ work by Firth, Hymes and Halliday on the relationship between situational context and language;
■ the way in which we adapt the language we use depending on audience.

## LOOKING AHEAD

We have illustrated the influence of the local situational context with reference to child-directed speech, foreigner talk and 'elderly speech'. Specific grammatical aspects of these are discussed and analysed in Sections B and C. In particular, Units B6 and B7 deal with the language of children and elderly people, and with second language acquisition. In Unit C6 we analyse children's writing and in C7 verb tense choices in different English language learning activities.

# Unit A4
# The wider socio-cultural context

In the previous unit, we looked at how the language of a communicative event is influenced by aspects of the local situation. However, such events also occur within a wider socio-cultural context, and features of this context will themselves have an impact on language. Particular social groups have different beliefs, values and ways of behaving, and these are often encoded in the forms of language used and the ways in which interaction is organised within this group. In turn, the language produced shapes the culture of the group. In this unit we will explore this relationship by focusing on grammatical choices within three kinds of group: national groups, groups of people who share a particular interest or occupation and groups of people who work together within an institution. We should acknowledge, however, that any attempt to characterise the culture or the language preferences of a 'national', 'interest', 'occupational' or 'institutional' group has to be considered a description of broad tendencies that ignores variation. A national group, for example, is made up of a wide variety of subgroups depending on ethnicity, gender, age, and so on, each of which may have its own culture and characteristic language, which may be different from those among the majority population.

## A4.1  THE INFLUENCE OF 'NATIONAL CULTURE'

Most people who have spent time in another country will have experienced the different patterns of communication associated with even everyday activities. Ruquaya Hasan (1989) has noted that while we might use the same term 'go shopping' for the service encounter in shops across the world, the behaviour and language associated with this activity will vary across different countries and cultures. When buying food in a British shop, it would be unusual to haggle over the price, or ask for a discount if we buy a larger quantity. In other countries, however, negotiation is often an expected stage of the purchase routine. Of course, in other contexts even in Britain, negotiating the price of purchases such as a car or a house is normal. Differences also exist between countries which may consider themselves to be (broadly) culturally similar, such as Britain and Australia. Eddie Ronowicz and Colin Yallop (1999) suggest that an Australian characteristic is to avoid being 'pushy', which has consequences for how shop assistants interact with customers:

> information about products will be supplied readily but special care will
> be taken to present it in the form of several choices and to avoid any hint

as to what decision should be taken. This is caused not only by the desire not to appear aggressive or self-important, but also by a deeper belief held dear by most Australians that everyone should not only be free to take their decisions, but that responsibility for those decisions and their consequences is a personal matter that should not be interfered with by others.

(Ronowicz and Yallop 1999: 125)

Another area in which there are obvious national differences is in the way we address one another. How we refer to each other, what titles and forms of address we use and how this is carried through to the system of pronouns reflects the society of which it is part, and also acts to construct that society. In addressing or referring to someone in Britain a careful judgement has to be made on whether to include their title (Mr, Mrs, Miss etc.) plus family name or use just their given name, knowing that we can cause discomfort or even offence by treating someone too familiarly or distantly. The choice is made more complex as the trend is towards informality, particularly among the young, influenced at least in part by the tendency in the United States and Australia to prefer given names over title plus family names even in formal contexts.

Choosing appropriate forms of address can prove particularly difficult when moving from one culture to another. Knowing when to use the familiar and polite pronouns that are found in many languages (e.g. French *tu/ vous*, German *du/ Sie*, Spanish *tú/ usted*) calls for sensitivity and can be problematic for speakers of languages (such as English) with only one second person pronoun (*you*). Some languages – such as Japanese, Korean and Javanese – express different levels of respect or politeness, depending on the relative status of the interactants, through the use of special gram-matical contrasts. While English expresses these through the use of titles such as 'Mr', 'Mrs', 'Ms', 'Miss', 'Doctor' and 'Professor', Japanese, for example, employs a number of suffixes attached to names:

– *san* is the 'neutral' form, used mainly for peers and acquaintances, although it is rather formal for use between friends. It is used for both males and females.
– *chan* is a primarily female diminutive form, used mainly to young girls, although teenage girls use it when addressing each other.
– *kun* is a primarily male diminutive form, used mainly to address younger males, although teenage girls use it to address their male peers.
– *sama* is a very polite form, used mainly for people with a much higher status. It is now little used in conversation.
– *sensei* is a form indicating respect, used mainly for teachers, medical doctors and politicians.

Learning how to use such contrasts without long-term exposure to their operation is difficult and, conversely, speakers of such languages can find it hard to come to terms with the relatively unsophisticated address systems of a language like English: how are appropriate respect and politeness to be expressed when so few linguistic resources are available? The tendency is to choose formal modes of address even when less formality would be appropriate.

**Task A4.1.1**

The following is based on something that actually happened. A middle-aged male Asian student came to do a Ph.D. at a British university, supervised by a respected male academic some years his junior. At their first meeting, the supervisor, intending to be friendly, asked the student to address him by his given name. The supervisor addressed the student in this way. During their next few meetings the student insisted on referring to the supervisor as 'Dr *Family name*'. The supervisor again, always in friendly fashion, asked to be called by his given name. The student then began to cancel meetings and avoid his supervisor, and so fell behind with his research. In subsequent discussions with the student it became apparent that he could not bring himself to address the supervisor by his given name alone as this would, in the cultural tradition in which he had been brought up, show disrespect. Nor, however, could he continue to address him as 'Dr *Family name*', as this seemed to be annoying the supervisor. For the student, it was better to avoid contact than, in his eyes, fail to accord appropriate respect or offend the supervisor.

➤ How do you think the problem should have been resolved? Have you ever encountered a similar situation?

Even within a particular society, terms of address change over time. If we examine texts from past periods of history we have to develop sensibilities to different contextual clues contained in the language. In Jane Austen's novels, for example, the nuances of forms of address would have been well known to her original readership. To the modern reader, however, the difference in status between 'Miss Bennett' and 'Miss Elizabeth Bennett' is not immediately apparent. The former, without the first name, refers to the eldest sister. Similar hierarchies still exist today in, for example, families with hereditary titles. The eldest son will inherit a title, which precedes his name, while younger brothers will remain plain 'Mr'.

## A4.2 THE INFLUENCE OF INTEREST AND OCCUPATIONAL GROUPS

When people participate in recurring communication situations they will tend to develop similar ways of talking and writing. They may use similar vocabulary and features of pronunciation and intonation, and develop characteristic patterns of grammar and ways of organising text and discourse. This may result partly from the subject matter, the objects and events that are spoken or written about, or from the value of using 'routines' or language formulae that provide a way of speeding up communication. Using the language of a particular group will also mark the speaker or writer as a member of that group, and so may be motivated by a wish to belong to or gain acceptance within the group. And, of course, developing a special way of communicating may also be motivated by a wish to exclude others. These sets of language items associated with discrete occupational or social groups are often referred to as **registers** (see also Unit A1, p. 12).

Here are three extracts illustrating different language registers:

1. 6 MY EXECUTORS AND TRUSTEES shall have the following powers in addition to all other powers over any share of the Trust Fund

    (a) POWER under the Trustee Act 1925 Section 31 to apply income for maintenance and to accumulate surplus income during a minority but as if the words 'my Trustees think fit' were substituted in sub-section (1) (i) thereof for the words 'may in all the circumstances be reasonable' and as if the proviso at the end of sub-section (1) thereof was omitted[2]

2. Yea. 171 38802 . . . Yea. Race 4 at Albion Park please. Ah, two units to win number 8. Two units to win number 11. Ah, number 6, six by six. Um, number 3, ten units a place. Ah, quinella please, 3 and 10 for ten units. Um, number 6 ten units to win. Um 5 um quinella please 5, 6 and 11 for four units the quinella. I think that's the lot thank you . . . Twenty units. Thank you very much. Bye.[3]

3. *Composition.* Two panes including one of eight first class and one pane of two 26p. *se-tenant*: Pane UIPW33 (8x1st (bright orange-red) two bands (blue fluor)) and two elliptical perf. holes on each vertical edge. One pane of two Millennium stamps *se-tenant*: Pane WP1239 (2x26p. two bands (blue fluor)). Printed in photogravure by Walsall[4]

The first is an extract from a will, and so is a written register of an occupational group – lawyers – who are specialised in drafting and interpreting this kind of document. The second is one side of a telephone conversation in Australia in which a client is placing bets with a salesperson on trotting races (where horses pull a carriage and their driver). The third is from a stamp catalogue, here giving information about a book of ten stamps and its contents. Each has particular characteristics of vocabulary, grammar, and, in the two written texts, punctuation, that make it distinctive. Unless we are part of the community which regularly participates in reading or writing wills, placing or receiving bets (in Australia), or reading or writing stamp auction catalogues, it is difficult to fully understand what is meant in these extracts. Any individual may, of course, have access to a number of registers; a lawyer may also bet on horses or collect stamps and stamp booklets!

The groups of people who share particular registers and use the kinds of text (both spoken and written) in which these registers occur, have been termed **discourse communities**. It can be fairly readily demonstrated that a notion of this kind has some validity. For example, the majority of people reading this book, we assume, will not have used (or be able to understand) the kind of stamp catalogue from which the last extract above is taken, so you are unlikely to consider yourself part of the discourse community which writes and reads this form of text. Yet to others it will be familiar. But while we might be able to say that we are 'in' or 'out' of a particular discourse community, and feel intuitively that such communities exist, giving a precise definition of discourse community can be problematic.

### ★ Task A4.2.1

➤ Think about your occupational and leisure interests. Consider whether there are any particular registers that you use in reading or writing that your friends or – if you are following a course – fellow students may not.

Various writers have defined discourse community in different ways. Some are wide and present difficulties in setting any boundaries for particular discourse communities. Bruce Herzberg suggests that the notion signifies:

> a cluster of ideas: that language use in a group is a form of social behaviour, that discourse is a means of maintaining and extending the group's knowledge and of initiating new members into the group, and that discourse is epistemic or constitutive of the group's knowledge.
> (Herzberg 1986: 1, reported in Swales 1990: 21)

while Patricia Bizzell (1992: 222) defines a discourse community as 'a group of people who share certain language-using practices'. John Swales (1990: 24–27) tried to address the problem of definition by proposing six defining characteristics of a discourse community:

1. it has a broadly agreed set of common public goals;
2. it has mechanisms of intercommunication among its members;
3. it uses its participatory mechanisms primarily to provide information and feedback;
4. it utilises and hence possesses one or more genres in the communicative furtherance of its aims;
5. in addition to owning genres, it has acquired some specific lexis;
6. it has a threshold level of members with a suitable degree of relevant content and discoursal expertise.

A related if broader notion is that of **communities of practice**, which are considered to share not only activities and tasks, but also values, beliefs and commitment to an underlying ideology. We might think of doctors practising orthodox Western medicine as such a community, or even practitioners of a particular alternative medicine such as homeopathy. Individuals are likely to be members of more than one community of practice depending on their work or social lives.

However we choose to label and define groups of this kind, of particular significance in our discussion of the relationship between groups and context is the concept of **genre**. The term genre is widely used to refer to a particular type of art form. So we might talk about 'a literary genre', 'the horror genre', 'TV thrillers of the Inspector Morse genre' and so on. More recently it has been used in language analysis to refer to the categories of text that mature speakers of a language recognise as distinct. These are usually labelled; for example, novels, newspaper editorials, political speeches, everyday conversations, radio phone-ins. Particular professional communities often have their own set of genres with which they regularly work. In the discourse community that works within tertiary education (the academic community) recognisable genres will include student-produced written genres such as the laboratory report, argumentative essay and thesis; written genres produced by academics such as the research article, research grant application; and spoken genres such as the tutorial, lecture, conference presentation and so on.

However, defining 'genre' in this way – and therefore classifying a text as belonging to one genre or another – is not without its difficulties. ('Genre', like 'discourse community', has been the subject of considerable debate.) The communicative purpose of a text is often taken to be the primary criterion in specifying a genre – in other words, if a text is to belong to a particular genre it should share the communicative purpose of the other texts so assigned. But deciding on the communicative purpose of a text can be problematic. John Swales (2001), for example, notes that while a shopping list (a genre type) would appear to be little more than a shorthand aide-memoire for the shopper it may also act as a mechanism for inhibiting impulse purchases on the basis that 'if it is not on the list, don't buy it' (Witte 1992). While a sales receipt (another genre type) seems to be no more than a receipt, it may have other purposes, such as monitoring inventory, calculating sales tax, offering discounts, providing seasonal greetings, and so on. Communicative purpose, then, may be complex and multi-layered.

Over time, comparable situations occur in which members of a discourse community have to meet certain communicative goals. This prompts comparable linguistic responses, and written and spoken genres develop as a consequence, using similar vocabulary, grammar, and organisational features. Newcomers to the discourse community will learn the features of the relevant genres, and so the genres become further established. This is not, of course, to say that genres do not change over time or that speakers or writers must strictly conform to what is typical.

Here is an illustration of an analysis of a particular genre from the academic community (Flowerdew and Dudley-Evans 2002). The genre is a rather specific one: letters sent by the editor of an international journal, *English for Specific Purposes*, to authors who had submitted a paper to be considered for publication. Each paper had been sent for review by anonymous reviewers, and their reports accompanied the editor's letter. The main aim of the letter is to tell authors whether the paper is to be accepted for publication, rejected, or (the usual option) that they are invited to revise and resubmit the paper for further consideration, and also to summarise the views of the reviewers and any suggestions they have for revision. John Flowerdew and Tony Dudley-Evans found that the editorial letters examined had a prototypical structure of four main stages (or 'moves'), reflecting the editor's communicative purposes, within which there were a number of smaller 'steps'.

| Moves | Steps | Example |
|---|---|---|
| 1 Prepare the reader for the decision (*obligatory*) | 1.1 Refer to submission *and/or* <br> 1.2 Apologise for delay *and/or* <br> 1.3 Interpret reviewers' report | 1.1 I am enclosing the two reports on the above manuscript. <br><br> 1.2 I must apologise for the delay in getting these to you. <br> 1.3 Both reports present very full and, I hope, helpful comments on your manuscript. |
| 2 Conveying the decision (*obligatory*) | 2.1 Accept *or* <br><br><br><br> 2.2 Offer resubmission *or* <br><br><br><br><br> 2.3 Accept as a research note *or* <br> 2.4 Reject (+/– mitigate; +/– justify) | 2.1 I think that this article will be acceptable after you have revised it taking the suggestions of the reports and this letter into account. <br> 2.2 I would be very interested in receiving a revised version of the paper, but, as the paper will have to be substantially different from this one, it would be necessary to send it out for further reports. <br> 2.3 I think that the suggestion of rewriting the paper as a Research Note made by the longer report is an excellent one. <br> 2.4 [I have now read the manuscript entitled . . .] I am afraid that it is not really suitable for publication in ESPJ. |
| 3 Making recommendations for revision/ improvement (*optional*) | 3.1 Refer reader to reviewers' recommendations *and/or* <br> 3.2 Make editorial recommendations | 3.1 Both reports are critical of the length of the literature review and of the fact that many of the references are quite old. <br><br> 3.2 I think that the review of the literature could be pruned without too much difficulty. |
| 4 Signing off (*obligatory*) | 4.1 Confirm decision *and/or* <br> 4.2 Mitigate bad news *and/or* | 4.1 If you do all this, we will certainly publish as soon as possible. <br> 4.2 I realise that this will come as a particular disappointment as you have put in a lot of work revising the manuscript. |

| Moves | Steps | Example |
|---|---|---|
| | 4.3 Apologise for delay *and/or* | 4.3 I am sorry that it has taken so long for me to get these comments to you. |
| | 4.4 Refer to enclosure *and/or* | 4.4 I enclose an annotated copy to indicate the changes I have suggested. |
| | 4.5 Refer to personal matter *and/or* | 4.5 [name of place] is mostly sunny, though distinctly cold for spring. |
| | 4.6 Present a deadline *and/or* | 4.6 If you make these corrections by the end of the year . . . |
| | 4.7 Suggest further contact *and/or* | 4.7 If you would like to discuss this further you have my e-mail address. |
| | 4.8 Give encouragement | 4.8 . . . as this is an original and very interesting piece of work. |

The organisation and language of these letters both reflect and also help to create the values and goals of the journal. These reflect the values and goals of the current and previous editors of the journal and its editorial and advisory boards, and are stated formally in the journal and on the publisher's website. These in turn will be influenced by the values and goals of the academic field (Applied Linguistics) and the academic community more generally.

For authors, publishing reports of their research in a journal such as *English for Specific Purposes* is a way of gaining and maintaining acceptance within the academic community. In many cases issues of job security and promotion are at stake. On behalf of the wider academic community, the editor acts as a 'gatekeeper' with the role of maintaining high academic standards. On the other hand, the role also involves breaking down barriers and assisting authors to gain access to the academic community by offering guidance on how to improve papers so that they become publishable. This dual role is reflected in the detailed advice given in the editorial letters, particularly perhaps to less experienced contributors. Responsibility to the wider community is also seen in the way in which the editor encourages resubmission, often being deliberately vague so as to express no commitment to publish the paper should it be resubmitted.

Part of the ethos of the journal is to encourage contributions from a wide range of countries and from non-native speakers of English, reflecting the international nature of the profession. Encouragement to continue and develop research and to resubmit papers where they fall short of a publishable standard are a major feature of the letters. Being part of a community is also reflected in the language of the letters which seeks to maintain good relations and avoid face-threatening communicative behaviour, so that various ways are used to 'soften' rejection and criticism. The editor may know the authors personally or be aware that, at conferences or educational visits, in the relatively small world of teaching English for Specific Purposes, their paths may cross in the future.

Of particular interest to us here (see also Unit C2) are grammatical features that are characteristic of each move or step and their place in realising the communicative purpose of that move. For example, Flowerdew and Dudley-Evans observe that a regular pattern in Move 3, making recommendations, is the use of 'I think' followed by a modal verb ('should', 'need to', 'could', 'can'), with a directive function, as in:

> I think that you should focus much more on these points . . .
> I think you need to take a little time . . .
> I think you could draw a parallel . . .
> I think you can cut the last part . . .

## A4.3  THE INFLUENCE OF THE INSTITUTIONAL CONTEXT

Another kind of community which may develop special characteristics of language and interaction is the large institution such as a hospital, university or large business. To illustrate, we will consider the contextual factors surrounding the production of genres in a multinational corporation, using work by Catherine Nickerson (2000). Nickerson views the social context for a multinational corporation as having a number of hierarchical levels, represented in Figure A4.1.

She suggests that certain situations will recur within corporations (such as the need to order products, deal with complaints, transfer employees within the organisation, negotiate contracts and draw these up). These situations will necessitate certain social (or rhetorical) actions (such as making an enquiry about the availability of materials and placing a written order, or making a recommendation to head office), which are undertaken by particular participants, depending on their position in the hierarchy. Managers, supervisors and technicians may typically be engaged in different forms of written and spoken communication. The recurring situations, social actions, and participants are factors which determine the genres, or 'typified communicative practices' (reports, letters, emails and so on), of the corporation, and in turn these genres may have characteristic linguistic features.

A number of contextual factors determine which situations recur. These include the type of business activity in which the corporation is engaged, and such factors as its size and structure (for example, whether or not the organisation is divided into separate departments), the technology available to it (for example, whether communication within the corporation is mainly through face-to-face contact or email), and methods of control (for example, how employees are supervised, monitored and rewarded). Also of influence are the national culture within which the organisation operates and its 'corporate culture' – what it sees to be its reason

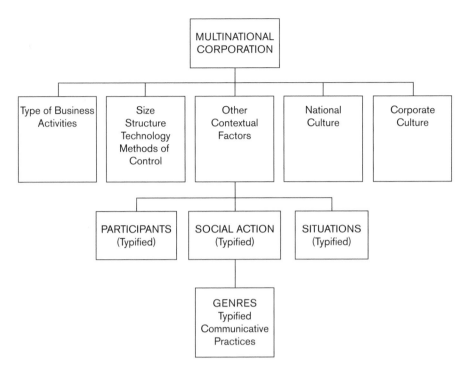

*Figure A4.1* The contextual factors surrounding a multinational corporation and the configuration of typified situations, participants and social action; genres.

Source: Nickerson 2000: 39

for being and what it hopes to achieve. As the contexts vary, so too do the genres produced and/ or their recurrent linguistic features.

We will explore briefly the last two of these areas: *national culture* and *corporate culture*. Ron Scollon and Suzanne Scollon (1995) have argued that in an anglophone corporate culture there is a concern to focus on objective facts and logical analysis, in a style which is 'clear, brief and sincere'. Scollon and Scollon trace this style back to the seventeenth century, in a conscious decision of the British Royal Society to take this as the preferred style for scientific communication. They report Thomas Sprat, Bishop of Rochester, who commented on the approach to language taken by the Royal Society in his *History of the Royal Society* as follows:

> They have therefore been more rigorous in putting in Execution the only Remedy, that can be found for this *Extravagance*; and that has been a constant Resolution, to reject all Amplifications, Digressions, and Swellings of Style; to return back to the primitive Purity and Shortness, when Men deliver'd so many *Things*, almost in an equal number of *Words*. They have exacted from their Members, a close, naked, natural way of Speaking;

positive Expressions, clear Senses; a native Easiness; bringing all Things as near the mathematicall Plainness as they can; and preferring the Language of Artizans, Countrymen, and Merchants before that of Wits, or Scholars.

(Kenner 1987: 117, cited in Scollon 1995: 99)

As Western science and technology developed, and with it business, this became the preferred style in both fields where 'effective' communication is needed.

However, different national cultures may have different priorities in business interaction. For example, Haru Yamada (1997) has suggested that United States and Japanese business meetings respond to different goals. In the United States, meetings are a response to the need to manage business tasks at hand and their goal is to bring about decisions. Japanese meetings, on the other hand, are a response to the need for an effective way of exchanging opinions, and their goal is to manage the ongoing relationship among colleagues. Japanese corporations have evolved other systems for making decisions, with employees' opinions being gathered outside meetings (Nickerson 2000: 40). These different goals influence the lexical and grammatical choices made in these contexts. For example, Japanese meetings will typically begin with a period of 'sounding out aims' in order to establish the cohesiveness of the group and to 'confirm goodwill among meeting members'. In American meetings, however, the 'real business' is done first, putting more interpersonal interaction at the end of the meeting, if there is a place for it at all (Yamada 1997: 118).

The culture and ideology of individual corporations, too, can be reflected in the language used within the organisation. Perhaps the clearest statement of this link is in the 'mission statements' of companies and organisations. The main aim of such statements, often written by senior management, is usually to present and promote the values and goals of the organisation and by doing so encourage employees, to whom it is primarily addressed, to accept these values and goals as their own. John Swales and Priscilla Rogers (1995) have looked at mission statements from two United States companies, Honeywell and the Dana Corporation, and shown how language choices are made in order to foster affiliation and identification with the company. One of these is the use of 'we', 'our' and 'ours' to refer to the company or its employees. For example:

We are committed to sustaining our focus on the controls business as we grow and change . . . (*Honeywell: Strategic Priorities*)

We will grow in selected markets by implementing our market strategies. (*Dana Corporation: The philosophy and policies of Dana*)

Interestingly, when the company's values and goals may conflict with those likely to be held by its employees, the authors of the mission statements avoid *we*. The following extracts are from the Dana Corporation:

(a) The purpose of the Dana Corporation is to earn money for its shareholders and to increase the value of the investment.

(b) It is highly desirable to outsource a portion of our production needs.

In (a), the company itself rather than 'we' is associated with profits. The alternative 'We earn money for our shareholders . . .' would suggest that individual employees work in order to make money for those who invest in the company – not something that many workers would wish to be reminded of. In (b), 'outsourcing' (paying people from outside the company to do parts of its work) is an issue of some controversy between workers and management, and not all workers would wish to be associated with the view that it is 'highly desirable'.

In this unit we have looked at:

**Summary**

- the relationship between language and socio-cultural context
- the influence of national culture on language choice
- the registers and genres of particular discourse communities and communities of practice
- the influence of institutional context, and the effects of national and corporate culture on language use within institutions.

## LOOKING AHEAD

The relationships between grammar and socio-cultural context will be explored further in various places in the book. In particular, Unit B2 focuses on institutional influence on language choice in radio phone-ins and doctor–patient interviews. We return to move analysis in Unit C2 in analysing letters of recommendation and business letters. The language associated with academic writing is examined both historically and in contemporary academic articles across a range of disciplines in Unit B3. In Unit C3 we analyse grammatical features of academic writing using a corpus approach.

# Unit A5
# Context in approaches to grammar

In Unit A1 we noted that grammatical descriptions are generally underpinned by a particular approach to grammar. Each approach makes assumptions about the nature of language and develops its own methods, techniques and terminology for grammatical analysis. This book is not the place to present a thorough comparative study of approaches to grammar. Our interest is instead focused on the relationship between grammar and context, and so in this unit we take a number of approaches to grammar (and to language more generally) and examine how far they consider this relationship and what they have to say about it.

## A5.1  FORMAL AND FUNCTIONAL APPROACHES

A useful starting point is the broad distinction that is often made between *formal* and *functional* approaches to grammar. Graham Lock (1996: 1), for example, suggests that a formal approach:

> sees grammar as a set of *rules* which specify all the possible grammatical structures of the language. In this approach, a clear distinction is usually made between grammatical (sometimes called *well-formed*) sentences and ungrammatical sentences. The primary concern is with the *forms* of grammatical structures and their relationship to one another, rather than with their meaning or their uses in different contexts.

A functional approach, on the other hand:

> sees language first and foremost as a system of communication and analyzes grammar to discover how it is organized to allow speakers and writers to make and exchange meanings. Rather than insisting on a clear distinction between grammatical and ungrammatical forms, the focus is usually on the appropriateness of a form for a particular communicative purpose in a particular context. The primary concern is with the *functions* of structures and their constituents and with their meanings in context.

The approaches to grammar we discuss briefly below represent a range from primarily formal to primarily functional, although, as we will see, most have both formal and functional characteristics.

## A5.2 TRADITIONAL GRAMMAR

The label 'traditional grammar' is often applied to grammatical descriptions produced by classical Greek scholars, through to major works of the late nineteenth and early twentieth centuries, such as Henry Sweet's *New English Grammar* (between 1892–1898) and Otto Jespersen's *A Modern English Grammar on Historical Principles* (1909–1949). Although traditional grammar is generally said to have been superseded by more modern approaches since the middle of the twentieth century, the influence of traditional grammar on many current grammatical descriptions and on the teaching of grammar to native and non-native speakers of English is considerable.

To give some idea of what a traditional grammatical description looks like, here are three extracts. (1) is from Sweet's *New English Grammar* (Part II: *Syntax*, p. 62) in a section contrasting the perfect with the future perfect; (2) and (3) are from Jespersen's *A Modern English Grammar* (Part II: *Syntax*), (2) on 'Person' (p. 131) and (3) on 'Shades of Meaning of Mass-Words with the Zero Article' (p. 438):

(1)  **2243** The perfect is used instead of the future perfect in clauses dependent on a sentence with a verb in the future, as in *by the time you have washed and dressed, breakfast will be ready*, and in other cases where the future meaning is clear from the context: *when will you come again? as soon as I have finished my work | I bet you half-a-crown that before nightfall I have seen him!*

(2)  4.41.  In the third person we have the forms

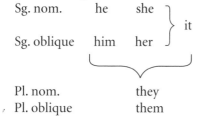

Sg. nom.    he    she ⎤
                              ⎬ it
Sg. oblique    him    her ⎦

Pl. nom.              they
, Pl. oblique          them

(3)  12.64. Mass words connected with zero may denote (1) an indefinite (undefined) quantity (part) of the thing meant. . . . Luke 22.19 And he took bread, and gave thanks, and brake it | Butler Er [Penguin] 48 Solitude had unmanned me already | . . .

While traditional grammars are concerned both with linguistic form and also grammatical meaning, acknowledgement of the relationship between context and grammar is limited. The variety of English that is described by Sweet is that 'in general use among educated people' (Part I, p. xi), and Sweet clearly sets himself up as the judge of educated usage. Jespersen's description is of the grammar of literary language, with all his illustrative examples taken from literary texts. (The examples in the extract above are from the Book of Luke in the Bible, and Samuel Butler's novel *Erewhon.*) The focus in both works, then, and in traditional grammar generally, is on a prestige variety of English: educated English in Sweet's work and literary English in Jespersen's. The implication is that anything outside this prestige variety is not acceptable and therefore not to be described in the grammar. There is little or no attempt, then, to describe which grammatical forms might be considered appropriate or possible in given social situations, and only very limited comment on potential differences between spoken and written English.

A further illustration of the neglect of context in traditional grammar is noted by Michael McCarthy (1994, 2001). Traditional grammars frequently describe paradigmatic choices, so that the subject personal-pronoun paradigm is given as *I*, *you* etc. (as illustrated for the third-person pronoun in extract (2) above), and *this*, *that*, *these* and *those* are presented together as determiners or pronouns. This way of representing oppositions will be familiar to most people who have studied foreign languages. However, the oppositions that arise in context may not be those suggested in traditional grammars. In the following example (McCarthy 2001: 55):

> Freda told me about Sally's problem. It?/this?/that? grabbed my attention immediately.

*It*, *this* and *that* form a paradigm of grammatical choices, each of which represents a different 'topical focus'. *It* simply keeps going the topic that is being focused on; *this* marks a shift to a new focus; *that* refers to a topic different from the one currently being focused on (McCarthy 1994, 2001). The paradigms that become available in actual discourse, then, are not necessarily the 'ready made' ones presented in traditional grammars, based on formal features, but are a reflection of the context in which they occur.

## A5.3 GENERATIVE GRAMMAR

The most influential formal approaches are those derived from the work of the American linguist Noam Chomsky (starting with the publication of *Syntactic Structures* in 1957), which come under the heading 'transformational-generative' grammar (or sometimes just 'generative', the label we will use below). Generative grammar differs from a traditional approach in a number of fundamental respects, and we will highlight three here.

First, the formal apparatus for representing language is radically different. While word class labels (noun, verb etc.) are similar, generative grammar defines grammatical classes in linguistic rather than notional terms. For example, while traditional grammar might define a noun as 'a word used for naming a person, place etc.' generative grammar defines it in formal terms, referring perhaps to the fact that a noun occurs before plural -*s* or its alternants, or after *the* or adjectives. And the representation of generative rules is far removed from anything found in Sweet or Jespersen's work. Here is an example of a 'phrase structure rule' (Celce-Murcia and Larsen-Freeman 1983: 11):

$$
NP \rightarrow \left\{ \begin{array}{l} (det)\ N\ (pl) \\ \\ pro \end{array} \right\}
$$

It is intended to represent the information that the noun phrase (NP) includes either an obligatory head noun (N) preceded by an optional determiner (det) and an optional plural inflection (pl), or a pronoun (pro). 'Transformational rules' are intended to show the relationship between sentences with the same meaning but a different grammatical form. A rule to show the link between active and passive sentence can be represented as follows (Crystal 1987: 97):

$$
NP1 + V + NP2 \rightarrow NP2 + Aux + Ven + by + NP1
$$

The left side represents an active sentence with the form noun phrase (NP1) followed by a verb (V) and a second noun phrase (NP2). The right side shows how this is transformed into a passive sentence with NP2 being placed at the beginning and NP1 preceded by 'by' at the end, and the verb changing from a past tense to past participle (V*en*) with an auxiliary before it.

Second, the widely accepted belief of traditional grammar was that a grammatical description could be produced by applying appropriate procedures (primarily observational techniques and a set of given grammatical classes) to a 'corpus' of language. As we have seen, in Sweet's case this corpus was the English used by 'educated people' (presumably with himself as the model), while Jespersen's corpus was a set of literary texts. Chomsky rejected the view that a grammatical description should account for what is observed in a body of data. Instead, he argued that a grammar should be able to generate all the grammatical but none of the ungrammatical sentences of a language. Generative grammars, then, are concerned with what is *possible*, and not with what *occurs* in language use.

Third, the concern of generative grammar is to represent the relationship between linguistic features and the innate ability of human beings to master language. It is assumed that people have an innate system of rules – in other words, a grammar – on the basis that human languages are so complex that learning them from scratch is beyond our capability, and that we must therefore have some special pre-disposition. Some of these rules are 'universal' in that all human beings possess them, while others are language-specific. Not all of the language produced by a native speaker will reflect their knowledge of a language (that is, a knowledge of its rules). Because of performance factors such as memory lapses, false, starts and so on, some speech data will be 'tainted' or 'degraded' (Ouhalla 1994: 7–8) and therefore not useful as evidence of innate knowledge.

Chomsky's view of the relationship between grammar and language in use in context was made clear in the first chapter of *Syntactic Structures*, where he says that: 'grammar is autonomous and independent of meaning' (Chomsky 1957: 17). In this view, then, grammar is independent of the study of the use of language in situations. Although some later work on generative grammar takes meaning to be an essential part of the grammar of the language (e.g. Baker 1995; Zribi-Hertz 1989) consideration of the use of the language in the real world is excluded.

## A5.4 SYSTEMIC FUNCTIONAL GRAMMAR

While generative grammars are primarily concerned with describing language as an object, and how this reflects the distinctive properties of the human mind, a functional grammar such as systemic functional grammar (SFG) places at its centre the social context of language, and explores how language is used and how it is structured for this use. (For other functional grammars, see, for example, Dik 1978, van Valin 2001.) SFG is mainly associated with the work of the British-born linguist Michael Halliday (e.g. 1973, 1978, 1994, Halliday and Matthiessen 2004). Halliday considers that the clause is the unit in which three different kinds of meaning are combined. These he calls **experiential** (concerned with content and ideas), **interpersonal** (concerned with the relationship between participants in the interaction and the speaker/writer's attitude towards the content) and **textual** (concerned with how language is used to organise the text itself). We can look at the clause from each of these three perspectives, and each suggests different ways of dividing up a clause and labelling its component parts. Thompson (2004) illustrates this by dividing and labelling (using SFG terminology) the components of the clause 'Did Jim take her calculator?'

| type of structure | | Did | Jim | take | her calculator? |
|---|---|---|---|---|---|
| experiential | → | | Actor | Process | Goal |
| interpersonal | → | Finite | Subject | Predicator | Complement |
| textual | → | Theme | | Rheme | |

The main grammatical resource for expressing the experiential function is **transitivity**, so analytical focus is on the kinds of processes being talked about and the participants involved. The main grammatical resource for expressing the interpersonal function is **mood** (declarative, interrogative or imperative), so analytical focus is on such things as the order of the subject and verb element. The main grammatical resource for expressing the textual function is **information structure**, so analytical focus is on which item to place first in the clause. The initial element, the **theme**, often picks up on information in the later element, the **rheme**, in a previous clause and thereby facilitates cohesion. The overall message of the clause is comprised of a combination of meanings expressed by the choices made in all three functions.

Like traditional and generative grammars, SFG recognises a hierarchy of grammatical units: words make up groups which make up clauses (see also Unit

A1). Above the clause, however, SFG analyses **clause complexes** (two or more clauses linked by coordination or subordination) rather than sentences. Description in SFG extends beyond the clause complex to the grammatical resources used to link parts of a text (both spoken and written) and make it hang together. These cohesive devices include reference, substitution and ellipsis, conjunction, and lexical cohesion (Halliday and Hasan 1976). The analysis of texts is common in SFG and the main aim is usually to discover how the social context in which it was created is reflected in the text (or what impact the text in turn has on the social context).

Context, then, is at the centre of SFG. Everything that is said or written is viewed as occurring within a context of use, and over time the uses of language are seen to shape its formal system. The interplay between language and context is also highlighted in SFG. Not only is language influenced by the context in which it is used, it is also considered to influence that context.

## A5.5  EMERGENT GRAMMAR AND PATTERN GRAMMAR

Finally in this section we outline two approaches to grammar that are radically different from traditional and generative grammars, although they share some of the features of SFG. They were developed around the same time and, although there are substantial differences in detail, they share the view that context and communication are at the core of grammar.

### *Emergent grammar*

Paul Hopper (1998) suggests that most views of grammar see it as an abstract system, held together by a set of rules, which exists prior to its use in discourse. It is therefore independent of the time and situation in which it is used, and meanings exist outside their contexts. It is assumed that in order to achieve effective communication, participants must share a knowledge of this system, although individuals may use it more or less effectively. From this perspective, a grammatical description tries to identify the principles by which elements of language (such as words) can be classified according to their distribution in larger elements (such as phrases or sentences). Some approaches may go on to relate features of the grammar to the invariable attributes of the human mind, while others explore how the features are used in social settings for communicative purposes. But in all such approaches it is assumed that the grammatical system exists first and is then deployed in communication.

Hopper's alternative view of an 'emergent grammar' reverses this order. He argues that the starting point of grammar is communication. In similar contexts, the resulting discourse will include routines or repeated patterns of language. It is the categories of these regularities that constitute grammar; grammar, then, *emerges* out of interaction (hence, 'emergent grammar'). Language is seen to be largely a collection of formulaic or routine constructions which speakers will borrow or adapt from their previous experiences of communication in similar circumstances on similar topics and with similar participants. To illustrate, here is an example of speech from Hopper's paper taken originally from Carterette and Jones (1974: 422):

> Well no the problem is and this is what the psychologist has mentioned to me. these kids wont wont show any hope like the see you take a normal uh the average retarded child i mean the one who doesnt have any handicaps like blindness or deafness or something like that. he will improve a little bit. maybe a lot. it depends on how badly disturbed he is. but these people wont because theyre still going to no matter what happens theyre going to be living in a fantasy world. because theyre blind. and they have to imagine and they keep asking one question after the other and then nothing they say makes any sense and nothing is relevant to the situation. and it never will be because they well there's just such a sharp line of differentiation between the normal blind and then the emotionally disturbed blind.

Hopper notes the following routines in this extract:

| | | |
|---|---|---|
| the problem is | has mentioned to me | these kids |
| you take | a little bit | maybe a lot |
| it depends on | no matter what happens | they're still going to |
| living in a fantasy world | one question after another | nothing they say makes any sense |
| relevant to the situation | sharp line of differentiation | emotionally disturbed |

Different routines will emerge relevant to the context. Routines such as 'the problem is' or 'a little bit' are likely to be found in a wide variety of contexts, while 'sharp line of differentiation' and 'emotionally disturbed' are likely to be found in fewer, more specialised contexts. When enough routines have a similar pattern, this pattern forms part of a subsystem of the grammar. Because speakers will have more or less experience of particular contexts, and therefore the routines associated with them, the grammar of each speaker will be different.

Seeing grammar as being derived from communicative purpose and context in this way makes us rethink conventional views of grammar in a number of important ways. First, as the categories of routines are the grammar, and as routines may or may not coincide with what is usually recognised as grammatical units (phrases, clauses etc.), we need to reconsider the relevance of these grammatical units and look for alternatives. Second, many previous grammatical descriptions try to be comprehensive, with the aim of describing the whole of the grammatical system. An 'emergent grammatical description' (if one could be written) would need to take into account the variability of context and could never achieve comprehensiveness. Third, rather than viewing grammar as an external, abstract system shared by speakers, grammar is internal to the individual and constantly changing as their experience of discourse in different communicative contexts increases. Fourth, if grammar represents categories of observed repetitions rather than a pre-existing abstract system, this view lends support to basing grammatical description on language in context (such as in a corpus approach, see Unit A9) rather than intuitive data.

### Pattern grammar

Echoing Hopper's claim that language users build up a set of context-related routines, John Sinclair (1991: 110), who has done extensive work on corpus linguistics, suggests that 'a language user has available to him or her a large number of semi-preconstructed phrases that constitute single choices'. He goes on to note that some of these are fixed (e.g. *of course, just now, on an empty stomach*), others allow different kinds of internal variation (e.g. *it's not in his nature to, it was scarcely in their nature to*), and that many uses of words and phrases tend to co-occur with particular grammatical choices (e.g. *set about* is closely associated with an -*ing* form, as in *set about leaving*).

Basing their work on Sinclair's observations, Gill Francis and Susan Hunston (e.g. Francis *et al.* 1996, 1998, Hunston and Francis 1999) have produced an approach which they term 'pattern grammar'. Through an investigation of large electronic corpora of spoken and written text (see Unit A9), they are able to identify frequently-occurring grammatical patterns associated with particular words (in particular, what follows the word) as well as listing words that are frequently found in these patterns. For example, one of the significant patterns associated with the verb *feel* is *feel + as if/though*, as in '*It feels as if/ though I'd never been away*', and other verbs found in this pattern are *act, appear, behave, look, smell, sound, speak, talk,* and *taste* (Francis *et al.* 1996: 121–122).

As a discourse progresses, words anticipate patterns that follow, so a reader or hearer has an expectation of what it is to come. For example, in

> I'm not very good at this sort of thing

the verb *be* ('*m*) anticipates an adjective (*good*); *good* anticipates *at* and a noun phrase (*this sort*); and *sort* anticipates *of* and a noun phrase (*of thing*). Taking us beyond the usual domain of grammar, other phrases anticipate larger-scale textual patterns. For example, the phrase '*you might expect*' very frequently anticipates some kind of contradiction, as in '*you might expect James to agree and write it off as an elaborate allegory. But he cannot resist building up his case for sticking another pin in an overcrowded map*' (Hunston and Francis 1999: 227).

### Task A5.5.1

➤ List the grammatical patterns which you think commonly follow the verbs *seem* and *hope*. (You can check your intuitions to some extent with data in Unit C3.)

Pattern grammar is based on the assumption that words are associated with particular patterns of language, and that these patterns can be observed in investigations of large corpora of text. Superficially, then, it would seem that lexis rather than communicative context is at the core of the approach. However, Hunston and Francis (1999: 240) illustrate how context is central in their work taking the improbable utterance '*My friend told*'. A pattern grammar explains the improbability of this utterance by saying that, from the corpus evidence, the verb *tell* does not occur without a following noun (except in the sense 'giving away a secret'). If we remember that a corpus represents what is done with language, then it is clear that if a pattern occurs frequently in the corpus, then it does so because contexts occur frequently where this pattern meets communicative requirements. Conversely, if a pattern is infrequent, this is because contexts rarely arise where it is needed.

Hunston and Francis are at pains to point out that if a pattern does not occur, this is not to say that contexts will never arise in which a pattern is needed. A simple illustration of how patterns change can be seen in the verb *enjoy*. This is usually found in the pattern 'verb + noun phrase', where the noun phrase is sometimes a reflexive pronoun. However, a relatively new use (in British English, although perhaps more well established in North America) is the phrase '*Enjoy!*', an informal phrase often used when you have given something to someone – in our experience, said most commonly by waiters in pizza restaurants! This seems to be an instance of grammar being created as new communicative contexts emerge.

As well as challenging some notions central to traditional grammatical descriptions, such as word classes, and units such as phrases and clauses, a pattern grammar has implications for how we teach English as a foreign or second language. It would suggest that, rather than focusing separately on the teaching of grammar and of vocabulary, we should help learners to develop awareness of frequently occurring patterns associated with particular words. So, for example, learners could be encouraged to predict or notice in real texts words that typically come after particular verbs or nouns.

**Summary**

In this unit we have looked at the extent to which the following approaches to grammar take context into account:

■ formal and functional approaches
■ traditional grammar
■ generative grammar
■ systemic functional grammar
■ emergent grammar and pattern grammar.

## LOOKING AHEAD

Systemic functional approaches to grammar are exemplified in Unit B3, where Michael Halliday discusses scientific writing, and Unit B6 in the extract by Clare Painter on child language. Pattern grammar is associated closely with corpus linguistics, which forms the basis of the extracts in B1 and B4 and the analysis in C3.

# Unit A6
# Presenting a view of the world through grammatical choices

So far we have looked at some fundamental ideas in talking about grammar (in Unit A1), and in the notion of context (in Units A2–A4), and we then went on to consider the place of context in some important approaches to grammatical description (in Unit A5). In this unit and the next we explore in more detail the way in which context is both represented and constructed by means of specific sets of grammatical choices. In this unit we focus on how **transitivity** can be manipulated to present different views of events, and in the next, A7, we look at grammatical resources for expressing interpersonal relations through **mood, modality**, and choice of **personal pronouns** and **reporting verbs**.

Here, then, we will consider ways in which we can express the same information in different ways by exploiting transitivity. Compare, for example, the following sentences:

a.  The police pushed the rioters back.
b.  The rioters were pushed back by the police.
c.  The rioters were pushed back.

In each case, two groups are involved, 'the police' and 'the rioters', and one action, 'pushing back'. In (a) 'the police' are the starting point of the clause, while in (b) and (c) it is 'the rioters' that are highlighted in this way. In (c), mention of 'the police' is omitted. Of particular interest to us here is *when* the grammar of English allows us to manipulate information in this way, and *what motivations* people have for choosing one means of ordering information or another.

## A6.1  WHAT IS TRANSITIVITY?

Before looking at what an analysis of transitivity can tell us, in this section we will briefly outline the notion of transitivity. If you are already familiar with this, you may wish to move directly on to A6.2, or read quickly through it to refresh your understanding.

A clause usually contains a verb group, indicating what sort of process or state is being talked about, and one or more noun groups, indicating the people or things being talked about. While most clauses contain a noun group functioning as **subject,** they may or may not contain a noun group functioning as **object**. For example, the verb *enjoy* and *lob* require an object to complete their meanings in the clauses:

a.  while France <u>enjoyed</u> *the glory of hosting the leaders of the world's richest nations* . . .

b.  the protestors <u>lobbed</u> *Molotov cocktails and stones* at the police lines . . .[5]

Verb phrases are underlined and objects are in italics. A clause containing an object is termed a **transitive clause** and a verb with an object a **transitive verb**. The verb *had rampaged* in the following clause doesn't have an object:

c.  when anarchists wearing black hoods and ski masks <u>had rampaged</u> through Geneva . . .

A clause without an object is termed an **intransitive clause** and a verb without an object an **intransitive verb**. Transitive verbs may have passive forms, as in

d.  In Lausanne, 31 miles along the side of Lake Geneva, *scores of protesters* <u>were arrested</u> . . .

e.  *an inquiry* <u>had been launched</u>.

while intransitive verbs can not. Many verbs, such as *suffer*, can occur with or without an object. Compare the text extract

f.  He <u>suffered</u> *multiple fractures* . . .

with the constructed clause

g.  He <u>suffered</u> terribly.

A special class of verbs which can be transitive or intransitive are termed **ergatives**. These allow the same noun group as object in transitive clauses and as subject in intransitive clauses (Stubbs 1996: 133). An example is the verb *march*.

Compare the text extract

h.  About 1, 000 people <u>marched</u> from the activist camp . . .

with the constructed clause

i.  The police <u>marched</u> *about 1,000 people* away from the city centre.

We can think of the people or things represented in the subject and object of the clause as the <u>**participants**</u> in the activity represented in the verb. The number and type of participants depends on the kind of process that is encoded in the verb. The verb 'lobbed' in b above designates a process that involves another thing (here, 'Molotov cocktails and stones'). A verb such as 'lobbed' relates to a <u>**material process,**</u> in that it describes a physical action. Different states of affairs are encoded in other classes of verb and these classes occur with different types and numbers of participants. For example, some verbs relate to **mental processes**, our inner mental experiences of sensing the world – the way we feel, perceive, think and talk about things – as in:

j.   I felt pretty silly wearing a plastic walnut shell on my head. (BNC: A3P)*

while others designate what are sometimes referred to as **relational processes**:

k.   He seems a level-headed lad with a great temperament for the game. (BNC: CH3)*

i.   Italy is the cradle of European civilisation. (BNC: A1F)*

*   The reference information given in brackets refers to the original text source in the British National Corpus (BNC).

Verbs indicating relational processes always have two participants, as their role is to relate one to the other. In the first, the verb *seems* relates a quality or feature to the sentence subject; in the second, the verb *is* sets up a relationship of identity between 'Italy' and 'the cradle of European civilisation'.

## A6.2   WHY IS TRANSITIVITY SUCH AN IMPORTANT GRAMMATICAL RESOURCE?

The particular importance of transitivity is that it makes available a number of options for representing information in different ways, and the choices we make can indicate our point of view. We will look at two aspects of this in this section: the *roles that we assign to participants*; and process of *nominalization* in the representation of participants.

### *Assigning roles*

The subject participant is essentially the 'actor' in the process and the object participant the 'acted upon', the person or thing that the action happens to. The positioning of 'actor' and 'acted upon' in the clause can be varied. Compare, for example:

a.   The police shot one Italian protester dead.
b.   One Italian protester was shot dead by the police.

In a, the 'actor' fronts the clause, whereas in b the 'acted upon' is brought to the front. We should note here that there isn't always a correspondence between the subject and 'actor' and the object and 'acted upon'. In, for example:

c.   One Italian protester died in the shootings.

the subject (*One Italian protester*) is the 'acted upon'.

More generally, we can manipulate which participant we wish to represent as the 'actor' and which participant the 'acted upon' with respect to a particular action. Here are extracts from the text in which the police and the demonstrators are the participants involved:

d.  Police clash with anti-capitalists after day of peaceful protest (Headline)
e.  police in Geneva and Lausanne fought with groups of anarchists and anti-capitalists.
f.  they [the police] fired volleys of teargas and plastic bullets and mounted baton charges [implied 'at the protesters'].
g.  police used teargas and plastic bullets to force them [the protesters] back from the hotel districts . . .
h.  scores of protesters were arrested after police used tear gas and plastic bullets . . .
i.  a group of about 30 clashed with police near the Rue du Strand.
j.  the protesters lobbed Molotov cocktails and stones at the police lines.

In extracts d–h, the police are represented as the 'actors' and the demonstrators as the 'acted upon' – or to put it another way, at the receiving end of the police actions. In i and j, however, the demonstrators are represented as the 'actors' and the police the 'acted upon'. The impression created in the article by the repeated representation of the police as the actors in the violent protest that took place is that the author views their presence as at least an incitement to the violence, if not the cause itself.

A further illustration comes from Michael McCarthy and Ronald Carter (1994: 156–157). The following three headlines report the same event, an incident during the miners' strike of 1984 involving the then head of the British National Coal Board, Ian McGregor. k is from the *Daily Telegraph*, a right-wing newspaper, l from the *Morning Star*, a Communist newspaper and m from the *Guardian*, a liberal independent newspaper:

k.  Coal supremo felled in pit fury
l.  McGregor scraps pit visit in face of angry demo
m.  NCB chief fit after incident at pit

In k, McGregor (the 'Coal supremo') is presented as the acted upon. No actor is mentioned (that is, it is not said who 'felled' him), although the implication is that the miners were responsible. In l, although an 'angry demo' is reported, direct responsibility for scrapping the visit is assigned to the actor, McGregor. In m, the information is presented more neutrally, with no indication or responsibility for the 'incident'. (In this extract 'fit' is a noun; that is, the NCB chief was very angry.) The way in which the information is presented in each headline reflects the view of the writer and, more generally, the ideology of the newspaper in which it appears.

We noted in 6.1 that certain classes of verb (material, mental and relational processes) typically occur with particular numbers and types of participants. For example, the usual state of affairs is that it is people who perform mental processes: that is, who feel, perceive, say, ask, and so on. However, by using such a verb a participant which is not a person can be projected as having this quality. In the examples below, a company (in n) and a newspaper (*Socialist Worker*) (in o) are portrayed as conscious by their co-selection with verbs denoting mental processes ('decide' and 'wonder'):

n.   The company has decided to axe 53 Mirror employees, which accounts for a tenth of the job cuts across the national and regional newspaper group announced last week.[6]

o.   HSE [Health and Safety Executive] documents seen by *Socialist Worker* say that this move, 'has raised issue of the process by which HSE exercises these powers, and what other factors other than simply worker safety need to be taken into consideration'. . . . But *Socialist Worker* wonders what these 'other factors' – mentioned in the HSE documents – are?[7]

 **Task A6.2.1**

➤ Before reading on, consider what effect this choice has in each case.

➤ Try to rephrase the sentences to substitute a conscious participant instead.

The effect in n. is to suggest that the decision was not taken by an individual, but by a group of people (here, senior managers) on behalf of the company as a whole. Although the text from which o is taken was presumably written by an individual (although the writer was not named), in using '*Socialist Worker* wonders' the question appears to be posed on behalf of the newspaper and, by implication, of all its readers. A challenge to the Health and Safety Executive made by *Socialist Worker* readers as a collective body, it seems to be suggested, has more impact than one made by a lone journalist.

### *Nominalisation*

Processes are most obviously realised as verbs. However, processes can also be nominalised – that is, realised as a noun – and these nominalisations can then become participants in other processes. For example, processes expressed by the verbs *accuse, extend, describe,* and *observe* can be expressed alternatively in the nouns *accusation, extension, description,* and *observation*. The process of nominalisation will usually have consequences for other parts of the sentence. For example, the process of 'accusing' could be expressed with the verb 'accuse' in (the constructed):

a.   Each side accused the other of being hell-bent on trouble. While this was happening the focus of last night's disturbances was the centre of Geneva.

or alternatively with the noun 'accusation' in (as appeared in the original text):

b.   Amid accusations from each side that it was the other which was hell-bent on trouble, the focus of last night's disturbances was the centre of Geneva.

If we use a verb to describe a process, then we need to give the verb a subject (and with some verbs an object, too), but if we use a nominalisation, the participants relating to that process can be left out. Compare the constructed examples:

c.   If women consume alcohol in pregnancy, this can lead to birth defects.
d.   The consumption of alcohol in pregnancy can lead to birth defects.

In c, the process is expressed in the verb *consume*, and in d the process is nominalized in *consumption*. The participant *women* is redundant in the message being conveyed – birth defects are hardly likely to result if men consume alcohol during women's pregnancy! – and the nominalised version allows us to omit this information.

Nominalisations are particularly common in the context of academic writing where they allow authors to compress a lot of information into a few words. In e below, both participants (subject and object) are nominalisations, here underlined:

e.   Lead hazard interventions have reduced children's blood-lead concentrations ... (Rust *et al.* 1999: 175).

The first could be expanded into a full clause, in which case the person or group responsible for intervening needs to be identified. We might, for example, expand it to:

f.   The Environmental Protection Agency has intervened in areas with hazardous levels of lead.

The second could be similarly expanded to:

g.   The amount of lead which is concentrated in children's blood.

and a fully expanded version of the original might then be

h.   The Environmental Protection Agency has intervened in areas with hazardous levels of lead to reduce the amount of lead which is concentrated in children's blood.

This longer version is probably unnecessary for the readership of this type of research article. However, one of the criticisms of academic (and other formal) writing is that it can be dense and difficult for the non-expert to understand, and undoubtedly nominalisations contribute to this. In the example we have used above it is reasonably easy for the lay reader to work out the underlying processes, but this is not always the case. The nominalisation underlined in the following example is hard to 'unpack':

i.  Another source of systematic mass uncertainty is <u>the possible deviation of the measured electron temperature from the local mean plasma temperature that enters the hydrostatic equilibrium equation</u>

(Markevitch *et al.* 1999: 257)

### Task A6.2.2

Before leaving the topic of nominalization it is worth considering the headline of the newspaper article about the G8 summit used in this unit:

CARNIVAL TURNS TO CONFRONTATION.

Here too we have a nominalisation, occurring after the verb.

➤ Consider how you might rewrite this using the verb *confront*. What is glossed over by using the nominalized form?

➤ Have a look at the headlines in your local newspapers and see if they make use of nominalisations. What contextual factors do you think are at work in the case of newspapers using nominalisations?

**Summary**

In this unit we have looked at the role of transitivity in representing and constructing context. In particular, we have focused on:

■  what transitive and intransitive verbs and clauses are
■  different ways of representing participants in an action as actor or acted upon
■  representing processes in nominalised forms.

### LOOKING AHEAD

Nominalisation is examined again in Unit B3 in the context of academic writing. It is also one of the devices used in 'little texts' such as newspaper headlines and small ads. You will analyse these in Unit C5.

# Unit A7
# Expressing interpersonal relations through grammar

In the previous unit, we saw that grammatical choices related to transitivity allow us to present in different ways information about the world and events that take place. But language is not just about communicating information: it is also about building relationships between people and about expressing personal views on the content of messages conveyed. This function, beyond conveying propositional content, is sometimes referred to as the **interpersonal** dimension of communication. Sociolinguists have characterised the interpersonal dimension using a number of variables related to the context in which communication takes place: whether there exists, or whether we wish to create, intimacy or distance between ourselves and those we are communicating with; whether there are status differences between participants; whether the context requires more or less formal communication; whether our communication has a high or low information content, or a high or low emotional content. Other related work has looked at how relationships and attitudes towards content are indicated linguistically. A number of grammatical areas provide resources for expressing interpersonal aspects of communication. These include: **mood**; choice of **pronouns**; **reporting verbs**; and the expression of such notions as possibility, probability, and necessity, which together are often referred to as **modal meanings** or, more simply, **modality**.

In what follows we will first look at how relationships are created and maintained between speakers and listeners, and between writers and readers in a discussion of mood and pronoun choice. Then we will look at how commitment to the truth of a proposition, and attitudes towards what others have said and written are expressed, focusing on modality and reporting verbs.

## A7.1 CREATING AND MAINTAINING RELATIONSHIPS

### Mood

Most clauses have a mood selection: that is, they are either indicative or imperative, and if they are indicative they can be either declarative or interrogative. (The subjunctive mood – e.g. I'd leave now if I were you – will not be dealt with here.) Here are some examples:

a.  It's half past seven.     (= declarative)
b.  Are you getting up?       (= interrogative)
c.  Get out of bed.           (= imperative)

Norman Fairclough (2001: 104–105) has argued that mood choice can position the speaker/ writer and listener/ reader in different role relations to each other. Declaratives, interrogatives and imperatives typically position the speaker/ writer as, respectively, the provider of information, the requester of information, and the person asking the listener/ reader to do something. The listener/ reader is in turn, respectively, the receiver of information, the provider of information, and the actor (assuming they comply). Of course, this situation is more complex because declaratives, interrogatives and imperatives do not necessarily function as statement, question and order. a and b above, for example, said by parent to a recalcitrant child, might both be intended as orders, while c, although having the form of an imperative, might be a reduced version of 'I'm going to get out of bed' (*A*: What are you going to do? *B*: [I'm going to] Get out of bed.).

In certain contexts, participants may have restricted access to particular mood choices. In the formal classroom, the teacher has the right to use imperatives, inter-rogatives and declaratives freely in their interaction with pupils:

Spell it.    How do you spell 'definitely'?    That's wrong.

However, when pupils speak to teachers, social convention has it that they don't use imperatives. While 'Could you spell it?' might be an acceptable question from pupil to teacher, a command to 'Spell it' is likely to be heard with disapproval. Further, pupils are only usually permitted to use declaratives in response to questions from the teacher. In both cases, breaking the convention would put the pupil in the (unacceptably) more powerful role. Similarly, in the diagnosis phase of a doctor–patient consultation, by convention the doctor is in the role of information requester and user of interrogatives. A patient's 'Why do you want to know?' or 'What are you doing with that?' might be heard as unusual or even being deliberately awkward, assuming a powerful role at a stage in the proceedings where the doctor, it is generally accepted, is in charge.

### *Personal pronouns*

Selection of personal pronouns is another resource for expressing interpersonal meaning, particularly for projecting the 'distance' or 'closeness' between speaker/ writer and listener/ reader. For example, in English *we* can refer to a variety of groups, such as the speaker and those spoken to, or the speaker and some others but not those spoken to.

To illustrate, here is an extract from an article in the *Sun*, a British daily newspaper with an informal, populist style. The *Sun* is fiercely nationalistic and as such does not want any further integration of Britain into the European Union. The article is written by a regular columnist, Richard Littlejohn, and here he is discussing the government's position on membership of the single European currency, the euro. Notice how he uses the pronouns *we* and *they* to make a distinction between himself and his readers on the one hand and the government (the referent of *they*) on the other.

d.  This . . . is necessary to preserve the fantasy that membership is merely a question of economics. That's rubbish. We know it. They know it. But they keep up the fiction.[8]

Littlejohn uses *we* to project a context in which he and his readers, whom he assumes agree with him, are positioned on the opposing side to the government. In creating this world in which there are two mutually exclusive groups, *we* and *they* (or 'us' and 'them'), he leaves no space for dissenting voices; *Sun* readers who side with the government do not, in Littlejohn's world, exist.

In advertising texts, too, personal pronouns are used to construct roles for readers:

e.  Travel Knits Smart, simple separates in a travel friendly blend give you greater mileage, fewer wrinkles.[9]

This advertisement from a clothes catalogue makes a direct address to the reader, using *you*. It assumes that 'you' are a reader who wants clothes for travelling that will still look smart when taken out of a suitcase. In other words the 'ideal reader' in the mind of the writer is being constructed as one who travels, perhaps for business, and therefore is in need of such clothes. Put crudely, such an advertisement is creating a context into which the unknown reader can enter the position of the ideal reader and then see the need for the clothes.

Both choices of pronouns and mood create a 'position' for the reader/listener. This position can be: in line with the opinions of a newspaper; as a customer for a product; as a patient suffering from an illness; and so on. While language choices can be made which seek to place us in these positions or to take on these personas, we need also to keep in mind that we have the choice to reject such positioning, as we all do on a regular basis in not buying everything that is paraded before us by advertisers. Our ability to construct our own interpersonal positions is a reminder that communication is a two-way process. Writers or speakers can try to manipulate how they or their messages are viewed, but they cannot ultimately control an individual's response.

## Task A7.1.1

➤  Take a newspaper article which clearly takes a strong view on a subject, or a number of advertisements. Identify personal pronouns, and consider what the choices suggest about how the writer positions himself or herself and others.

## 7.2 TAKING A STANCE ON PROPOSITIONS

### *Modality*

Modality is the expression of possibility or obligation through the use of modal verbs such as *may, can, could, will* and *should*, semi-modals such as *have to, be going to, have got to*, and other adjectives, adverbs and nouns expressing modal meanings such as *probably/probable/probability* and *possibly/possible/possibility*. Traditionally, two types of modality are distinguished (e.g. Greenbaum 1996: 260): **epistemic** and **deontic**. Epistemic modality is to do with the speaker's judgement of the truth of a proposition, such as its necessity or possibility. Deontic modality is to do with some kind of human control over the proposition, such as ability, permission or obligation. Here are examples in which epistemic modality is signalled with *likely, may* and *quite clear*.

a. The first of what is *likely* to be thousands of crosses was planted at Belfast's Garden of Remembrance yesterday. (BNC: CBM)*
b. Marcos's remains *may* be brought to the Philippines. (BNC: A1G)*
c. It is *quite clear* that the opposition's spending plans will lead to higher inflation. (BNC: BM4)*

Here are some examples in which deontic modality is signalled with *can't, must*, and *necessary*:

d. Elaine *can't* talk. (BNC: A1X)*
e. Even when farmed, wild boar *must* be genetically pure and reared in conditions which approximate the wild. (BNC: A3C)*
f. Is it *necessary* to be so rude to Paul? (BNC: KDO)*

* The reference information given in brackets refers to the original text source in the British National Corpus (BNC).

While both types of modality are regularly found in speech and writing, in certain contexts modality is found relatively frequently. In academic writing, for instance, markers of epistemic modality are generally more common than in conversation (see Biber *et al.* 1999, 483ff.). For example, the following extract is the opening of a discussion about evaluation in language teaching taken from a paper in a collection of academic articles. Each sentence has been given a letter for ease of reference.

 **Task A7.2.1**

➤ Read text extract 1 below and underline the modality markers.

➤ Consider in each case what meaning they add.

1a. Evaluation for purposes of accountability is mainly concerned with determining whether there has been value for money, in other words whether something has been both effective and efficient. b. The main aim is to report on a product and give an evaluative judgement whether something is intrinsically a 'good thing' or not. c. Generally the information derived from evaluation for purposes of accountability is not used in any major way to improve the functioning of the curriculum or class-room practice. d. Rather it informs decisions as to whether something is to continue or be discontinued. e. If, for example, sponsors or heads of institutions are not satisfied with the implementation of a particular project, then cuts may be made. f. Thus, if a particular reading scheme is introduced, evaluated a year later, and then judged to be ineffective, it is highly likely that a school will discontinue supporting this venture.[10]

The modality markers are in sentences a *mainly*, b *main*, c *Generally*, e *may*, f *highly likely*, *will*.

The opening sentences include '*mainly* concerned', '*main* aim', and '*Generally*', all of which alert us to the writers' wish to withhold full commitment to the propositions in the sentences. Why this should be becomes clear if the text is read without them. While the text would remain coherent, the writers would be stating things very categorically and leaving themselves open to challenges such as 'Is evaluation *only* concerned with determining whether there has been value for money or are other aspects involved?' By using *mainly* they are **hedging** their assertion: that is, withholding their complete commitment to the truth value of the proposition. They are showing an awareness that there may be other aspects to evaluate but, on the other hand, they are also showing their belief that determining value for money is the main factor. Withholding full commitment to the propositions in the second half of the paragraph is accomplished through *may*, *highly likely* and *will*. These are necessary as the sentences are speculative and phrased as conditions, 'If X, then Y'. However, *may* in the first conditional sentence is still a choice as *will* or *must* could be substituted and make a much stronger assertion. In the final sentence an *it*-clause is chosen and the adverb *likely* is modified to make it stronger through the addition of *highly* which matches the strong likelihood associated with the following *will*.

The reason for the frequency of modality markers in academic writing is well illustrated in the following extract from the discussion section of an article from a medical journal. Modality markers are in italics:

2 The presence of normal or near normal PT/APTT *suggests* that no change in factors VIII or V (*sic*). Decreased factor VIII levels in 5 cases (with associated increase in APTT/PT in 1 case and hypofibrinogenemia in 1 case) *could be explained* on the basis of development of factor VIII inhibitors and acquired hemophilia in RA that has been at times severe enough to result in life threatening bleeding and q3 absence of factor VIII from the serum. . . . Our results demonstrate that apart from mild and

isolated abnormalities of coagulation, DIC of any severity is not seen in patients with RA without vasculitis and as such is *very unlikely* to contribute to the pathogenesis of the disorder.[11]

The discussion of research findings in articles such as this may become the basis for the development of future treatments of patients. In such a context it is essential that claims are not made which are not justified, and so writers are careful to word their explanations and interpretations with due caution.

 **Task A7.2.2**

There is much criticism of scientists in the media for 'getting things wrong'.

➤ Listen to interviews with scientists on the radio or television and look at reports of scientific findings in newspapers. Is hedging used in the way that you have seen it used in extracts 1 and 2 above? Is there a difference between the way scientists present their findings and the way journalists report them?

Of course, it is not only writers of academic texts who hedge 'on the record' claims that could later be proved wrong. Politicians, too, choose words with care so that they give no hostages to fortune by saying things that could cause them trouble in the future. Here is part of a speech on joining the euro given by the United Kingdom Chancellor of the Exchequer. Notice in particular his use of the modal *could*:

> With Britain in the euro, business *could* benefit through greater access to a more integrated European capital market. And if, on the basis of sustained and durable convergence, we *could* lock in stability for the long term, then business *could* see a cut in the cost of borrowing on a sustainable basis with a long-term boost to cross-border investment flows and foreign direct investment in the UK.[12]

## *Reporting*

We end this unit by looking at another grammatical choice that can be used to convey the writer's commitment to or view of a proposition said or written by someone else: choice of reporting verb. Our first illustration again comes from academic writing. Extracts 3 and 4 below are taken from the introduction to a research article, paragraphs 3–6, analysed by Geoff Thompson (1994). In it there is a report of previous research on children 'in care': that is, children taken from their families and looked after in special homes or by foster parents. The author's controversial view is that people who take decisions on whether black children should be taken into care are often influenced by racism. Paragraph and sentence numbers have been added for ease of reference, and relevant sections put in italics. Some sentences without reporting are omitted.

3. (3) [3.1] There have been a few research studies which have focussed on the issue of black children's admission into the care system. [3.2] *These have principally shown* that black children are much more likely to come into care than white children.

(4) [4.1] *A group of studies which indicate* the greater likelihood of admission for black children were carried out by researchers at the University of Bradford who observed the admission patterns of children into Bradford Social Services Department. [4.2] *The first study conducted in the late 1960s found* that children of 'mixed origin' were eight and a half times more likely to come into care than 'white indigenous' and 'Afro-Caribbean and Asian' children (Foren and Batta 1970). [4.3] *A subsequent study conducted in 1975 obtained similar findings* (Batta, McCulloch and Smith 1975). [4.4] *Both studies revealed* that children of 'mixed origin' came into care at an earlier age and tended to stay in care for longer periods. [4.5] *A third study of Bradford's child care population conducted in 1978 confirmed* the findings of the earlier research with regard to children of 'mixed origin' (Batta and Mawby 1981).

In paragraphs 3 and 4 (sentences 3.2 and 4.1–4.5) the author reports studies using reporting verbs *shown, found, obtained . . . findings, revealed,* and *confirmed* (*indicate* is perhaps a little less positive than the others) that show a positive attitude to their findings and conclusion; that is, that she feels that they are true.

4. (5) [5.1] Although *research studies have asserted* the high presence of black children in the care system, it is not clear whether black children are disproportionately represented. [5.2–5.4 omitted] [5.5] *A report by the Commission for Racial Equality (1977) suggested* demographic and geographical factors as well as the lower socio-economic position of black families. [5.6] *Boss and Homeshaw found*: 'disturbing indications of a heavy-handed approach by both the police and the court towards coloured children, particularly West Indians' (1975: 355). [5.7] *Moreover, they also found* that: '. . . proportionally more care orders and supervision orders were made on this particular group than was consistent with their overall numbers of court appearances' (1975: 355).

(6) [6.1] *Despite the above findings, the researchers feel* that since black families are predominantly young, demographic reasons alone could account for the high proportion of black children in care. [6.2] *Other studies have also offered explanations* which are primarily related to the nature and type of families (McCullough, Batta and Smith 1979; Fitzherbert 1967). [6.3] The picture is one therefore where *the structures and lifestyles of black families are viewed* in negative terms and *are perceived to be* the major contributory factors which result in black children's admission into care. [6.4 omitted] [6.5] *It has been found* that while social workers are more likely to explain the admission of black children into care in terms of individual or family pathology, parents themselves de-emphasise such factors and highlight their poor socio-economic situation (Pinder and Shaw 1974; Adams 1981).[13]

In contrast to paragraphs 3 and 4, in 5 and 6 (sentences 5.2, 5.5 and 6.1–3) the author reports other writers in a more neutral way with *have asserted, suggested, feel, offered explanation, are viewed* and *are perceived to be*. Essentially, she does not accept their conclusions and, as she does not show that she accepts them, she is left free to disagree. The acceptance of writers' findings but not their conclusions is also expressed in 5.6, 5.7 and 6.1. She begins by reporting findings with the verb *found* in 5.6 and 5.7, indicating support, but then shows that she disagrees with the writers' conclusions in *Despite the above findings, the researchers feel. . . .* The extract ends in 6.5 with a further positive report in *It has been found . . .*, accepting conclusions which are then discussed further in the next paragraph.

If we move away from the relatively subdued world of academic writing to the more emotive world of journalism we can see that reporting verbs are used more explicitly to convey the journalist's impressions of how words were said or what value to ascribe to them. While *said* is common, other choices allow the journalists to interpret events for the readers and thus colour our view of what took place. Here are a number of illustrative extracts from British national daily newspapers. Reporting verbs are again put in italics.

5. Yesterday an increasingly exasperated Tony Blair *spat out* his rejection of claims . . . that he duped his colleagues and the public (*Daily Mail*, 3 June 2003)
6. An influential committee of MPs *demanded* a law to limit the number of Whitehall special advisors (*Daily Mail*, 3 June 2003)
7. Owen *pleads* for calm (*Daily Mail*, 3 June 2003)
8. Mr Howard . . . *accused* the government of 'being divided and on the run' (*Daily Telegraph*, 10 June 2003)
9. The researchers *stressed* that television had to some extent replaced radio as source of constant background noise (*Daily Telegraph*, 10 June 2003)
10. Parent governor Patricia McDonald, 44, *stormed*: 'This is a barmy idea.' (*Sun*, 10 June 2003)

In most cases we have no access to the exact words spoken or the way in which they were said. We do not know, for example, whether Tony Blair actually 'spat out' his rejection (that is, said it in an angry way), or whether this is the journalist's interpretation or what the journalist would wish us to believe. Even where a quotation is given, the reporting verb gives the journalist's interpretation of either the implication of what was said (was Mr Howard actually 'accusing' the government or just describing the current situation?) or the manner in which it was said (did Patricia McDonald actually 'storm' or say this in a calm way?).

 **Task A7.2.3**

➤ Find a newspaper article which reports what politicians have said. Examine whether the choice of reporting verbs reflects whether the journalist (and perhaps the newspaper more generally) supports or opposes what was said.

In this unit we have looked at how grammatical choices are involved in the construction of an individual's persona in any given communicative context. In particular, we have focused on:

- how such dimensions as power and exclusivity can be manipulated through choice of

  - mood
  - pronouns.

- how we can show our views on events and try to influence the views of others through choice of

  - modality
  - reporting verbs.

## LOOKING AHEAD

Interpersonal relations are relevant in many of the readings in Section B and the analyses in Section C. The role of power and questions, for example, is significant in the radio phone-ins described in Unit B2. Modality, stance and hedging are particularly significant in academic writing, as discussed in Units B3 and C3. How we portray ourselves in relation to others in similar or different social, gender, age, or national groups is the focus of Units B8, B9, C8 and C9. The personas we create for ourselves in electronic communication are explored in Units B4 and C4.

# Unit A8
# Standards and varieties

Socio-cultural and situational aspects of context come together in looking at different regional varieties of a language and 'standard' language. When we talk about a standard in language (such as 'Standard English'), we have in mind a norm or model of language from which 'non-standard' language deviates. The usual implication is that 'standard' represents correctness (particularly in grammar), that alternatives are in some way incorrect and that in educational contexts at least we should aspire to using the standard model. This is often specified formally in curricula. For example, the British National Curriculum specifies a number of attainment levels which the majority of children are expected to have achieved by specified ages. The descriptions of the attainment levels for English speaking and listening include the following references to standard language from Levels 3 to 8 and beyond:

*Level 3*: They are beginning to be aware of Standard English and when it is used.
*Level 4*: They use appropriately some of the features of Standard English vocabulary and grammar.
*Level 5*: They begin to use Standard English in formal situations.
*Level 6*: They are usually fluent in their use of Standard English in formal situations.
*Level 7*: They show confident use of Standard English in situations that require it.
*Level 8*: They show confident use of Standard English in a range of situations, adapting as necessary.
*Exceptional performance*:
They show assured and fluent use of Standard English in a range of situations and for a variety of purposes.[14]

Although the National Curriculum encourages children to acquire flexibility in their language use according to context, two points are clear from the extracts above and from other information in the National Curriculum document: that an ability to speak in Standard English is an important educational target; and that 'Standard English' refers specifically to British English.

In this section we will explore two related issues. First, we will look further at the notion of 'Standard English' – how it has been characterised and the reactions to language which deviates from it – and then go on to look at varieties of English that have developed in different national contexts around the world.

## A8.1  STANDARD ENGLISH

Writing on this topic, Peter Trudgill (1999) took as his title 'Standard English: what it isn't', suggesting that it is helpful to clarify what Standard English is by saying what it is not. First, it is not a language in itself, but a variety of English, albeit a prestigious variety. Second, Standard English is not an accent; it has nothing to do with how we pronounce the language. In Britain some people connect Standard English with Received Pronunciation (RP), which is a largely non-regional dialect associated with speakers from higher socio-economic groups. However, Standard English can be found in use throughout Britain and in many other countries worldwide and the majority of its speakers use their own regional accents. Third, Standard English is not a style, in that it can be used either formally or informally and in all contexts in between. For example, our language would be more formal while presenting a research paper at a conference (a) than later when describing that presentation over lunch with a friend (b), though in both cases we are speaking Standard English:

a.   In this presentation I will highlight the different patterns of theme used by students during electronic conferencing and by those same students when writing essays.
b.   I was talking about the research project with Caroline and how students string their ideas together when they're talking online and how they do it differently when they're writing essays for their tutors.

Fourth, Standard English is not a register, or a variety of language that is determined by topic, such as the register of law or the register of computing. Standard English is used across registers and, conversely, it is possible to find non-Standard English used in particular registers.

Having said what it is not, what is it? It can be characterised as the kind of English written in published work and generally taught in English-speaking schools. It is spoken in national news broadcasts and where published writing is most influential, in educational contexts. As we saw in Unit A1, Standard English is the variety described in grammar reference books, with non-standard forms sometimes referred to but distinguished in some way. Trudgill argues that Standard English is in fact a **dialect**, as we would describe Scouse, Cockney or Geordie in Britain or the dialects of Boston or New York City in the United States. Standard English is distinct from these dialects, however, in a number of ways. First, it does not have an associated accent. Second, it is a social rather than a geographical dialect, even though it comes in a number of forms such as Scottish Standard English, American Standard English, English Standard English or Singapore Standard English. Although there may be some differences in grammar between these forms, the differences are small in comparison to the similarities. Third, it is much more widespread than any other dialect of English.

Trudgill suggests that there are relatively few grammatical differences between Standard English and other dialects, although these have particular social significance. They include the following.

1.  Standard English does not distinguish between main and auxiliary forms of the verb *do* whereas many other dialects use *I do, he do* as auxiliary forms and *I does, she does* as main verb forms.
2.  Standard English marks the third person singular present tense verbs, usually by the addition of an *s: I go* versus *she goes*. Other dialects either use zero for all persons or *-s* for all persons.
3.  Most non-standard dialects permit the use of multiple negation: *I don't want none.*
4.  In Standard English reflexive pronouns are based on both possessive pronouns, e.g. *myself* and objective pronouns, e.g. *himself*. Most non-standard dialects use only possessive forms, e.g. *hisself, theirselves.*
5.  Standard English does not distinguish between the singular and plural pronoun *you.* Some dialects maintain a distinction between *thou* and *you* or have developed a new form *youse.*
6.  Standard English has irregular forms for the verb *be* in present and past tense forms. Many non-standard dialects use one form for all persons, such as *I be, you be, he be.*
7.  In Standard English many irregular verbs have a past participle form different from the past tense form, e.g. *he has seen* and *she saw*. Many non-standard dialects make no distinction between these forms, e.g. *he has seen* and *she seen.*
8.  Standard English has two demonstrative pronouns, *this* (near to the speaker) and *that* (away from the speaker). Many other dialects indicate nearness to the listener (*that*) and distance from both speaker and listener (*yon*).

 **Task A8.1.1**

➤ If you are familiar with a non-standard variety of English, think about how many of these features are used by its speakers.

➤ What other non-standard features does it have?

Of course, difficulties can arise in deciding which grammatical forms are characteristic of Standard English and which are not, particularly in speech. For example, in spoken English the rules of subject–verb concord are frequently ignored after the dummy subject *there*, as in:

The majority of it's wood and there's three large windows in it (BNC: KB7)*

---

\* The reference information given in brackets refers to the original text source in the British National Corpus (BNC).

This particular usage of *there's* followed by a plural noun phrase has been observed in the speech of Standard English speakers in different countries. This seems to be related to the use of *there's* as a ready-made 'chunk' of language which is likely to come to mind in conversation where planning time is restricted. In this way *there's* is similar to phrases in other languages such as *il y a* and *es gibt*, as Jenny Cheshire (1999: 138) points out:

> [*There's*] would then be comparable to French *il y a* or German *es gibt*, neither of which exhibits agreement with the following noun phrase. In more formal speech styles, where speakers have time to plan what they intend to say, and where speaking turns may be distributed more routinely than in informal conversation, the expression of grammatical agreement could become more important than the communicative need to take or keep the floor whilst preserving the pace of speech . . . In these styles, the option of choosing a prefabricated phrase could be bypassed.

It is important to note that this informal usage, while deviating from usual descriptions of Standard English, is very common. Some researchers of spoken language have contended that it is *not* a non-standard form, and that it is more a case of the current writing-based grammatical descriptions being unable to cope with how unplanned speech is shaped. This is the view taken by Carter and McCarthy and by Biber and colleagues in their extracts in Unit B1.

## Task A8.1.2

➤ Consider your own use of language and the variety you use. If you use more than one dialect, try to explain why you select one dialect and not another.

What is accepted as Standard English changes over time. This can be illustrated, for example, by comparing language in the 'quality' press at different periods. Like many newspapers, the *Guardian* publishes a style guide for its journalists, which includes (among a great deal of other information) some guidance on grammatical usage. In its first style guide, published in 1928, the following information was given about the so-called 'split infinitive':

> Split infinitives should be avoided – that is, the separation of the verb from its preposition. "To run swiftly" or "swiftly to run" is correct; not "to swiftly run."

However, by 2003, its style guide includes the following advice:

> It is perfectly acceptable to sensibly split infinitives, though to always do so may sound inelegant – so use common sense. And remember George Bernard Shaw's reaction after an editor tinkered with his infinitives: "I don't care if he is made to go quickly, or to quickly go – but go he must!"[15]

While this suggests that split infinitives are becoming part of Standard English, some people still find them unacceptable.

In fact, challenges to Standard English are often met with hostility, both in Britain and (as we will see in A8.2 below) elsewhere. Debate about English language standards has recently (at the time of writing) been a matter of heated discussion in the media in connection with the spread of the language of text messaging (more formally 'short message service' [SMS], or less formally just 'texting') to contexts outside communication by mobile phone. One newspaper article[16] included the following comments on texting from various people involved in education:

> The majority of teachers would support a crackdown on this sloppy form of writing. . . .

> There must be rigorous efforts from all quarters of the education system to stamp out the use of texting as a form of written language so far as English study is concerned . . .

> 'texting' must not be allowed to become acceptable written English – it will only further erode the language.

The article went on to give part of an essay written in text language by a 13-year-old girl at a Scottish secondary school, under the subheading 'cn u trnsl8 a txt sa?' It read:

> 'My smmr hols wr CWOT. B4, we usd 2 go 2 NY 2C my bro, his GF & thr 3 :-@ kds FTF. ILNY, its gr8.

> Bt my Ps wr so {:–/ BC o 9/11 tht they dcdd 2 stay in SCO & spnd 2wks up N.

> Up N, WUCIWUG – 0. I ws vvv brd in MON. 0 bt baas & ^^^^^.

> AAR8, my Ps wr :–) – they sd ICBW, & tht they wr ha-p 4 the pc&qt . . . IDTS!! I wntd 2 go hm ASAP, 2C my M8s again.

> 2day, I cam bk 2 skool. I feel v O:-) BC I hv dn all my hm wrk. Now its BAU . . .'

 **Task A8.1.3**

> ➤ Before you read on, try to 'translate' the text message into Standard English.

Here is the 'translation' given in the newspaper article:

My summer holidays were a complete waste of time. Before, we used to go to New York to see my brother, his girlfriend and their three screaming kids face to face. I love New York, it's a great place.

But my parents were so worried because of the terrorism attack on September 11 that they decided we would stay in Scotland and spend two weeks up north.

Up north, what you see is what you get – nothing. I was extremely bored in the middle of nowhere. Nothing but sheep and mountains.

At any rate, my parents were happy. They said that it could be worse, and that they were happy with the peace and quiet. I don't think so! I wanted to go home as soon as possible, to see my friends again.

Today I came back to school. I feel very saintly because I have done all my homework. Now it's business as usual . . .

Concern about the widespread infiltration of text messaging conventions into written English may, however, be misplaced, as 'predictive texting' becomes more common and sophisticated. Further developments in text messaging technology seem sure to follow, as they have with the autocorrect and grammar-checking facilities in word-processing software. While it seems certain that our accepted notion of standards in language will be influenced by electronic forms of communication, it is very hard to predict in any detail and with any certainty what this impact might be.

## Task A8.1.4

➤ As we were writing this unit, a commentator on BBC Radio 5 Live said: 'Texting is ruining our children's grammar!' Do you agree with this view?

## A8.2 LANGUAGE VARIETIES

There are many ways of looking at the idea of language **variation**. In this unit so far we have looked at variation between standard and non-standard language. Alternatively, we might look at the way in which language varies in speech and writing, or we might look at variation in different **registers** of English, comparing, for example, journalistic language and the language of academic text. In this section, however, we consider the kind of variation that is produced when a language comes into contact with another language. In particular, we look at **varieties** of English which have grown up in many countries as English has been exported around the world and taken up in different ways by different communities to be used alongside local languages and in some cases to supplant them. In North America and

Australasia, for example, the large number of British migrants and their political domination has created English native-speaker populations. Geographical and historical separation and interaction with speakers of other languages has led these varieties to develop differences from British English. In addition, they substantially affected the indigenous languages.

Two important concepts of relevance here are those of **pidgins** and **creoles**. A pidgin is a language that develops as a means of communication between groups of people who do not share a common language. Pidgins are usually used in order to facilitate a narrow range of communicative functions involved in, for example, trade or administration. Consequently, compared to other languages they have a limited grammar and vocabulary. The forms of a pidgin are mainly taken from or influenced by the languages spoken by the communities in contact (although most tend to come from the prestige or more widely used language rather than the local language), while other features emerge which are unique to the pidgin. Pidgins based on English, Spanish and Portuguese developed during colonial periods and other times of extensive trading contact in regions such as the East and West Indies, Africa and the Americas. If a pidgin becomes spoken as a speech community's mother tongue, then it is known as a creole. As they are used for a much wider range of communicative purposes than pidgins, creoles have a wider range of grammatical structures and a more extensive vocabulary. Many present-day creoles are spoken in the Caribbean by the descendants of African slaves, although they also exist in other parts of the world.

For example, in Australia many Aboriginal languages have completely died out, often to be replaced not by Standard Australian English (AusE), but by Aboriginal English (AbE). Contact between English-speaking settlers and Aboriginal groups resulted in a form of English pidgin, beginning with a basic vocabulary and grammar but becoming more sophisticated over time. With the disruption of aboriginal societies through dispossession and disease, local languages were gradually replaced by the English pidgin, sometimes as a **lingua franca** between different Aboriginal groups. When children were born into this pidgin-speaking community and became native speakers of pidgin, the language took on the status of a creole. This is now usually thought of as a dialect of Australian English but separate from it. It is suggested by some researchers that the evolution of this new dialect has helped Aboriginal people to communicate across their original linguistic communities about the experiences and the changes to their lifestyles brought about by European settlers. By developing their own dialect of English they have created a means for maintenance of their culture and their separateness from the colonising cultures. Ian Malcolm (2001: 218) argues that:

> [English] has gone through a progressive process of indigenisation which has enabled it to serve certain functions of Aboriginal cultural maintenance. AbE and AusE carry contrasting historical and cultural associations, and their separateness has been consistently maintained by Aboriginal speakers. Since the reasons for this still remain, it is likely that Aboriginal English

will continue to be maintained as a distinct dialect, although many of its speakers will maintain bicultural competence through the maintenance of Australian English as a part of their repertoire.

We see here, then, evidence of a wide cultural context that has given rise not just to lexical and grammatical selection within a dialect, but to the development of a new dialect. Aboriginal English is a new dialect of Standard Australian English, which is itself a relatively newly recognised variety of English, albeit one with very close ties to British English and American English.

Other new varieties of English are also recognised, particularly in former British colonies like India and Singapore, although the status of these varieties is often a matter of contention in the countries in which they are spoken. In Singapore, for example, the local variety that has developed as a means of informal communication between the various ethnic and language groups in the country is known as 'Singlish'. It derives features from a number of local languages, particularly Chinese and Malay. However, it is often compared unfavourably with Standard Singaporean English, which is much closer grammatically and lexically to other varieties of English. For example, the National University of Singapore has a 'Promotion of Standard English' (PROSE) website[17] which highlights, in a clearly critical way, features of Singlish. Singlish is described as

a layman's . . . term that could mean any of the following:

- **Colloquial Singapore English** that is used in informal contexts by someone who is highly competent in educated Singaporean English or Standard Singaporean English.
- **Lower (mesolectal and basilectal) varieties** of Singaporean English used by the less competent speakers, producing utterances such as 'He my teacher', 'Why you say me until like that?' and 'I got not enough money'. (Note: *Basilect* and *mesolect* are terms used by sociolinguists, usually in the study of creoles. A basilect is a variety most remote from the prestige variety – here Standard Singaporean English – and a mesolect is closer to the prestige variety.)
- **Interlanguage or developmental varieties** of English produced by some language learners at the beginning stages.

Standard English is defined as:

English that is internationally acceptable in formal contexts. In other words, someone speaking Standard English should be understood easily by educated English speakers all over the world.

(It is worth noting here that the website does not make clear whether 'Standard English' refers to Standard Singaporean English or some other, unspecified, variety of English.)

Examples of Singlish with the Standard English equivalents are also given, including:

- *Singlish*: Why you never bring come?
  *Standard English alternative*: Why didn't you bring it?

- *Singlish*: He take go already.
  *Standard English alternative*: He has taken it with him.

- *Singlish*: How come nobody tell us this exam is open book one?

  *Standard English alternative*: Why didn't anybody tell us this is an open book exam?

Regular criticisms of Singlish by Singapore government officials and in newspaper editorials are other strands of the authorities' promotion of the use of Standard Singaporean English over Singlish. Their argument is that while Singlish has assisted in promoting inter-ethnic exchange and the forging of a Singaporean identity, it fails as a language for international communication because it is difficult for non-Singaporeans to understand, and is therefore seen as a handicap in economic expansion. This policy has extended to banning Singlish from television and advertisements, while strongly promoting the use of Standard Singaporean English in schools and higher education. What we can observe happening here then is the government labelling one Singaporean English dialect as inferior to another and reducing the situations in which the less valued variety can be used.

**Summary**

In this unit we have looked at:

- the notion of Standard English and difficulties in defining it
- challenges to Standard English and reactions to them
- pidgins and creoles
- other language varieties.

## LOOKING AHEAD

In looking at Standard English, we have identified influences of the wider socio-cultural and more local situational context. These contextual influences on grammar in new electronic forms of communication such as texting and email are considered further in Units B4 and C4. Gender, age and social class are also significant factors in how people react to Standard English and variations from it. These, together with discussion of international varieties of English, are considered further in Units B8, B9, C8, and C9.

# Unit A9
# Corpus approaches to the study of grammar

## A9.1   CORPORA IN LANGUAGE STUDY

Collections of texts stored on computers and accessed using specialist software have significantly changed the way language can be researched and enhanced our understanding of grammatical patterns found in particular contexts. These collections of texts, generally known as **corpora** (the singular form is **corpus**), can be searched and accessed in a number of ways, but a commonly used approach is to produce a series of **concordance lines**. Here is an illustration of how concordance lines might appear on a computer screen.[18]

*Figure A9.1* Concordance lines for *wanted*

The search term, otherwise known as the **keyword** or **node**, is the word *wanted*. Even in this small sample we can see that *wanted* is frequently followed by *to* and a verb in the infinitive.

One of the main applications of corpora in language study has been in the writing of dictionaries. Corpora can help dictionary writers identify new words, and find out which words and phrases (and which meanings of a word or phrase where it has a number) are used most frequently. More recently, large corpora of many millions of words have also been used in the writing of descriptive grammars (see Unit A1) such as the *Collins COBUILD English Grammar* (Sinclair 1990), and the *Longman Grammar of Spoken and Written English* (Biber *et al.* 1999) We noted in Unit A1 that many grammatical descriptions appeal to intuition in deciding what is grammatical or ungrammatical, and in creating illustrative examples. However, dealing with language in this way divorces it from its meaning in its local and wider linguistic context. A corpus, in contrast, provides language that has been used, with key words embedded in their textual context (or 'co-text'). Examining words in these contexts offers us a way of learning more about how words combine to make meanings for communicative purposes.

## A9.2 CORPORA IN THE STUDY OF GRAMMAR IN CONTEXT

We move from talking generally about the use of corpora in language study to ways in which corpus analysis can help us understand more about the relationship between grammar and context. We will focus specifically on work that has used corpora in looking at: grammatical patterns across contexts; the characteristics of grammar in speech; changes in grammatical usage over time; grammar in learner English; and grammar in translation. Then the final piece of work presented in this section highlights the blurring of the boundary between grammatical and lexical meaning that is a product of the corpus approach.

### *Grammatical patterns across contexts*

Corpus studies of grammar in context often compare a particular grammatical feature across two or more collections of language produced in different contexts. For example, Sidney Greenbaum and colleagues (1996) analysed complement clauses – that is, clauses that complement verbs and adjectives, as in *I believe <u>that it is too late</u>* (complementing the verb *believe*) and *I am aware <u>that it is too late</u>* (complementing the adjective *aware*) – in six corpora: spontaneous natural conversations, unscripted monologues (lectures and talks), broadcast discussions, personal letters, academic writing and non-academic writing. The table below focuses on one part of their work, in which the stylistic option of including or omitting *that* in complement clauses (*I believe [that] it is too late; I am aware [that] it is too late*) is analysed. The following figures are given:

■ The size of each corpus in number of words;
■ The number of occurrences of complement clauses in which *that* is included or omitted ('zero *that*') for each corpus expressed as a figure per thousand words. This allows a direct comparison across the corpora, which are of different sizes.
■ The percentage of clauses in which *that* is included or omitted for each corpus;
■ In brackets, the actual number of occurrences of *that* and 'zero *that*' complement clauses in each corpus.

## Task A9.2.1

➤ Look at the similarities and differences in the relative frequencies of *that*-inclusion and *that*-omission across the corpora and comment on them.

*Table A9.1* Analysis of complement clauses with *that* included or omitted.

| Category | No. of words | That | Zero that | Total |
|---|---|---|---|---|
| Non-academic writing | 8,508 | 4.7/ 85.1% (40) | 0.8/ 14.9% (7) | 100% (47) |
| Academic writing | 8,588 | 3.8/ 91.7% (33) | 0.3/ 8.3% (3) | 100% (36) |
| Letters | 8,190 | 2.1/ 22.4% (17) | 7.2/ 77.3% (59) | 100% (76) |
| TOTAL WRITTEN | 25,286 | 3.5/ 56.6% (90) | 2.7/ 43.4% (69) | 100% (159) |
| Monologues | 11,198 | 5.7/ 68.8% (64) | 2.6/ 31.2% (29) | 100% (93) |
| Broadcast discussions | 11,161 | 10.2/ 57.6% (114) | 7.5/ 42.4% (84) | 100% (198) |
| Conversations | 41,406 | 2.8/ 31.5% (117) | 6.1/ 68.5% (254) | 100% (371) |
| TOTAL SPOKEN | 63,765 | 4.6/ 44.6% (295) | 5.7/ 55.4% (367) | 100% (662) |
| Total | 89,051 | 4.3/ 46.9% (385) | 4.9/ 53.1% (436) | 100% (821) |

Adapted from Greenbaum *et al.* 1996: 83, Table 6.4a; 84, Table 6.4b

You might have noticed a generally higher frequency of *that*-clauses (both with *that* included and omitted) in speech and writing. However, there is a greater tendency to include *that* in writing than in speech. Further, the choice to omit *that* is taken in less formal contexts in both speech and writing, in letters and conversations, whereas in more formal contexts in both speech and writing, the tendency is to include it.

Calculating the relative frequency of occurrence of a particular grammatical feature is, of course, only the starting point of cross-corpus comparison. Where significant differences are observed, we can go on to investigate these further using, among other methods, analysis of relevant concordance lines. In this way, a more detailed exploration of possible relationships between grammar and context can be undertaken.

### *Grammar in speech*

Language corpora have predominantly been made up of written text. There are obvious additional difficulties in compiling a corpus of speech, including having to record and transcribe it, and practical problems in representing features of speech such as pauses and overlapping turns in conversation. However, spoken corpora have been collected, and studies of these have begun to influence our ideas about the grammar of speech and how this is distinct from the grammar of well-formed writing. Particularly influential in this work has been research on the *CANCODE* (Cambridge and Nottingham Corpus of Discourse in English) corpus of spoken English led by Ronald Carter and Michael McCarthy. The corpus was designed to reflect language use in five broad contexts based on the type of relationship among participants (McCarthy 1998: 9). For example, transactional relationships are those where speakers make plain their needs and move towards fulfilling those needs outside the contexts of professional, socialising or intimate relationships. Spoken texts are also categorised according to the goal of the interaction: for example, primarily a one-way information flow; interactive and collaborative, trying to accomplish a task; or collaborative, exploring ideas and attitudes. The table below shows the categories of speech events in CANCODE, together with example contexts.

*Table A9.2* Categorisation within the CANCODE corpus

| *Context-type* | *Goal-type* | *Example* |
| --- | --- | --- |
| Transactional | Information provision | Tourist information requests for information |
| Professional | Information provision | Company sales conference, informal informational talks |
| Pedagogical | Collaborative ideas | University small-group tutorial |
| Socialising | Collaborative task | Relatives and friends preparing food for a party |
| Intimate | Collaborative ideas | Mother and daughter discuss family matters |

Source: McCarthy 1998: 10

This systematic approach to the corpus allows attention to be paid both to the characteristic grammatical structures of speech, and also differentiation between recognisable genre types, such as stories, arguments, and so on. One area that is found to be typical of grammatical constructions in naturally occurring speech is situational ellipsis. Ellipsis is the omission of certain words which can be retrieved from the context. In the case of situational ellipsis, it is the shared physical context and the face-to-face nature of conversational interaction that promotes ellipsis particularly of pronouns (examples 1 and 2) and auxiliary verbs (example 3). The omitted material is enclosed by angled brackets <. . .>:

1   <your> Handbag is it, what else then?
2   <they> Put the phone in as well for you, did they?
3   <do you> Think it's your house or something?

(McCarthy 1998: 64)

You can read more about analysis of speech in the CANCODE corpus in Unit B1.

### *Grammatical changes over time*

Other kinds of investigation include comparing grammatical usage in corpora of language from different time periods. For example, Geoffrey Leech (2003) has compared the uses of English modal and some semi-modal verbs over a thirty-year time span in both British English and American English, using four one-million-word tagged corpora of written texts from between 1961 and 1991. The corpora were comprised of texts of three types: from newspapers (e.g. news reports and editorials), from general prose (e.g. religious texts, texts to do with skills and hobbies), and learners' fiction (e.g. academic texts and a variety of literary texts). A tagged corpus such as this is one in which a label is attached to each word to indicate its word class or part of speech; for example, the label NN1 is commonly used to indicate singular common nouns and NP1 to indicate singular proper nouns. This information allows us, for example, to search for a keyword having a specified grammatical class, and to more easily identify the grammatical classes of words surrounding the keyword. Tables A9.3 presents some of Leech's findings.

The results suggest that in British English the use of *will, can,* and *could* has remained steady, but that there has been a decline in the use of *must, may, shall, ought to* and *need.* The trend is less clear for *would, should* and *might.* Overall the trend seems to be for a decreasing use of modal auxiliaries.

### Task A9.2.2

➤   Compare the findings for British and American use and decide whether the trends are the same or different.

➤   Think of reasons why this might be the case.

*Table A9.3* Frequencies of modals in four British and American written corpora

|  | British English | | | American English | | |
|---|---|---|---|---|---|---|
|  | 1961 | 1991 | Difference % | 1961 | 1991 | Difference % |
| would | 3028 | 2694 | −11.0 | 3053 | 2868 | −6.1 |
| will | 2798 | 2723 | −2.7 | 2702 | 2402 | −11.1 |
| can | 1997 | 2041 | +2.2 | 2193 | 2160 | −1.5 |
| could | 1740 | 1782 | +2.4 | 1776 | 1655 | −6.8 |
| may | 1333 | 1101 | −17.4 | 1298 | 878 | −32.4 |
| should | 1301 | 1147 | −11.8 | 910 | 787 | −13.5 |
| must | 1147 | 814 | −29.0 | 1018 | 668 | −34.4 |
| might | 777 | 660 | −15.1 | 635 | 635 | −4.5 |
| shall | 355 | 200 | −44.7 | 267 | 150 | −43.8 |
| ought (to) | 104 | 58 | −44.2 | 70 | 49 | −30.0 |
| need(n't) | 87 | 52 | −40.2 | 40 | 35 | −12.5 |
| Total | 14667 | 13272 | −9.5 | 13962 | 12287 | −12.2 |

Source: Leech 2003: 228

The figures suggest that overall American use of modal auxiliaries in 1961 was less than for British English at that time, and the decline between 1961 and 1991 has been greater than for British English. From this analysis Leech concludes that British use of modals has followed the trend of American use but at a slightly slower pace. Such an investigation raises further questions for research such as whether the same trends are observed in spoken English, and (assuming a similar amount of modal meaning is expressed) what expressions of modal meaning have replaced those modals that have declined in use. Of course, figure such as these do not show anything about variation in the trends identified across text types. For example, *shall* continues to be used widely in legal texts in both United States and United Kingdom contexts.

### Grammar in translation

The growing internationalisation of business and government (as in the expansion of the European Union) has increased the demand for documents to be translated into multiple languages, and **parallel corpora**, or collections of texts and their translations in other languages, are proving useful in both the training of translators and the practice of translation. Specialised software allows a text and its translations to be aligned so that a word or phrase in one language can be retrieved together with its equivalent in other languages (e.g *Paraconc* and *Multiconcord*). **Parallel concordances** can then be produced with all possible translations in a corpus of a key word or phrase readily visible, allowing us to see how it has previously been translated. An illustration of what can be observed is given by Marie-Madeleine Kenning (1998). Grammars of French distinguish between the pronouns *me, te, lui, nous, vous,* and *leur,* used for animates, and the pronouns *y* and *en,* used for inanimates. However, Kenning raises the question of whether this distinction is relevant in the case of stressed, or emphasised, pronouns. For example, while an acceptable translation of

As Pierre had not arrived, I left without him.

is

Comme Pierre n'était toujours pas là, je suis partie sans lui.

(*lui* replacing *him*), native speakers of French would be less inclined to use a pronoun with an inanimate antecedent, preferring to recast the sentence, as in

As I could not find my book, I left without it.

Je suis parti sans mon livre, puisque je n'arrivais pas à le trouver.

[I left without my book, as I didn't manage to find it.]

In investigating this issue, Kenning used two parallel corpora – one English, the other French – consisting of two works of fiction, three chapters of a fictional work, and a popularised version of an academic text. She searched for stressed *it* in a particular linguistic context, after prepositions (e.g. *behind it*, *through it*), and observed the French equivalents. There were only seventeen cases in which pronouns were also used in French with an inanimate antecedent, and of these nearly half came from one text in which the pronoun replaced *mer* (sea) where it was personified:

Non contente d'être un lieu de travail, elle (la mer) s'approprie tout entiers hommes, femmes, enfants qui vivent d'elle . . .

Not content to be just a workplace, it took complete possession of the men, women and children who lived from it. . . .

In many more cases, however, *it* is not replaced with a pronoun. Instead, there may be repetition of a lexical item, use of a synonym, a recasting of the sentence with a different pronoun, and so on. In the following example *un rideau* (a curtain) is replaced by *ce rideau* (this curtain) rather than a pronoun:

elle découvrit un rideau bas qu'elle n'avait pas encore remarqué; derrière ce rideau se trouvait . . .

she came upon a low curtain she had not noticed before, and behind it . . .

Parallel corpus work of this kind, then, can provide the kind of detail that grammars rarely include, and offer a valuable resource in translation.

### *Grammar in learner English*

A further application of corpora is as an aid to language learning and teaching. While most of the published work in this area is on learning and teaching English as a foreign language, which is what we will focus on here, corpus applications in the teaching of other languages are increasingly common (see, for example, Dodd 2000 on teaching German).

Essentially, corpora have two main uses in language teaching and learning. First, the data from the corpus, perhaps in the form of concordance lines, can be given directly to students as part of a process of inductive learning about how the language is used. This is sometimes called 'data-driven learning' (Johns 1994). Second, teachers can analyse a corpus themselves in order to inform the design of teaching activities or materials, or simply to provide authentic examples. Collections of the language written or spoken by learners allow difficulties to be highlighted, and these can then become the focus for teaching. Additional insights can be gained by comparing learner language and corpora of native-speaker language produced in similar contexts or for similar purposes.

For example, Figure A9.2 is a sample of concordance lines illustrating the difficulties faced by learners with the word *rise*. The keywords are *rise* (both noun and verb forms), and other parts of the verb, *rose* and *risen*. The corpus is a relatively small collection of eighty written texts comprising 22,000 words produced by a multinational group of Masters in Business Administration (MBA) students at the University of Birmingham. The texts, describing and accounting for changes in world imports over a thirty-year period, were written as part of an initial diagnosis of language proficiency.

```
 1 ver food imports have again on the rise due to population problem at few countri
 2 e next century will see a constant rise in the importance of services being supp
 3 it.  The demand of new energy will rise sharply. 25 As both the pie charts of wo
 4 n of world imports after 1987 will rise continually in the machinery, equipment
 5 lution, deforestation, etc. can be risen simultaneously.  Moreover, if the propo
 6 , equipment, manufactures also has risen because almost every country, especiall
 7 , it was found that its import was risen up slightly.  in the opposite way, food
 8 ell.  This kind of commodities has risen its share from 10% in 1965 to approxima
 9 and the services sectors have also risen. Based on the information in the charts
10 n 1965 and 1987.  Their proportion rose from about 40% in 1965 to about 50% in 1
11 ry and equipment but also services rose its importance in 1987. According to the
12  decreased. In 1987, services part rose. For the future, my prediction makes as
```

*Figure A9.2* Concordance lines for *rise*, *risen* and *rose* from learner corpus

The main difficulty for students seems to relate to transitivity. The verb *rise* is intransitive, so doesn't take an object and doesn't have a passive form. However, in lines 5, 7, 8 and 11 students treat it as a transitive verb. In 5 and 7 it is made passive, and in 8 and 11 the verb is followed by an object.

In another corpus study of the writing of international MBA students (referred to as the learner corpus below), we compared aspects of the language used in their dissertations with language used in published journal articles in the same academic field (the journals corpus). The students had been encouraged by their subject tutors to use this kind of writing as a stylistic 'model' for their own language. Here we focus on the uses of extraposed *it*-clauses, of the type *it is assumed that* and *it is important to* (Hewings and Hewings 2002). We found that the MBA students used this grammatical structure more frequently and for different purposes than in the published writing. For example, the pattern *it + is/become + adjective* is used in both corpora to express a strong conviction about the importance or necessity of something, but is considerably more frequent in the learner corpus. The adjectives used in this pattern by the students in the learner corpus and by the academics in the journals corpus are given below, together with the number of occurrences in each corpus.

Learner corpus
*necessary* (10), *obvious* (10), *clear* (9), *essential* (5), *impossible* (6, including 1 *not possible*), *crucial* (2), *vital* (2), *inevitable* (1), *critical* (1), *difficult* (1), *imperative* (1), *unacceptable* (1), *undeniable* (1).

Journals corpus
*clear* (6), *essential* (2), *inevitable* (2), *necessary* (1), *not possible* (1), *possible* (1), *evident* (1), *unrealistic* (1), *vital* (1).

In the learner corpus the pattern seems to be primarily used to impress upon the reader the value of the students' own research, claiming that their findings have significant consequences for the establishment of good business practice. In the journals corpus it is relatively infrequent but, when used, mainly labels some feature of the present situation as 'clear', 'evident' etc., rather than making claims about the importance of the researchers' own findings. In reading the dissertations, there is a general impression that students make a much greater and more overt effort to persuade readers of the truth of their statements than do the published writers in the journal articles. One way in which this comes about is the use of *it*-clauses to state claims forcefully – but perhaps more forcefully than is appropriate.

### Grammatical and lexical meaning: blurring boundaries in corpus studies

When we use concordance lines to produce grammatical descriptions, the boundary between what is grammatical meaning and what is lexical meaning can become unclear. To illustrate, see Figure A9.3 on page 90 for a sample of eight concordance lines for the keyword *commit*.

Describing the grammar of *commit*, we might note that it is used here transitively (that is, with an object), and this object might be a singular or plural countable noun (*an act*, *offences*) or with an uncountable noun (serious *crime*, *suicide*). However, we might also observe that *commit* tends to co-occur with words which have

```
1 grievous bodily harm if they commit a deliberate foul resulting
2 he is committing or about to commit an act likely to endanger li
3 ion and one of conspiracy to commit deception. The deception cha
4 ose who drink alcohol do not commit offences of violence thereaf
5 r an IRA bombing she did not commit, or the accused in the Matri
6 ce of hacking with intent to commit serious crime - including al
7 ventually starve to death or commit suicide. Although skeletally
8 fect environment in which to commit these offences.' Detective I
```

**Figure A9.3** Concordance lines for *commit*

Source: Partington 1998: 67

unfavourable connotations, such as *foul, deception, offences,* and so on. As *commit* usually occurs with such 'negative' lexical items, *commit* itself takes on this negative meaning. Other verbs, conversely, tend to have positive associations. *Provide,* for example, frequently combines with words to do with care, food, money, help and shelter (Partington 1998: 68). Whether information on the tendencies of words to combine in certain ways and with certain meanings is part of grammatical or lexical meaning is a matter of debate. What is certain, however, is that corpus exploration allows us both to check our intuitions about the use of language in context, and also to identify patterns of use that we may not otherwise be aware of.

**Summary**

In this unit we have looked at:

- how corpora of written and spoken text can be used in investigating grammar and context
- applications of corpus investigation in:
    - comparing a particular grammatical pattern across corpora of texts produced in different contexts
    - identifying the grammatical characteristics of conversation
    - identifying grammatical change over time
    - translating texts
    - studying learner English.

## LOOKING AHEAD

Examples of corpus studies and opportunities to undertake analysis of concordance lines are found in a number of later units. Unit B1 focuses on analysis of spoken corpora, including the CANCODE corpus. An investigation of conditional structures in corpora of doctor–patient interaction and medical articles is reported in Unit B2. In Unit B3, academic writing is analysed in corpora taken from a number of different disciplines. In Unit C3, also on academic writing, comparative statistics and concordance lines are provided for you to carry out your own analyses.

# SECTION B
## Extension

Section A presented key ideas, assumptions, terminology and methods used in exploring the relationship between grammar and context. We also introduced research that has been particularly influential in this area. Section B gives you the opportunity to read in more detail about related research in extracts from published papers. While all the authors seem to accept that the study of both grammar and context are fundamental to an understanding of language in use, not all have the same view of either grammar or of context. Consequently you will notice different terminology and approaches adopted, and that some extracts are more focused on grammar while others concentrate on aspects of context.

Each unit of this section presents extracts from one or more papers around a context-related theme. Unit B1, for example, looks at grammatical features in the context of conversation, Unit B2 in institutional contexts, and so on. Where appropriate, the introduction to each extract highlights aspects of data or research methodology that are of particular interest in exploring the relationship between grammar and context.

Units B1–B5 explore grammatical choices in different modes of communication – speech, traditional print and electronic text. The extracts in Unit B1 on grammar in conversation also serve to illustrate the growing significance of electronic corpora in language study. Analysis of concordance lines allows us to see the immediate grammatical context for different lexical items, and where a corpus has been compiled to reflect different interactional contexts, further information can be gleaned. Features of spoken interaction are examined further in Unit B2 through two very different contexts: radio phone-ins and doctor–patient consultations. These examples demonstrate how grammatical choices are constrained by the type of interaction that is typical of or expected in particular settings. In the radio phone-in we see how the generally more powerful position of a person asking questions can be undermined by the institutionalised format of the phone-in. In the doctor–patient consultations the communicative relevance of different conditional constructions is exploited in interpersonally difficult exchanges. Units B3 and B4 look at grammatical patterns in different forms of writing in contexts such as academic research papers and textbooks, electronic messages and novels. Unit B3 in particular, on academic writing, demonstrates that we can continually narrow or refine our definition of context from, say, academic writing to academic writing for research journals, to academic writing in journals on twentieth-century Australian fiction. Unit B4 discusses features of electronic language. The final unit in this subsection deals with both spoken and written texts produced in contexts where it is necessary to omit or modify aspects of the grammar – commentaries on fast-moving sporting events and dating advertisements placed in newspapers and magazines.

Units B6 and B7 deal with aspects of grammar in the context of language learning and loss. The research reported in Unit B6 looks first at the relationship between language development and cognitive development in young children. The second extract focuses on the specific grammatical patterns associated with subordination and how these are deployed by children working on different writing tasks. The final extract deals with language loss in elderly people with dementia. Here we see that a study of grammatical and discoursal features helps to indicate the stage of dementia that a person has reached. Returning to language learning, Unit B7 looks at the effect of classroom context and specific teaching strategies on the acquisition of a second or foreign language.

The final units, B8–B10, deal with the relationships between social and regional context and grammatical choices. Unit B8 investigates 'non-standard' grammatical choices in the language of young people and notes that both age and gender are significant factors. Unit B9 presents an extract from a paper first published in 1959 linking grammar and social class, which was very influential in the early exploration of how grammar helps both to convey and to construct our view of the world. The second text in this unit takes up one aspect of the original paper and systematically investigates the use of adverbials in the conversations of two contrasting social groups. Unit B10 moves away from local regional or social differences in language to variation resulting from historical and geographical separateness. Grammatical variation can be seen in so-called 'new Englishes' developing in countries such as Singapore, Hong Kong and India. More remote from English, but still influenced by it, are pidgins and creoles such as those used in Melanesia and Hawaii. In these languages grammatical developments are taking place as they extend into new contexts – particularly writing.

Each text is accompanied by activities designed to help focus your reading. For some texts we provide tasks to be carried out before you read, and for all of them we provide tasks for you to do as you read, to highlight the most important elements of the reading. Tasks designed to be carried out after you have read the text encourage you to reflect on the material there and on its relationship with other research, and also on the methodologies used and conclusions drawn. Are the methodologies ones which you feel are adequate to substantiate what is said? When you come to do your own analysis in Section C, you will find that relating particular aspects of context to particular aspects of grammar can be challenging.

# Unit B1
# Grammar in conversation

In Unit A9 we saw that one of the exciting ways in which the study of language has developed in recent years has been the application of computational techniques allowing the analysis of large amounts of natural language data. Corpus analysis allows the researcher to look in detail at recurring patterns of use and how these patterns relate to what we called in Unit A2 the 'local linguistic context'. For many years the focus in corpus studies was on what texts to include within a corpus and the technicalities of storing and retrieving them. The fruits of that careful ground-work are now becoming clear as we start to see previously unsuspected grammatical regularities, and this is particularly apparent in relation to spoken language.

The three extracts in this unit all use corpora to investigate whether traditional grammatical descriptions are adequate to describe and account for the grammar of naturally occurring speech. Once we move away from an analysis of constructed sentences to 'real' language, past approaches to grammatical analysis are often found wanting as we suggested in Unit A1. This is particularly the case for spoken language and especially conversation where false starts, hesitations and reformulations are the norm. In Text B1.1, Ronald Carter and Michael McCarthy discuss the spoken data that makes up a minicorpus of their larger CANCODE corpus (see Unit A9 for details). The mini-corpus consists of two and a half hours of transcribed talk from a variety of male and female speakers from different backgrounds and of different ages. They have classified the types of data into that associated with service encounters (shopping, talking to an accountant, etc.), narratives (recounting stories or events), casual conversation, and what they call 'language in action' (talk accompanying tasks such as food preparation, moving furniture, etc.). In this subset of their full data, they isolated four grammatical features to exemplify their contention that speech has its own grammatical norms. These four features are discussed in Text B1.1 below.

 **Task B1.1.1**

Before reading Text B1.1, carry out the following activity:

➤ On the basis of your reading of Section A, try to predict some of the grammatical features more characteristic of spoken interaction than of writing.

As you read Text B1.1 carry out the following activity:

➤ Carter and McCarthy argue that it is important to recognise that the grammar of speech has many characteristics different from those found in writing. Make a note of the features that they associate with the grammar of speech. Illustrate each feature with an example from the text or – preferably – one of your own. Classify the features in terms of how common they are in their four genres (service encounters, narratives, casual conversation, and language in action) where this information is given in the text.

➤ Make a list of the reasons that Carter and McCarthy give why particular grammatical features are more common in certain genres than others.

You might find it helpful to put your answers to these questions in a table such as this:

| Grammatical features | Examples | Genres | Reasons for distribution between genres |
|---|---|---|---|
| Ellipsis | i) [Would] Wednesday at four be okay (auxiliary verb ellipsis)<br>ii) Mm [we] saved a fortune (subject pronoun in fixed expression) | Common in: Language in action, informal service encounters, casual talk<br>Uncommon in: Narratives | Talk which is related to the situation at the time favours situational ellipsis.<br>Narratives are too far removed from the present and therefore need to make all elements clearer. |

**Ronald Carter and Michael McCarthy (1995) 'Grammar and the spoken language', in *Applied Linguistics*, vol. 16, no. 2: 141–158.**

Text B1.1
R. Carter and
M. McCarthy

## 1 Ellipsis

Ellipsis, the omission of elements otherwise considered required in a structure, occurs widely in the mini-corpus. Here we shall concentrate on just one kind of ellipsis, what Quirk *et al.* (1985: 895 ff.) (hereafter QUIRK) refer to as *situational ellipsis*. . . . Situational ellipsis is particularly apparent in casual data. It is also notably present in language-in-action data, where not only the participants but the objects and entities and processes talked about are typically prominent in the immediate environment. There is also situational ellipsis in our service-encounter examples. It is notably *absent* from the narrative data, where the participants and processes of the story are usually separated in time and place from the moment of telling.

There are over 80 places in the mini-corpus where one or more items of structure which would be expected in the formal written mode do not appear, but whose referents are retrievable from the immediate situation. Of these places, 65 are ellipses where subject pronouns are retrievable from the contextual environment. In 41 of these 65 cases, a copular or auxiliary verb is also absent where it might be expected in written text . . . These types of pronoun and/or pronoun + operator absences are well described in existing grammars (e.g. see QUIRK), although the tendency is to explain them as

R. Carter and
M. McCarthy

elements of informality. QUIRK simply states that situational ellipsis is 'restricted to familiar (generally spoken) English' (ibid.: 896). While it may be true that such ellipses do not occur in highly formal contexts, it is also true that the wholly *informal* and, by any account, 'familiar' narratives in our mini-corpus do not have them either, and so the formality/informality or familiarity distinction is anything but the whole story. We would argue that genre and context are the two key factors that mediate beyond the choice of formality/familiarity. The narrative genre, with its spatio-temporal displacement, no matter how informal or familiar, cannot easily retrieve its elements from the immediate context and thus spells out explicitly the participants and verbal operations which may be assumed to be retrievable from the environment in other, more situation-dependent forms of talk, such as language-in-action, informal service encounters, and casual talk, where participants are face to face. Extract (1), from a service encounter, illustrates such retrievability:

(1)    [At a dry-cleaner's. <02> is leaving a pair of trousers for cleaning]

<01>   Wednesday at four be okay

<02>   Er yeah that's fine . . . just check the pockets a minute

Initial *will* or *would* from <01>'s turn and *I'll* from <02>'s second clause are not realized. Our conclusion is that a proper description of a feature such as situational ellipsis, and any description claiming pedagogical usefulness, should be able to state those environments in which the types of ellipsis described tend to and tend not to occur, as well as stating the structural restrictions on what elements in the clause may and may not be ellipted.

Even on the purely structural questions of what is permissible or not in situational ellipsis, existing grammars fail to take into account some interesting features of correlation between grammar and lexis. In the mini-corpus, it is noticeable that, on many occasions, items are ellipted from what are often termed lexical phrases (Nattinger and DeCarrico 1992), institutionalized expressions (Lewis 1993: 94), or fixed expressions (identified by the normal criteria of lack of syntactic or lexical productivity; see McCarthy 1992). QUIRK (899) does permit this for the definite and indefinite article with fixed and idiomatic expressions, but our data show ellipsis of other items too . in the environment of fixed expressions. Nattinger and DeCarrico (ibid.) argue that such expressions are fundamental in the construction of text, and, indeed, it is their very fixedness and cultural commonality which makes them good candidates for ellipsis; the unspoken elements of the message can always he assumed to be known. Some examples follow, with relevant fixed expressions manifesting ellipsis in italic:

(2)

<01>   We did quite well out of it actually

<02>   Great

<03>   Mm *saved a fortune* [ellipted: *we*]

(3)

<01>   How many pillows do you have, one two

<02>   I have one Graeme won't have any

<01>   Yeah right okay *good job* you said [ellipted: *it's/it was a*]

R. Carter and
M. McCarthy

. . . We would argue that any description of ellipsis in spoken language is incomplete which does not investigate fully and render an account of this essentially culturally embedded feature of lexico-grammatical form. . . .

## 2 Left dislocation and topical information

Left dislocation is one of the names commonly used for the phenomenon where items semantically co-referential with the subject or object of the clause are positioned before the subject. An example from our data is:

(4)

<01>  Well Sharon, where I'm living, *a friend of mine*, *she's* got her railcard, and . . .

Here, *a friend of mine* is 'copied' in the subject pronoun *she*. There are seven clear examples in the mini-corpus (uttered by seven different speakers in seven different extracts) where the pronoun subject of the clause is co-referential with an initial noun phrase uttered before the main clause gets under way, as in example (4), and again here in example (5):

(5)

<01>  The one chap in Covent Garden who I bought the fountain pen off he was saying that he'd . . .

where *he* copies the whole of the preceding long noun phrase. Examples (4) and (5) fit in with Geluykens' (1992) model for left dislocation, where *a friend of mine* in (4) would be termed the 'referent', *she* would be termed the 'gap', and *'s got her railcard* the 'proposition'. But other comparable phenomena, labelled 'quasi-left dislocation' by Geluykens (ibid.: 131) are also apparent in our data, and merit a closer look. For example, the initial noun phrase may be only indirectly related to the subject, which need not be a pronoun copy, as in (6):

(6)

<01>  *This friend of mine*, *her son* was in hospital and he'd had a serious accident . . .

Or there may be discord of person and number between the front-placed noun phrase and the main-clause subject, as in (7), but which does not seem to hamper pragmatic decoding by the listener(s):

(7)

<01>  *That couple that we know in Portsmouth*, I don't hear of *her* for months then . . .

. . . The point about these canonical examples of left dislocation and the less clear but related examples is that they have in common the utilization of an available 'slot' before the core constituents of the clause (Subject, Verb, Object/Complement, Adjunct, in whatever order they occur) are realized. Indeed, it would seem to be a misnomer and a misleading metaphor to talk of *dislocation* for it suggests that something has been pushed out of place to a somewhat aberrant position. We would argue that left-placed or fronted items of this kind are perfectly normal in conversational language, and are

R. Carter and
M. McCarthy

quite within their 'right place'. The phenomenon occurs especially in the narrative genre, where ten of our total of fourteen examples of this type of feature occur. It is apparent that speakers use the available slot to flag a variety of items of information that will be helpful to the listener in identifying participants, in linking current topics to already mentioned ones, in reactivating old topics, and generally anchoring the discourse, offering what Quirk *et al.* (1985) call 'a convenience to hearer' (QUIRK: 1417). This is a quintessential example of 'grammar as choice', where the speaker chooses to fill an available slot for textual and interpersonal motives. [The proclivity of this slot to carry topic-prominent items leads us to term it the *topic*.]

### 3 Reinforcement: the tail slot

Just as there seems to be an available slot at the front of the clause, which we have called the *topic*, so too, when all the core clause constituents have been exhausted, is there a final available space which speakers often choose to fill with different types of information. Tags occupy this slot. A typical example is the reinforcement tag (e.g. 'You're stupid, *you are.*'). But also recurrent in the mini-corpus are amplificatory noun-phrases, the reverse, as it were, of the topic-slot noun phrase and a subsequent copying pronoun. Some examples follow:

(8)

<01>  It's lovely

<02>  Good winter wine *that*

(9)

<01>  It's very nice *that road up through Skipton to the Dales* [<02> Yeah] I can't remember the names of the places

(10)

<01>  And he's quite a comic *the fellow*, you know

<02>  <Is he    yeah>

(11)    [<01> is the host, <02> a dinner guest]

<01>  Look get started you know putting all the bits and pieces on

<02>  <Bits and pieces on

<01>  Cos otherwise they tend to go cold *don't they pasta*

Eleven such nominal post-clause items occur in the mini-corpus, uttered by eight different speakers across seven different extracts. The speakers come from Wales, Northern England, and Southern England, suggesting it is not confined to one dialect. Example (11) demonstrates that the nominal items are not mutually exclusive with tags. It will also be noted that examples (8) to (11) are all in contexts where evaluative statements are being made. So too are the other seven examples not quoted here. This fits in with Aijmer's (1989) study of *tails*, as she calls the phenomenon, and as we shall do hereafter. Tails, in Aijmer's data and in ours, tend to occur with phatic, interpersonal functions, usually in contexts of attitudes and evaluations.

R. Carter and
M. McCarthy

Tails are therefore an important part of what may be called *interpersonal grammar*, that is to say speaker choices which signal the relationships between participants and position the speaker in terms of his/her stance or attitude. Tails may therefore be compared with *topics*, and a model for the clause in conversation may be posited which offers the structural potential shown in Table B1.1.

The topic and the tail are optional, but when utilized, carry important interpersonal functions, as our and others' data show. With this model, elements commonly found in conversational data need not be scattered around the descriptive apparatus or relegated to minor or marginal sections of the grammar, but achieve their proper place as items of 'real' language. . . .

*Table B1.1*  Structural potential of the clause in conversation

| Sequence | Pre-clause | Clause | Post-clause |
|---|---|---|---|
| Function | TOPIC | CORE | TAIL |
| Constituents | S-tp/O-tp/RI | S/V/O/C/A | TAG/S-tl/O-tl |
| Forms | NP/NFC | NP/VP/ADVP | NP/VP |

S-tp and O-tp = subject or object in the topic slot: S-tl and O-tl = subject or object in the tail slot; RI = related item; and TAG = any of the types of English sentence-tags (see Bennett 1989). S/V/O/C/A represent the core clause constituents (subject, verb, object, complement, and adjunct), which may be re-ordered for a variety of thematic and focusing purposes (e.g. object-fronting; see Hietaranta 1984). NP = noun phrase; NFC = non-finite clause; VP = verb phrase; and ADVP = adverbial phrase.

## 4 Indirect speech

Indirect speech is an area which, on the face of it, seems thoroughly covered in the grammars we have surveyed. Hundreds of examples abound of the type 'X said that Y', where the reporting verb (typically *say* or *tell*) is in the simple past tense and the sequence of tense rules apply to the reported clause. And yet in our mini-corpus, eleven examples of indirect speech (uttered by eight different speakers in eight different extracts) have the reporting verb in past continuous, Some examples follow:

(12)

    <01>  I mean I *was saying* to mum earlier that I'm actually thinking not for the money but for the sort of fun of it really trying to get a bar or a waitressing job I *was saying* to you wasn't I |<02> Yeah| in the summer well over Christmas or Easter

(13)

    <01>  Tony *was saying* they should have the heating on by about Wednesday

(14)

    <01>  Where were, yeah because I *was saying* to Ken that you wouldn't be in a pub at twelve o'clock in Corby would you you would have to be in somebody's house

(15)

<01> Yes Maureen and Derek *were telling* me you have to get a taxi

. . . We note that *say* and, in example (15), *tell* may be used in this way, that the report may be of what the speaker him/herself said or what another said, and that past simple could have been used, but with a distinctly different force: the past simple seems to give more authority to the actual words uttered, while the past continuous seems more to report the *event* of the uttering (exploiting perhaps the basic foregrounding and backgrounding functions of past simple and past continuous, respectively). Once again, though, what is interesting is that no examples of indirect speech in the *narrative* extracts have past continuous. We checked ten other narrative extracts not in the mini-corpus and none of them have any occurrences either. All our examples occur in the casual genre, except one, which crops up in the middle of a language-in-action sequence. All the indirect speech reports in our narratives are introduced by report-ing verbs in past simple or so-called historical present (see Johnstone 1987 on this). This may hint at a truly reporting function for past simple reporting verbs, where what someone said *and* what words they used (although creatively reconstructed) are considered important. On the other hand, past continuous *say* and *tell* show a tendency to emphasize message content rather than form, and to report or summarize whole conversational episodes rather than individual utterances. At the moment, our con-clusions must be tentative until much more data can be analysed. As a feature of spoken English grammar, it seems, past continuous reporting verbs have slipped through the grammarians' net. We would argue that this is precisely because: (a) most notions of reported speech are taken from written data (including literary text); and (b) that where spoken data have been consulted, there has been an overemphasis on oral narrative, which is simply unlikely to yield such examples if the present corpus is anything to go by, and an over-emphasis on broadcast talk, where indirect speech is likely to be of a truly quotational type, where form and content are both important (e.g. news reporting).

**Task B1.1.2**

Having read text B1.1, carry out the following activities:

➤ Listen out for examples of the grammatical features that Carter and McCarthy have noted. Consider whether your examples occur in the situational contexts/genres that they have found. If they do not, explain why they occur in these different contexts/genres.

➤ Carter and McCarthy 'argue that genre and context are the two key factors that mediate beyond the choice of formality/familiarity'. Think about a variety of situations that you are familiar with where there are different levels of formality or familiarity between the participants. Does the concept of genre (interviews, service encounters, dinner table conversation etc.) help in accounting for the grammatical choices? Try to gather some examples of speech which support your point of view.

Text B1.2 is the result of an extensive corpus study by Douglas Biber and colleagues which has resulted in a body of work contrasting the grammatical frequencies of different structures in four broadly based varieties or registers – news, fiction, academic prose and conversation (see Units A1 and A4). Unlike Carter and McCarthy, they did not distinguish different contexts at a fine level of detail. However, their findings indicated such differences in the grammar of speech from that of the written registers that they devoted a whole section of their work to a discussion of the type of structures characteristic of speech. In the extract below they distinguish between the body of a speaker's message which carries the main content, and optional preceding and following elements which they refer to as 'prefaces' and 'tags'. They ascribe the function of these elements to the need for a speaker to cope with planning complex messages in the short time available in conversation. Using the example:

*Preface*  North and south London
*Body*                                          they're two different worlds
*Tags*                                                              aren't they? In a way

they note that these utterances do not have the carefully crafted and integrated structure typical of sentences. They are instead discussed in terms of clausal or non-clausal units (see Unit A1).


## Task B1.2.1

As you read Text B1.2, carry out the following activities:

➤ Make a list of the different types of preface and tag. Give an example and note whether it is common, if this information is given.

➤ Note down what terms Carter and McCarthy use for prefaces and tags.

(*Note*: the bracketed information at the end of examples indicates whether they are taken from British English (BrE) or American English (AE). The symbol † shows that an example has been truncated to save space.)


## Douglas Biber *et al.* (1999) *The Longman Grammar of Spoken and Written English*, Harlow, Pearson.

Text B1.2
D. Biber *et al.*

### 1 Prefaces and other utterance launchers

Utterance launchers is a term we can use for expressions which have a special function of beginning a turn or an utterance. They include prefaces in addition to other locutions which are integrated into the syntactic structure of the utterance they introduce . . . In general, they have a role not only in propelling the conversation in a new direction but also in providing the speaker with a planning respite, during which the rest of the utterance can be prepared for execution. These conversational launching-devices include fronting, noun phrase prefaces, discourse markers, and overtures.

D. Biber *et al.*

## A **Fronting**

The grammatical shape of clausal units is overwhelmingly conformant to the dominant SVO/P/A word order of English (where O or P or A is a complement of the verb), and the exceptions to this order (disregarding ellipsis) are rarely found in conversation. The variant word order O/P/A SV known as topicalization or fronting is found only under highly restricted conditions, illustrated in the following example (the fronted object is emboldened):

> 1  A: *You always remember numbers. Don't you? Car numbers and telephone numbers and –*
>
> B: **Car numbers** *I remember more by the letters than the numbers* (BrE)

. . . Fronting is a device for information management: it capitalizes on word order flexibility to give thematic prominence to one element in the immediate context. However, such flexibility is very limited in present-day English.

## B  *Noun phrase prefaces co-referential to pronouns*

Noun phrase prefaces . . . are more common in conversation than fronting is, combining a topicalizing function with the division of a clause frame into two more easily managed chunks. The following examples illustrate the device of noun phrase prefaces co-referential to a pronoun in the following clause:

> 2  **This little shop – it's** *lovely* (BrE)
>
> 3  **Those Marks and Sparks bags**, *can you see* **them** *all?* (BrE)
>
> 4  *you know,* **the vase**, *did you see* **it**? (AmE)

The preface plus body could be replaced, in more orthodox sentence grammar, by a single clause in which the prefatory noun phrase replaces the co-referential pronoun in the clausal unit: e.g. example 2 corresponds to *This little shop is lovely.* . . .

## C  *Discourse markers and other prefatory expressions*

Commonly an utterance opens with a single prefatory word, which has the function of orienting the listener to the following utterance, especially in relation to what has preceded. Such prefatory words can be of various types: they may be inserts (discourse markers such as *well* and *right*, interjections such as *oh*, and response forms such as *yeah* and *okay*) or they may be classed as adverbs (stance adverbs such as *anyway* or linking adverbs such as *so* and *then*).

In fact, the boundaries between these categories are far from clear-cut in conversation and many words are multifunctional in their discourse role. Some examples are:

> . . .
>
> A: *erm, that was immediately after the war, you know, the first war*
>
> B: **Right** *– did your wife come from the same area?*

A: **Well**, *in a way, although her parents were* Scotch (BrE)

**Oh**, *I should have let you read the paper, I never thought of it.* (AmE)

. . .

A: **Okay**, *I'll meet you over there. / Alright.*

B: **So** *I'll see you at the house.* (AmE)

Sometimes such particles are used in combination:

. . .

**Yeah. So anyway** *it's supposed to be more aerodynamic I guess.* (AmE)

**Okay well then**, *shoot, shoot, it's not going to be* Star Wars. (AmE)

We use the term 'discourse marker' also for a further category of utterance launchers consisting of more than one orthographic word. Usually these are similar in form to comment clauses. Common examples are:

**I mean, look (here), mind (you), see, you know, you see**

For example:

. . .

A: I **mean** *are these the same, these are the same?*

B: Uh huh. *Those are kind of further back.* (AmE)

## D Overtures (longer expressions)

On other occasions, the speaker uses a longer expression from a stock of ready-made utterance openers available in the language:

1 But **the trouble is** *a lot of engineering, a lot of engineering is now making into that.* (AmE)

2 **I'll tell you what** *I've just had a thought.* (AmE)

Such multi-word expressions are a more explicit way of signalling a new direction in the conversation; the list is more open ended than that of discourse markers. Further examples, with a rough indication of the pragmatic force they signal, are:

| | |
|---|---|
| *I would have thought* | (politely putting a point of disagreement) |
| *Like I say* | (repeating a point the speaker made earlier) |
| *The question is* | (presenting an issue in an explicit, forceful way) |
| *There again* | (adding a contrasting point to an argument) |
| *What we can do is* | (proposing a joint course of action) |
| *You mean to say* | (asking for confirmation of a point the speaker finds difficult to believe) |
| *Going back to . . .* | (returning to an earlier topic) |

D. Biber *et al.*

Other overtures are: *No wonder, For one thing, The (only) thing is, As a matter of fact.* Here are a few examples:

. . .

Hm. **The question** *is how many people are willing to spend a lot of money for this CD-ROM.* (AmE)

*I have a room, I could do that, I could go upstairs but* **there again***, you're shut off from everything aren't you* (BrE†)

*Not to worry. Not to worry. Erm –* **what we can do is** *er – use something here.* (BrE)

**you mean to say***, we're paying two and half thousand pounds worth of repairs, I says, and they're not done?* (BrE†)

**Going back to** *the subject of their parents thinking about it. How did you find you know having someone living in your house and things like that?* (BrE)

*Because people don't want to buy a repossessed house.* **For one thing** *they think it's unlucky.* (BrE)

*I don't mind driving it <= the car> down there, but the thing is how am I gonna get back if I drive it down.* (BrE†)

. . .

## 2 Tags

We turn now to 'Qualification of what has been said'. The tendency to add elements as an afterthought to a grammatical unit, especially a clausal unit, can be illustrated by a number of different strategies which can be characterized as the adding of tags, or retrospective qualifications loosely attached to the preceding clausal material . . .

### A Retrospective comment clauses

*And then they're open seven days a week* **you say***.* (BrE)

*Mm I wouldn't go into Amanda Close* **I don't think** (BrE)

The speaker here adds a comment clause which in effect modifies the stance of the preceding clause: it is a kind of propositional hedge.

### B Retrospective vagueness hedges

*And it was her second car that she'd ever had* **sort of thing***.* (BrE)

*North and south London they're two different worlds aren't they?* **in a way***.* (BrE)

Final hedges such as these indicate that the speaker would like the hearer to take the preceding message 'with a pinch of salt', i.e. not to understand it as absolutely or literally true.

D. Biber *et al.*

## C  Question tags

Question tags have an interactive function of eliciting the hearer's agreement or confirmation. They can also be seen as having a role of retrospective qualification:

Well, that little girl's cute **isn't she**? (AmE)

You get more done that way **huh**? (AmE)

You had a nice trip though **yeah**? (AmE)

Here the qualification is pragmatic. The speaker begins by making an assertion then retrospectively turns its force into that of a question.

## D  Noun phrase tags

A further type of tag takes the form of repeating a noun phrase with further elaboration, presumably to clarify a reference that might otherwise be unclear:

He's had **a blind** put up – **a special blind that that leads straight across the fanlight**. (BrE)

You always remember **numbers**. Don't you? **Car numbers and telephone numbers and —** (BrE)

As the opposite of noun phrase prefaces, noun phrase tags frequently take the form of an appended noun phrase co-referentially linked to a pronoun in the body of the clause:

I mean **it** was the only one with its own kitchen, **the one I was gonna have**. (BrE)

I just give **it** all away didn't I Rudy **my knitting**? (BrE)

Oh I reckon **they're** lovely. I really do **whippets**. (BrE)

The major motivation for this device seems to be the need to clarify reference retrospectively. It appears that the use of a personal pronoun is the first resort of the speaker, who at the end of the clausal unit may suspect (perhaps through a non-verbal signal from the addressee) that its reference is unclear to the addressee. Hence the appending of a clarifactory noun phrase.

## Task B1.2.2

Having read Text B1.2 carry out the following activities:

➤ Consider whether Biber and colleagues use the term 'tag' in a way that is different from your understanding of it. If this is so, in what way is it different?

➤ In Text B1.1, Carter and McCarthy analysed a number of different spoken genres while in Text B1.2 Biber and colleagues look at conversation more broadly. Consider the advantages of these different approaches. What research questions could be answered more appropriately by them?

Our final extract in this unit looks at negation in spoken discourses; that is, how clauses are made negative by adding elements such as *not* or *no*. Gunnel Tottie examines linguistic features that co-occur with negation and offers some explanations.

## Task B1.3.1

As you read Text B1.3 carry out the following activities:

➤ You will notice that Tottie highlights the frequency of mental verbs co-occurring with negation in speech. What examples can you think of to illustrate this co-occurrence?

➤ Decide whether you agree with her explanation that it is a sign of speaker 'involvement'.

**Text B1.3**
**G. Tottie**

### Gunnel Tottie (1991) *Negation in English Speech and Writing: A Study in Variation*, London, Academic Press, Inc.

### Frequency of negation and speaker involvement

It is interesting to try to relate the proportions [shown in Table B1.2] to underlying situational and interactional parameters as well as to psychological factors, i.e., production and processing constraints. It is certainly the case that production constraints account for many of the repetitions: Speakers must cope with production and planning at the same time and sometimes resort to repeating the same item over and over again while searching for new linguistic material, or else, repetition is used for self-repair. Repetition is also often used more or less consciously as a floor-holding device, or entirely deliberately, for emphasis. Repetition also typically occurs as the sequel to an explicit denial. In that case, however, it is not as a rule the same lexical item that is repeated but the repetition is functional and consists of an explanatory statement as in **no** / *Marilyn does **no** teaching*.

*Table B1.2* Survey of speech-specific factors

|  | Mental verbs | Explicit denials | Questions | Supports | Repetitions | Rejections | Imperatives |
|---|---|---|---|---|---|---|---|
| Total | 68 | 63 | 36 | 34 | 16 | 7 | 1 | 225 |
| Percentage | 30 | 28 | 16 | 15 | 7 | 3 | .5 |

Explicit denials and rejections are clearly products of the communicative situation in which they occur: The fact that at least two speakers are present, instead of just a solitary writer, provides the opportunity for questions to be asked, for negative as well as positive answers to be given, for statements to be denied, and for offers and suggestions to be made, accepted, or rejected. Explicit denials and rejections are functions of the situation, demonstrating that conversation is used for very different ends than writing normally is.

Perhaps the most interesting group of factors contributing to the high incidence of negative expressions in conversation is that consisting of collocations of negatives with mental verbs, and of negative expressions in questions and as supports. All of those uses of negation testify to the cooperative effort that goes into conversation. By means of negative questions, especially tag questions, speakers seek corroboration from listeners, and by means of supports (of which the negative ones are only one type), listeners provide such corroboration, making it easier for speakers to continue.

The use of mental verbs, often with first and second person subjects as pointed out by Chafe (1982), is another facet of the interactive character of conversation: Speakers' reference to their own and their interlocutors' mental processes is a manifestation of the higher emotional load of conversation than of typical writing, which is informative in character (cf. also Biber 1988: 105f.). The use of mental or 'private' verbs is another sign or speakers' INVOLVEMENT, and it is certainly no accident that mental verbs collocate with negation, which adds to the emotional character of what is said, and which contributes to the avoidance of bluntness and to the achievement of what Fraser (1980) calls 'conversational mitigation.' In conversation, speakers and listeners cooperate to achieve certain goals, by doing essentially other things with words than writers do, and also doing them according to certain rules laid down by society. When a speaker makes a refusal by saying I *don't know if* I *will* . . ., that is not just a sign of uncertainty or groping for words, but an important device serving to save the face of the person making the offer and enabling participants to continue the conversation without bad feelings.

## Task B1.3.2

Having read text B1.3 carry out the following activities:

➤ Read the following examples of conversation and classify the underlined negatives using Tottie's list of speech-specific factors.

   a.  Mm, pretty quick are<u>n't</u> they? (BNC: KB5)
   b.  Do<u>n't</u> forget that clock's gone about five minutes slow. (BNC: KB7)
   c.  She does<u>n't</u> like people smoking in her house. (BNC: KB7)
   d.  A: Does Ricky go in there? B: <u>No</u>, he's <u>never</u> been there. (BNC: KB7)
   e.  A: I do<u>n't</u> like the downstairs one so much. B: <u>No</u>, I like this much more. (BNC: KB7)

➤ Tottie's final example 'I don't know if I will . . .' is explained in terms of saving the face or feelings of the person who is being refused. Consider how different contexts might affect the way a refusal is made. Will there always be an effort to save someone's face?

➤ Look back over the three texts in this unit and list the different reasons that are given for the grammar of speech having different characteristics from the grammar of writing. Decide whether you find them all equally convincing. Reflect on your own speech and consider when you use features such as ellipsis, tags or negation and what psychological or contextual reasons seem to account for your choices.

➤ All three texts in this unit have used corpus analysis. State what grammatical features they have uncovered and how their findings might contribute to the discussion of grammatical acceptability and Standard English introduced in Units A1 and A8.

**Summary**

These three texts illustrate in detail the ways in which we are able to adapt our grammatical choices to the context in which we are using the language. Of all the contrasts in context, that between speech and writing is perhaps the clearest. We have seen here that there are many features that are particular to speech or are more common in speech than in writing. This has been found by looking at their relative frequencies of occurrence within large corpora. By then examining the co-text surrounding a particular instance of language use researchers can start to look for the motivations behind choices. These include: obtaining more planning time when speaking, signalling to the hearer what is being focused on at a particular point in a conversation, and providing additional interpersonal dimensions.

In this unit we have looked at:

Contexts

■ Corpus studies of the grammar of informal speech.

Linguistic features/grammatical structures

■ Ellipsis
■ Left dislocation of topic
■ Reinforcement of the topic at the end of an utterance
■ Use of past continuous in indirect speech
■ Prefaces (or 'topics') and other utterance launchers
■ Tags (or 'tails')
■ Negatives and speaker cooperation strategies.

# Unit B2
# Grammar in speech in institutional settings

In Section A we introduced the notion that the grammatical choices we make are related to a variety of contextual features, from the local linguistic context through to the wider socio-cultural context. We saw in Unit B1 that one of the clearest influences on grammatical choice is whether the interactants are speaking or writing. In this unit we narrow our focus to speech in two specific institutional contexts: radio phone-ins and medical consultations. In labelling these contexts 'institutional' we mean that the function of the language used is limited and to some extent routinised. In addition, the roles of the participants are clearly defined and their linguistic options therefore constrained. In the type of radio phone-in investigated here, there are three typical participant roles: the 'host' or 'presenter' of the programme whose role includes introducing the 'questioner' to the studio 'guest'. In the medical consultations the major participants are doctor and patient. The roles adopted by or assigned to the participants allow them to exercise different degrees of control over the discourse, as we saw in Unit A7. It is this relationship between language and power that is highlighted in the first reading in this unit by Joanna Thornborrow (2002) on the management of talk in radio phone-ins. Rather than taking extended extracts from this paper (and the one by Gibson Ferguson which follows) we will present shorter extracts with examples that bear closely on the relationships between grammatical choice and power in institutional contexts.

## Task B2.1.1

As you read the dialogues and discussions below, carry out the following activities:

➤ Note what the common stages of interaction are at the beginning of a question in a radio phone-in programme.

➤ Consider what features are often associated with the language of callers who do not use a question-framing stage. How does this position the questioner in relation to the others in the interaction?

Thornborrow's paper, one part of a book dedicated to institutional discourse, discusses the control of dialogue exercised by those who ask questions and how this is disrupted by the dynamics of radio phone-ins. In this kind of phone-in it is the programme host who controls who is allowed to speak, when and about what, and who acts as a mediator between a caller and the guest being questioned on the show. This mediation subverts the normal relationship between caller and call-receiver. Normally when we receive a phone call we expect the caller to initiate a topic that we can identify as the reason for the call. If it is a friend, the reason may well be to exchange news of friends and family; or if it is a colleague then we might expect some topic to do with work. In phone-in programmes, however, there is a three-way interaction and therefore a different way of participating has to be negotiated. In particular, the questioner is placed in a less powerful position than is usual because the topic of their call will already be known to the host and to the guest.

Thornborrow undertakes a close analysis of a number of calls to a radio phone-in on BBC Radio 1 to the then British prime minister, Margaret Thatcher, and observes the way in which callers adapt to their role in the three-way interaction. Many go through three stages – greeting, transition, and question framing – as in example 1. (SB is the phone-in host.)

1.

*SB:*    thank you for coming and let's get straight to the calls Keith M—
( . ) from Barnstaple in North Devon good evening

*Caller:*  hello yes uh my question uh to the prime minister is on health
(.hh) I'm a nurse [—]

(p.72)

As Thornborrow (2002: 73) notes in her comments on this extract we can see the caller starting from the initial greeting sequence with the host and then using a buffer or transitional device 'yes uh', to move towards the question. This is framed with 'my question uh to the prime minister is . . .'. Thornborrow attributes this question framing to the callers realigning themselves as questioners, despite the knowledge that the question is already known to the host and guest. This framing, where a speaker uses initial position to signal information about the topic, is similar to left dislocation and topical information (Carter and McCarthy) and prefaces or utterance launchers (Biber *et al.*) that were introduced in Unit B1. In the case of phone-ins, the caller is signalling that a question is about to be asked; they are flagging that the introductory sequence is over and that they are moving on to the main business. Some callers go through longer framing sequences than others – giving information about themselves or their circumstances. In example 2 the caller uses three frames (underlined) to draw attention to the non-serious nature of the question.

2.

*Caller:*  that's right (.h)er <u>(mine's) a bit of a light weight question this</u> er <u>I
just wondered</u> er Mr Kinnock has er recorded a video (.) er with
Tracy Ullmann er David Steel has [er app]eared=

*SB:*                                   [(((laughs))]

*Caller:* =_in one as well <u>I wondered</u> if y–you'd chance to let down your
hair whether or not you'd appear in a video?

(p. 74)

Not all questioners use this sequence and Thornborrow's evidence is that questions
not preceded by a framing device tend to be grammatically much more complex
with a more formal style as exemplified in examples 3 and 4.

3.

*Caller:* does the prime minister think that in the current employment
situation (.) where a university degree is no longer a guarantee of a job (.)
that the conservative's intended (.) student loan scheme (.) is justified.

(p. 74)

4.

*Caller:* = (Mrs) Thatcher. in view of yesterday's party election broadcast (.)
I would ask you (.) if you think that the manner in which you pushed you
to the forefront (.) rather than your policies (.) leaves you open to personal
attack

(p.73)

In 3 the caller uses the more formal third-person form of address ('does the prime
minister think' rather than 'do you think'), and in both 3 and 4 complex and
complete clause structures probably indicate that the callers have carefully prepared,
possibly scripted, what they are going to say. Rather than frame their questions with
reference to themselves or their situation, these callers refer to wider contextual
elements such as the current employment situation or the previous day's party
election broadcast. This is a pattern commonly found before questions in political
interviews conducted by professional journalists. In terms of how this relates to
issues of status and power relations in the case of radio phone-ins, Thornborrow
(2002: 76) concludes:

> Callers who choose a more formal register for their questions may be using
> this formality to construct a firmer interactional status for themselves as
> questioners and, consequently, to construct a more symmetrical framework
> of interaction with the other more institutionally powerful participants.

What we see here then is that the setting of a radio phone-in circumscribes the
type of interaction that can take place. The unusual situation of a caller asking a
question to someone who already knows what that question is going to be and
having their role mediated by the host of the show leads to certain interactional
patterns being repeated. The most common is the three-part sequence of greeting,
transition, and question frame. This is usually accompanied by utterances of an
informal nature, grammatically simple and perhaps incomplete. However, questioners can position themselves vis-à-vis the host and guest differently. By dropping

the question framing element, by making reference to the wider social context, not just personal context, and most significantly by choosing to use formal and complex grammatical structures, the questioner can take a more equal position within the interaction.

## Task B2.1.2

Having read the above, carry out the following activities:

➤ According to Thornborrow, most phone-in question sequences begin with three stages: greeting, transition, question framing. Consider other institutionalised interactions from different contexts. Try to predict the stages that are common. You might like to think about, for example, having a check-up at the dentist, booking concert tickets over the phone or asking a question after a lecture.

➤ Thornborrow argues that using a more formal register creates a 'more symmetrical framework of interaction with the other institutionally powerful participants'. Think of other institutional situations where some participants have greater power to control the interaction. Is increasing the level of formality the only strategy that the less powerful interactant can employ?

Our second example on the relationship between institutional setting and grammatical choices investigates medical discourse. A number of studies in recent years have analysed aspects of both spoken and written medical discourse. Some of the studies of medical writing have applied corpus analysis techniques (e.g. Gledhill 2000, Luzon Marco 2000) while much of the analysis of speech has focused on detailed qualitative description (e.g. Roberts and Sarangi 2003; Sarangi and Roberts 1999). Here we look at a study by Gibson Ferguson (2001) which explores both spoken and written interaction using a corpus-based approach, highlighting the communicative significance of certain grammatical patterns.

The sensitivity of much that is discussed between doctors and patients can lead to particular ways of talking designed to lessen embarrassment, or to be encouraging or comforting. In Ferguson's study we see that *conditional* structures are deployed in a variety of ways to help in this difficult area of communication. The work compares conditionals in a corpus of 34 doctor–patient consultations, totalling approximately 30,000 words, and two similarly sized corpora of written medical discourse from medical journal articles and from journal editorials, although we concentrate here on his findings from the spoken corpus.

## Task B2.1.3

Before you read the material on conditionals, carry out the following activity:

➤ Conditional structures (*if . . . then . . .*) are traditionally associated with expressing hypotheticality. Ferguson identifies five additional functions in doctor–patient consultations. Try to predict some of these other functions or think of examples where conditional structures are used for purposes other than hypothesising. Now, as you read, carry out the following activities:

➤ Note the most common function of conditionals. Why is the conditional used so frequently?

➤ Analyse the verb choices in one example for each of the functions of conditionals, e.g.

*If you go outside, Sister will fix you up* (present . . . *will* + infinitive).

A conditional sentence typically consists of two clauses – the *if clause* and the *then clause*. The relationship between these two clauses is one of dependency, such as cause and effect, enablement, inference, or some other looser connection. Traditionally, conditionals have been described in terms of the degree of hypotheticality expressed through verb choices in the two clauses:

■ first conditional: present + future (*if it rains, we'll go home*);
■ second conditional: past + would (*if it rained, we would go home*):
■ third conditional: past perfect + would have (*if it had rained, we would have gone home*).

(Ferguson 2001: 64)

In practice, however, this simple paradigm of so-called hypothetical conditionals does not describe the variety of tenses used and the different meanings conveyed. For example, in addition to the three combinations of verb forms above, Ferguson also found evidence of four others in his three corpora: present + present; present + modal; past + past; past + modal. This greater variety of forms was most common in the written genres. For example, in the methods section of journal articles he found that conditionals with the form past + past were frequently used to express co-occurrence of situations which were dependent on each other:

A child was classified as food-intolerant if the answer was 'yes' to both questions (p. 71)

Conditionals, then, take on a variety of forms and functions and these are distributed differently between written and spoken genres in the same institutional setting – medicine. We will now concentrate on the findings from the corpus of doctor–patient consultations, where the variety of forms was greatest. Table 1 exemplifies the function of conditional sentences in this corpus.

Here we see that hypothesising is only one function of conditionals in doctor–patient consultations. The table shows that the major use is in polite directives. The

*Table B2.1* An overview of the functions of conditionals in doctor–patient consultations

| Function | Number of instances | Examples |
|---|---|---|
| Polite directives | 20 (10 without apodosis [i.e. a main clause]) | *If you go outside, Sister will fix things up.* *If you pop through there . . .* *If you go up, you'll be sort of facing that direction.* *If you ask at the desk.* |
| Patient description of symptoms (habitual co-occurrence/conjunction of two situations) | 13 | *She said I screw up my eyes all the time if I'm driving the car or so on.* *If I'm turning a dishcloth or anything out, it's pretty painful at the wrists.* *I feel sick all the time if I don't have the tablets.* |
| Prediction or prognostication | 12 | *If that is the case, then the whole thing will just sort of fizzle out.* *I think you'll be lucky if that resolves, to be honest.* *. . . the problem is if you operate she might finish up with a stiff toe.* |
| Hypothesising in context of explaining reasoning about diagnosis, management or treatment | 8 | *I don't think she'll have damaged the tendon because if she had the toe would tend to get pulled right down, though it is tending to pull a wee bit down.* *If there'd been a foreign body or anything like that, then I'd have said look I think we should do something about that.* |
| Doctor's elicitation of patient symptoms (habitual co-occurrence/conjunction of two situations) | 7 | *Do you have any pain if you sneeze or cough?* *If she runs around a lot – has been more active, it's been swollen?* *If you have one, what happens.* |
| Asserting a habitual co-occurrence/conjunction of two situations | 6 | *If they have a gap in their palate, it's very obvious when they speak. If you've got a child who's not speaking properly, you don't just assume it's bad speech.* *If it doesn't disappear, you're left with something like a glove finger.* |
| Subtotal=66 Others unclassified Total conditional= 77 | 11 | |

(Ferguson 2001: 78)

use of a conditional mitigates what is in fact a directive from the doctor to the patient. The *if*-clause makes it seem as if the proposed action is optional and will only take place if the patient is willing. In fact, it is an indirect order which the patient is unlikely to feel able to disobey.

The second most common use of conditionals is in patients describing symptoms. These conditionals do not signal hypotheticality, but rather that one event always causes or is associated with another. Ferguson uses the example:

> If I'm sort of thinking about something else while I'm eating, then it . . . doesn't work properly.

to show that the main clause typically states the symptom and the subordinate *if*-clause specifies the circumstances that give rise to the symptom (p.77). These are similar in form to the conditionals used by doctors to elicit information from patients about their symptoms.

Predicting the outcome of a condition or treatment is another common function of conditional sentences. Typically the main clause contains 'will' or another modal verb and states the outcome which depends on the condition stated in the *if*-clause.

> If you operate, she might end up with a stiff toe.

(p.77)

The next example illustrates the use of conditionals to explain the reasoning behind a course of action or a diagnosis. Ferguson explains the example and then goes on to discuss a final type of conditional not mentioned in the table.

> It's just that if it took a long time to heal, that sometimes makes one wonder whether there's been some foreign body in it.

Here, the doctor, having just rejected the possibility of a foreign body in the wound, explains to the patient's mother why this possibility had occurred to him in the first place; namely, because of the time taken for the wound to heal . . . The sentence may be understood as . . . [an] example of . . . an 'epistemic' conditional, where the relation of antecedent to consequent is one of premise and conclusion rather than of cause and effect in the socio-physical domain.

Finally, it is perhaps worth remarking on a use of conditionals not represented in [the] Table. This is their use in contexts of reassurance, which, not unexpectedly, recur fairly often in consultations. That conditionals function as one of a number of resources for expressing reassurance may be attributed to the fact that the [*if*-clause] allows the speaker to present interactionally difficult content as hypothetical rather than actual. In other words, the doctor, suspecting a particular problem, may choose to present it as hypothetical and provisional, thereby rendering potentially unpleasant information less threatening. An interesting case from the data is illustrated in: [a6]

> All right. I don't think you'll need to come in and stay or anything like that, but I think we should bring you in as an outpatient for

some further tests because, obviously, in a man of 47, if this was a circulation problem, then we ought to be sure of what's going on.

> The previous context here makes clear that the patient most probably does indeed have a circulatory problem. It is interesting, then, that the doctor not only uses a conditional to indicate a lack of diagnostic certainty but also selects a past tense to strengthen the hypotheticality of the [*if*-clause], presumably for the interactional reasons we have indicated.
>
> (Ferguson 2001: 79)

This discussion of the function of conditionals gives us an insight into how flexibly we can use particular grammatical forms. By combining different tenses we are able to express subtleties of meaning, and this is well illustrated in the last example. Ferguson's examples from medical discourse show how both form and function vary in different genres according to the context of interaction and the meanings that need to be conveyed.

 **Task B2.1.4**

Having read the material on conditionals, carry out the following activities.

➤ In the previous unit Carter and McCarthy noted that despite the many descriptions of the grammatical forms of reported speech, there had not been any comment on the use of the present continuous tense in reporting. Similarly, Ferguson highlights that there are more patterns of verb choice in conditional forms than have traditionally been described in grammars. Consider what explanations there might be for these omissions.

➤ At the beginning of this unit we said that institutional contexts resulted in language use being to some extent routinised and having more limited functions. Decide whether your experience confirms this. Can you think of a situation where someone does not conform to the expectations of the institutional setting? What happens to communication as a result?

In this unit we have seen demonstrated that the institutional nature of a particular setting can have systematic influences on the grammatical choices of interactants. In the radio phone-in, the usual position of initiating topics held by a caller is undermined by the mediating role of the programme host and the knowledge that the question or topic is already known to all the contributors. However, analysis of callers' language showed that the use of more complex grammatical sentences, including subordinate clauses, allowed them to reclaim some of the initiative. Ferguson's research showed that within the different genres of medicine conditional forms were widely used for a variety of functions. He established that functions and therefore their associated forms were distributed differently between genres. The examples from doctor–patient consultations showed particularly well the range of functions that conditional forms may have and possible motivations for making these choices.

In this unit we have looked at:

Contexts

■ Institutional settings

■ radio phone-ins
■ doctor–patient interviews.

Linguistic features/grammatical structures

■ questions
■ utterance-framing strategies
■ function and form of conditionals.

117

# Unit B3
# Grammar in written academic contexts

Much of the research into the influence of context on grammar has been conducted in relation to academic writing. This has been prompted by two main concerns: to discover the characteristics of academic – and particularly scientific – writing, and possible reasons why these features are found; and to help students to communicate well in different academic subject areas. Below we include three extracts which focus on particular grammatical characteristics of academic writing and their relationship to the academic context.

The first extract is by Michael Halliday, who is responsible for much of the work on systemic functional grammar (SFG) which was introduced in Units A1 and A5. Here he looks at features of scientific English, particularly *grammatical metaphor*, and how such metaphors may have developed from 'congruent', or non-metaphorical, expressions of events and processes. You have already looked at nominalisation, which is an important process in grammatical metaphor, in Unit A6. In this extract we see that grammatical metaphor involves more than just nominalisation, though the length and complexity of *noun groups*, or *nominal groups* as Halliday calls them, is central. You will notice that many of the grammatical terms used by Halliday have capital letters. Also, Halliday and his associates refer to the part of speech 'verb' by their functional label 'process'. These specifics of SFG terminology need not concern us here.

 **Task B3.1.1**

As you read Text B3.1, carry out the following activities:

➤ Make a note of what a grammatical metaphor is, giving an example to illustrate it.

➤ Consider what arguments Halliday gives for the development of grammatical metaphor.

➤ Think about your own academic writing and see whether you recognise any of the features that Halliday discusses in your own work.

M.A.K. Halliday (1993) 'Some grammatical problems in scientific English', in Halliday, M.A.K. and Martin, J.R. (eds) *Writing Science: Literacy and Discursive Power*, London, Falmer Press: 69–85.

Text B3.1
M.A.K. Halliday

## Grammatical metaphor

High lexical density and ambiguity . . . are both by-products of a process I shall refer to as 'grammatical metaphor'. This is like metaphor in the usual sense except that, instead of being a substitution of one *word* for another, as when we say **you're talking tripe** instead of **you're talking nonsense**, it is a substitution of one grammatical class, or one grammatical structure, by another; for example, **his departure** instead of **he departed**. Here the words (lexical items) are the same; what has changed is their place in the grammar. Instead of pronoun **he** + verb **departed**, functioning as Actor plus Process in a clause, we have determiner **his** + noun **departure**, functioning as Deictic plus Thing in a nominal group. Other examples are **her recent speech concerned poverty** instead of **she spoke recently concerning poverty**; **glass crack growth rate** instead of **how quickly cracks in glass grow**. Often the words may change as well as the grammar, as in the last example where **how quickly** is replaced by **rate** – we do not usually say **glass crack growth quickness**; but the underlying metaphor is in the grammar, and the lexical changes follow more or less automatically.

I am not suggesting that there will always be some absolute, non-metaphorical form to which these grammatical metaphors can he related; metaphor is a natural historical process in language and modes of expression involving different degrees of metaphor will always exist side by side. We can often take two or three or even more steps in rewording a grammatical metaphor in a less metaphorical, more congruent form; for example, we might say that 'cracking' is really a process – something happening – rather than a thing, so that **cracks in glass**, with **cracks** as a noun, is a metaphor for **glass cracks** with **cracks** as verb. As another example.

(m) |The 36 class only appeared on this train| in times of reduced loading, or engine failure.

could be reworded as **when loadings were reduced, or the engine failed**; but we might then reword the first part over again as **when the load was smaller** or even **when fewer goods were being carried**.

What is the nature of this rewording? One way of thinking of it is by imagining the age of the reader, or listener. In talking to a 9-year-old, we would never say **in times of engine failure**; we would say **whenever the engine failed**. Notice that we have not had to simplify the vocabulary; there are no difficult words in the first version – it is the grammar that is difficult for a child. Similarly we would change **slow down the glass crack growth rate** to **make the cracks in glass grow more slowly**, or **stop the cracks in glass from growing so quickly**. What we are doing, when we reword in this way, is changing the grammar (with some consequential changes in vocabulary) by making it *younger*. Children learn first to talk in clauses; it is only later – and only when they can already read and write with facility – that they are able to replace these clauses with nominal groups.

As far as we can tell, this also reflects what happened in the history of the language. In English, and other languages of Europe, the older pattern is the clausal one; and it is based on certain principles of wording which we might summarize as follows:

119

1 processes (actions, events, mental processes, relations) are expressed by verbs;
2 participants (people, animals, concrete and abstract objects that take part in processes) are expressed by nouns;
3 circumstances (time, place, manner, cause, condition) are expressed by adverbs and by prepositional phrases;
4 relations between one process and another are expressed by conjunctions.

For example:

| participant | process | circumstance | relation between processes | participant | process | circumstance |
|---|---|---|---|---|---|---|
| **the cast** | **acted** | **brilliantly** | **so** | **the audience** | **applauded** | **for a long time** |
| \|noun\| | \|verb\| | \|adverb\| | \|conjunction\| | \|noun\| | \|verb\| | \|prepositional phrase\| |

If this is now reworded metaphorically as:

| the cast's brilliant acting | drew | lengthy applause | from the audience |
|---|---|---|---|
| \|noun\| | \|verb\| | \|noun\| | \|prepositional phrase\| |

a number of changes have taken place: The processes **acted** and **applauded** have been turned into nouns, **acting** and **applause**; the participant **the cast** has become a possessive, while **the audience** has become part of a prepositional phrase. The circumstances **brilliantly** and **for a long time** have both become adjectives inside nominal groups; and the relation between the two processes, showing that one of them caused the other, has become a verb, **drew**. This makes it sound as though acting and clapping were things, and as if the only event that took place was the cause relation between them (. . . **acting drew** . . . **applause**). All these changes illustrate what is meant by grammatical metaphor.

This kind of metaphor is found particularly in scientific discourse and may have evolved first of all in that context. It is already beginning to appear in the writings of the ancient Greek scientists; from them it is carried over into classical Latin and then into medieval Latin; and it has continued to develop – but to a far greater extent – in Italian, English, French, German, Russian and the other languages of Europe from the Renaissance onwards. And although it has spread across many different registers, or functional varieties, of language, in English at least the main impetus for it seems to have continued to come from the languages of science.

Why did scientific writers, from Isaac Newton onwards, increasingly favour such a mode of expression? – one in which, instead of writing 'this happened, so that happened', they write 'this event caused that event'? These were not arbitrary or random changes. The reason lies in the nature of scientific discourse. Newton and his successors were creating a new variety of English for a new kind of knowledge; a kind of knowledge in which experiments were carried out, general principles derived by reasoning from these experiments, with the aid of mathematics; and these principles in turn tested by further experiments. The discourse had to proceed step by step, with a constant movement from 'this is what we have established so far' to 'this is what follows from it next', and each of these two parts, both the 'taken for granted' part and the new information, had to be presented in a way that would make its status in the argument clear. The most effective way to do this, in English grammar, is to construct the whole step as a single clause, with the two parts turned into nouns, one at the beginning and one at the end, and a verb in between saying *how* the second follows from the first . . .

Here is a contemporary example, taken from the *Scientific American*:

The atomic nucleus absorbs and emits energy only in quanta, or discrete units. Each absorption marks its transition to a state of higher energy, and each emission marks its transition to a state of lower energy.

Notice how, in the second sentence, each clause consists of (i) a 'taken for granted' part, nominalizing what has been said before (**the atomic nucleus absorbs energy → each absorption; the atomic nucleus emits energy → each emission**); (ii) a 'new information' part, pointing forward to what is to come, and also nominalized (**its transition to a state of higher / lower energy**); and (iii) the relation between them, in the form or a verb (**marks**). Frequently the 'taken for granted' part summarizes the whole of a long previous discussion; for example, the same article contains the sentence:

The theoretical program of devising models of atomic nuclei has of course been complemented by experimental investigations.

This has exactly the same pattern; but here the 'taken for granted' part (**the theoretical program . . . atomic nuclei**) is referring back to many paragraphs of preceding text.

If we reword these so as to take the metaphor out, the entire balance of the information is lost. For the last example we might write:

We devised models of atomic nuclei, in a program of theoretical [research], and in addition of course we investigated [the matter] by doing experiments.

But this would give us no indication that the first part was a summary of what had gone before, or that the last part was going to be taken up and developed in what followed. What is equally important, it would fail to make it clear that each step – devising theoretical models and investigating experimentally – is to be understood as a unity, a single phenomenon rather than an assembly of component parts.

## Task B3.1.2

Having read Text B3.1, carry out the following activities:

➤ Repackaging the information in clauses into noun groups is a feature particularly associated with science writing. Consider whether you have found scientific or academic writing generally difficult to understand. Decide whether the concept of grammatical metaphor provides a full explanation of why this might be the case.

➤ In Halliday's view, grammatical metaphors are not just different ways of expressing something, they actually represent a different way of seeing how the world works – *things* rather than *actions* are foregrounded. Compare this explanation with the discussion of transitivity in Unit A6. Does how we represent the world through grammatical choices indicate how we see the world and, by implication, constrain our vision of the world? Do you think that by using particular grammatical structures we are prevented from seeing things from a different perspective?

Much recent work on academic writing has studied distinctive modes of expression in particular disciplines. Rather than see all academic writing as having similar characteristics, researchers have looked at the differences between, say, physics and biology or history and English literature. Linguistic analysis is used as a way of understanding how members of a discipline view their subject. In addition, the interactive nature of academic writing is stressed. Writers need to develop appropriate relationships with their readers, presenting themselves and their work in ways deemed acceptable by their fellow academics. How this is accomplished varies between disciplines and also in response to the type of text (genre) being written.

In Text B3.2, Ken Hyland discusses the use of a feature he calls 'directives' (e.g. *consider, see, you should*). His research is based on a large corpus of writing collected across eight disciplines: philosophy (Phil), sociology (Soc), applied linguistics (AL), physics (Phy) and microbiology (Bio). These disciplines represent a relatively broad cross-section of academic practices from 'hard' fields, where knowledge is based on abstract conceptualisations, to 'soft' fields, where knowledge is based on concrete experience. The writing is from three different genres: research articles (RA; totalling 1.4 million words), textbooks (TB: 481,000 words) and final-year undergraduate student project reports (PR: 628,000 words). He supplemented the analysis of texts with information on disciplinary writing practices gathered in interviews with students and staff. His evidence shows that certain types of directives are more common in particular genres and disciplines than others. Before reading on, can you think why this might be the case?

 **Task B3.2.1**

As you read B3.2, carry out the following activities:

➤ Note the three grammatical forms that directives commonly take.

➤ Note the three functions that directives commonly fulfil.

➤ Consider the reasons given for the 'heavy use of directives in the hard disciplines'. Why do you think scientists use few rhetorical devices to 'explicitly engage their readers'?

➤ Consider what Hyland means when he says 'Directives in the science and engineering subjects can . . . help writers to maintain the fiction of objectivity'.

**Ken Hyland (2002) 'Directives: Argument and engagement in academic writing', in *Applied Linguistics*, vol. 23, no. 2: 215–239.**

Text B3.2
K. Hyland

The view that academic writing is an interactive accomplishment is now well established. A writer's development of an appropriate relationship with his or her readers is widely seen as central to effective academic persuasion as writers seek to balance claims for the significance, originality, and correctness of their work against the convictions and expectations of their readers . . . One important means of accomplishing these goals is the use of *directives*, defined here as utterances which instruct the reader to perform an action or to see things in a way determined by the writer. . . .

## Forms and functions of directives

For this study directive force was seen as typically realized in the surface structure of an utterance in three main ways: by the presence of an imperative, example (1); by a modal of obligation addressed to the reader, example (2); or by a predicative adjective expressing the writer's judgement of necessity/importance controlling a complement *to*-clause, example (3):

(1) *Consider* the Achilles paradox. (Phil Research Article)

   *Note* that B is dimensionless, hence the chart of Figure 18.8 can be used. (ME text book)

(2) The first relation in the set *should* always be used when the stress is not proportional to the load. (Bio Project Report)

   Together, these acts produce a total speech act that *must* be studied in the total speech situation. (AL Text Book)

(3) Since a large amount of investment has been attracted, *it is necessary to* understand its impact on the economy. (Economics Project Report)

   This means *it is essential to* characterize the large signal model of the HBT as a function of operating and ambient temperatures. (EE Research Article)

While these devices may convey different degrees of emphasis, they all carry the authority of the writer in specifying how the reader should participate in the text or perform some action outside it.
   . . . My analysis of rhetorical contexts reveals that directives can be classified according to the principal form of activity they direct readers to engage in, giving three main types: textual, physical, and cognitive. First, directives allow academic writers to guide readers to some *textual act*, referring them to another part of the text or to another text. They can also be used to instruct readers to perform a *physical act*, either involving a research process or real world action. Third, directives can steer readers to certain *cognitive acts*, where readers are initiated into a new domain of argument, led through a line of reasoning, or directed to understand a point in a certain way. Figure 1 summarizes this scheme and gives some typical realizations.
   So while the use of directives is governed by, and helps to govern, the relationship between the writer and assumed readers, the purposes they realize modify this relationship considerably. An imperative deployed to guide a reader through a text is

Extension

radically different from an instruction to undertake a real-world action, and different again from an injunction to understand a point in a particular way. . . .

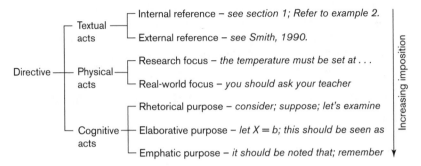

*Figure B3.1* Categories of directives

## Rhetoric and reasoning: directives across disciplines

The use of directives varies enormously across the disciplines. In some fields they represent a major rhetorical resource, a way of setting out arguments and inter-acting with readers which have become regular practices . . . In other fields they do not routinely figure as patterns of reasoning and interaction. Table B3.1 shows frequencies ranging from over 55 per 10,000 words in the mechanical engineering and physics textbooks down to only 10 in sociology . . . Overall, the hard science texts contained almost twice as many directives per 10,000 words and over 65 per cent of directives in both textbooks and student reports occurred in the science and engineering texts . . .

*Table B3.1* Disciplinary variations in use of directives (per 10,000 words)

| Field | Textbooks | Field | Articles | Field | Reports |
|---|---|---|---|---|---|
| Mechanical Eng. | 55.6 | Electronic Eng. | 29.0 | Info. Systems | 24.4 |
| Physics | 50.9 | Philosophy | 27.3 | Mechanical Eng. | 23.7 |
| Biology | 46.8 | Physics | 21.1 | Biology | 11.8 |
| Electronic Eng. | 36.3 | Mechanical Eng. | 19.6 | TESOL | 9.2 |
| Philosophy | 24.1 | App. Linguistics | 19.5 | Economics | 8.9 |
| Marketing | 22.0 | Sociology | 16.1 | Social Sciences | 7.7 |
| App. Linguistics | 13.8 | Marketing | 12.6 | Marketing | 3.9 |
| Sociology | 10.1 | Biology | 12.3 | Public Admin. | 3.3 |
| Overall | 31.7 | | 19.1 | | 10.5 |

K. Hyland

It is difficult to pick out clear disciplinary patterns from the functional distributions. The summary in Table B3.2 shows a noticeable division between hard and soft fields in the proportion of directives given to physical acts, and in fact over 80 per cent of all cases occurred in the science texts. The soft disciplines, with the exception of philosophy, tended to contain more textual directives and biology was the only hard science where writers used directives to guide readers to external sources in any numbers. Philosophy, applied linguistics, and marketing had higher proportions of cognitive directives, although the cases adjusted to 10,000 words show that the physics, mechanical, and electronic engineering texts had more than twice as many forms of all disciplines except philosophy.

*Table B3.2* Summary of functions by discipline (per cent)

| Field | Textual acts | | | Physical acts | | | Cognitive acts | | |
|---|---|---|---|---|---|---|---|---|---|
| | TB | RA | PR | TB | RA | PR | TB | RA | PR |
| Physics | 29.8 | 24.4 | – | 26.6 | 29.8 | – | 43.6 | 45.8 | – |
| Biology | 67.0 | 55.7 | 7.9 | 20.3 | 22.2 | 77.9 | 12.7 | 22.1 | 14.2 |
| Mechanical Eng. | 9.1 | 13.1 | 5.8 | 36.9 | 33.6 | 79.7 | 54.0 | 53.3 | 14.5 |
| Electronic Eng. | 11.1 | 11.6 | – | 50.5 | 40.0 | – | 38.4 | 48.4 | – |
| Info. Systems | – | – | 5.4 | – | – | 79.3 | – | – | 15.3 |
| Philosophy | 1.1 | 16.3 | – | 14.8 | 2.8 | – | 84.1 | 80.9 | – |
| Sociology/ Soc. Sci. | 45.4 | 68.1 | 35.4 | 14.8 | 2.5 | 38.2 | 39.8 | 29.4 | 26.4 |
| Public Admin. | – | – | 38.7 | – | – | 11.4 | – | – | 49.9 |
| App. Ling./ TESOL | 24.9 | 55.3 | 52.8 | 8.9 | 10.0 | 24.9 | 66.2 | 34.7 | 22.3 |
| Marketing | 17.7 | 52.2 | 62.5 | 21.9 | 8.2 | 18.8 | 60.4 | 39.6 | 18.7 |
| Economics | – | – | 45.7 | – | – | 14.2 | – | – | 39.9 |
| Overall | 23.3 | 36.4 | 21.0 | 28.3 | 15.4 | 58.4 | 48.4 | 48.3 | 20.6 |

[The additional fields of information systems, public administration and economics represent student writing that is allied to the eight disciplines in the RA and TB corpora.]

. . . While I acknowledge there may be numerous reasons for disciplinary variations, I will try to show that such preferred rises can be seen, in part, as reflecting the broad areas of inquiry associated with the hard and soft fields. I will focus on typical writer–reader engagement practices, conventions of dialogic positioning, and the meanings attached to succinctness and precision.

K. Hyland

### Directives and reader engagement

One reason for the heavy use of directives in the hard disciplines may be that this is one of the few rhetorical devices that scientists use with any regularity to explicitly engage their readers. Writers' attempts to invoke reader participation take a number of forms and can include personal pronouns, questions, digressions, hedges, and emphatics. These conventions of personality however have been shown to differ across disciplines and are particularly low in science and engineering papers (Swales 1990, Hyland 1999, 2000). This is in part because of very different ways of conducting research and of persuading readers to accept results.

Generally speaking, hard science writers are attempting to establish empirical uniformities through research practices which typically involve familiar procedures, broadly predictable outcomes, and relatively clear criteria of acceptability (Becher 1989, Whitley 1984). As a result, they can rhetorically purge their authorial presence in the discourse, playing down their role to strengthen the objectivity of their interpretations and replicability of procedures while highlighting the phenomena under study. Scientific writing is therefore often informally regarded as impersonal, as writers commonly avoid projecting themselves into their discourse to take an explicit stance towards their topic and findings. Instead, they often prefer to locate their interpretations in the results of statistical or laboratory analyses. All writing however, needs to solicit reader collusion: it must work to draw an audience in, carry it through an argument, and lead it to a particular conclusion. Directives enable writers in the hard sciences to do this without expressing a clear rhetorical identity:

> (4)  *Note* the transverse stress acts to fracture the monolith along the flow, direction. (ME RA)
>
> . . . *compare* lanes 1 in Fig. 3A and B.     (Bio RA)
>
> The analysis given in our paper *should be* considered in the context of a more general problem of nonstationary phenomena . . .     (Phy RA)
>
> It *is necessary to* take into account the dT'/dUp derivative when calculating . . . (EE RA)

Directives in the science and engineering subjects can therefore help writers to maintain the fiction of objectivity by avoiding explicit attitudinal signals while simultaneously allowing them to adopt an authoritative command of their data and their audience . . . *Directives, in other words, permit authorial intervention in a discourse.* They offer a means to directly address readers, particularly by selectively focusing their attention on an aspect of research procedure or instructing them to interpret an argument in a certain way, without personalizing the dialogue.

### Positioning and attention

. . . Perhaps the most imposing use of directives involves positioning readers, directing them to some cognitive action by requiring them to *note, concede,* or *consider* some aspect of an argument. Typically these directives lead readers towards the writer's conclusions by setting up premises (5) or emphasizing what they should attend to in the argument (6):

(5)    *Suppose* we have two explananda, E1 and E2.     (Phil RA)

*Consider* a sequence of batches in an optimal schedule. *Suppose* there is a non-full batch in the k-th position.     (EE RA)

*Think about it.* What if we eventually learn how to communicate with . . .
(Soc TB)

(6)    . . . *mark that* it is possible to interpret the larger symmetry in terms of supersymmetric quantum mechanics.     (Phy RA)

In cluster analysis *it is important to remember* that there is no single solution; only solutions that are more or less useful for a particular context.
(Mkt RA)

Please *note that* gender is not specifically discussed here, because . . .
(Soc RA)

This kind of explicit manipulation of the reader clearly carries risks however (as the politeness marker used to mitigate the last example suggests) and is rarely found in the student texts.

As I have noted, while such reader positioning occurs in all disciplines, it is mainly a feature of the hard sciences. Maintaining an effective degree of personal engagement with one's audience is an equally valuable strategy in the soft disciplines of course, but there it contributes to a very different authorial persona. Because the variables that soft fields deal with are often less precisely measurable, and their practices are more explicitly interpretive than in the hard sciences, persuasion may depend to a larger extent on an ability to invoke a credible and engaging persona (Hyland 2000). So while the ability to rhetorically construct an appropriate degree of confidence and authority is an important part of effective communication this is tempered with respect for the possible alternative views of readers and their right to hold these views. As a result, the writer's ability to manipulate an audiences' reading of a text through directives, so invoking an implied authority, is perhaps more circumscribed as both the applied linguist and marketing respondent observed:

You take control with imperatives, you tell them what to think, and I don't think that will always go down too well.     (Mkt interview)

I am aware of the effect that an imperative can have so I tend to use the more gentle ones. I don't want to bang them over the head with an argument I want them to reflect on what I'm saying. I use 'consider' and 'let's look at this' rather than something stronger.     (AL interview)

. . . Philosophy is an exception to the other soft-knowledge research papers, with only a quarter of the directives in articles leading the reader to references and virtually none in textbooks. Here rhetorical and elaborative cognitive forms made up 68 per cent of all devices in the articles and 74 per cent in the textbooks, working to direct the reader to understand the exposition in a certain way. This strategy combines with a heavy use of features such at boosters, first person pronouns, and inclusive *we* in philosophy, all of which contribute to a high degree of personal involvement to create a sense of communal intimacy, as these examples suggest:

(7)     *Suppose we consider* that there is a finite basis for our reasonable beliefs. *Let us assume*, for the sake of argument, that, in the actual world, full compliance with a . . .

*Suppose now*, that – as I think – at the end of our story, the ship of Theseus and the ship of Stathis share the same parts.

*We must consider* the semantic justification of the rule of adjunction.

Philosophical discourse differs from many other disciplines in that it does not seek to accomplish 'closure' by reaching consensus on a particular interpretation of an issue. Reading philosophy involves following a path without end where the writer's argument does not settle matters but simply contributes to a continuing conversation. Participation in this discourse, and the addition of an elegant argument, are central to being a philosopher . . . Relationships are accomplished by way of a highly intrusive stance to create, or appeal to, a world of shared understandings and the sense of a closely knit community of peers. Directives in philosophy, then, appear to help reduce the distance between participants and to stress participation in a shared journey of exploration, but it is always clear who is leading the expedition.

### Succinctness and precision

A major distinction between hard and soft knowledge areas is the extent to which succinctness and precision are valued, or even possible. Because of the linear, problem-oriented nature of natural sciences, research tends to be highly focused, with heavy investments in equipment and expertise devoted to specific goals. Consequently much research occurs within an established framework of theoretical knowledge and routine practices which means writers can presuppose a certain amount of background, argument, and technical lexis in their writing (Bazerman 1988) . . . Hard knowledge research papers are typically half the length of those in the soft disciplines, and there are clear reasons for economy of expression in these fields. Directives offer writers this kind of economy (cf. Swales *et al.* 1998) and devices such as *consider, suppose, let* statements, and so on allow them to cut to the heart of an argument without more space consuming locutions . . . In contrast, knowledge making in the humanities often needs to be accomplished with greater elaboration, its more diverse components reconstructed for a less cohesive readership. Time and space constraints are less urgent and directives perhaps less necessary to preserve them.

Related to this apparent preference for economic and straightforward argument style in the hard fields is a strong need for precision, particularly to ensure the accurate understanding of procedures. Hard knowledge research typically involves the precise application of specific methodologies in seeking to solve particular disciplinary problems and 93 per cent of all research focus directives occurred in the hard sciences. Respondents frequently mentioned that the manipulation and measurements of materials had to be systematic and exact, and writers had little hesitation in instructing readers exactly how these procedures should be carried out, particularly through the use of modals:

(8)   . . . the above definitions for the B2 index *should be* multiplied by a factor of 0.83.   (ME RA)

. . . attention *must be* paid to the standard membrane microstrip and for low free-space radiation loss.   (EE TB)

. . . To sum up, the hard knowledge fields not only contained far more directives, but these were also more likely to function as a means of guiding readers through a procedure and to the conclusions of the writer. Both these frequencies and more impositional functions are partly influenced by traditions of precision, tight space constraints, and highly formalized argument structures in the hard fields. These features, in turn, are related to their sources in mathematics, shared research practices and understandings; and the rapid growth of scientific knowledge. It can also be surmised, however, that conventions of impersonality, which focus readers on the text not the writer, also contribute to engagement styles which allow writers to interact with readers while stressing the phenomena rather than their textual personalities. In other words, some fields permit greater authorial presence than others and the use of directives emphasize that social relationships within discourse communities exercise strong constraints on a writer's representations of self and others.

## Task B3.2.1

Having read Text B3.2, carry out the following activities:

➤ Look back through this unit and identify directives that we or the extract authors have used. Classify them using Hyland's system.

➤ Compare your findings with those of Hyland relating to the field of Applied Linguistics in textbooks and research articles. Consider how you would explain your findings.

➤ Hyland has discussed variation in the use of a grammatical feature in relation to discipline and genre. Other researchers have also identified variation within genres in the same discipline. Look at where we have used directives in this book and decide whether there is any pattern. Do directives occur in certain places and not others? Is there an obvious reason for this?

➤ If you have access to other types of academic writing from other disciplines, look for directives and how they are used. If they are not common, does the writer use other methods of engaging the reader?

➤ Hyland concludes that 'social relationships within discourse communities exercise strong constraints on a writer's representations of self and others'. Look back at any experiences you have had writing or reading in other disciplinary discourse communities. Were you aware of different expectations within that type of writing community?

The next extract in this unit also looks at how writers position themselves within academic writing in different disciplines. Yu-Ying Chang and John Swales investigated features which have sometimes been frowned on by authors of style manuals and writing guidebooks, being considered too informal in this context. They compiled a list of the eleven most frequently mentioned of these features and then looked in detail at their use in three disciplines – statistics, linguistics and philosophy. The features identified in order of frequency were:

1. imperatives directed at the reader;
2. the use of the first person pronouns (*I, we*) to refer to author(s);
3. broad reference such as *this, these, those,* etc. which can refer to lengthy and sometimes unspecified sections of earlier text;
4. split infinitives where an adverb comes between *to* and the stem of the verb;
5. beginning a sentence with a conjunction such as *And* or a conjunctive adverb such as *However*;
6. ending a sentence with a preposition;
7. run-on sentences and expressions (e.g. ending a list with *etc.*);
8. sentence fragments – that is, sentences with lack a vital component such as subject, verb, or object;
9. contractions (*won't, aren't, you're*);
10. direct questions;
11. exclamations.

They identified a general trend towards greater use of informal features in published academic writing, but the extent of this use varied between the disciplines examined. They interviewed discipline specialists to discuss why this might be the case.

 **Task B3.3.1**

Before reading Text B3.3, carry out the following activities:

➤ Look at the list of features above identified by Chang and Swales and decide whether you use any of them in your own academic writing.

➤ Chang and Swales looked at informality in three disciplines: statistics, linguistics and philosophy. Consider which discipline you expect to use informal grammatical features the most and think of reasons why this might be the case.

As you read Text B3.3, carry out the following activity:

➤ Chang and Swales offer explanations for why some disciplines use more informal language than others. Make a note of the main reasons given for each discipline and say whether you think these reasons are convincing.

**Yu-Ying Chang and John M. Swales (1999) 'Informal elements in English academic writing: threats or opportunities for advanced non-native speakers?', in Candlin, C. N. and Hyland, K. (eds.) *Writing: Texts, Processes and Practices*, London, Longman: 145–167.**

Text B3.3
Y.-Y. Chang and
J.M. Swales

## Interdisciplinary differences

Table B3.3 shows that Statistics was the field which had the highest frequency of the occurrence of main-text imperatives; Linguistics was second and Philosophy third. When these frequencies of imperatives were compared with the other grammatical features listed in Table 1, an intriguing correlation between the use of imperatives and the other ten grammatical features emerged. Philosophy, although it had the fewest occurrences of imperatives, was the field where the other ten informal grammatical features were used the most frequently. On the other hand, mathematical statisticians, who used the most imperatives, used the other ten features *far less frequently* than the authors from the other two disciplines. A further text analysis, however, reveals that although these philosophers used fewer imperatives than the statisticians and the linguists, they exhibited a higher degree of rhetorical flexibility in their use of imperatives: they manoeuvred more different types of imperative verbs (e.g. *concede, like, accept,* and *agree*), and embedded these verbs in more various, syntactic and textual contexts (cf. Chang 1997).

. . . It appears that the philosophers, by employing almost all the ten features the most frequently and manipulating imperative sentences in the most varied ways, exhibit a more informal and interactive writing style (cf. Bloor 1996). They achieve their intended rhetorical purposes through the alternation of linguistic moods (the interchange among *imperatives, declaratives* and *interrogatives* in a paragraph, for example), and through the manipulation of overt personal pronouns and sentence rhythm (e.g. *initial conjunctions, sentence fragments* and *contractions*). Our Philosophy informant, as a senior member in the Philosophy discourse community, provided us with a probable explanation of this writing style:

> Philosophy has to be more rhetorical in a way because it's dealing with issues where there isn't, an established way of settling . . . There, if you want to give demonstrations in philosophy, you would have to be doing something more like therapy to get people over philosophical confusions.
>
> (Gibbard, interview, 1997)

Therefore, this stylistic choice of contemporary philosophers could be considered to be the closest reflection of a postmodernist view of knowledge: 'Our certainty will be a matter of *conversation* between persons, rather than a matter of interaction with nonhuman reality' (Rorty 1979: 157, our emphasis).

On the other hand, researchers in Statistics seem to continue to believe in the empiricist and positivist assumption that scientific studies are factual, and hence best designed to be faceless and agentless; their insistence on formal style thus still remains (cf. Biber 1988: 192–195). To be prudent scientists, the statisticians avoid using features which reveal personal involvement or emotion (e.g. *first person pronouns, direct questions* and *exclamations*) and features which are claimed, by some authors of writing manuals and guidebooks, as reflecting incomplete thought and poor knowledge of grammar (e.g. *run-on expressions* and *sentence fragments*). The rather formal

Table B3.3 The use of the eleven grammatical features in the three disciplines

| | Statistics | | Linguistics | | Philosophy | | Total | | |
|---|---|---|---|---|---|---|---|---|---|
| | No. of uses | No. of persons | No. of uses | No. of persons | No. of uses | No. of persons | No. of uses | No. of persons | % of persons |
| imperatives | 285 | 10 | 264 | 10 | 90 | 10 | 639 | 30 | 100 |
| I/my/me | 29 | 4 | 307 | 9 | 684 | 10 | 1020 | 23 | 77 |
| unsupported this | 97 | 9 | 316 | 10 | 230 | 10 | 643 | 29 | 97 |
| split infinitives | 1 | 1 | 0 | 0 | 0 | 0 | 1 | 1 | 3 |
| forbidden first words | 57 | 7 | 229 | 10 | 446 | 10 | 732 | 27 | 90 |
| initial and | 1 | 1 | 16 | 6 | 120 | 10 | 137 | 17 | 57 |
| initial but | 15 | 5 | 102 | 8 | 232 | 10 | 349 | 23 | 77 |
| initial so | 14 | 3 | 21 | 4 | 44 | 8 | 79 | 15 | 50 |
| initial or | 1 | 1 | 3 | 2 | 24 | 8 | 28 | 10 | 33 |
| initial however | 26 | 7 | 87 | 7 | 26 | 6 | 139 | 19 | 63 |
| final prepositions | 3 | 2 | 20 | 8 | 21 | 9 | 44 | 19 | 63 |
| run-on | 6 | 2 | 28 | 8 | 21 | 5 | 55 | 15 | 50 |
| sentence fragments | 0 | 0 | 4 | 4 | 11 | 6 | 15 | 10 | 33 |
| contractions | 0 | 0 | 21 | 5 | 71 | 6 | 92 | 11 | 37 |
| direct questions | 9 | 3 | 62 | 8 | 153 | 9 | 224 | 17 | 57 |
| exclamations | 0 | 0 | 1 | 1 | 5 | 3 | 6 | 4 | 13 |

Y.-Y. Chang and
J.M. Swales

and impersonal tone in their textual presentations therefore serves to maintain an *appearance* of objectivity and neutrality since they seem to believe that knowledge is an *accurate* representation of the real world. As for Linguistics, its status as a field not comfortably categorized as either humanities, sciences or social sciences seems to be well reflected in its textual presentations. In general, the linguists also use all the features employed by philosophers, only that they use them less frequently, and hence exhibit a writing style less saliently informal than the philosophical style discussed above.

## Task B3.3.2

Having read Text B3.3, carry out the following activities:

➤ Decide whether the findings of Chang and Swales support the view of science writing that Hyland outlined in Text B3.2. Consider where they overlap, contradict or extend each other.

➤ Look back at Text B3.1, written by Michael Halliday, an established and highly respected grammarian. Note the features that he uses from the Chang and Swales list. Decide whether you consider his style acceptable and whether you yourself would write an essay using that style. Are certain styles acceptable from some people but not from others? Why might be the case?

Chang and Swales identify one of the consequences of the greater informality they were discussing as being increased difficulty for non-native speakers. However, the problem of deciding when to choose formal or informal linguistic features is one which even native English speakers find problematic. What we have seen here in these extracts is that writing for academic purposes by both professional academics and students, although relatively narrowly focused, is nevertheless subject to many influences, including the overall academic context, the disciplinary context, the genre of the text, and the interpersonal positioning of writer and audience.

In this unit we have looked at:

**Summary**

Contexts

■ Academic writing

   ■ historical development of scientific style
   ■ disciplinary differences in textbooks, research articles and reports
   ■ acceptability or otherwise of informal features in published academic writing.

Linguistic features/grammatical structures

■ Grammatical metaphor

- nominalisation.
- Directives
    - imperatives
    - modals of obligation
    - predicative adjectives.
- Informal style (e.g. first-person pronouns, split infinitives, contractions, exclamations, etc.).

# Unit B4
# Grammar in written communication:
# Literature and electronic language

> All this – the river and flowers, running, which was something she rarely did these days, the fine ribbing of the oak trunks, the high-ceilinged room, the geometry of light, the pulse in her ears subsiding in the stillness – all this pleased her as the familiar was transformed into a delicious strangeness.[19]

> Sorry, cant tlk, wsnt mn2b on comp. lotr wa amzn. I lve legolas, his elephant thng ws gr8! U enjoy it? Wt else u bn up2? Spider ws terifyin + im scard of spiders neway! tb[20]

The carefully crafted passage of prose is in stark contrast to the text message with its staccato form and non-traditional spelling. In both, however, the writer is communicating to an unseen reader and making use of the conventions of different media. The novel is traditionally written with attention to details of form, spelling, punctuation and the effect of the language in conveying subtle messages. A major influence on the language of texting, on the other hand, is economy of communication, in both the number of characters used and the time taken to write messages. In this unit we will explore how various forms of written communication, both on paper and in electronic media, create their own contexts for language use, promoting different types of interaction and different uses of grammatical resources.

We start the unit with a type of written text with which we are all familiar to some extent – the novel. The author of a novel has the responsibility for creating the context in which the action takes place and for drawing the reader into the story. Text B4.1(a) gives us an insight into the role of language in this process. It is taken from a book on stylistics, a sub-discipline which brings together the study of literary texts with the tools of linguistic analysis. The novel being discussed is *The Old Man and the Sea* by Ernest Hemingway. The analysis by Paul Simpson shows how, by looking at grammatical choices, it is possible to see how an author achieves particular stylistic effects. Simpson contrasts the grammatical patterns used in sections of the narrative dealing with the old man's thoughts and consciousness with those used in passages describing physical activity, focusing on the contribution that patterns of transitivity make to these activity passages. The extract starts with a short passage from the novel and Simpson asks the reader to keep in mind the traditional question associated with transitivity analysis – 'who or what does what to whom or what and where?' The analysis is based on systemic functional grammar (SFG) which is briefly described in Unit A5. Simpson uses SFG terms, but it is not necessary to understand all the terminology in order to follow his argument.

## Task B4.1.1

Before reading Text B4.1, carry out the following activities:

➤ Reread the section on transitivity analysis in Unit A6, keeping in mind how the analyses discussed in the unit exemplify the question central to transitivity analysis: 'Who or what does what to whom or what and where?' Also remind yourself about the different types of verbs or 'process' types and how these relate to the number and type of participants in a clause.

➤ Look at the quotation from Hemingway that begins Text B4.1. Identify the actor(s) in the main clauses and who or what is acted upon.

Now, as you read Text B4.1, perform the following tasks:

➤ Simpson notes that 'Often, the ACTOR role is ellipted'. Look again at the Hemingway quotation and count how many times the subject of the clause is ellipted.

➤ Consider whether or not you agree that all but one of the clauses express the physical (material) actions of the old man.

➤ Look for any clauses expressing mental states or activity.

**Text B4.1**
**P. Simpson**

### Paul Simpson (1993) *Language, Ideology and Point of View*, London, Routledge.

(1) He knelt down and found the tuna under the stern with the gaff and drew it toward him keeping it clear of the coiled lines. (2) Holding the line with his left shoulder again, and bracing on his left hand and arm, he took the tuna off the gaff hook and put the gaff back in place. (3) He put one knee on the fish and cut strips of dark red meat longitudinally from the back of the head to the tail. (4) They were wedge-shaped strips and he cut them from next to the backbone down to the edge of the belly. (5) When he had cut six strips he spread them out on the wood of the bow, wiped his knife on his trousers, and lifted the carcass of the bonito by the tail and dropped it overboard.

Following up the 'who does what' axiom reveals a number of dominant stylistic traits in the passage. Almost invariably, the old man is the 'doer', doing some action to some entity. The clauses in which he features are all in the simple past and are normally arranged in a sequence which reflects the temporal sequence of the events described.

They contain virtually no interpretative intrusions by the narrator. In short, they reflect pure neutral narrative and with a single exception, all express material processes of doing. In all of these material processes, the old man is the ACTOR so the processes are of the *action* type. As nothing 'just happens' to him in any of these clauses, and he is firmly in control of everything he does, then a full description will specify that these clauses express material action processes of *intention*. Here are breakdowns of some typical patterns:

| | ACTOR | PROCESS | | |
|---|---|---|---|---|
| 1 | He | knelt down . . . | | |

| | ACTOR | PROCESS | GOAL | CIRCUMSTANCES |
|---|---|---|---|---|
| 2 | he | took | the tuna | off the gaff |

| | ACTOR | PROCESS | GOAL | CIRCUMSTANCES |
|---|---|---|---|---|
| 4 | he | cut | them | from next to the backbone |

Often, the ACTOR role is ellipted when clauses are strung together, although it is still easily inferred through reference to preceding clauses. The symbol Ø can be used to denote this sort of implicit agency:

| | ACTOR | PROCESS | [connector] | | |
|---|---|---|---|---|---|
| 1 | He | knelt down | and | | |

| | ACTOR | PROCESS | GOAL | CIRCUMSTANCES | [connector] |
|---|---|---|---|---|---|
| | Ø | found | the tuna | under the stern . . . | and . . . |

| | ACTOR | PROCESS | GOAL | CIRCUMSTANCES |
|---|---|---|---|---|
| | Ø | drew | it | toward him |

Another feature of this highly stable pattern of transitivity is the invariable use of the active voice. Passive variants, where the GOAL element is fronted and the ACTOR either shifted rightwards or removed completely, are never used. Indeed, in the context of the passage as a whole, conversions to the passive would seem a little odd:

5(a)  When six strips had been cut, and they were spread out by him on the wood of the bow . . .

Of a total of seventeen processes expressed in this paragraph, only one is non-material. This is a relational process which occurs in the first clause of sentence 4. By way of contrast with the dominant material – action – intention pattern, here is a breakdown of this clause:

| | CARRIER | PROCESS | ATTRIBUTE |
|---|---|---|---|
| 4 | They | were | wedge-shaped strips |

... One of the stylistic consequences of the dominant material paradigm, where mental and other processes signifying reflection and deliberation are suppressed, is that it creates a highly 'actional' descriptive framework. Now, in the context of the longer passage in which this paragraph appeared, it was shown that this type of description alternated systematically with paragraphs of speech and thought presentation. This offers an excellent illustration of the convergence of transitivity and point of view. There is a controlled oscillation between sequences of material processes depicting an externalized view of events, sequences of verbalization processes in the form of the represented speech of the old man and sequences of mental processes representing intrusions into the old man's consciousness ... This regular pattern ... is not restricted to a few paragraphs but to the entire central section of the novel.

### Task B4.1.2

Having read Text B4.1, carry out the following activities:

➤ Simpson maintains that this passage contains 'virtually no interpretive intrusions by the narrator ... they reflect pure neutral narrative'. Decide whether you agree with this and whether writers can ever succeed in keeping themselves out of their texts.

➤ Simpson notes that this descriptive type of passage alternates with representations of the old man's speech and his thoughts, and that different process types (verbs) are associated with the different passages. This paragraph is dominated by material processes of doing (e.g. *knelt, took, put*), while in other passages verbal process (e.g. *said, shouted*) and mental processes (e.g. *thought, remembered*) are dominant. Choose three paragraphs from different parts of a novel and note the types of verbs and who the main actors are. Look for any variations in different parts of the novel and then try to suggest explanations for the choices made by the author.

From a long-established form of writing, our attention now turns to the newer context of communicating using computers. The lexical and grammatical impact of the new medium has given rise to the coining of new terms such as 'Netspeak' or 'electronic language'. Such language is far from being a single variety and later in this unit you will read an extract from research into the particular features found in the electronic language of Bulletin Board Systems. Before turning to that extract, we will look at arguments, put forward primarily by David Crystal (2001) in his book *Language and the Internet*.

Once computer communication spread beyond its originators in the United States defence community, language use associated with it came under many and various influences as online cultures multiplied and became differentiated. According to Brenda Danet (2002: 8) groups of technically minded but essentially playfully motivated 'hackers' were significant in their use of language, particularly in these early years:

Hackers love to play with words and symbols, and are known for punning and other clever, irreverent uses of language. The expression 'snail mail' for ordinary paper mail is just one of their neologisms which have become part of the vocabulary of many participants in online culture.

Crystal describes the various forms of language use on the Internet collectively as 'Netspeak'. He also links the evolution of Netspeak to a relatively young and computer-literate population, although computer literacy has now spread to all age groups, as the advent of so-called 'grey gamers', retired people playing computer games, indicates. As the users of computers and the Internet become more disparate it becomes less helpful to think of Netspeak only as the playful jargon of young hackers.

## Task B4.1.3

➤ Below, Crystal discusses electronic language, speech and traditional forms of writing. Before you read the extracts, consider whether, in your experience, electronic communication is more like speech or writing – or something different?

➤ As you read make a chart, similar to the table below, listing the characteristics of 'Netspeak' as outlined by Crystal. Using your own experience and Crystal's comments, classify the different characteristics for the types of 'Netspeak'. We have given our responses for the first few characteristics in the table.

|  | The Web | email | Chat rooms | Virtual worlds |
|---|---|---|---|---|
| interactive | sometimes | yes | yes | yes |
| time-governed | no | no |  |  |
| transient |  |  |  |  |
| urgency/ energetic force |  |  |  |  |

One of the common ways of characterising Netspeak is to view it as written speech. To test this description Crystal looks at which characteristics it shares with writing and which with speech. He divides Netspeak into four: the Web, email, chatrooms and virtual worlds (usually fantasy games) in order to describe their different features. He deals first with their similarities to speech:

Some of the Web's functions (e.g. sales) do bring it much closer to the kind of interaction more typical of speech, with a consequential effect on the kind of language used, and many sites now have interactive facilities attached, in the form of e-mail and chatgroup facilities.

In contrast to the Web, the situations of e-mail, chatgroups, and virtual worlds, though expressed through the medium of writing, display several of the core properties of speech. They are time-governed, expecting or demanding an immediate response; they are transient, in the sense that messages may be immediately deleted (as in e-mails) or be lost to attention as they scroll off the screen (as in chatgroups); and their utterances display much of the urgency and energetic force which is characteristic of face-to-face conversation. The situations are not all equally 'spoken' in character. We 'write' e-mails, not 'speak' them. But chatgroups are for 'chat', and people certainly 'speak' to each other there – as do people involved in virtual worlds.

(Crystal 2001: 29)

Crystal also details the contextual features of chatrooms, email and virtual worlds which are different from face-to-face conversation.

- There is a lack of simultaneous feedback as messages are first composed and then sent. There is no opportunity for the recipient to give feedback equivalent to a nod or frown while the message is being typed.
- Interaction on the Internet is much slower than in conventional speech. In email and asynchronous chatgroups respondents are rarely online at the same time, so a response may arrive hours, days or even weeks later. Even in synchronous chat or games in which participants are at their computers at the same time there is always a certain time delay or lag between messages being sent and received. If these time delays are perceived as long (more than five seconds) they can disrupt the flow of communication, leading an interactant to wonder why they have received no reply.
- Lags in synchronous electronic interaction disrupt the normal turn-taking conventions of conversation particularly where several participants are involved. Situations can arise where messages arrive out of sequence due to software or hardware problems relating to an individual's computer. This makes it not only difficult to follow a conversation, but almost impossible to participate in it.
- There is no equivalent on the Internet of variations in how we speak – intonation, loudness, pauses, tone of voice which carry much of the information about how an utterance is to be interpreted. Some attempts have been made – for example, emoticons, little faces made up of punctuation marks and designed to convey a message about the attitude of the writer to what is being said. Others try to use repeated letters (*hiiiiii, sooooo*), repeated punctuation (*why????????*), abbreviations (<g> for grin or <lol> lots of laughs, both indicating that a remark should not be taken too seriously) or capital letters to convey this additional emotional content. They are, however, very unsubtle when compared to the range of options that a face-to-face interactant would have.

Crystal (2001: 41) sums up the relationship between Netspeak and speech as follows:

> Addressing someone on the Internet is a bit like having a telephone conversation in which a listener is giving you no reactions at all: it is an unnatural situation, and in the absence of such feedback one's own language becomes more awkward than it might otherwise be.

Netspeak also exhibits differences from traditional writing, and these are least pronounced on the Web. On the Web writer and reader are not known to each other; there is a time lag between writing and reading; messages can be reread many times; paragraphs, sentences and punctuation are usual; feedback is either non-existent or delayed; writing can be revised by the writer before being made public and often contains elaborate grammatical constructions; writing can be combined with other visual elements such as graphs and pictures. In other types of Netspeak there is often greater shared knowledge between writer and reader – either through family, work or friendship groups, or as interactants in a game. Messages in synchronous chat and virtual worlds is generally ephemeral and rarely reread. In email the situation is less clear cut. Some email is deleted immediately after it is read; other email is stored for many years. The attention to features such as punctuation, spelling and grammatical well-formedness is also different. Emails and professionally orien-tated chatgroups or listservers associated with work are generally closer to the norms of traditional writing. Messages in synchronous chat, on the other hand, show similarities with texting, using a mixing of letters and numbers, new and briefer spellings and lots of abbreviations. Crystal concludes that Netspeak should not be categorised as a written or a spoken medium but rather as a genuine 'third medium':

> Once we take the different Internet situations into account, then the Web is seen to be by far the closest to written language, with chatgroups furthest away, and the other two situations in between. The differences are striking . . . but on the whole, Netspeak is better seen as written language which has been pulled some way in the direction of speech than as spoken language which has been written down. However, expressing the question in terms of the traditional dichotomy is itself misleading . . . Netspeak is more than an aggregate of spoken and written features . . . it does things that neither of these other mediums do, and must accordingly be seen as a new species of communication.
>
> (Crystal 2001: 47–48)

## Task B4.1.4

Having read the material above, carry out the following activities:

➤ Crystal sees 'Netspeak' as a new species of communication. Arguably, however, the context of chatgroups is different from the context of email or the Web and will lead to different forms of communication. Decide whether it is more helpful to think in terms of an all-embracing term like 'Netspeak' or to consider different types of electronic communication separately.

➤ Looking back at the table of characteristics that you compiled while reading about Crystal's work, try to think of which grammatical features you would expect to be associated with them.

Text B4.2, by Milena Collot and Nancy Bellmore, focuses on grammatical features in a particular type of electronic language – that used by people interacting on electronic Bulletin Board Systems (BBSs).

> BBSs have no fixed or identifiable membership . . . The subject matter . . . covers a vast expanse, ranging from discussions of art to political debates and personal advice columns. BBSs are organized into 'conferences', identified by an appropriate title, which gather all messages with a common theme.
>
> (Collot and Belmore 1996: 13)

The extract starts with a table setting out the contextual factors (e.g. participant roles, topic, purpose, etc.) which influence communications on BBSs in general and the particular features of the BBS that they investigated. Following the table, Collot and Belmore introduce their method of analysis which is based on work by Douglas Biber in the 1990s. This pre-dates his larger-scale grammar which you read an extract from in Unit B1.

 **Task B4.2.1**

Before reading Text B4.2, carry out the following activity:

➤ Look at Table 1 in Text B4.2 and consider what influence these contextual considerations will have on grammatical choices.

As you read Text B4.2 carry out the following activities:

➤ Note what Collot and Belmore describe as a 'key feature of Biber's approach' and decide how well this fits in with what you have read of Crystal's work.

➤ Look carefully at the second table in Text B4.2 and identify which features show the greatest variation between Biber's corpus and Collot and Belmore's Electronic Language Corpus based on communications from BBSs. You can do this most easily by looking as the feature deviation score (FDS). Scores which are near zero are similar while bigger numbers (both positive and negative) show the greatest differences.

**Milena Collot and Nancy Belmore (1996) 'Electronic language: A new variety of English', in Herring, S. (ed.)** *Computer-Mediated Communication: Linguistic, Social and Cultural Perspectives,* **Amsterdam, John Benjamins: 13–28.**

Text B4.2
M. Collot and
N. Belmore

## 3 Descriptive framework

### 3.1 *Biber's multidimensional-multi-feature model* (MD-MF)

*Table B4.1* Components of the speech situations which characterize Bulletin Board Systems

*Participants*
    *Roles*
        Addressor, addressee, audience
    *Personal characteristics*
        Diverse
    *Group characteristics*
        Canadian and American

*Relations among participants*
    *Social relations*
        Egalitarian
    *Personal relations*
        Generally friendly
    *Degree of shared interests*
        High
    *Degree of shared knowledge*
        Variable but often high

*Setting*
    *Physical context*
        Participant's own desktop
    *Temporal context*
        Any time of day or night
    *Extent to which space and time are shared by participants*
        Zero

*Topic*
    Topics are classified into 'conferences' and vary accordingly

*Purpose*
    To request and give information, to make announcements, to engage in discussion

*Social evaluation*
    *Attitude towards communicative event*
        Acknowledgment of the unique nature of the event
    *Attitude towards content*
        Varies according to topic

*Relations of participants to the text*
    *Type 1*
        Planned text, prepared beforehand
    *Type 2*
        Unplanned text, composed on-line

*Channel*
    Keyboarding

Adapted from Biber 1988

M. Collot and
N. Belmore

An empirical study of Electronic Language requires a suitable model for the study of situationally determined language variation, and an adequate corpus. The model chosen was Biber's multidimensional-multi-feature (MD-MF) analysis as described in his *Variation Across Language and Speech* (1988) . . .

Biber's particular innovation has been the analysis of computer-readable corpora to determine sets of linguistic features whose presence or absence correlates with what he calls 'textual dimensions'. A textual dimension is a functional categorization which cuts across traditional genre classifications. The assumption is that if a particular set of linguistic features consistently co-occurs in a group of texts, that set of features serves a particular communicative function. For example, academic prose, press reportage and official documents, however much they may differ in other respects, all have in common such features as a varied vocabulary and a high frequency of prepositional phrases, but a low frequency of such features as first and second person pronouns and present tense verb forms. Biber's analysis indicates that these features characterize all prose, regardless of genre, that is intended to be highly informational.

The principal technique used in Biber's approach is exploratory factor analysis. The purpose of factor analysis is to reduce a large number of variables, in this case, linguistic features, to a small set of derived variables, or factors. Factor analysis reveals which linguistic features tend to co-occur and which tend to be mutually exclusive. Each such set of features is a factor, and underlying each factor is a textual dimension. By summing the frequencies of each of the linguistic features in a text belonging to a particular genre, a factor score can be computed for that text . . . The average factor score for all texts in a genre yields what Biber calls the mean dimension score for the particular genre. . . .

Biber identified six factors and thus six dimensions. He labels each dimension in terms of what he considers the communicative function of the linguistic features associated with that dimension. One such dimension is 'involved versus informational production'. A text which rates high on the 'involved' end of the scale would contain, among its most prominent features, a relatively large number of private verbs like 'believe', 'feel' and 'know', i.e., verbs which express states or acts which are not observable (Quirk *et al.* 1985:1181), contractions, first and second person pronouns, hedges like 'sort of' and 'kind of', *if*-clauses, and emphatics like 'for sure' and 'a lot'. Conversely, a text which rates high on the 'informational' end of the scale would be characterized by many nouns, attributive adjectives, and prepositional phrases, longer words, and many different words. The score of different genres on each dimension allows a comparison of genres both within and across dimensions.

A key feature of Biber's approach is that it does not assume a simple dichotomy between speech and writing. His characterization of texts in terms of the relation between communicative function and linguistic features reveals that there is no absolute distinction between speech and writing. Thus, written genres such as personal letters are more similar to spoken genres such as face-to-face conversation than they are to other written genres, and in each dimension he has found that written and spoken texts overlap.

Biber applied his model to . . . the one-million word Lancaster-Oslo-Bergen (LOB) corpus of written English (Johansson *et al.* 1978, Johansson *et al.* 1986), the 500,000-word London–Lund corpus of spoken English (Svartvik 1990), and a collection of personal and professional letters. [The] model makes it possible to [pose the] question . . . 'Where does Electronic Language fit on each of the dimensions identified by Biber?'

## 3.2 The Electronic Language corpus (ELC)

M. Collot and
N. Belmore

Once a descriptive framework had been selected, the next task was the compilation of an adequate corpus of Electronic Language . . . Preliminary texts were downloaded from an international BBS called Input Montreal . . . The final corpus came from nine different conferences and contains about 200,000 words . . . The corpus consists of two subsets, 'off-line' (90,075 words) and 'other' (115,618 words). Off-line messages are pre-written and can be positively identified by the presence of a tag, inserted after the last line of a message, which indicates that an electronic mail reader was used . . .

Table B4.2 displays an extract from the comparative statistics for Biber's corpus and the ELC. Features which are common in Biber's corpus are usually common in the ELC; features which are rare are usually rare in the ELC. However, as would be expected in a subset of English with unique situational constraints, there are some striking differences. FDS is the feature deviation score.

*Table B4.2* An extract from the comparative statistics for Biber's corpus and the ELC

| Linguistic feature | Biber Mean | ELC Mean | Biber Std. Dev. | ELC Std. Dev. | FDS |
|---|---|---|---|---|---|
| Past tense | 40.1 | 28.0 | 30.4 | 11.6 | −0.4 |
| Time adverbials | 5.2 | 5.9 | 3.5 | 3.1 | 0.2 |
| First person pronouns | 27.2 | 57.5 | 26.1 | 21.2 | 1.2 |
| Third person pronouns | 29.9 | 25.5 | 22.5 | 9.4 | −0.2 |
| Agentless passives | 9.6 | 7.0 | 6.6 | 5.2 | −0.4 |
| THAT verb complements | 3.3 | 7.0 | 2.9 | 2.9 | 1.3 |
| Present participial clauses | 1.0 | 1.2 | 1.7 | 1.0 | 0.1 |
| THAT relative–object position | 0.8 | 1.7 | 1.1 | 0.9 | 0.8 |
| Sentence relative | 0.1 | 1.9 | 0.4 | 1.4 | 4.5 |
| Prepositions | 110.5 | 118.2 | 25.4 | 62.3 | 0.3 |

. . .

## 5 Results

Any attempt to interpret the findings of this study on the basis of previous research on speech and writing would have to heed Biber's admonition that there is no absolute difference between speech and writing. Electronic Language displays some of the linguistic features which have been associated with certain forms of written language, and others which are more usually associated with spoken language. The genres which it most closely resembles are public interviews and letters, personal as well as professional.

M. Collot and
N. Belmore

## 5.1 *Textual dimensions*

### 5.1.1 Dimension 1: Informational vs. involved production

In Biber's factorial structure, nouns, word length, prepositions, high type/token ratios and attributive adjectives were all assigned substantial negative weights. A high frequency of these features would therefore represent a great density of information. In the ELC, the frequencies for these features were largely comparable to Biber's corpus, with the exception of nouns, which were far more frequent in the ELC (225 per 1000 words) than in Biber's corpus (180 per 1000 words). However, if we consider the features in Factor 1 with positive weights, the balance is redressed. The ELC is replete with indicators of involvement such as first and second personal pronouns, contractions, hedges ('sort of', 'kind of') and amplifiers ('utterly', 'very'). Thus, although one of the primary purposes for participating in a BBS is to seek and impart information, the language in which this information is couched is more similar to that of spontaneous genres such as interviews, spontaneous speeches, and personal letters, than it is to that of informative genres such as official documents, academic prose, or press reportage. Figure B4.1 shows the position of the ELC (underlined) on Biber's continuum for Dimension 1.

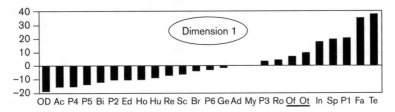

*Figure B4.1* Informational vs. involved production

Abbreviations for Figures 2 through 7:

| | | | |
|---|---|---|---|
| Ac | Academic prose | Ot | Other ELC |
| Ac | Adventure fiction | P1 | Personal letters |
| Bi | Biographies | P2 | Popular lore |
| Br | Broadcasts | P3 | Prepared speeches |
| Ed | Editorials | P4 | Press reportage |
| Fa | Face-to-face conversations | P5 | Press reviews |
| Ge | General fiction | P6 | Professional letters |
| Ho | Hobbies | Re | Religion |
| Hu | Humor | Ro | Romantic fiction |
| In | Interviews | Sc | Science fiction |
| My | Mystery fiction | Sp | Spontaneous speeches |
| OD | Official documents | Te | Telephone conversations |
| Of | Off-line ELC | | |

## 5.1.2 Dimension 2: Non-narrative vs. narrative

M. Collot and
N. Belmore

There are a number of features with strong positive weights on this dimension, and none with negative weights. Biber sees all of these features as markers of narrative action. For example, past tense and perfective aspect describe past events, while third person pronouns (other than 'it') refer to animate, typically human referents. Public verbs like 'admit' and 'say' are also important on this dimension, because they function as markers of reported speech, while synthetic negation ('he said nothing' vs. 'he did not say anything') is often seen as the preferred style in literary narrative. In the ELC, all of these features are considerably less frequent than in Biber's corpus. As a result, the ELC has a relatively low score on this dimension. With respect to narrative features, the genres it most resembles are professional letters, telephone conversations, press reviews, and interviews . . . Figure B4.2 shows the position of the ELC on Biber's continuum for Dimension 2.

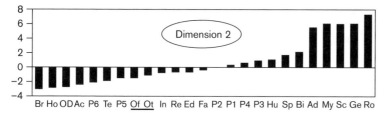

**Figure B4.2** Non-narrative vs. narrative discourse

## 5.1.3 Dimension 3: Situation-dependent vs. explicit

The features which carry large positive weights on this dimension are relative constructions. WH-relative clauses in object position ('the man whom Sally likes'), pied-piping relative clauses ('the manner in which he was told'), and WH-relative clauses in subject position ('the man who likes popcorn') are all seen as devices for the explicit, elaborated identification of referents in a text. In contrast, the three features with negative weights – time and place adverbials such as 'later', 'yesterday', 'above' and certain other adverbs – are considered markers of reference to times, places and events which can only be correctly interpreted if the addressee has sufficient knowledge of the text (e.g., 'see above') or the external circumstances ('just below us here') to be able to infer, on the basis of context, the intended message. The scores for this dimension reveal that the ELC lies between the two extremes. It has the same or nearly the same score as humor, press reportage and interviews . . . Figure B4.3 shows the position of the ELC on Biber's continuum for Dimension 3.

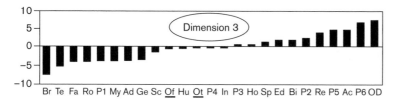

**Figure B4.3** Situation-dependent vs. explicit

147

M. Collot and
N. Belmore

5.1.4 *Dimension 4: Overt expression of persuasion*

This dimension is characterized by prediction and necessity modals, suasive verbs ('command', 'demand'), conditional subordination, and infinitives, most commonly used as adjective and verb complements, which are seen as marking the speaker's attitude towards the proposition encoded in the infinitive clause ('happy to do it', 'hope to see you'). In the ELC, many of these features have a higher frequency than in Biber's corpus. However, three features are less frequent: suasive verbs, necessity modals and split auxiliaries ('they are objectively shown to'). As a consequence of these differences, the ELC is situated between personal letters and editorials, near the high end of the scale. Figure B4.4 shows the position of the ELC on Biber's continuum for Dimension 4.

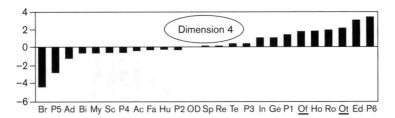

*Figure B4.4* Overt expression of persuasion

5.1.5 *Dimension 5: Non-abstract vs. abstract information*

Agentless passives, BY-passives, past participial clauses ('built in a single week') and past participial clauses with relative deletion ('the solution produced by this process') are the most important features associated with abstract information. No feature has a large negative weight on this dimension. According to Biber, these forms are frequently used in procedural discourse, where emphasis on the agent is reduced because the same agent is presupposed across several clauses. These features are generally as rare in the ELC corpus as they are in Biber's. However, two features which factor analysis reveals as frequently co-occurring with passive constructions – conjuncts ('however', 'in contrast') and adverbial subordinators ('since', 'while') – do occur considerably more frequently in the ELC than in Biber' s corpus, and thus account for the ELC's relatively high score on this dimension. However, neither of these features appears to play a major functional role . . . therefore . . . the ELC score on this dimension [should] be interpreted with caution. Figure B4.5 shows the position of the ELC on Biber's continuum for Dimension 5.

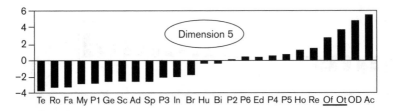

*Figure B4.5* Non-abstract vs. abstract information

M. Collot and
N. Belmore

### 5.1.6 Dimension 6: On-line informational elaboration

Four features underlie this dimension: demonstratives, THAT clauses as verb complements, THAT relative clauses in object position, and THAT clauses as adjective complements. Biber sees the co-occurrence of these features as marking informational elaboration in relatively unplanned types of discourse, hence the word 'on-line'. The ELC has a greater number of all four features than Biber's corpus. Accordingly, the ELC scores fairly high on this dimension, between spontaneous speeches and editorials. The off-line subset is at the same level as professional letters. Figure B4.6 shows the position of the ELC on Biber's continuum for Dimension 6.

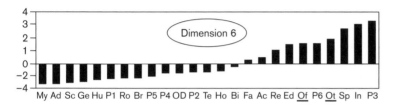

**Figure B4.6** On-line informational elaboration

## 5.2 Situational features

There seem to be at least four situational features which play an important role in explaining the linguistic manifestations of the ELC. The first is the degree of common interests and shared knowledge among the participants. People who have been using a BBS for a while know each other's nicknames, mannerisms and ideas. They have followed each other's arguments on different subjects and have accumulated a wealth of shared knowledge . . . This may account for the high degree of involvement in the ELC, as well as for its relative situation-dependency, despite the fact that participants are separated by time and space.

The second important feature is the purpose of communication, which is to request and impart information and to discuss specific issues. These purposes seem to play an important role in shaping Electronic Language as a non-narrative and highly persuasive discourse type.

The third important component of the speech situation is the tripartite nature of the roles played by the participants, which include an addressor, an addressee and an audience. This may explain the similarities between the ELC and public interviews, in which the interviewees respond specifically to the interviewer but do so for the benefit of a wider audience. Finally, the fact that time and space are not shared by the participants may explain the resemblance between the ELC on the one hand and personal and professional letters on the other.

## Task B4.2.2

Having read Text B4.2, carry out the following activities:

➤ Consider what the type of statistical analysis undertaken by Biber and by Collot and Belmore tells us about electronic language and traditional forms of communication.

Other researchers have looked at specific grammatical features and investigated them in other forms of electronic language. For example, Ann Hewings and Caroline Coffin (2004) compared the findings from Biber *et al.* (1999) on personal pronouns in conversation and in academic prose with their use by students in traditional written essays and in discussions which took place through an asynchronous electronic conference. Greater use of personal pronouns is one of the factors associated with involved rather than informational language and occurred more frequently in the electronic conference messages than the essays. The same is true in face-to-face oral interviews and tape-mediated test interviews in language assessment.

➤ Think about your own use of computers and some of the grammatical variables discussed in the extract. Try to identify any patterns in your own electronic language and judge whether these vary depending on the type of interaction you are involved in.

**Summary**  In this unit we have looked at:

Contexts

■ Literary novels
■ Electronic communication(the Web, email, and chatgroups).

Linguistic features/grammatical structures

■ Transitivity
■ Disruption of turn-taking in electronic communication
■ Alternatives to paralinguistic features
■ Bulletin Board System features (e.g. past tense, time adverbials, first- and third-person pronouns, agentless passive etc.).

# Unit B5
# Grammar in restricted communications

Our title for this unit refers to the language used in contexts where various restrictions, particularly of space or time, result in the message being compressed, with consequences for grammatical choices. One clear example was the old telegram style of writing where, for example, articles and finite verbs were often missed out. In this form of communication the sender had to pay for each word sent and, consequently, the maximum information was packaged into the shortest number of words. Here is an authentic telegram text:

> MUM FELL. HURT BACK. IN HOSPITAL. RING HOME.

We can see how this has been compressed if we imagine how someone might have given the same news verbally:

> Your mum's had a fall and hurt her back. She's in hospital. You've got to ring home.

Grammatical adaptations in restrictive contexts such as this are widespread and found in both speech and in writing, as you will see in the extracts below on sports-announcer talk and dating advertisements in newspapers.

In B5.1 by Janet Holmes you will read about some specific features of 'play-by-play' description by sports announcers commentating on the action of a sports match. Holmes highlights syntactic reduction and word order inversions as typical.

**Task B5.1.1**

As you read Text B5.1, carry out the following activities:

➤ Make sure you understand the difference between 'play-by-play description' and 'colour commentary'.

➤ List the reasons given for the grammatical characteristics of play-by-play commentary. Write an example of each.

**Janet Holmes (2001) *An Introduction to Sociolinguistics*, second edition, Harlow, Longman.**

### Sports announcer talk

When people describe a sporting event, the language they use is quite clearly dis-tinguishable from language used in other contexts. The most obvious distinguishing feature is generally the vocabulary. Terms like *silly mid on*, *square leg*, *the covers*, and *gully*, for instance, to describe positions, and *off-break*, *googly* and *leg break* to describe deliveries, are examples of vocabulary peculiar to cricket. But the grammar is equally distinctive. This is especially true of the kind of sports announcer talk which is known as 'play-by-play' description.

Play-by-play description focuses on the action, as opposed to 'colour commentary' which refers to the more discursive and leisurely speech with which commentators fill in the often quite long spaces between spurts of action. Play-by-play description is characterised by telegraphic grammar. This involves features such as syntactic reduction and the inversion of normal word order in sentences. . . .

### Syntactic reduction

*Example 1*

*From baseball or cricket commentaries.*

(a) [It] bounced to second base
(b) [It's] a breaking ball outside
(c) [He's a] guy who's a pressure player
(d) McCatty [is] in difficulty
(e) Tucker [is] taking a few ah stuttering steps down the wicket from the bowler's end but Waugh [is] sending him back

While describing the action they are observing, sports announcers often omit the subject noun or pronoun, as in (a), and frequently omit the verb *be* as well, as utter-ances (b) and (c) illustrate. Utterances (d) and (e) omit only *be*. There is no loss of meaning as a result of this syntactic reduction, since the omitted elements are totally predictable in the context. The referent is unambiguous – in (a) *it* refers to the hit, and in (b) *it* could not refer to anything other than the bowler's pitch.

### Syntactic inversion

*Example 2*

*From baseball or cricket commentaries.*

(a) In comes Ghouri
(b) And all set again is Pat Haden
(c) On deck is big Dave Winfield
(d) Pete goes to right field and back for it goes Jackson

Reversal or inversion of the normal word order is another feature of sports announcer talk. This device allows the announcer to foreground or focus or the action and provides him or her . . . with time to identify the subject of the action – an important piece of information for listeners . . .

### *Routines and formulas*

*Example* 3

> a little wider on the track the favourite Race Ruler
> Twilight Time is behind those
> Breaking up behind is Noodlums' Fella
> and he went down
> and one tipped out was My Dalrea . . .

Each of these [lines] is composed of a set of pre-determined formulas into which the horses' names are slotted . . . The narrow range of syntactic and lexical choices made by the commentators can be illustrated by looking at the possible ways of communicating (a) that the race has started and (b) where the horses are positioned. These are both elements of the 'play-by-play' description of the race and both are conveyed formulaically. The 'start' formula and the 'horse locator' formula can be described as follows:

(a)  Start formula

and they're away (and racing now)

or

and they're off (and racing now)

(b)  The horse locator fomula

(horse's name) wide on the outside (horse's name)

or

(horse's name) over on the outside horse's name)

or

(horse's name) parked on the outside (horse's name) . . .

The specific features of the formulas are not arbitrary, but motivated by the demands of the context. For example, . . . syntactic inversion . . . also occurs as a feature of race-calling formulas, e.g. *one tipped out was* My Dalrea. It gives the speaker time to identify the person or horse before having to name them. The use of passives allows the speaker to follow the natural order in naming the horses. *Taro is followed by* Sunny, rather than out of order *Sunny follows* Taro.

**Task B5.1.2**

Having read Text B5.1, carry out the following activities:

➤ Holmes claims that syntactic reduction, inversion of normal word order in sentences and routines and formulas are characteristic of play-by-play sports commentary. Consider whether you would expect to find all of these characteristics in all types of play-by-play commentary or whether this would depend on the type of sport being played.

➤ Listen to sports commentaries on the radio and on the television and decide whether they make use of different grammatical constructions. Consider what aspects of the context influence the grammatical choices made.

In the next extract, we will see how a compact written genre – the dating ad(vertisement) – fulfils some of the functions of meeting and getting to know a prospective partner, which is more usually done verbally and face to face. Like sports announcer talk there are certain routines and conventions: abbreviations are common (wltm – would like to meet; UR – you are; Ldn – London; Beds – Bedfordshire); syntactic reduction often involves omitting personal pronouns and auxiliary verbs; and the ads themselves usually follow a common format outlined by Justine Coupland (1996):

| | | |
|---|---|---|
| 1 | Advertiser | **Bright brunette, 28** into gigs, film, food. |
| 2 | *seeks* | Seeks |
| 3 | Target | slim M |
| 4 | Goals | for marriage, kids, messy divorce. Ldn. |
| 5 | (Comment) | |
| 6 | Reference | 23444[21] |

Carol Marley identifies a number of ways in which this typical pattern is modified, and in Extract B5.2 she discusses the use of questions to increase the interactional quality of the text. She bases her discussion on work by Geoff Thompson and Puleng Thetela (1995) on advertisements in general.

 **Task B5.2.1**

As you read Text B5.2, carry out the following activities:

➤ Make sure you understand what is meant by 'prospection'.

➤ Find the difference in the prospected responses between the two types of text-final question identified by Marley.

➤ Look at the examples given and identify where material has been ellipted. Categorise the ellipsis, for example of articles, pronouns, finite verbs, etc.

**Carol Marley (2002) 'Popping the question: questions and modality in written dating advertisements', in *Discourse Studies* vol. 4, no. 1: 75–98.**

Text B5.2
C. Marley

### Questions as interaction

The questions found in my corpus divide into three main types, the first two of which can be distinguished by their placement in the text of the ad itself.

### *Text-final questions*

As with the commercial data examined by Thompson and Thetela, one strategy adopted by my ad writers is to end the text, though not the interaction, with a question. The question sets up an expectation of a response and hands over to the reader the responsibility for completing the interaction by providing this prospected response. In Thompson and Thetela's data the response required was usually minimal and pre-shaped by the preceding text, essentially seeking agreement. The text-final questions in my data, however, do not appear to be quite so straightforward; they further divide into two types, the first of which can be seen in Examples 1 and 2.

*Example 1*

> **Attrac., 29yo, warm**, tender, loving, M, WLTM female 30–35, Enjoys music, theatre, pubs, clubs, etc. <u>Companionship, romance?</u> Ldn.

*Example 2*

> **Creative, attract. single** dad, 31, socialist. Seeks sim. female <u>to share new dawns. love?</u> . . . Ldn.

These questions do indeed leave the reader responsible for continuing the interaction by adopting the role of answerer and making the next move in the exchange, but the answers they prospect do not seem to be so restricted to merely minimal agreement. The questions here effectively function modally, presenting possibilities for nego-tiation rather than definitive yes/no propositions: their occurrence in the Goals slot means they lead the reader beyond the present of both the text itself and the immediate response to it. Instead they prompt speculation on the potential of the future relationship that could result from responding.

The second type of text-final question, by contrast, focuses much more on the present and an immediate response to the text. Again, though, the response required seems to be rather more than a minimal agreement . . .

*Example 3*

> **Still dreaming. Unique** boy seeks HIS girl. He's 34, blond, blue-eyed. She's simply adorable. <u>Will she reply?</u> Mcr.

Extension

*Example* 4

> **Friendship! We are** 2 intellectual & humorous black ladies aged 31 wanting mental stimulation. <u>Can U help!</u> Bristol.

The response required by this type of question, occurring in the Comment rather than Goals slot, is less speculative than with the first type. As in Thompson and Thetela's data, agreement is necessary but in these cases it is not sufficient. The challenging nature of these questions can now be better – but still not fully – accounted for: responsibility for completing the interaction is handed over to the reader as a result of their text-final positioning. The appropriate response they strongly prospect consists not just of agreement, nor of mere speculation on the future, but also of making the next move in the genre-chain' (Shalom 1997) and actually replying to the ad itself.

This effect is particularly clear in Example 6, with its direct appeal to the reader for help, but perhaps less immediately obvious in Example 3, where the third-person question may at first glance appear to be rhetorical. Rhetorical questions themselves have traditionally been explained as a means of engaging the reader more vividly with the text. From the present perspective, this can be explained at least partly by the expectation of response that questions bring with them and the discoursal pressure mentally to supply a response of one's own, if one is not provided by the current 'speaker'. Such pressure is augmented here by the text-final placement of the question, inviting the reader to take up the conversational baton and consider how well she herself fits the description of the advertiser's dream woman as 'simply adorable'. If she does identify herself with the advertiser's ostensibly third-person target, then answering the question in the affirmative becomes equated with actually replying to the ad. It is worth noting here the important element of conditionality that is present in both examples. Only those who meet the advertiser's criteria – in Example 4, being able to provide mental stimulation – are targeted as potential respondents.

While both types of text-final question leave the reader to conclude the interaction, another group of questions regularly occurs in text-initial position, opening rather than serving to conclude the ad.

### Text-initial questions

The great majority of dating ads in my corpus follow the sequence of Coupland's textual framework and open with the Advertiser slot; the self-description thus forms the thematic point of departure for the ad as a whole (Halliday 1994). One way to focus instead on the partner sought is to use the passive voice to thematize the other-description. An alternative, more speech-like, strategy is to use a text-initial question in the Target slot to address prospective partners directly and immediately engage them in interaction. Such questions in my data almost always take the form of' yes/no questions, as shown in Examples 5 and 6.

*Example* 5

> **<u>Like music</u>** <u>& dance?</u> Gay male, mid 30's, 5'11". Seeking someone same age fun. Beds.

*Example 6*

> **Are you open** minded, warm, mature, 25–40. Attentive, loving man, 29, WLTM you. No ravers. Lndn.

Again these questions cast the reader in the role of answerer, and the ensuing text shows that they are assumed to have provided the minimal response of agreement; but again the questions themselves seem not so much constraining as involving. Their occurrence in the Target slot means the reader is directly drawn into checking their own suitability against the criteria the advertiser provides, as opposed to being able to read more conventional third person partner descriptions precisely as descriptions of a third-party 'other'. Being able to meet the criteria in these cases effectively becomes a prerequisite for taking further fully licensed part in the interaction. Responding with an affirmative 'preferred second pair part' (Levinson 1983) rules the answerer in for further exchange as an addressee of the kind the advertiser seeks. (A negative reply, by the same token, rules the respondent out of such fully legitimate participation, but the impulse of the question is towards eligibility rather than exclusion. Few of us would want to consider ourselves narrow-minded, cold and immature!) The same implicit conditionality, an 'if so, then' connection, operates here as in the text-final challenges. But in these cases it operates not between reading the ad and responding to it, but between the writer's opening demand for information in a first exchange and their giving of information about themselves in a second exchange. Unlike the text-final questions, then, with these questions, responsibility for the continuation of the interaction lies with the writer rather than the reader.

From this perspective, text-initial questions exert a greater degree of interactional management than text-final ones, by assuming that at least one reader has been able to supply the match the advertiser seeks and extending the interaction into one or more further exchanges. But both kinds of question, although they seem quite readily to allow the 'wrong' answer as a means of weeding out unsuitable potential respondents, nevertheless exert a fairly high degree of management by exploiting the relative constraints of yes/no questions to delimit the range of possible responses.

## Wh- *questions*

Wh- questions are in principle much more open in terms of the freedom allowed the responder to answer as they choose from a wider range of' possible formulations. Thompson and Thetela (1995) observe that they therefore represent 'a slightly riskier strategy' for an advertiser to adopt (p. 114) and indeed they are found vastly less frequently in my data than polar questions. When they do occur, two factors render their application very similar to polar questions: the preceding text significantly restricts their scope in terms first of addressee and second of preferred response. As the next two examples show, they are effectively designed to elicit a response that locates the reader as the desired other, with the appropriate next move being projected as something equivalent to 'I'm here':

*Example 7*

> **Attract. grad.** 37, wonders if there are any articulate, caring, funny men left. Where are you all? Lond.

*Example 8*

> **Choicest blend /Earl** Grey, <u>where is Camomile's special cup of tea?</u> I'm prof'. 38, NW. UR caring, intellig., kind. L'pool.

The increased pressure to respond positively by offering oneself perhaps becomes more apparent if an alternative formulation of Example 7 is considered. It might be argued that the question here in fact stands for a declarative and the example could be rewritten as follows:

> Attractive graduate, 37, wonders if there are any articulate, caring, funny men left. I haven't been able to find any. London.

A statement such as this sets up an expectation of no more than acknowledgement by way of response, whereas the interrogative form actually chosen more explicitly invites the reader, addressed as 'you', first to assess himself in terms of the positive (and widely aspired to) qualities the advertiser wonders about. If the assessment is affirmative (as would seem likely), then the reader has the information sought by the writer and the second stage would be to identify and offer himself in response.

The function of questions in my data, then, can be summarized as follows. They all exert a greater degree of management of the interaction than declarative statements, either by appealing for, or challenging, a reader to respond or by assuming that an appropriate response has been supplied. In the latter case of text-initial questions, the reader effectively becomes a co-conversationalist as a result of the high degree of control exerted by the writer. W*h*- questions are probably least controlling in this sense, with text-final questions ranked somewhere in between these two positions.

 **Task B5.2.2**

Having read Text B5.2, carry out the following activities:

➤ Consider how you would respond to the questions in these advertisements, and whether you find yourself mentally answering the questions and entering into the interaction.

➤ Compare these questioning advertisements with the more common format given before the extract or with any dating advertisements that you can find. Look particularly at verb choices. Consider what the choice of a verb such as *seek* used in a declarative rather than an interrogative might signal.

The extracts from Holmes and Marley have categorised some of the ways in which restricted texts succinctly convey complex messages using an adapted grammatical repertoire. In Unit A8 you saw how text messaging also relies on developing a shared understanding of grammatical and lexical resources adapted from the norm for writing. You will be able to pursue this further in Unit C4 on electronic communication and C5 on 'little texts'.

**Summary**

In this unit we have looked at:

Contexts

- Sports commentaries
- Dating advertisements.

Linguistic features/grammatical structures

- Syntactic reduction
- Syntactic inversion
- Routines and formulas
- Text-final questions
- Text-initial questions
- *Wh*-questions.

# Unit B6
# Grammar in developing and disintegrating language

In Unit A3 we looked briefly at the effect of audience on language choice, including the influence of the age of participants. In this unit, we explore this influence in more detail through three research studies into the language of: pre-school children, children from seven to nine years, and older people suffering from dementia. In these studies we can see first the development of increasing sophistication in the grammatical structures of children in both speech and writing and in the final study, the way in which declining grammatical and other linguistic abilities are linked to and indicative of the stages of dementia. The three studies show the interconnection between language and cognition – how language demonstrates our understanding of the world around us and enables or constrains our further development.

Text B6.1 is a naturalistic study of parent–child talk by Clare Painter into the developing language of her son, Stephen, between the ages of two years and six months (2;6) and five years (5;0). She recorded conversations over that period and analysed and interpreted them using the concepts and categories of Halliday's (1994) systemic functional grammar. Earlier (Unit B3) we read Halliday's explanations of how scientific language evolved in complexity in ways not dissimilar to the language development of a child. Painter's work was influenced by Halliday's study of child language development (1978) and discusses his view that from babyhood we are building a complex set of options to enable 'meaning making'. She further argues that the linguistic changes we can observe both signal cognitive development in the child and importantly enable further such development. Without developing resources for meaning making human beings cannot make sense of or influence the contexts in which they find themselves.

 **Task B6.1.1**

As you read Text B6.1, carry out the following activities:

➤ Decide how far you agree with Halliday that we develop options for 'meaning making'.

➤ Make a note of the sequence that a child goes through in learning to classify things.

➤ Note three grammatical patterns that Painter identifies and at what age they occurred in Stephen's talk.

**Clare Painter (2004) 'The development of language as a resource for learning', in Coffin, C., Hewings, A. and O'Halloran, K. (eds.) *Applying English Grammar: Corpus and Functional Approaches*, London, Arnold.**

Text B6.1
C. Painter

As Halliday (1981) argues, in the process of learning language, a child is also learning *through* language. In other words, language is both a meaning system to be built up by the child, and also the means by which the child builds up other meaning systems – those that constitute our 'knowledge of the world'. Moreover the need to understand experience and to build knowledge constitutes one of the primary motivations to develop language further (Halliday 1975). Thus an examination of a learner's changing texts will reveal not only instances of the developing linguistic system but instances of the speaker's use of the system as means of understanding nonlinguistic phenomena, showing how the system expands as a result of the child's cognitive explorations . . .

**Construing phenomena I: building taxonomies**

When children begin to use their first words, they are beginning to build a resource for naming the things they see and experience in the world around them. A common noun, such as *cat*, an adjective like *big*, or a verb like *open* names a class of things, qualities or actions respectively. Thus language from the beginning enables the myriad distinct, individual instances of the experience of phenomena to be generalised (under the guidance of others) as *categories* of everyday 'knowledge of the world'. Once a child starts learning to talk, words that name categories are needed every time he or she speaks. However, I wish to focus initially on those utterances which overtly identify or classify something by name. First let us look at Examples 1a–c produced by Stephen in the second half of the third year, between 2;6 and 2;8. (Note that throughout, Stephen is 'S', his mother is 'M' and his father is 'F').

*Example 1   Naming*

1a.  2;6  (S enters childcare centre and addresses staff member, A)
      S:  I've got a paper
      A:  Oh let's have a look. What's on the paper? (opening folded sheet) Do you know'?
      S:  Um, that's words (pointing) that's words

1b.  2;7  (S pointing at the traffic from the car)
      S:  A taxi, another taxi . . . a tru- no, a van

1c.  2;8  (S examining pattern on rug)
      S:  That's a square. What's that?
      M:  That's a circle

C. Painter

In the early period of learning English as a mother tongue these are typical utterances where things are being classified by naming. They are typical in that the child can enquire about or tell how to categorise some observed phenomenon, first by bringing it into shared attention, either through physically pointing and/or through verbal pointing (with *this*, *that*, etc) to some material entity in the context. Then a 'relational' verb (see Halliday 1994: 112*ff*)) such as *be* is used with a name to construe the category to which the observed instance belongs. The clause type can be analysed as having two 'participant' roles brought into a relationship by *be*, as shown below:

### Analysis 1 Early context-dependent relational process for naming

| **that** | **'s** | **a circle** |
|---|---|---|
| Participant 1 | Relational Process | Participant 2 |
| verbal 'pointer' | = | category |

Clearly examples 1a–1c serve to construe the relation between a lexical symbol and the observed material phenomenon for which it stands. But, as Hasan (1985) has argued, working out what a lexical word 'stands for' cannot proceed without simultaneously working out how different categories relate to each other. For example, to be able to use the word *van* appropriately depends on working out its relations to other relevant words (known as 'co-hyponyms'), such as *truck*, *station wagon*, *car*, and this can hardly be done without simultaneously construing a semantic space which might he realised by a superordinate word like *vehicle* or *traffic*. So through these utterances where Stephen was practising naming he was also necessarily construing the things of his experience into taxonomies (hierarchies of class and subclass) . . .

The next developmental step in the use of language to construe categories builds upon experience with the kinds of texts described so far. The need to make sense of experience is the challenge which has led Stephen to classify its various aspects through naming and describing utterances. But having, in this way, built up a linguistic resource to create a taxonomically organised knowledge of the things of his everyday experience, that linguistic resource is then available for use to do something more.

This can be seen if the earlier classifying utterances are compared with Example 2 from a year later:

### Example 2 Classifying categories

2. 3;8 (S is examining animal jigsaw puzzle pieces)
        S: There isn't a fox and there isn't – is a platypus an animal?
        M: Yes
        S: And is a seal is an animal?
        M: Yes (shepherding S to bathroom)
        S: And is er–er er–er—
        M: You do your teeth while you're thinking

The difference in this text is that both participants in the classifying clauses are realised by noun groups which name categories, as shown below:

## Analysis 2 Relational process: both participant roles construing categories

| is | a platypus | an animal |
|---|---|---|
| Relational Process | Participant 1 | Participant 2 |
| = | (category) | (category) |

The first participant role here is not a referring word like *this*, picking out some observable thing from the context, but constructs a class lexically. Two levels of taxonomic hierarchy are thus brought into a relation. There are numerous recorded examples of such utterances from Stephen, but none was recorded before age 3;5. (The later appearance of such clauses is also attested by other case studies, such as Macnamara (1982) and Painter (1984).)

What has happened, then, is that the deployment of the grammar of 'relational' clauses (using *be* and *have*) in order to make sense of material reality has led inevitably to a new orientation towards making sense of the linguistic potential itself, by examining the relations between lexical categories, as in Is *a platypus an animal*. But this, in turn, requires a further extension of the meaning resources. For example, in the fourth year, even when attention was still focused on categorising specific observable things, the impetus to explore the meaning potential required something new. This was the development of some means to make explicit the positive criteria upon which an entity was being assigned to a particular lexical class. This was done through a new use of *because* to create what Halliday and Hasan (1976) refer to as an 'internal' conjunctive relation. This can be exemplified by the following texts, from the second half of the fourth year, after 3;7. The relevant utterances are underlined:

## Example 3 The use of 'internal' causal links

3a. 3;9 (M refers to airship overhead as 'spaceship balloon')
   S: Not a spaceship — an airship —
   <u>cause a spaceship has bits like this to stand it up</u>

3b. 3;11 (S is pointing at page numbers)
   S: That's fifteen <u>because it's got a five</u>;
   that's fourteen <u>because it's got a four</u>

In these examples *because* has the 'internal' conjunctive meaning of 'I know [it's an airship] because . . .'; 'I can tell [it is the number 15] because . . .', where the relation is between a claim and its evidence (Halliday and Hasan 1976). And while the 'external' use of *because* (*e.g.* Do *this because* . . .; I *want this because* . . ., etc.) had already appeared, this internal conjunctive option was a fresh move. The importance of the internal link is that it serves to explain the speaker's reasoning for asserting or inferring something – in this case the reason for placing something in a particular category. . . .

The changes in the use of the meaning potential [exhibited in these examples] are significant not only in creating new forms of text but in enabling new ways of thinking and learning. I would argue that there is in fact a spiralling relationship between linguistic and cognitive development whereby experience with text provides the impetus for new cognitive possibilities that the language may then need to expand

C. Painter

further to meet. In other words, the use of classifying clauses, such as *that's a car*, and describing clauses, such as *Daddy's got bristles*, enables the child to categorise phenomena, which in turn challenges the child to reflect on the basis for inclusion in categories and the relation of one category to another. To meet this challenge requires an expansion of the language to encompass 'internal' causality (*it's an X because . . .*) and the option of classifying clauses where – instead of reference to something observable – one category is expressed as a subordinate of another (*a platypus is an animal* etc.).

 **Task B6.1.2**

Having read Text B6.1, carry out the following activities:

➤ Consider the question: If we accept the view that learning and language are interdependent, what consequences does that have for how we educate children?

➤ In Unit A5 you read about the influential linguist Noam Chomsky and his view that human languages are so complex that learning them from scratch is beyond our capability, and that we must therefore have some special predisposition to learn language. This leads to the understanding that grammar is independent of meaning and of the situations in which meanings are made. Compare Chomsky's view of grammar and language learning with the views of Halliday and of Painter and say which you find more convincing.

From classifying and causation in the speech of a young child we move on to subordination in the writing of seven nine-year old children in a study by Paula Allison and colleagues. The study builds on work by Harpin (1976) which identified first the shift from simple coordination of clauses with *and* to the more elaborate and flexible device of subordination. These he found to steadily increase in frequency through the age range 7–11 years. It also draws on research which indicates that at this age children begin to make use of grammatical structures that are rarely found in speech. So by looking specifically at subordination we can see how children extend their ability to connect ideas and events and to shape their language to the context of writing and, as this extract shows, to the context of the particular tasks that they are given.

A group of 22 children were set five writing tasks to be carried out over a period of six weeks.

Task 1 – The saddest/happiest day of my life: an autobiographical account.

Task 2 – The Day of the Storm: a recount of a version of the Bible story of Jesus calming the storm, which was first read to the children.

Task 3 – I found a hole yesterday: the continuation of a story starter provided by a picture and the first few lines of the story.

Task 4 – The Bike Ride: The children were given a story map that depicted a child starting out on a bike ride. The task involved choosing a route for the bike ride and writing a story of what happened along the way.

Task 5 – How to play: an account of how to play a game well known to the child, for someone who had never played it before

The resulting texts were divided up into clauses with the range in length being from seven to 80 clauses, and a median of 17. Subordinate clauses, defined as any clause which was dependent on a main clause, were counted and classified as either adverbial, nominal or relative.

**Task B6.2.1**

As you read Text B6.2, carry out the following activities:

➤ Note the effect of context – the type of task – on the use of subordination. Decide which type of task appeared to require or encourage the greatest use of subordination.

➤ This study draws on research by Perera (1984) which indicates that 7–11-year-olds are in the process of using grammatical structures associated only with writing and not found in speech. Look for examples to support or refute this in the extract.

**Paula Allison, Roger Beard and John Willcocks (2002) 'Subordination in children's writing',** *Language and Education, An International Journal,* **vol. 16, no. 2: 97–111.**

Text B6.2
P. Allison,
R. Beard and
J. Willcocks

**Types of subordinate clause**

Following Harpin, the subordinate clauses used were classified into three types: adverbial, nominal, relative . . . Examples:

When *she got to her Gran's* she was soaking wet — ADVERBIAL clause of time

She was thinking *how to get across* —          NOMINAL clause acting as object

I saw a tree *that someone had pulled out* —     RELATIVE clause modifying the
                                                 noun 'tree'

In the present study, the children generally made far less use of relative clauses than of either adverbial or nominal clauses – so much so that, in spite of the very small size

P. Allison,
R. Beard and
J. Willcocks

of the sample, both of these differences were highly significant statistically (P=< 0.0001) using the Friedman two-way Anova . . .

There was a wide range within the group . . . Every child used adverbial clauses at some stage and many used them in each piece of writing. Adverbial clauses of time (*when*, *after*), and of reason (*because*) were most common, but clauses of condition were used quite regularly in the 'How to Play . . .' task. A similar pattern of distribution appears in relation to the use of nominal clauses. These were used most frequently in direct speech and also after such words as 'thought', 'mentions', decide' or 'hope'. According to Harpin (1976: 70–71), the latter use may reflect an increasing proportion of indirect speech in children's writing at this age.

A rather different pattern of distribution appears . . . in relation to the use of relative clauses. According to previous research, the smaller range of use of relative clauses may reflect the fact that many of the children were only just beginning to use such clauses in their writing. In fact, over half the group (13) used a total of two relative clauses or fewer. At the same time, two children used relative clauses in most of their writing, but the same two children, whilst scoring highly in subordination generally (24%/28%), used fewer nominal clauses than the other children.

Of course, the present investigation was not a developmental study, being rather a snapshot of the stage of development reached by a small group of children at one particular time. Nevertheless important developmental clues lie in the wide differences in subordinate clause usage between individual children, for they were all still a long way from the mature levels of writing skill which they could reasonably be expected to achieve in years to come.

## Subordination within writing tasks

. . . In the 'How to Play . . .' task, the children tended to write relatively short pieces and yet they generally used as many subordinate clauses as they used in other pieces which were often longer . . . Consequently their 'How to Play . . .' writing was richer in subordination and, in particular, in the use of relative clauses (a total of 25 in all), than their writing for any of the other tasks (where there was a range of from 3 to 15) . . .

The lowest median percentages were in the writing undertaken for the two 'story projection' tasks, 'Hole' and 'Ride', one involving a continuation of a story starter and the other a story projection based on a story map. The relatively small sample size limited the possibilities of statistical analysis, but the emerging difference between the use of subordination in the procedural writing, the two recounts and the two projected stories may repay further investigation in larger-scale studies. This study provided some indication that the type of task had an influence on the way children used subordination and this issue will now be taken up in the profiles of individual children.

## Some individual profiles

The following section draws upon an analysis of the work of some individual children. . . . The analysis is concerned with children's use of three kinds of subordinate clause (adverbial, nominal and relative) and short excerpts from the writing of different children is used as illustration.

P. Allison,
R. Beard and
J. Willcocks

## Adverbial clauses

Some children appeared to need more help with connecting ideas using simple adverbial clauses. Gary, for instance, in 'The Bike Ride', used 20 clauses, only three of which were subordinate: one nominal after 'said'; and two adverbial connected by 'because' and 'when'. 'Then' was used eight times and 'so' five times. 'So' could perhaps be seen as introducing subordinate clauses, but the relationships between clauses was generally in relation to temporal and causal relationships (e.g.' . . . so I went on. So I went down . . .'). The only exception to this was used in 'I saw some sheep (so I went all the way back home to get my dog)'. Many clauses were almost subordinated, but Gary was not able to give sufficient attention to how ideas are connected and his writing appeared rather disjointed. He appeared to need more guidance in connecting ideas using simple adverbial clauses.

Laura, on the other hand, was more confident in using common adverbial clauses, especially those introduced by 'because' and 'when'. In her piece on 'The Day of the Storm' she used an adverbial clause of result begun by the connective 'so . . . that'. Having used the structure once:

I was so tired *that I laid down on a pillow* . . .

She soon repeated it in a different context:

My friend Carly was so frightened *that she went down the steps* . . .

It might be significant that the story which was read aloud as part of the task uses the same structure three times. Laura seemed to have taken note of the structure and begun to make more use of it herself.

Other children seemed to respond to the opportunities provided by a specific task by beginning to experiment in using common adverbial clauses in different ways. In his piece on 'The Saddest Day', Mark used 'when' to introduce a subordinate clause of time six times, but not always in the same way. He showed he was able to put the subordinate clause at the beginning of a sentence:

*When Sarah heard about Fella dying* she was very sad.

and used this construction several times elsewhere in the text. But he also embedded the same clause in the main clause:

but *when we got in the car* I cried.

The subordination of other children seemed to respond to the demands of a particular task. In 'How to Play', Scott's subordination index was 41%; in 'The Bike Ride' and in 'I found a hole yesterday', it was 0% and 4% respectively. In 'How to play', he used an adverbial clause of condition three times with the connective 'if'. He also showed he was able to embed this structure in a main clause:

or *if it is the other way round* you turn the black over.

SECTION
B

P. Allison,
R. Beard and
J. Willcocks

## Nominal clauses

Most children used nominal clauses for direct speech, leading to the high percentage in some pieces of writing.

Samantha: The Bike Ride:

> . . . Then Sarah saw a man. The man said to Sarah 'My name is Joe. What's yours.' Sarah said 'My name is Sarah'. 'Would you like to come home with me' said Joe. 'Yes please.' said Sarah. 'We can go in my tractor' said Joe. 'What about my bike' said Sarah. 'You could ride it' said Joe. 'Yes I will' said Sarah. Joe took Sarah to his house . . .

Direct speech seemed to be a feature of much of Samantha's writing and this is accurately punctuated. Although this piece began with a narrative, she took the first opportunity to revert to speech. Some children in the group seemed to be beginning to make the transition from direct to indirect speech and used different words to introduce nominal clauses.

Robert used:

> I didn't <u>know</u> *what heaven was*

> I <u>thought</u> *she went on holiday*

> I <u>wish</u> *there wasn't a word called dead.*

Carly used nominal clauses for direct and indirect speech:

(1) direct speech: Her Mum said *why don't you take some food?*

(2) transition from direct to indirect speech:

She said to her mum *that it was quite a long way.*

(3) indirect speech:

Rachel asked her mum *if she could go and sleep at her friend's house.*

Only a few children were using nominal clauses not connected with speech:

Natalie: So they found out *what it was*, a mouse . . .

## Relative clauses

Children appeared to vary considerably in their confidence in using relative clauses. There were a few examples of children beginning to use them, but they often remained 'speech-related', in that the clauses followed a non-standard form:

- and then there was this wall *what you had to touch*
- The number *what you get* you take that number

P. Allison,
R. Beard and
J. Willcocks

Some children were able to use relative clauses in more complex structures:

- At the end *who wins* is the one *who have all their counters in the other place*.
- I told her all the things *that had happened* and all the things I *saw*.

Susan was one of the few children who appeared very confident in the use of relative clauses.

- there was a brown bean *that sat down*
- the little house *where mother washed up*
- the man *who was driving a tractor along the road*

In her piece of writing, 'How to Play Monopoly', she was able to use relative clauses in different ways in order to help her in dealing with the procedure:

> You have to get a person to be a banker. A banker is a person *who gives you money and who you give money to*. You have to roll the dice if you land on a square it might say roller coaster and there will be a price underneath. If you want to go on the roller coaster you pay the price *it says on the bottom*. You have some little houses and if you do not want to go on the roller coaster you put a house on the square *that says roller coaster* . . .

From these examples it can be seen that the children's writing showed a variety of features which indicated their varying grasp of different grammatical structures. Some of these structures maybe closely related to those of speech and may not be expressed in standard forms. There were also signs of some children using a rather literary style, possibly because they were transferring structures they had read (or heard read) into their own writing.

## Task B6.2.2

Having read Text B6.2, carry out the following activities:

➤ Given the number of factors associated with children's choice of subordination, decide whether you think it is reasonable to claim that more elaborate or sophisticated use of subordination indicates development in a child's communicative ability.

➤ In Unit A3 we discussed the effect of local situational context on grammar. Look back at that unit and then list as many of the contextual influences on the writing of the children in this study as you can. Consider whether some are likely to have a greater influence than others.

While the first two papers in this unit have looked at language change in the early years of life, the third investigates changes in older people who are suffering from dementia. Katinka Dijkstra and colleagues used an analysis of local text and wider discourse features to chart the relationship between changes in language use through progressive stages of the disease. The grammatical and discoursal features that they noted came largely from the existing literature on Alzheimer's disease and dementia more generally. They recorded changes across three groups of suffers – those in the early, middle and later stages of the disease – finding that discourse level and utterance level features of conversation were affected by the particular stage of dementia.

### Task B6.3.1

Before you read Text B6.3, carry out the following activity:

➤ Look back over A1.2. Notice, in particular, the discussion of grammatical forms and speech.

As you read Text B6.3, carry out the following activities:

➤ Keep in mind the characteristics of spontaneous speech that you have read about. In relation to the utterance-level features investigated, decide whether you would expect these features to occur in your own speech.

➤ Look carefully at Table B6.1. Consider whether the features marked as 'High' or 'Low' in the *Early* column correspond to features of your own language use.

➤ Compare the *Early* and *Middle* columns and identify which features change from 'High' to 'Low' or 'Low' to 'High' in these columns. These indicate which features of language are affected first. Decide whether these early changes occur more at the discourse or the utterance level.

The discourse features investigated were: overall numbers of words used; number of unique words; number of information units which were relevant, truthful and non-redundant (e.g. *I went to school in New Jersey*); conciseness as measured by the number of words in each information unit; the number of elaborations of the topic under discussion (e.g. *No, I went to grade school first of course and then high school*); disruptive topic shift (e.g. *And they're both with the Lord. You are a good looking woman*); topic maintenance measured by dividing the number of elaborations by the number of disruptive topic shifts; and finally, global coherence as measured by the number of utterances that were on topic (Dijkstra *et al.* 2002: 63).

The utterance level features investigated were: incorrect pronominal reference; aborted or incomplete phrases not revised within two succeeding sentences; empty phrases with little or no content (e.g. *First and then and that and that was all*); repetitions; indefinite terms; revisions, that is incomplete phrases that were revised and completed within two succeeding sentences; local coherence, that is the number of utterances that are semantically connected to the preceding sentence; and finally, cohesion, which was divided into temporal (correct verb tense), referential (correct pronominal reference), simple causal (simple conjunctions), and complex clausal (complex conjunctions) (Dijkstra *et al.* 2002: 64).

Text B6.3 is a table showing how features of the conversations of elderly nursing-home residents with dementia change over the stages of the disease. Only characteristics which showed a statistically higher or lower occurrence are included.

**Katinka Dijkstra, Michelle Bourgeois, Geoffrey Petrie, Lou Burgio and Rebecca Allen-Burge (2002) 'My recaller is on vacation: discourse analysis of nursing-home residents with dementia',** *Discourse Processes*, **vol. 33, no. 1: 53–76.**

Text B6.3
K. Dijkstra,
M. Bourgeois,
G. Petrie,
L. Burgio and
R. Allen-Burge

*Table B6.1* Discourse profiles for residents in early-, middle- and late-stage dementia

| Level | | Early | Middle | Late |
|---|---|---|---|---|
| *Discourse* | | | | |
| 1. | Words | H | | L |
| 2. | Unique words | H | L | L |
| 3. | Information units | H | H | L |
| 4. | Conciseness | H | H | L |
| 5. | Elaborations | H | L | L |
| 6. | Disruptive topic shifts | L | L | H |
| 7. | Topic maintenance | H | | L |
| 8. | Global coherence | H | L | L |
| | | | | |
| *Utterance* | | | | |
| 1. | Incorrect pronominal referents | L | L | H |
| 3. | Empty phrases | L | L | H |
| 4. | Repetitions | L | | H |
| 6. | Indefinite words | L | L | H |
| 7. | Local coherence | H | H | L |
| 8. | Cohesion | | | L |
| | a. Temporal | H | | L |
| | b. Referential | | H | L |
| | c. Simple causal | H | | L |
| | d. Complex causal | H | | L |

Note
H = significantly higher occurrence; L = significantly lower occurrence.

## Task B6.3.2

Having read Text B6.3, carry out the following activities:

➤ Find reasons for the authors' belief that discourse level features appear to deteriorate faster than utterance level features.

➤ If you are familiar with any children under the age of ten, consider how they would score on the features investigated in Text B6.3 and what reasons there might be for this. For example, you might consider whether they would use many unique words, whether they were good at topic maintenance, or whether they had problems with pronominal referents.

➤ Do you think that the development of language in children follows similar (but reversed) stages to the loss of language in people suffering with dementia? Consider how you might try to investigate this.

By looking at the column 'Middle' we can see which features of language start to deteriorate first. The number of unique words and elaborations start to decrease at the same time as global coherence also declines at the discourse level. Most utterance-level features remained less affected at this stage and only showed up statistically in the later stages. So, for example, in the later stages, sufferers can be expected to use more incorrect pronominal referents, utter more apparently empty phrases, use more indefinite words, and so on. This study of sixty older people complemented other existing studies and strengthened the case for there being patterning in language loss. In dementia sufferers the pattern of loss becomes notice-able when discourse level characteristics start to suffer disruption. Features such as global coherence and topic elaboration require most cognitive resources and are an early indicator of the progress of the disease. It is only in the later stages that utterance level features start to show be affected to a similar degree.

In Texts B6.1 and B6.2 we saw examples of how individual and group based studies show that children's language gradually extends and develops in a broadly common sequence. Text B6.2 also illustrated that by manipulating the context – in this case the type of task – it was possible to influence the use of particular grammatical resources. Just as there seems to be a sequence in the way that children acquire language, so there seems to be a pattern to the way in which people with dementia lose certain language abilities.

**Summary**

In this unit we have looked at:

Contexts

■ Language development in children, both speech and writing
■ Language loss in adults with dementia.

Linguistic features/grammatical structures

■ Grammatical features of child language development

  ■ using BE to classify objects (e.g. *That's a circle*)
  ■ relating different noun groups using BE (e.g. *a platypus is an animal*)
  ■ internal conjunctions expressing reason (*That's a fifteen because it's got a five*)
  ■ adverbial, nominal and relative subordinate clause use.

■ Discoursal level features of language loss (e.g. topic maintenance, global coherence etc.)
■ Utterance level features of language loss (e.g. incorrect pronominal referents, local coherence etc.)

# Unit B7
# Grammar in second-language learning

In the previous unit we looked at the development of grammatical structures in the speech and writing of children and at the deterioration of communicative ability in the speech of people with dementia. We saw in these approaches that some degree of sequencing can be observed in both acquisition and loss of structures. This finding is also central to work on second-language acquisition (SLA). Theorists have maintained that people acquire the structures of their second language (L2) in a reasonably fixed order. In Text B7.1 below, Rod Ellis and Celia Roberts approach SLA research from a sociolinguistic perspective which highlights the importance of choice in language use, arguing that choice leads to variable language behaviour where a user can opt to use one grammatical or lexical form rather than another. Context is thought to influence choice and, therefore, acquisition.

They look at both linguistic and situational components of context. Their 'linguistic context' refers to both the surrounding words in an utterance and the wider discourse structuring of a text or spoken interaction. 'Situational context' at the macro level is an investigation of **domains** such as language associated with the school, family, church, etc. There are, however, problems of identifying language behaviour and choices that are influenced directly by domain. Consequently, the situational context needs also to be examined at the micro level: that is, 'by correlating the use of specific linguistic features with narrowly defined social categories to do with the scene, [or setting] and the participants of the situational context' (Ellis and Roberts 1987: 9). (See also Unit A2 on the components of context.)

In discussing SLA, researchers often refer to the language being learnt either as the **L2** or the **target language** and the type of target language generated by learners during their learning as **interlanguage**. In the first section below, Ellis and Roberts relate aspects of the interlanguage to the domains in which learners interact.

## Task B7.1.1

As you read Text B7.1, carry out the following activities:

➤ Discover Ellis and Roberts's view on L2 knowledge following a standard route. Find the evidence they use to support their view.

➤ Ellis and Roberts isolate domain as an important contextual factor in SLA. Consider the advantages and disadvantages resulting from naturalistic versus classroom domains.

➤ Explain how context affects variability. If you speak another language, consider whether you are aware of using that language more carefully and more accurately in some contexts than in others.

Text B7.1

R. Ellis and

C. Roberts

**Rod Ellis and Celia Roberts (1987) 'Two approaches for investigating second language acquisition', in Ellis, R. (ed.) *Second Language Acquisition in Context*, London, Prentice-Hall International.**

### Domain and interlanguage development

Strong claims have been advanced (e.g. Krashen 1981) that the development of L2 knowledge follows a more or less standard route, This route, it is claimed, is evident in a fixed order of development of grammatical morphemes such as plural -s, past tense -ed, and articles, and also in a fixed sequence of development for transitional structures such as negatives or interrogatives, which involve the acquisition of a series of interim rules before the target language rule can be mastered. It has been suggested that the universality of this route is the result of the way the L2 learner processes input data. The learner is predisposed to construct his interlanguage in fixed ways.

Not all SLA researchers agree with Krashen that there is a 'natural' route of development, and the extent to which interlanguage development can vary is an issue currently receiving much attention. In particular, researchers are interested in whether different learning conditions can affect the order of development. One way of investigating this is by comparing how interlanguage develops in different domains.

One type of comparison that can be made is between SLA in a naturalistic domain and SLA in a classroom domain. There are now a number of reviews of the research which has undertaken this comparison (e.g. Long 1983, Ellis 1985). Where route of development is concerned, the general picture which emerges can be summarized as follows:

(1) In general the route of development is impervious to context. That is, there is general agreement that the order in which a set of morphemes are acquired or the stages through which learners pass in acquiring transitional structures like negatives or interrogatives, is not affected by the learning domain. Also, the error types found in naturalistic and classroom SLA are the same.

(2) Certain structures are influenced by instruction, however. For example, third person -s and plural -s appear to be used more accurately (and, therefore, possibly acquired earlier) by learners who receive instruction.

In addition, the available evidence suggests that instructed learners learn more rapidly than uninstructed learners (cf. Long 1983) and also go on to achieve higher levels of proficiency. Instruction may not be able to 'beat' the natural order of development in any significant way, but it may enable the learner to pass along it more rapidly. There are a number of possible explanations for this. One is that if instruction is timed to

R. Ellis and
C. Roberts

take place when the learner is developmentally 'ready' to acquire a particular structure, acquisition takes place more easily than if the learner is left to 'discover' the rule for himself. Another explanation is that formal instruction may sensitize the learner to the presence of specific formal features in the input, which otherwise, left to his own resources, he might not attend to. A third explanation is that in the classroom the learner is exposed to a more formal register of language use which provides a different kind of data to work on and facilitates the development of features that are infrequent or insignificant in the kind of informal language use experienced naturalistically.

It is becoming clear that we can expect some differences in interlanguage development according to learning domain. These differences will probably be manifest more in the rate and success of acquisition than in the sequence of development or the central processes of interlanguage rule-formation. However, the effects of learning domain are likely to operate in subtle ways. It is becoming clear, for instance, that the effects of instruction on SLA are very complex. A lot more research will be needed to establish when and how classroom learners differ from naturalistic learners. Also, research is needed to explore how differences in the learning conditions within each of these broad domains affects SLA. We already have evidence to suggest that naturalistic learners experience very different contexts for acquiring the L2 (cf. Schumann 1978) and these affect the level of proficiency attained. We need more finely grained comparisons of learning domain to discover how learner-internal (i.e. innate factors) interact with learner-external (i.e. environmental) factors.

## The linguistic and situational context and interlanguage development

It is possible to identify a number of different kinds of rules which comprise the interlanguage of an L2 learner. These are:

### (1) Formulaic structures

These are linguistic units which have no internal structure and which are acquired and used as unanalyzed wholes. Formulas which figure in the interlanguage of many learners of L2 English are, 'I don't know' and Can I have a –?'. Arguably, formulaic structures do not constitute rules in the normal sense of this term.

### (2) Categorical interlanguage rules

These are invariable rules which differ from those found in the target language. For example, at any early stage of development, L2 learners may have a single categorical rule for verbs – the unmarked, simple verb form (e.g. 'come') – which is used in all contexts irrespective of how the target language is used.

### (3) Variable interlanguage rules

These are rules that account for the systematic distribution of two or more variants, one or both of which is/are not found in the target language. For example, learners in the process of acquiring English negative structures may alternate, at some point,

R. Ellis and
C. Roberts

between the neg + verb pattern and the aux + neg + verb pattern . . . in a systematic way.

### (4) Categorical target language rules

These are invariable rules found in the target language. For example, there is a categorical rule for German that requires the verb to be end-positioned in subordinate clauses. Such rules may not be acquired until late on in SLA. In some learners they may not be acquired at all.

### (5) Variable target language rules

These are rules that account for the systematic distribution of two or more variants which are also found in the target language grammar. An example is the rule that describes the use of full and contracted copula (cf. Labov 1970). We know very little about how or whether L2 learners acquire such rules. With these different types of rules in mind, we can try to specify how the linguistic and situational context affects SLA . . .

Any interlanguage system is likely to manifest a large number of variable rules of type (3). Variability is an inherent property of interlanguage systems. Examples can be found to show that both the linguistic and the situational context determine the distribution of variants in an interlanguage variable rule. For example, Ellis (1986) has shown that one L2 learner of English whose interlanguage contained a variable rule for third person -s (the variants being -s and the simple verb form), distributed these variants according to whether the preceding element was a pronoun or a noun phrase subject, as shown in Table B7.1. Here, then, is a clear example of how the learner's variable output is governed by linguistic factors.

*Table B7.1* Percentage suppliance of two variants by one L2 learner according to linguistic context

| Linguistic context | Variant | |
| --- | --- | --- |
| | -s | simple form |
| Pronoun subject | 81% | 19% |
| Noun phrase subject | 39% | 61% |

There is abundant evidence, too, to show that factors to do with the situational context influence when the L2 user uses one form as opposed to another. For example, Fairbanks (1983) reports that a Japanese learner of English rarely used third person -s in casual speech (using, instead, the simple form) but supplied it consistently in his careful style, even overgeneralizing it to contexts requiring the plural verb form. Third person -s, therefore, constitutes a variable interlanguage structure which is influenced both by the linguistic and the situational context . . .

One way in which interlanguage development takes place is by the gradual elimination of variability. This is because variable rules are more evident in interlanguage than in

R. Ellis and
C. Roberts

the target language. But it is important to realize that variability is never entirely eliminated, even in the learner who proceeds to target language competence, as the target language itself contains a fair number of variable rules. It is a mistake to view SLA as targeted exclusively on the acquisition of categorical rules. It is targeted on those patterns of variability that exist in the target language variety. Thus successful SLA will involve the acquisition of target language variable rules (i.e. type 5). This obvious truth has been neglected, in general, by SLA researchers, and perhaps even more so by teachers, For example, studies which have investigated how learners acquire English copula have treated the copula rule as a categorical one. They have sought to determine whether acquisition has or has not taken place by seeing whether learners supply the copula in obligatory contexts (i.e. in utterances where the presence of the copula is required in native speaker performance). However, the copula is best accounted for by a variable rule, which specifies the probability of the full or contracted copula occurring in different linguistic contexts. Ellis (1986) has shown that a learner can achieve apparent native-like control over the copula, if this is measured in terms of suppliance in obligatory contexts, but not achieve total control if this is measured in terms of native-like variable use. In short, we know very little about how L2 learners acquire variable target language rules.

So far we have been considering how interlanguage variability – viewed syncronically – can be accounted for. We will now examine the relationship between context and interlanguage development . . .

When a form first appears in an interlanguage, it does so in restricted contexts. As the learner gains greater control over the form its use spreads to other linguistic contexts. Thus, for instance, the rule for third person -s may first be restricted to contexts where the subject of the verb is a pronoun. Later the learner extends the rule to contexts where the subject is a noun phrase. This change occurs as a gradual process in much the same way as historical change. It is possible to identify how the contexts are developmentally ordered by examining the accuracy with which a specific form such as third person -s is used in each context at a single point in time. Thus initially we find that third person -s is used with greater accuracy with pronoun than with noun phrase subjects.

However, the true picture is much more complicated. This is because when a form first appears it is likely to do so in contexts where some previously acquired form is used. Initially this gives rise to *free variation*. Gatbonton (1978) provides a framework for describing what appears to happen. In her *diffusion model* there is an 'acquisition phase' and a 'replacement phase'. In the former the learner first acquires a specific form which he uses in a number of different linguistic contexts. Then he acquires a second form, which is used in the same contexts. By the end of the acquisition phase, therefore, the learner has two forms operating in free variation. In the replacement phase the learner first restricts one of the forms to a specific context, while continuing to use both forms in all other contexts. Later both forms come to be restricted to their respective contexts. Gatbonton shows how her model can be applied to L2 phonological development, but there is no reason why it cannot also be used to describe grammatical development.

Finally, we will consider how variability according to situational context is related to interlanguage development. Tarone (1982) suggests that there is a 'pull effect' from the learner's careful style in the direction of the vernacular style. That is, new forms may enter the learner's interlanguage in the careful style and then gradually spread to other more informal styles. For example, third person -s may first be evident in carefully monitored speech . . . but later become apparent in unattended speech. Thus

R. Ellis and
C. Roberts

the accuracy levels of third person -s in different styles at any one developmental point provide an indication of the degree of control which the learner has achieved over this form at this stage.

The claim that stylistic variability and interlanguage development are related must be treated circumspectly, however. While it appears an entirely plausible claim from what is known about the nature of language use in general, it has not yet received any clear empirical support. Further caveats are in order. It would be wrong to suggest that *all* forms emerge first it the careful style. Some forms may be acquired directly into the vernacular style. Indeed, the spread of forms may work in the opposite direction – from the vernacular style to the careful style. Also it should be recognized that there will be within-style variability, which is also contextually determined . . .

In conclusion, we can say that the study of interlanguage has gained enormously from sociolinguistic approaches which have sought to relate language use to context. In this approach the formal mastery of the L2 is to be seen as embedded in its communicative mastery. It is our belief that context is of crucial importance for understanding how interlanguage develops and that the study of variability provides a way of observing both what the learner's linguistic competence consists of at any one time and also how this competence changes over time.

 **Task B7.1.2**

Having read Text B7.1, carry out the following activities:

➤ Consider what factors might influence the acquisition of past simple tense forms in English.

➤ Compare the contexts in which a learner of English is trying to acquire the simple past tense form with the contexts experienced by a young child learning English as its first language. Consider the similarities and differences, and how these might explain the differences in language development.

Ellis and Roberts's study points to the importance of context and the influence of domains. In addition, early on in the extract they indicate that the acquisition of certain grammatical structures can be influenced by instruction. This issue was investigated by Peter Master, who chose to evaluate the learning of one of the more difficult aspects of English grammar – the article system. He used a quasi-experimental research methodology involving three control groups and an experimental group that was given systematic teaching on six aspects of the article system. All groups were given a pre- and post-test and the experimental group showed a significant increase in scores. Text B7.2 gives details of the grammatical aspects of the article system focused on and then part of the concluding discussion.

 **Task B7.2.1**

Before reading Text B7.2, carry out the following activity:

➤ Look back a few pages in this book and write out a short extract underling all the occurrences of *a, an* and *the*. Try to explain why a particular article choice was made in each case.

As you read Text B7.2, carry out the following activity:

➤ Look at the examples of article use given by Master and decide whether they account for all the uses you identified in your extract.

**Peter Master (1994) 'The effect of systematic instruction on learning the English article system', in Odlin, T. (ed.) *Perspectives on Pedagogical Grammar*, Cambridge, Cambridge University Press.**

Text B7.2
P. Master

1. the countable–uncountable and singular–plural distinctions

   Example:  There is a tree (singular countable) in my garden.
   There are [∅] flowers (plural countable) in my garden.
   There is [∅] grass (uncountable) in my garden.

2. the indefinite [a(n), ∅]–definite [the] distinction

   Example:  There is a tree (indefinite) in my garden. The tree (definite) is losing its leaves.
   There are [∅] flowers (indefinite) in my garden. The flowers (definite) are blooming.

3. the premodified–postmodified distinction

   Example:  A *mangy old cat* (premodified) came into the room.
   The cat *which lives down the street* (postmodified) came into the room.

4. the specific–generic distinction

   Example:  I received a book (specific) for my birthday.
   A book (generic) makes a great gift.

5. the common noun–proper noun distinction

   Example:  A doctor (common noun) came to see me.
   [∅] Dr. Smith (proper noun) came to see me.

6. the idiomatic phrase–nonidiomatic phrase distinction

   Example:  He is always on [∅] edge. (idiomatic phrase)
   He lives on the edge of town. (nonidiomatic phrase)

. . . The significant increase in score on the posttest by the experimental group suggests that the article system can indeed be learned and that it is perhaps the *systematic* presentation of the article system that makes the difference. Pieces of information about the system, rather than an approach that teaches the entire system, can often lead to confusion when the student is called upon to produce written text. The reason is that many aspects of the system tend to operate simultaneously, and it is rare to find a text in which only one or two article rules are applied . . .

The significant increase may be partly due to the effort to focus on the functions of the articles as well as their formal characteristics. Widdowson (1988) says in this regard that teaching only the formal linguistic properties is not appropriate in the language classroom. Grammatical instruction must focus on the function of grammar as it serves the intended meaning of an utterance.

 **Task B7.2.2**

Having read Text B7.2, carry out the following activities:

➤ Consider the context in which this research took place. Decide what additional information you need to know in order to evaluate what other factors may have influenced the acquisition of the article system.

➤ 'Grammatical instruction must focus on the function of grammar as it serves the intended meaning of an utterance'. Recall whether, in your experience as a language learner, you have focused in a classroom setting on learning both form and function and, if so, whether you found this helpful or confusing.

The final paragraph of this text is perhaps the clearest indication of the study's contextualising approach. The focus on function that is highlighted as so important can only be realised if some type of context is envisaged; for example, whether a specific instance is being discussed (e.g. an eye infection) or a generalisation is being made (e.g. *Infection is usually caused by bacteria*). Without an understanding of the effect of context, either implicit or (preferably) explicit, research suggests that second language learners will be unable to make principled grammatical choices.

**Summary**

In this unit we have looked at:

Contexts

- Second-language acquisition
    - the effect of informal and classroom domains on acquisition
    - the effect of systematic teaching on acquisition.

Linguistic features/grammatical structures

- Interlanguage (e.g. formulaic structures, categorical interlanguage rules etc.)
- The article system.

# Unit B8
# Grammar and gender

There is a considerable body of sociolinguistic research which has related patterns of speech to social context and geographical area. Features of pronunciation, for example, vary in relation to where a speaker comes from (e.g. the hard *a* sound in 'bath' [/bæθ/] for a British speaker from the Midlands or north of England, in comparison to the softer *a* [/ba:θ/] used in the south-east); who they are interacting with (e.g. friend, colleague, social equal or superior); the setting of the interaction (at work, home, school, police station); and so on. Similarly, grammatical choices are also seen to vary with *gender*, the focus of the extracts in this unit. In particular, there has been much discussion since the 1970s on the speech patterns of women and their relation to women's status within society, following work by the American linguist Robin Lakoff (1975).

Extract B8.1 is a report of a research project carried out in Australia in the late 1970s which relates the changes in grammatical structures used by adolescent boys and girls to their perceptions of prestige varieties of the language, generally the standard language, and varieties with 'covert prestige' a term coined by Trudgill (1972) to indicate non-standard vernacular uses which have prestige in certain communities.

**Task B8.1.1**

As you read Text B8.1, carry out the following activities:

➤ Make a note of the findings discussed by Eisikovits in relation to age and gender.

➤ Decide whether these findings support the previous research reported in the Discussion section in Text B8.1.

Text B8.1
E. Eisikovits

**Edina Eisikovits (1998) 'Girl-talk/boy-talk: sex differences in adolescent speech', in Coates, J. (ed.) *Language and Gender: A Reader*, Oxford: Blackwell.**

## Methodology

The data for this study consist of more than fifty hours of tape-recorded conversation. The sample of informants was made up of twenty males and twenty females, equally divided into two age groups, a younger group . . . average age thirteen years eleven months and an older group . . . average age sixteen years one month. All were Australian-born of Australian-born parents and were long-term residents of inner-Sydney working class suburbs . . . Their parents had occupations relatively low in social status; for example, cleaner, canteen assistant, truck driver. The informants were interviewed in pairs with the view of obtaining as broad a picture of their natural language as is possible within the limitations of a tape-recorded situation. In addition, those of the younger group . . . still at school two years later were interviewed a second time, . . . thereby providing a small developmental group against which changes over apparent time could be compared.

In all, twelve grammatical variables were examined in the larger study of Inner-Sydney English (ISE) from which these data were drawn (Eisikovits 1981), but for the purposes of this chapter, three highly stigmatised variables have been isolated for consideration. It should be noted, however, that the patterns evident with respect to these three variables were similarly evident with respect to other grammatical variables examined in the larger study.

The three variables to be considered in detail here are:

1 non-standard past tense forms such as *seen* and *done*, as in:

He woke up and seen something.

2 multiple negation; for example,

They don't say nothing.

3 invariable *don't*; for example,

Mum don't have to do nothing.

The occurrence of these forms is quantified using the paradigmatic Labovian model, that is:

$$\% \text{ frequency} = \frac{\text{number of occurrences of non-standard form}}{\text{total number of potential occurrences} \ldots}$$

[The results have been omitted. They showed that overall the differences between girls' and boys' use of nonstandard forms diverges over time.]

E. Eisikovits

## Discussion

The existence of such different patterns of usage of non-standard forms among the two sex groups poses an obvious problem: why should an increase in age bring about such different patterns of usage among male and female speakers? Why is it only the girls who decline in their use of such forms as they grow older whereas, if anything, the boys increase their usage of such forms? If such forms are seen simply as developmental features we would expect a consistent decline with age among both groups. Clearly, at least two separate but intersecting factors are involved here: one developmental and the other relating to sex differences. Studies of sex variation in phonology in the past (Labov 1966, Shuy, Wolfram, and Riley 1966, Trudgill 1972) have tended to suggest that women regularly use more socially prestigious speech than men. Such sensitivity among female speakers is particularly evident in lower middle class and upper working class speech (compare Wolfram 1969).

In addition, women have been shown to evidence greater stylistic variation than men. Studies by Wolfram (1969), Labov (1972), and Trudgill (1972), have shown that lower middle class women – especially younger females in the process of social mobility – are likely to evidence particular sensitivity to prestige norms in more formal speech situations.

Such sensitivity to social and stylistic variation is acquired by the child in various stages. Labov (1964, 81) presents a tentative model of language acquisition which incorporates the child's growing awareness of and control over variation in language. He specifies six levels of development; (i) the basic grammar, (ii) the vernacular, (iii) social perception, (iv) stylistic variation, (v) the consistent standard and finally, (vi) the acquisition of the full range. These stages are not entirely separate entities but are markers along a continuum of change. From Labov's model we would expect the informants in this study to be at stages (iii) and (iv); that is, initially at the stage of perceiving the social significance of speech and then gradually learning to modify their own speech in line with these perceptions. Such a view would account for the particularly high frequency of non-standard forms among the younger female group as well as for the decrease with age apparent in the use of such forms by the female informants. However, if this model is used to account for the use of non-standard forms here, we would expect a consistent decline with age among both the male and female groups. Hence, we are still left with the problem of accounting for the usage of the male speakers who, unlike their female counterparts, do not appear to modify their speech in the direction of the prestige standard.

One possible explanation for this is that the two groups do not share the same prestige standard; that is, forms perceived positively by one group are not similarly viewed by the other. Smith (1985, 83), citing research evidence from Labov (1966) and Trudgill (1972), suggests that such a difference in prestige norms may be widespread:

> Given the fact that men and women typically occupy quite different social niches, and are often clearly differentiated even in those they share, it would not be surprising to find that the sexes are habituated to different sets of context-dependent speech norms, and that their speech, and their impression of others' speech, reflect these differences.

Certainly, the attitudes and perceptions evidenced by the two sex groups in this study show some striking differences. Although both boys and girls were interviewed at similar points in their lives – the two older groups were at the conclusion of their high school education so that they were all looking outwards to the broader community – their orientations and 'world views' differ significantly.

Among the older girls there is a serious and conservative acceptance of the responsibilities of adulthood. All are concerned with fitting in with society and its expectations rather than, as two years earlier, with the conflicts with it. No longer are they rebellious in their attitudes towards family, school, and society in general. All see themselves as having 'grown up' – a process which for the girls means 'settling down'. This change is aptly summed up by 1E: 'I think I've settled down a lot. It's better not being in trouble anyway.' . . .

That this new conservatism is extended to attitudes to language may be seen in 1E's changed view of swearing. Asked what her fights with her boyfriend are about, she replies:

> Oh, petty things. Like, oh, sometimes he swears at me and I don't like swearing anymore. An he'll swear at me so we have a fight about that.

Even more telling are her later comments:

1E:   We went – I've seen 'One Flew Over the Cuckoo's Nest' – can't even say 'cuckoo' properly. That was a good show. The only thing is they swear a lot in it.
INT:   And that really bothers you?
1E:   Mm. Sometimes, like, sometimes I'll be in the mood for it an other times I'll think, you know, 'I don't wanna say that.' 'Cause when you listen t'other people it sounds terrible, you know . . .
INT:   You don't think about that when you're 13 or 14 doing it yourself.
1E:   No, you don't. When you get older, you think, 'Oh Jesus, what did I ever say that for?'

Among the boys, however, a rather different perception emerges. They, too, see themselves as having grown up, but for them this does not necessarily mean settling down or conforming to family or societal expectations of 'good' behaviour. Instead, it is more usually seen as a movement towards self-assertion, 'toughness' and an unwillingness to be dictated to . . .

Many spoke about on-going conflict with the police, the school, teachers, and to a lesser extent, parents, relating these stories with defiance and bravado. Incidents in which they were able to outwit authority were recounted with pride as evidence of toughness and skill. Never was there any admission of earlier errors as foolishness as there was among the older girls. Indeed, where family conflicts had diminished, this was because of reduced parental controls on the boys' actions rather than any recognition on their parts, as with the girls, of the validity of their parents' viewpoints. Consider, for example, the following dialogue: . . .

INT:   What about homework?
1D:   If I wanna do it, I do it. If I don't Mum don't care.
2D:   They make me sisters an that do their homework.

This extract would suggest that not only are the older boys less conformist than their female counterparts but also that this independence is given tacit support by their parents and the community at large. Unlike the girls, they are encouraged to be independent and tough. Clearly, different behavioural norms as well as different social perceptions exist for the two sexes. Given these differences, it is hardly surprising that the two groups differ in their attitudes to and use of language. We have already seen the growing conservatism of the girls in their attitude to swearing. The boys on the other hand tend to move in a contrary direction: . . .

INT:    You were in trouble for the same thing?
5D:    Yeah, for swearing.
INT:    What did they do to you?
5D:    Oh, they just took me inside an smacked me. That's all.
INT:    What about now?
5D:    If I swear in front of me mother now she don't say nothing.

Such different social and linguistic perceptions may provide an explanation for the two groups' differing usage of non-standard forms here. That is, while the girls are increasingly ready to accept external social norms – a conformity mirrored in their readiness to modify their speech in line with external prestige norms – the boys are not so accepting. Indeed, they are learning to assert themselves, to express their opposition to authority and the middle class establishment – an opposition similarly mirrored in the maintenance/increase in their use of non-standard forms . . .

**Conclusions**

What all this would suggest is that for the girls the norms which they become increasingly aware of are in line with those of external social usage. [. . .] The boys, however, [. . .] appear to use non-standard forms to affirm their own masculinity and toughness and their working class anti-establishment values. . . . What we have then is very strong evidence for age and sex differences in this variety of Australian adolescent speech – differences which reflect different social and linguistic norms held by the two sex groups. The extent to which these norms are held by Australian adolescents in general and not just residents of the inner-city area of Sydney is a question well worthy of future investigation.

**Task B8.1.2**

Having read Text B8.1, carry out the following activities:

➤    'The informants were interviewed in pairs with the view of obtaining as broad a picture of their natural language as is possible within the limitation of a tape-recorded situation'. Consider whether the term 'natural language' captures the type of interaction Eisikovits was recording. Decide what contextual factors you would need to take into account to describe and define more accurately the type of language she was recording.

➤    Eisikovits claims to have strong evidence for age and sex differences in the variety of speech used by this group of Australian adolescents. Consider any other group (e.g. middle-aged, middle-class professionals, university students on the same course, shop workers in your local supermarket) and decide whether there are any obvious differences in the speech of men and women in the group. Consider how you might obtain data to test out your views.

Eisikovits's work supports the view that girls' and women's talk changes and accommodates to the norms of the standard language. However, more recent research stresses that the factors influencing grammatical choices which have been associated with gender are in fact much more complicated:

> Speakers' usage may vary in relation to age or social class or a whole host of other variables, as well as in relation to gender. In terms of explanations, there is now a strong feeling that it is inadvisable to treat 'women' or 'men' as monolithic categories.
>
> (Coates 1998: 10).

An illustration of an investigation of this complexity is found in the second extract in this section, where Stephen Levey looks at the use of the discourse marker *like* in the speech of girls and boys. He relates the higher proportion of uses of *like* in the speech of girls, not to norms of accommodation towards a prestige or standard variety, but to conversational strategies which encourage collaboration in the negotiation of meaning. *Like* is not just a marker of vagueness or inarticulateness, but rather it creates a space for the addressee to fill in and therefore participate more (verbally or non-verbally) in the interaction. He discusses its affective role; that is, the part it plays in expressing the stance of the speaker towards what they are saying.

 **Task B8.2.1**

As you read Text B8.2, carry out the following activities:

➤ Make a list of the functions identified by Levey for the discourse marker *like*.

➤ Discover what arguments Levey uses to account for the greater use of the discourse marker *like* by girls than by boys.

**Text B8.2**
**S. Levey**

**Stephen Levey (2003) 'He's like "Do it now!" and I'm like "No!", some innovative quotative usage among young people in London', *English Today*, vol. 73, no. 19 (1): 24–32.**

**Variation in the children's use of *like***

Previous studies have highlighted a significant correlation between age and frequency of usage of discourse *like*. Although scholars who have investigated the discourse functions of *like* generally concede that it occurs more often in the speech of young

S. Levey

people than that of older people, little has been said about its use in the speech of pre-adolescents . . .

The examples below (taken from a corpus of recordings of 500 10-to-11-year-old pupils in a London school situated in a working-class area) show that *like* is used to bracket units of talk in spontaneous discourse (see Schiffrin 1987:31) and is positionally mobile as shown by its appearance before or within different constituents in an utterance:

1   Before a noun phrase
    they had to jump *like* a metre away from the actual acid

2   Before an adjective
    he was *like* nice to all the rest

3   Before an adverb
    girls act like they're *like* really pretty <u>and all that</u>

4   Before a prepositional phrase
    . . . and I was *like* under water for a few seconds

5   Preceding reported speech
    when my brother yells, he's *like* 'Do it now!' like that and I'm *like*, 'No!'

6   Before a main clause
    *like* he starts putting all them three in really hard matches

7   Before a subordinate clause
    cos *like* if he misses a shot, he starts punching people

8   At the end of a clause
    . . . and when they're children *like*, their children act as if they're the parents

. . . In example 1 above, *like* appears to convey the meaning 'approximately' and retains traces of the established grammatical use of *like* in phrases such as 'its more like five miles away'. . .

The preferred syntactic slot for *like* in the speech of the 10/11-year-old children I recorded is before or within a noun phrase. This seems unsurprising in view of the fact that previous studies claim that the long-established prepositional use of *like* is the starting point for its subsequent development as a discourse marker . . .

Another important reason why *like* commonly appears before a noun in my data is that it serves to highlight the introduction of new entities into discourse (Dailey-O'Cain 2000: 61–62) as in the example below:

9   they put *like* this bandage stuff round it

In examples such as the one above, Miller and Weinert (1995:365) claim that *like* functions as a non-contrastive focusing device . . . In the vast majority of the children's data *like* focuses on constituents which occur to the right of it including not only phrasal constituents, but also whole clauses and, arguably, entire discourse topics . . .

Because discourse *like* more generally functions as a marker of non-equivalence, nonliteralness, or 'looseness', in the sense that it indicates a discrepancy between the speaker's actual utterance and what the speaker has in mind (see Andersen 1997:41), it is not hard to see why it has developed a non-verbatim quotative function. There is clearly an association between a marker of non-literalness and quotation given that reported utterances following quotatives are rarely literal or verbatim reports of speech but are more generally the quoting speaker's constructed interpretations of what was said or thought (see Tannen 1989). Thus, in example 5 above, the girl's use of quotative *like* enables her to exemplify a stereotypical response from her brother . . .

Furthermore, it is also significant that, in example 5 above, quotative *like* is used to give discourse prominence to an utterance expressed with strong emotion and token mimicry (i.e., by adopting the pitch, tempo and voice quality of the reported speaker) . . . The girl uses exaggerated prosody to stylize and caricature her brother's aggression, and implicitly conveys her current attitude towards what she perceives as negative behaviour on the part of her brother.

From the discussion above, it should be apparent that *like* has developed a variety of pragmatic uses which are not simply associated with pause-filling. . . .

## *Like* as an index of conversational involvement

Previous studies of discourse variables have shown that their occurrence is constrained by differences in contextual style. For example, Holmes (1986:15) notes that the discourse marker *you know* appears most frequently in sections of relatively sustained narratives or accounts of speakers' personal experiences which are intended to entertain or maintain the interest of the addressee. Similarly, it seems plausible to argue that the frequency of discourse *like* in the children's narratives is due in no small part to its addressee-oriented uses for creating involvement in conversation.

A closer look at the pragmatics of *like*, particularly from the perspective of its role in interpersonal dynamics, suggests that it may be exploited in discourse to build conversational solidarity and negotiate inter-speaker common ground, Discourse *like* not only appeals to hearers to interpret an utterance as a less than literal rendering of the thoughts of the speaker; it also invites the collaboration of the hearer in the negotiation of meaning. By pragmatically signalling the subjectivity of the speaker's utterance, *like* requires the addressee to actively participate in determining the range of implications or scope of interpretation of the non-literal proposition framed by *like*. The speaker assumes the hearer will be able to supply, 'whatever unstated understandings are required to make recognizable sense of the speaker's talk' (Garfinkel 1967:3). Lack of explicitness in informal discourse therefore accomplishes social goals: being understood without explicitly stating what one means contributes to sense of involvement through mutual participation in sense-making (Tannen 1989:23). The maintenance of a social rapport between conversational participants and the establishment of a shared perspective probably takes precedence over the exchange of information in informal discourse (see Coates 1987:126).

The interactive and affective characteristics of *like* provide some insight into why this discourse particle is perceived to be so frequent in the speech of young people. Previous research on the interactional style of young people has highlighted its emotional and implicit nature. Nordberg (1984:20) claims that young people's conversations characteristically express views, values and feelings more frequently than adult conversations. Affective styles of speech make greater use of communicative devices such as *like* which enable speakers to express their emotional and subjective involvement in what they are saying . . .

As far as patterns of sex differentiation are concerned . . . the girls in my study use discourse *like* more frequently than the boys: in the computerised corpus, the girls use discourse *like* with a frequency of 10 occurrences per 1000 words in their personal narratives, whereas the boys use it with a frequency of 7 per 1000. One possible explanation for this difference is that the girls make greater use of *like* to seek interactional alignments which may help to establish a sense of rapport between speaker and addressee. I have already outlined how, from a pragmatic point of view, discourse *like* depends on the collaboration of the addressee to infer the range of meaning implicated by the proposition in its scope. The inferences which the speaker is required to make in order to comprehend the speaker's unstated meanings presupposes similarity of interlocutors' experience and knowledge. Wouk (1998:403–4) points out that the use of a marker which presupposes conjoint knowledge has the effect of increasing the sense of solidarity between discourse participants since solidarity is created by appealing to the commonality between co-participants in conversation.

The girls' use of *like* for affective and solidarity-building purposes is compatible with a body of linguistic evidence indicating that in Western cultures women employ a co-operative conversational style more than men, and appear to place greater emphasis on affective involvement in conversational interaction than males (see e.g. Holmes 1990:260–1). This is not to say, however, that a solidary and supportive interactional style is an inherent characteristic of female speech, as research from a variety of non-Western cultures shows that an involved conversational style is encountered in both male and female speech (see Britain 1998:48). The connection between interactional styles and linguistic practices obviously needs to be considered in relation to the cultural and social background in which it is embedded.

Research on pre-adolescent social behaviour in western societies has noted girls' and boys' conscious engagement in gender differentiation in the school environment, with boys becoming more obsessed with competitive physical games and girls showing greater involvement in social engineering (see Eckert 1997). Furthermore, the movement towards an increasingly peer-dominated social order prior to the onset of adolescence encourages extensive interaction in single-sex peer groups, which probably offers a crucial context for gender differentiation in speech and the crystallization of distinct styles of speaking (see Romaine 1999:196). The behaviour of the girls I recorded is consistent with that observed by Eckert (1997) in her study, with girls placing greater importance on negotiating alliances and cohesiveness than the boys.

From a linguistic perspective, one important concomitant of the girls' apparent greater emphasis on sustaining social cohesion in their peer group is the affective value they attach to speech. It is striking, for example, in the results I have obtained so far, that the girls in my study tend to make proportionally greater use than the boys not only of discourse *like* but also of phrase-terminal tags (see example 3 above) and reported speech in their narratives of personal experience. Phrase-terminal tags and reported dialogue (see Overstreet 1999 and Tannen 1989) have also been found to contribute to the creation of involvement in informal discourse, which suggests that these features co-occur because they are employed to achieve specific interactional effects. Similar findings are reported in other studies of the conversational behaviour of adolescents. Cheshire and Williams' (2002) research on the strategies used by adolescents to introduce new information in discourse has highlighted the use of addressee-oriented forms to mark noun phrases as requiring the involvement of the hearer in identifying referents through the use of discourse markers such as *like* and phrase-terminal tags such as *and stuff*. It is significant that in their examination of a number of syntactic features in speech, Cheshire and Williams (2002) generally found that girls adopted a more affective orientation than boys in their conversational interactions.

 **Task B8.2.2**

Having read Text B8.2, carry out the following activities:

➤ The discourse marker *like* 'invites the collaboration of the hearer in the negotiation of meaning . . . Without explicitly stating what one means contributes to [a] sense of involvement through mutual participation in sense-making'. Consider whether, in your experience the use of so-called 'vague language' such as *like*, *you know* and *and stuff* always contributes to your sense of involvement in a conversation, and whether such language devices could also be used to make people feel an outsider.

➤ Levey is careful to situate his findings within a Western cultural context. If you are familiar with another language and culture, examine any grammatical characteristics of that language that may be specifically or more commonly associated with the speech of women than that of men. Try to give an explanation for this.

We can see from both these extracts that how an individual varies their speech is influenced by a variety of factors, and also that by making choices an individual is aligning themselves with others in a group. Here, grammatical choices have been examined as constructing roles associated with the female gender. In the next unit we go on to look at an additional influence on grammatical variation, social class.

**Summary**

In this unit we have looked at:

Contexts

■ Gender and age (e.g. conformity and non-conformity to standard language norms; boosting of conversational involvement).

Linguistic features/grammatical structures

■ Non-standard past tense forms
■ Multiple negation
■ Invariable *don't* (e.g. *Mum don't have to do nothing*)
■ *Like* as a discourse marker.

# Unit B9
# Grammar and social class

*Social Class.*
*p 191.*

In Un[...]ons that could be linked
to gen[...]that it was very difficult
to isol[...]r such variation. Other
attem[...]lating them to grammar
choice[...]rch that has focused on
social

The fi[...]ernstein, an educational
sociol[...])s. The paper from which
this e[...]d shows how Bernstein
was b[...]iguage in society and in
educa[...]l to as *public language*, a
langu[...]groups in society, including a[...]his language gave rise to
thinking which is not favoured in educational contexts and so entrenches social
disadvantage. The extract starts with a list of characteristics of public language based
on his observations of adolescents from working-class areas of London.

## Task B9.1.1

As you read Text B9.1, carry out the following activities:

➤ Try to think of reasons for any of the characteristics of a public language listed
by Bernstein other than their association with lower-socioeconomic groups.

➤ Bernstein was not an applied linguist and moreover was writing over forty years
ago. His terminology was therefore different from that with which you may be
familiar. Consider what Bernstein is implying by the term 'formal' language,
and find terms used to describe 'public' and 'formal' language at the present
time.

➤ Drawing on your own experience, consider whether language variety has a
strong influence on educational success. Do you consider that people have a
choice over the variety of language that they use?

**Basil Bernstein (1971)** *Class, Codes and Control*, **vol. 1,** *Theoretical Studies Towards a Sociology of Language*, **London, Routledge & Kegan Paul.**

### A public language: some sociological implications of a linguistic form

Characteristics of a *public* language are:

(1) Short, grammatically simple, often unfinished sentences, a poor syntactical construction with a verbal form stressing the active mood.

(2) Simple and repetitive use of conjunctions (so, then, and, because).

(3) Frequent use of short commands and questions.

(4) Rigid and limited use of adjectives and adverbs.

(5) Infrequent use of impersonal pronouns as subjects (one, it).

(6) Statements formulated as implicit questions which set up a sympathetic circularity, e.g. 'Just fancy?' 'it's only natural, isn't it?' 'I wouldn't have believed it'.

(7) A statement of fact is often used as both a reason and a conclusion, or more accurately, the reason and conclusion are confounded to produce a categoric statement, e.g. 'Do as I tell you' 'Hold on tight' 'You're not going out' 'Lay off that'.

(8) Individual selection from a group of idiomatic phrases will frequently be found.

(9) Symbolism is of a low order of generality.

(10) The individual qualification is implicit in the sentence structure, therefore it is a language of implicit meaning. *It is believed that this fact determines the form of the language.*

These characteristics interact cumulatively and developmentally reinforce each other, and so the effect of any one depends on the presence of the others. The use of a public language is most probably a function of a particular social structure, although psychological and physiological factors will in any given case modify the usage. This language-use is not necessarily the result of a limited vocabulary but arises out of a sensitivity to a way of organizing and responding to experience. Thus two children of four, one of whom comes from an unskilled or semi-skilled home and the other from a middle-class home, might share a similar vocabulary, but the way they relate the words they know will show differences. Further, an individual may have at his disposal two linguistic usages, a *public language* and a *formal* language, or he may be limited to one, a *public* language, depending upon his social group.

Language is considered one of the most important means of initiating, synthesizing, and *reinforcing* ways of thinking, feeling and behaviour which are functionally related to the social group. It does not, of itself, prevent the expression of specific ideas or confine the individual to a given level of conceptualization, but certain ideas and generalizations are facilitated rather than others. That is the language-use facilitates development in a particular direction rather than inhibiting all other possible directions. A *public language* does not imply a common vocabulary. . . . The term *public language* refers to a common linguistic mode which various forms of communication, dialects, etc., share. I shall examine the behavioural implications of individuals who are *limited* to a *public* language.

The first four characteristics will be considered. The short, grammatically simple, syntactically poor sentence which is the typical unit of a public language does not facilitate the communication of ideas and relationships which require a precise formulation. The crude, simple verbal structure around which the sentence is built points to a possible difficulty inherent in the language-use in the expressing of processes. There may be two important implications of this handicap. An approximate verb of a lower logical order may be used to characterize a given process, whilst the verbal construction may fix the process in an inappropriate time as the result of the insensitivity to tense. This form of language-use is continuously reinforced from the very beginnings of speech, and as the individual learns no other possibility, subjectively, there is little or no experience of inadequate characterization. In fact when a more appropriate formulation is pointed out to the user of a *public* language the latter may insist that this is precisely *what he meant*. In a sense this is true, for what the individual wished to characterize, he did. The reformulation represents a second order characterization (that of a *formal* language), which is alien to the original speaker who will attempt to reduce the second order to the first. When this cannot be done the second order will be considered unnecessary, irrelevant, perhaps silly or the hearer will be bewildered. It may be that the percentage of nouns to verbs is higher in the *public* language than in a *formal* language, quite apart from the fact that a *public* language has a very limiting vocabulary. If this is so, then a *public* language tends to emphasize *things* rather than *processes*.

Because of a simple sentence construction, and the fact that a *public* language does not permit the use of conjunctions which serve as important logical distributors of meaning and sequence, a *public* language will be one in which logical modification and stress can be only crudely rendered linguistically. This necessarily affects the length and type of the completed thought. Of equal importance, the reliance on a small group of conjunctions (*and, so, then, because*) often means that a wrong conjunction is used or an approximate term is constantly substituted for a more exact logical distinction. The approximate term will then become the equivalent of the appropriate logical distinction. As there is a limited and rigid use of adjectives and adverbs, individual qualifications of objects (nouns) and individual modifications of processes (adverbs) will be severely reduced. . . .

The fifth characteristic indicated that there would be infrequent use of impersonal pronouns as subjects of sentences. I am thinking here of the pronoun 'one'. The use of the pronoun 'one' as subject implies the objectification of the experience which is verbalized. The subject is made general and so freed from the confines of a personal experience. 'One' also indicates an attitude to the relationships which confront the individual. In a special sense it involves a reaching beyond the immediate experience, a transcending of the personal, and brings the individual into a particular relationship with objects and persons. Impersonality becomes an important aspect of the possibilities flowing from the language. However with a *public* language it is much more probable that the pronouns 'we' or 'you' will serve an apparently similar function to 'one'. They are in fact not similar, nor are they a simple substitution; for 'we' or 'you' refer to the local experience, the local social relationships, the immediate normative arrangements, and are bounded by the personal. The social and logical frames of reference are different, being insular and restricted. The possibilities inherent in 'one' are absent; possibilities which are of both social and logical importance.

The sixth characteristic [a24] referred to statements which set up a sympathetic circularity, which may be initiated in several ways, but the dialogue always takes the form of a repetition of a thought by the conversants which maximizes the affective element of the relationship and at the same time restricts the ambit and the order of the discussion.

The seventh characteristic of a *public* language refers to the frequency with which a statement of fact is used both as a reason and a conclusion; more accurately, the reason is confounded with the conclusion to produce a categoric statement . . .

Characteristics eight and nine follow naturally from the [tendency of a *public* language to enhance the solidarity of the social relationship]. A *public* language is one which contains a large number of idiomatic, traditional phrases from which the individual chooses. Instead of an individual learning to create a language-use within which he can select to mediate his individual feeling, a *public* language-user tends to attach his feelings to social counters or tags which maximize the solidarity of the social relationship at the cost of the logical structure of the communication, and the specificity of the feeling. For traditional phrases, idioms, etc., tend to operate on a low causal level of generality in which descriptive, concrete, visual, tactile symbols are employed, aimed at maximizing the emotive rather than the logical impact.

Finally, the tenth and most important characteristic may be regarded as the determinant of the previous nine. In a *public* language the individual qualification creates a language of implicit meaning. The individual qualification will be made primarily through expressive symbolism or through a selection from the possibilities inherent in a *public* language, which is tantamount to saying that it rarely occurs at all via the language; for the *public* language is primarily a means of making *social* not *individual* qualifications. If some of the characteristics are examined – short, grammatically simple, syntactically poor sentence construction; inappropriate verbal forms; simple and repetitive use of conjunctions; rigid and limited use of adjectives and adverbs; selection from a group of traditional phrases – the very means of communication do not permit, and even discourage, individually differentiated cognitive and affective responses. *This is not to say that speakers of this language interact in a completely uniform manner, for the potential of a public language allows a vast range of possibilities*, but it provides a language-use which discourages the speaker from verbalizing his discrete relationships with the environment. The individual qualification is realized through a means which offers an immediacy of communication; that is, by expressive symbolism, together with a linguistic form which orients the speaker to a relatively low causal order, to descriptive concepts rather than analytic ones. The result of this mediating process orients the speaker to a distinct relationship with objects in the environment and so to a different *order* of learning from that which accompanies a formal language. With a *formal* language meaning is logically explicit and finely differentiated, whilst with a *public* language meaning is implicit and crudely differentiated. By the term 'differentiated' reference is made not simply to the range of objects which are elaborated or significant but to the logical order of the elaboration or significance. That is, to the matrix of relationships which arouse and condition responses.

In fact when an individual learns a *public* language he *learns* to perceive the possibilities symbolized by language in a distinctive way. Language is perceived *not* as a set of possibilities which can be fashioned subtly and sensitively to facilitate the development of a unique, individual experience. Language is *not* a means to verbalize relatively precisely the experience of separateness and difference. Rather, with a *public* language the individual from an early age interacts with a linguistic form which maximizes the means of producing social rather than individual symbols, and the vehicle of communication powerfully reinforces the initial socially induced preference for this aspect of language-use. It is language-use which encourages an immediacy of interaction, a preference for the descriptive rather than the analytic, a linguistic form such that what is not said is equally and often more important than what is said. A critical difference between the two speech forms is that whereas in a *formal* language subjective intent may be verbally elaborated and made explicit, this process is not facilitated in a *public* language.

As the structure of a public language reinforces a strong inclusive relationship, the individual will exhibit through a range of activities a powerful sense of allegiance and loyalty to the group, its forms and its aspirations, at the cost of exclusion and perhaps conflict with other social groups which possess a different linguistic form which symbolizes *their* social arrangements. The structure of a *public* language inhibits the verbal expression of those experiences of difference which would isolate the individual from his group and channels cognitive and affective states which might be a potential threat . . .

It is necessary to state at this point that the type of *public* language described and analysed here will rarely be found in the *pure* state. Even if such an 'ideal' language-use were to be spoken it would not be used in all situations within the local group. Modifications *within* the form would occur, most certainly, depending upon whether the situation is defined as social or personal. It is suggested that what is found empirically is an orientation to this form of language-use which is conditioned by socially induced preferences.

**Task B9.1.2**

Having read Text B9.1, carry out the following activities:

➤ We are not given any indication in Text B9.1 as to how Bernstein compiled his ten characteristics of public language. Try to discover similarities between any of these listed characteristics and grammatical features associated with contexts discussed earlier in this book.

➤ In Text B6.1 you examined child language development in relation to cognitive development. Consider how Bernstein's view that a public language 'orients the speaker to a distinct relationship with objects in the environment and so to a different *order* of learning from that which accompanies a formal language' relates to the views on language as a resource for making meaning expressed by Halliday and Painter.

In a later (1971) comment on his earlier work, Bernstein identified shortcomings in this study. For example, he described the list given at the beginning of the extract above as 'a rag-bag, possessing no linguistic respectability' (1971: 2)! He also acknowledged the role of contextual features, in addition to social class, in influencing the patterning of grammatical and lexical choices. The lack of acknowledgement of these additional factors at the time led to much criticism of Bernstein's work after it was published. His studies were taken by some to suggest that linguistic codes such as 'public language' were deficient. His views were extrapolated to suggest that working-class speech indicated an inability to think at higher levels. The significance of this paper, though, lay in Bernstein's insights into the way in which the socialisation of the individual within the group through 'public language' led to disadvantage in the educational system. More recently, his insights into the link between ways of communicating and ways of understanding have been seen as far-sighted and are particularly influential in theorising in systemic functional linguistics.

At a more specific level, his identification of certain grammatical characteristics of 'public language' has led to a number of studies which have helped to refine the link between class and language. Text B9.2 is from a report by Ronald Macaulay which focuses on Bernstein's fourth characteristic – rigid and limited use of adjectives and adverbs – and systematically compares adverb use in middle- and working-class speakers from two studies conducted in the Scottish cities of Ayr and Glasgow.

 **Task B9.2.1**

As you read Text B9.2, carry out the following activities:

➤ For the five types of adverb identified by Macaulay in Table 1, write down an example to illustrate each type and note which group of people in the studies reported use it most and least frequently.

➤ Draw a table like the one below to indicate the frequency of adjective use per thousand words in the different groups. Decide whether the findings with regard to adjectives show similarities or differences to those on adverbs and whether this is what you would expect.

|  | Ayr | | Glasgow | |
|---|---|---|---|---|
|  | *Middle-class speakers* | *Working-class speakers* | *Middle-class speakers* | *Working-class speakers* |
| **Adults** |  |  |  |  |
| **Adolescents** |  |  |  |  |

Text B9.2
R. Macaulay

**Ronald Macaulay (2002) 'Extremely interesting, very interesting, or only quite interesting? Adverbs and social class', *Journal of Sociolinguistics* vol. 6, no. 3: 398–417.**

## The Data

### 1. *Adverbs in -ly*

*Adults*

Table B9.1 gives the frequency of adverbs in *-ly* for the Ayr sample, from Macaulay (1995: 44), and for the Glasgow adult sample. It can be seen that while there are minor differences, the general pattern is remarkably similar in both, with the middle-class speakers using derived adverbs in *-ly* more than twice as frequently as the working-class speakers . . .

*Table B9.1* Relative frequency of derivative adverbs in *-ly* in Ayr and Glasgow

|  | Ayr | | | | Glasgow | | | |
|---|---|---|---|---|---|---|---|---|
|  | Lower-class | | Middle-class | | Working-class | | Middle-class | |
|  | # | Freq. | # | Freq. | # | Freq. | # | Freq. |
| Manner | 28 | 0.40 | 82 | 1.61 | 11 | 0.22 | 32 | 0.93 |
| Time/Freq. | 41 | 0.58 | 70 | 1.38 | 19 | 0.38 | 33 | 0.96 |
| Degree | 47 | 0.67 | 121 | 2.38 | 35 | 0.69 | 42 | 1.22 |
| Sentence | 76 | 1.08 | 174 | 3.42 | 92 | 1.82 | 197 | 5.74 |
| *really* | 55 | 0.79 | 106 | 2.08 | 93 | 1.85 | 104 | 3.03 |
| Totals | 247 | 3.52 | 553 | 10.87 | 250 | 4.97 | 408 | 11.89 |

Freq. = per 1,000 words

Figure B9.1 shows that for the Glasgow adults the individual frequencies reflect the general pattern with two outliers, one middle-class woman with a frequency of 6.5 and one working-class woman with a frequency of 12.2. Figure B9.1 also shows that it is the middle-class men who are the most frequent users of these adverbs . . .

Macaulay (1995) also examined the use of adjectives by the two groups of speakers in Ayr and found that the middle-class speakers used adjectives with a frequency of 22.41 per thousand in contrast to the lower-class speakers with a frequency of 11.74. The figures for the Glasgow sample show the middle-class speakers with a frequency of 34.16 and the working-class speakers with a frequency of 24.74. Once again, the pattern is repeated, though the distance between the groups is less in Glasgow.

*Adolescents*

What about the adolescents in Glasgow? The overall frequency of derivative adverbs in *-ly* for the Glasgow adolescents is given in Table B9.2. Although the overall frequency

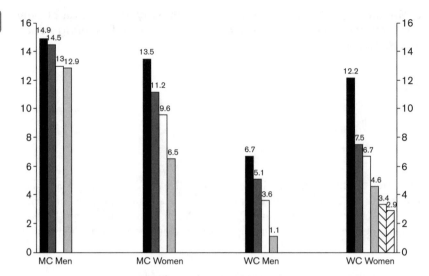

*Figure B9.1* Frequency of use of adverbs in *-ly* by 18 Glasgow adults (freq. = per 1,000 words)

of use is lower than in the adult sessions the pattern of social class differences is similar and the difference is still substantial. The individual figures are shown in Figure B9.2. Here the outliers are two middle-class boys who use very few adverbs in *-ly* and one working-class boy who uses these adverbs with a frequency of 8.2. It is the other two middle-class boys that use these adverbs most frequently, like the middle-class men.

*Table B9.2* Frequency of adverbs in *-ly* in Glasgow adolescent conversations, by gender and social class

|  | N | Freq. |
|---|---|---|
| Middle-class girls | 84 | 8.1 |
| Middle-class boys | 101 | 8.8 |
| Working-class girls | 50 | 3.7 |
| Working-class boys | 29 | 3.9 |
| MC adolescents | 185 | 8.4 |
| WC adolescents | 79 | 3.9 |

Freq. = per 1,000 words
[NB: No data on adolescents in Ayr was collected.]

Given the overall higher frequency with which these adverbs are used in the middle-class sessions, it is not surprising that the variety of adverbs is greater. In the middle-class adult conversations there are 74 different adverbs in *-ly* used; in the working-class conversations, 37 different adverbs are used. Of the total, 22 adverbs are used by both groups, the most frequent being *really* (MC 3.03/WC 1.85) and *actually* (MC 2.8/WC 0.74). In the case of the adolescents, the middle-class speakers use 32 different adverbs in *-ly*, and the working-class 21, with 15 used by both. As with the adults, the most frequent are *really* (MC 3.14/WC 0.85) and *actually* (MC 0.73/WC 0.57). However, the list of adverbs unique to either social class group does not suggest that the source of the

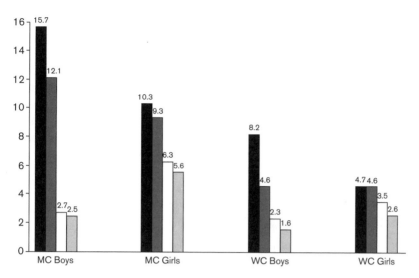

*Figure B9.2* Frequency of use of adverbs in *-ly* by 16 Glasgow adolescents (freq. = per 1,000 words)

difference lies in education. It is unlikely that educational differences account for the failure of working-class speakers to use adverbs such as *badly, clearly, fairly, happily,* etc. or their use of such adverbs as *automatically, basically, entirely,* and *literally* that do not occur in the middle-class conversations . . .

As regards the use of adjectives, the social class difference found among the adults is repeated in the adolescent conversations. The middle-class adolescents use adjectives with a frequency of 29.79 per thousand words and for the working-class adolescents the frequency is 21.86. The social class differences that were found in the Ayr interviews have thus been repeated in the Glasgow conversations, among both adults and adolescents . . .

What evidence is there in the transcripts to support the hypothesis that the middle-class speakers use adverbs in *-ly*: (1) to be more explicit; (2) to express intensity; or (3) to signal the speaker's evaluation? The Oxford English Dictionary gives as its definition for the word *explicit* in relation to knowledge: '[d]eveloped in detail: hence, clear, definite.' In the Glasgow middle-class conversations there are examples of derived adverbs that might come under this heading, as in the examples in 1:

1.  a.  they're *slightly* different but they're *exactly* the same colour (10R)

    b.  and it's *immediately* at the roadside (16L)

    c.  it just goes downhill *slowly* (16L)

    d.  a wee bit ambiguous here and there but *generally* okay (11L)

In the examples in 1 the speakers appear to be trying to make the point clearly. There are, however, similar examples in the working-class sessions, as shown in 2:

2. a.  you would just go along until you get to *roughly* the first street (15L)

b.  there's *really* nothing to see in it but it's *really* quiet (18L)

   c.  two *completely* different people (13R)

   d.  he's aboot – he's *nearly* as tall as – taller than John must be aboot six two – six four or something (14R)

There are not many examples in either set of conversations and if this is what Bernstein meant by explicitness, then it does not appear to explain the social class difference in the frequency of derived adverbs. I will return to the significance of details later.

   As regards intensity, the examples in 3 are taken from the middle-class interviews in Ayr (Macaulay 1991: 125):

3.   a.  I found it *extraordinarily* boring (IM)

   b.  I got *absolutely* sick of doing nothing (IM)

   c.  but this zombie of a mother – *completely apathetic* (WG)

   d.  a *terribly* crippled bent old woman (DN)

These examples support Labov's (1984) view of these adverbs as expressing intensity. There are 25 clear examples in the Ayr middle-class interviews but only three in the working-class interviews. Similar examples can be found in the Glasgow middle-class conversations:

4.   a.  and she was apparently *absolutely* horrendous (10L)

   b.  who's got *absolutely* no sense of golfing etiquette (11L)

   c.  whereas the lady describing it thought it was *absolutely* perfect (11L)

   d.  you're either running around going d– *absolutely* scatty chasing your tail or (10R)

However, there are similar examples in the working-class sessions, though fewer, and most of the examples come from one man (18L):

5.   a.  I was there it was – oh it was *absolutely* brilliant (18L)

   b.  oh I mean it's amazing it's *absolutely* fantastic (18L)

   c.  it seemed to me to be a *perfectly* good place (18L)

   d.  everything's all just draining doon like that you know just *completely totally* unwinding (13R)

So, there is some support for the view that the use of derived adverbs to express intensity contributes to the difference in frequency between the two social classes.

   What about Powell's (1992) notion that adverbs are used to express the speaker's evaluation? The most obvious examples are evidentials, as in examples 6a and 6b but more important are examples such as the hedge in 6c and the intensifier in 6d where the personal attitude is clearly stated:

R. Macaulay

6.  a.  but *funnily* enough I gave out (10L)

    b.  *interestingly* enough that one of these programmes on the telly (16R)

    c.  I thought *technically* it was brilliant but – but it was boring (12L)

    d.  San Francisco's actually quite chilly . . . it's – it's *amazingly* chilly (16L)

The examples in 6 are from the middle-class sessions. There are a few in the working-class conversations as well:

7.  a.  *funnily* enough we got that one (13R)

    b.  but hmm *unfortunately* my trade went (18L)

    c.  urban decay I mean you can get right into that *politically* (18R)

    d.  but as I say I *normally* drink whisky (13R)

However, there are few examples in either set of conversations, so the explanation for the difference in frequency is unlikely to lie here. However, some of the adverbs used by the middle-class Glasgow adults suggest an attitude of confidence in making categorical judgments that is less apparent in the working-class conversations: *amazingly, awfully, badly, drastically, enormously, overly, properly* and *terribly*. Even the other adverbs can have this effect when combined with adjectives as in the examples [omitted], the kind of effect Louw (1993) describes as 'semantic prosody.'

8.  L10:  mmhm her mother had me in stitches one day

        when I bumped into them in town

        and I think I'd had a *particularly* bad day with Kim

        and she was telling me all about her Fiona

        and what she was like at Kim's age

        who – and she was *apparently absolutely* horrendous

In 8 the adverbs emphasize the categorical judgments expressed by the adjectives . . . The Glasgow middle-class adults use adjectives with a frequency of 34.16 per thousand words and the working-class adults with a frequency of 24.74. However, the difference is greater when evaluative adjectives (Hunston and Sinclair 2000) are compared. The middle-class adults use evaluative adjectives with a frequency of 12.88 per thousand words and the working-class adults with a frequency of 8.67. Moreover, there is a difference in the kind of evaluative adjectives used. In the working-class conversations 52 percent of the adjectives are simple words of approval or disapproval (e.g. *good, bad, nice*): in the middle-class conversations only 36 percent of the evaluative adjectives are of this kind. The middle-class adults use adjectives such as *horrendous, horrible, hellish, chauvinistic, unattractive, messy, impressive, interesting, tremendous, fantastic, substantial* and *impeccable*, but none of these or similar adjectives is used by the working-class adults.

**Task B9.2.2**

After reading Text B9.2, carry out the following activities:

➤ Macaulay's work indicates that working-class speakers use adverbs less frequently than middle-class speakers, especially those adverbs which indicate intensity and evaluation. Try to find reasons why this should be.

➤ Decide whether the findings for women and girls in both social groups support what you have read about class and gender influences on grammatical forms. Think of alternative or additional reasons for the variations shown in the tables and figures.

➤ Consider how you might collect data to investigate either the influence of gender or the influence of class on grammatical forms, and whether you are able to keep the influences distinct.

We have quoted selectively here to give you an insight into how studies can be conducted which pursue the detail of the relationship between grammatical choice and social class. Macaulay begins by recording and analysing differences and goes on to discuss the discourse styles of the two classes. He notes that middle-class speakers in the study use adverbs (and adjectives) in emphatic statements, making quite clear their opinions and their attitudes. They also soften their statements with hedges of various kinds. On the other hand, he also reports that working-class speakers in the study avoid these strategies and depend upon an accumulation of details to make their points. For example, greater use of quoted dialogue by working-class speakers allows the hearer greater freedom to make their own interpretation rather than have an interpretation imposed on them as in the middle-class speakers' use of evaluative adjective and adverbs. Similarly, in the Glasgow working-class conversations there was a tendency to provide the hearer with a lot of information. This contrasted with middle-class strategies which made clear their attitudes and opinions (*very user-friendly really; it's actually quite nice for swimming*) through the use of adverbs. Clearly then, the notion of working-class language being in any way inferior or deficient in its communicative ability is called into question by a study such as this. However, it strongly supports the view that different social groups employ different discourse strategies which have different grammatical realisations.

**Summary**

In this unit we have looked at:

Contexts

■ Contrasting working class and middle class varieties.

Linguistic features/grammatical structures

- Features of public (working-class) language (e.g. grammatical simplicity, utterances which are often not complete sentences, rigid and limited use of adjectives and adverbs, etc.)
- *-ly* adverbs used in order to be explicit, to express intensity, and to signal evaluation.

# Unit B10
# Grammar in international varieties of English

The geographical locations in which English is used have widened over the centuries influenced by colonisation, trade and the growth of English-language-dominated media. Both the effects on local languages and on the English language itself have been profound. For example, as noted in Unit A8, the use of English by English-speaking traders, colonial officials, plantation owners, missionaries and so on in contacts with local populations led to both new languages and new varieties of English. In the first extract Stephan Gramley and Michael Pätzold explain the conditions that give rise to *pidgins* and *creoles* in these contexts.

**Task B10.1.1**

As you read Text B10.1, carry out the following activities:

➤ Make sure that you are clear about the differences between a pidgin and a creole – their historical development, who speaks them, where and why.

➤ Gramley writes of the continuum from minimal pidgin to true creole. To illustrate this, make a note of the grammatical characteristics of Melanesian Pidgin English and of the more elaborated creolized pidgin Tok Pisin.

Text B10.1
S. Gramley and
K.-M. Pätzold

**Stephan Gramley and Kurt-Michael Pätzold (2004)** *A Survey of Modern English*, **second edition, London, Routledge.**

### Definition of pidgins and creoles

The attempt to explain what pidgin and creole languages are leads in three different directions: the linguistic, the social and the historical.

### *Pidgins*

From the **linguistic point of view** pidgins are second languages; no one has a pidgin as their mother tongue. This is so because pidgins grow out of contact situations in

S. Gramley and
K.-M. Pätzold

which none of the people who need to communicate with each other have an established language in common. (If an already existing language is chosen, possibly in a simplified form, this will be known as a lingua franca; this did not happen in the cases reviewed here.) Motivated by the necessity of communicating, pidgin speakers have made do, by taking the majority of the vocabulary from the most prestigious of the languages involved, the so-called lexifer language, and resorting to grammatical patterns which may be [. . .] a common denominator of sorts . . .

In comparison with the native languages of their speakers, pidgins are less elaborated. This means that they have a smaller vocabulary, a reduced grammar, and a less differentiated phonology. Furthermore, pidgins are used in a much more limited set of circumstances and are stylistically less varied than first languages. In Melanesian Pidgin English (now often called Tok Pisin) or in Hawaiian Pidgin English (Hawaiian PE), for example, this looks as follows.

- Reduced vocabulary leads to extensive use of paraphrase and metaphor, e.g. in Tok Pisin: /skru biləg arm/ 'screw of the arm' is the word for elbow, just as /gras biləg hed/ 'grass of the head' means hair.
- As compared with StE there is a simplified and changed phoneme inventory: often missing are, for example, /ð/ and /θ/, cf. Hawaiian PE /tʰri ijá/ 'three years'. Often mentioned also is the lack of consonant clusters and the resultant sequences of consonant, vowel, consonant, (vowel), as in early Tok Pisin *pelet < plate*.
- Inflections are rare as compared with StE; for example, there is no plural {-S} in Hawaiian PE /tʰri ijá/ 'three years'.
- Syntactic reduction as compared with StE frequently leads to the lack of the copula, of prepositions, of determiners and of conjunctions, e.g. Hawaiian PE: *I think one year me school teacher* 'I think that I was a school teacher for one year'; *Baby name me no like* 'I did not like the baby's name'.

When historically, from the fifteenth century, Europeans ventured out into the (for them) newly discovered lands of Africa and Asia, they met with and had to communicate with peoples [speaking a wide variety of different languages]. To do this they relied largely on pidgins sometimes called trade jargons. The same need for communication with a polyglot population grew with the establishment of plan-atations. Those established in the Caribbean area as well as Brazil and what is now the southern United States relied on the massive importation of slaves from West Africa . . . In all of these places pidgins which drew on English for their lexicon came into existence . . .

The social situation in which these pidgins were spoken was characterized by the very limited needs and circumstances in the trading posts in West Africa. Consequently, it is no wonder that the registers which developed were equally limited: fewer contexts, fewer topics, more limited social relations . . .

Quite a number of pidgins have been able to survive long enough to develop beyond the stage of a trade jargon. This was especially the case in the plantation situ-ation, where pidgins were used not only to facilitate communication between master and servant, which was surely very limited, but also among the various labourers, who seldom shared a common mother tongue. These pidgins gained in stability and entered into a process of linguistic and functional elaboration.

S. Gramley and
K.-M. Pätzold

## Creoles

At the 'end' of this process of elaboration lies the creole, which is a pidgin that has become the first language of its speakers. This means that it may be a mother tongue or a primary language, i.e. the speakers' dominant language. A creole is an enriched, expanded and regularized language; it has the full complexity characteristic of any natural language. This seems to have happened quite rapidly on the plantations of the New World. African slaves who were able to communicate with each other only in a pidgin had children for whom this language was the only or the main medium available. They clearly added to the vocabulary and they gradually established a relative stability of grammatical forms and phonological norms. In West Africa, for example, Pidgin English is the home language of some people in urban areas (and the mother tongue of children in these homes) in urban areas. When it is used so constantly in the routines of daily life, it may be expected to be relatively more greatly expanded. However, pidgin is also widely employed as a market language. Here it may be considerably simpler. Pidgin and creole, in other words, can stand at the two ends of a linguistic continuum which stretches from true elaborated creole to a minimal pidgin/trade jargon. Tok Pisin, the pidgin-creole of New Guinea, is a native language in the towns and is becoming progressively more elaborated. It exists, however, in ever more simplified and pidgin-like forms as one moves into the rural and mountainous areas. It is this continuum and the historical relationship between a pidgin and its creolized form which distinguish a creole from any other natural language. Viewed on its own, as an independent linguistic system, there is nothing about a creole which is essentially different from any other natural language . . .

The grammar of Tok Pisin has re-expanded, as is typical of elaborated and, especially, creolized pidgins:

### Verbs

| | |
|---|---|
| *i* | before predicates (except first and second person singular (example: see next); |
| *-im* | marker of transitive verbs (from English *him*) (*samting i bin katim tripela hap* 'something divided it into three pieces'); |
| *i gat* | existential *there is/are* (*i gat tripela naispela ailan* 'there are three nice islands'); |
| *I stap* | progressive–existential marker: |

> – *trak i stap long rot*  'The truck is on the road'
> – *mi stap we?*  'where am I?'
> – *mi stap gut*  'I am well'
> – *mi dring i stap*  'I am drinking';

| | |
|---|---|
| *pinis* | completive or perfective aspect (after the predicate) (from English *finish*) |
| *bin* | past marker (pre-verbal) (*samting i bin katim* 'something divided it'); |
| *bai(mbai)* | future marker (pre-clausal) *bai mipela i save* 'we will know'; |
| *save* | modal of ability (*mi save rait* 'I can write'); |
| *laik* | immediate future marker (*traik i laik go nau* 'the truck is about to leave'); |
| *laik* | 'want to' *em i laik i go long trak* 'he want to ride on the truck'. |

S. Gramley and
K.-M. Pätzold

## Adjectives

*-pela*    marker of attributive adjectives; only added to monosyllabic ones (*naispela* 'nice');

∅    no adjective marker = adverb (*gut* 'well');

*móa*    comparative marker (*liklik móa* 'smaller', *gutpela móa* 'better');

*long ol*    superlative marker (*liklik long ol* 'smallest').

## Nouns

*ol*    plural maker (*ol sip* 'the ships');

*wanpela*    singular article (*wanpela lain* 'a line').

## Personal pronouns

*Table B10.1* The personal pronouns of Tok Pisin

|  | singular | plural | |
|---|---|---|---|
|  |  | exclusive | inclusive |
| first person | mi | mipela | yumi |
| second person | yu | yúpela |  |
| third person | em | ol |  |

## Conjunctions

| *na* | and | *o* | or |
|---|---|---|---|
| *tasól* | but, if only | *sapós* | if |

## Task B10.1.2

Having read Text B10.1, carry out the following activities:

➤ The evolution of pidgins and creoles has resulted largely from nineteenth-century colonisation. If you have any historical knowledge of your own language, consider whether it has been changed in any ways by the influence of a language belonging to a politically, economically or militarily dominant group, and also whether there was a point in the history of your language where it could have been described as a pidgin or creole.

➤ Gramley and Pätzold discuss the creole continuum where trade jargon and pidgin give rise to more elaborated creoles which are the primary language for their communities. Recent evidence suggests that some creoles have come into existence without a preceding pidgin stage. Consider what linguistic, historical or social factors might account for such a rapid development.

➤ The historical context in which creoles had their origins was trade and colonial expansion. Nowadays, creole speakers – like many other people – are travelling more and may settle in parts of the world where the lexifer or prestigious dominant language in their creole came from. In the United Kingdom, for example, Jamaican creole is commonly spoken in some areas. Think about how this is affecting the dominant language and whether the effects are felt in all contexts or in only a limited number of them. Try to identify any grammatical features that are being adopted from the creole into the dominant language.

➤ In the discussion of creoles and pidgins so far, we have implicitly concentrated on their development in face-to-face situations. Consider what further grammatical elaboration is likely when creoles are used in writing.

A specific example of the way in which Tok Pisin is becoming more elaborated to meet different communicative needs is the emergence of new ways of marking relative clauses. This has been examined by Stephen Levey (2001) in relation to *Wantok*, a newspaper published in Tok Pisin since 1970. He examined a corpus of extracts from the newspaper for the periods 1971–74 and 1990, 1994 and 1998. Over this time there has been a trend towards increasing use of relative clauses (e.g. 10.06/1000 words in 1971 compared to 21.62 in 1998). Not only has the use of relative clauses increased, but explicit syntactic marking of the structures has also emerged, in particular the use of 'husat' and 'we'.

The examples below taken from the *Wantok* corpus illustrate the extremes of [relative clause complexity and marking] in modern written Tok Pisin:

(2) < Wantok 90> M.F. em narapela gutpela straika [0 ol birua i mas lukaut gut]

M.F. is another good striker [(who) the opposing team must watch out for]

(3) < Wantok 94> Ol lain long siti [husat i no gat gaden] i save go long maket bilong baim ol kaukau na kumu.

City dwellers [who do not have a garden] usually go to the market to buy sweet potatoes and vegetables.

In sentence (2) above, the two clauses are juxtaposed with no overt marking and the syntactic relationship between them is inferred. By contrast, in sentence (3), the relative clause is integrated or embedded within the main clause, and the relative pronoun 'husat' ('who') is an overt morphological indication of the relationship between the main clause and the embedded clause. This example represents the highest degree of embedding, where a relative clause modifies a subject and there is no resumptive or copy pronoun in the continuation of the matrix clause following the relative clause (see Bruyn 1995: 151).

(Levey 2001: 256)

This has been associated with the need to ensure that the referent in the head noun phrase is explicitly linked to the elaboration contained in the relative clause and that there is no room for doubt.

Levey associates the increasing use of more elaborated and syntactically explicit relative clauses with a number of trends. The one we have summarised above is the influence of the written newspaper media which require a language that can be both precise and concise. A second influence is that of more innovative uses of language found in urban varieties: 'recently, anglicized urban sociolects have emerged as focal points for the diffusion of certain linguistic innovations. In both the spoken and the written language there is evidence of restructuring in the direction of English' (Levey 2001: 251). Both of these are also associated with the increases in literacy and the use of Tok Pisin in an expanding number of different written registers:

> The results of my investigation suggest that recent developments in relative clause formation strategies in media Tok Pisin are intimately linked with stylistic expansion. The increasing use of 'husat' and 'we' in written Tok Pisin can be considered a consequence of the evolutionary trends which are shaping the language as it expands to meet new stylistic requirements. The availability of two additional strategies for marking relative clauses can be viewed as effective linguistic solutions to the task of manipulating and structuring complex, cohesive written discourse.
>
> (Levey 2001: 265)

Not only has English been highly influential in the development of pidgins and creoles around the world; it has also been subject to local change which over time has led to new standard varieties, sometimes referred to as 'Englishes', as we saw in Unit A8. We now turn to an investigation of changes in relative clauses in one of these Englishes.

Varieties of English are often divided into traditional and new. Traditional varieties are associated with the United Kingdom and countries such as Australia, Canada, and the United States of America, where English replaced indigenous languages and the language of the majority of the population has now been English for many generations. New Englishes are associated mainly with countries which were colonised by the United Kingdom and which subsequently adopted English as one of their major languages. In countries such as Singapore and India, the variety of English that is used now has been influenced by its close association over many years with speakers of other languages. All these varieties are continuing to evolve, and this is demonstrated by Mark Newbrook in a study of the changes taking place within relative clauses. Text B10.2 is an edited list of the changes that have been observed in relative clauses in English around the world. Newbrook draws mostly on examples from research in Australia, Singapore and Hong Kong.

 **Task B10.2.1**

➤ As you read Text B10.2, consider the features of relative clauses listed by Newbrook. Recall whether you have come across any of these. If you have, do you associate them with any particular varieties of English, or contexts of use?

Text B10.2
M. Newbrook

**Mark Newbrook (1998) 'Which way? That way? Variation and ongoing changes in the English relative clause', *World Englishes*, vol. 17, no. 1: 53–59.**

### Features of variation

(a) Omission of subject relative pronouns

1. This is the student did it. (*who/that*)

(b) Use of 'redundant' subject relative pronouns in non-finite 'reduced relative' clauses

2. This is the student who admitted last year.

(c) Omission of prepositions with relative pronouns as prepositional completives

3. That was the accident which/that she was hurt.

4. There are some words which/that there are no equivalents. (for *for which . . .*, *which/that . . . for*)

5. That was the accident she was hurt.

(d) Use of 'where' or 'whereby'

6. This is an environment whereby the emphasis is on survival.

7. This is a basis where we can go on.

(e) Avoidance of 'that' with human antecedents

Forms such as 8 and 9 are often seen as 'wrong' by Singaporeans.

8. This is the person that I saw there.

9. There were several students that handed work in late.

This is a somewhat unusual 'Singaporeanism,' as it involves the avoidance of a pattern found (and deemed fully acceptable) in Standard British English.

(f) Hypercorrect use of 'whom' for 'who'

Another feature that is particularly salient in Singapore (though it does occur, apparently less frequently, in other English-using countries) is an originally hyper-correct preference for *whom* over *who* in subject function in deeply embedded clauses. This is a more specific manifestation, or perhaps an extension, of the general Singaporean tendency to prefer the formal variant *whom* over less formal *who* wherever both are standard . . .

(g)  Use of 'that's' as possessive of relative 'that'

10.  There's the girl that's book I borrowed.


## Task B10.2.2

Having read Text B10.2, carry out the following activities:

➤  Some of these variations in relative clauses occur in particular geographical locations and not others. Find explanations for why this should be the case.

➤  In the light of what you have read about language variation in Units B8–B10, consider the statement made in Unit A8:

> When we talk about a standard in language (such as 'Standard English'), we have in mind a norm or model of language from which 'non-standard' language deviates. The usual implication is the 'standard' represents correctness (particularly in grammar), that alternatives are in some way incorrect.

Give your opinion as to whether 'incorrect' is an appropriate description for social or regional varieties that differ from a 'Standard language'.

These changes are not found in all varieties and the reasons for change are many and different. In some cases, the change can be related back to the influence of the first language. This is the explanation offered for the relative frequency in Hong Kong of (b) the use of 'redundant' subject relative pronouns in non-finite 'reduced relative' clauses. However, interference is not suggested as an explanation for (e), the avoidance of *that* with human antecedents, which is only common within the new varieties in Singapore. One of the explanations for this may be Singapore's exposure to North American media as it is a usage that is also non-standard in the United States. However, this needs to be treated cautiously because as Newbrook (1998: 51) points out 'it is very much harder to learn a strategy of avoidance from a source which does *not* display the feature to be avoided than to learn the use of a form from a source which *does* display it'. Omission of subject relative pronouns (a), is one of the rarer cases where there is evidence that it occurs in both the United Kingdom, Australia and in the new varieties. In Hong Kong it is already virtually accepted as standard usage, though is much less frequent in Singapore, although for no apparent reason. In the United Kingdom it appears to be confined to spoken

English, but in Australia it is increasingly occurring in student writing and in more informal printed material. Newbrook speculates that in due course it may come to be accepted as fully standard in both the United Kingdom and Australia.

It should be highlighted that causes of variation are often complex. Some are influenced by local languages, customs and educational systems, others have appeared and no satisfactory explanation is available. In some cases, geographically and linguistically disparate varieties are exhibiting the same changes. One interesting speculation from Newbrook is that the new varieties in East Asia may now be coming under the influence of the Australian English standard rather that the British English standard. This takes us almost full circle. The English language was exported around the world primarily by British colonialism, but it is now countries formerly colonised, such as the United States and Australia, which are having significant impacts on the changes taking place in the language. The geographical, political and economic context has moved on and grammatical changes follow in their wake.

**Summary**

In this unit we have looked at:

Contexts

- English-influenced creoles and pigins, particularly Tok Pisin from Melanesia
- Developments in written creoles
- New English varieties (e.g. in Singapore, Hong Kong and India).

Linguistic features/grammatical structures

- Expansion of pidgin grammar through creolization (e.g. development of past tense markers, particles to indicate future completive and perfective aspects, etc.);
- Relative clause markers in Tok Pisin;
- Relative clause variation across different Englishes (e.g. omission of subject relative pronoun, omission of required prepositions with relative pronouns, etc.).

# SECTION C
## Exploration

This section helps you to go beyond reading and thinking about the work of others to being active researchers – looking at how your grammar and that of others influences and is influenced by context.

Exploration in the area of grammar and context requires careful data collection, selection and analysis, and we encourage you in this section to reflect on these requirements. Often patterns in the grammar only become apparent in long texts or in a large collection of different texts. This has presented us with a problem in designing this section. We have had to choose short texts as illustrative material in order to help you practise your analytical techniques in an efficient way, but this is not representative of how research on grammar and context is typically carried out.

Each unit in Section C is structured around data, activities and feedback to help you progress towards becoming more independent in your language studies. All the units contain a *Background* section giving details about the data, where it comes from, and which particular earlier units it links in with. Then you will be given a series of tasks in *Task* sections. The *Focus* section in each task guides you through the analytical processes necessary to research the *Data* provided in the next section. At the end of the first activity you will find a *Commentary* which discusses what we have found in looking at the same data. You may have found the same or other things. It is important to stress that to help you understand and reflect on language it is necessary to undertake the activities before looking at the commentary. In some units you will find two or three more activities with feedback which will give you more structured practice of analysis. Occasionally there is also a *Research note* to give you additional guidance on appropriate aspects of research methodology. Later tasks in each unit will require you to bring together the ways of looking at data that you have practised and to undertake an independent analysis with no final commentary.

Unit C1 introduces analysis of grammar in conversation, looking at a number of extracts recorded in a family home. Attention is drawn to grammatical features such as incomplete utterances, reported speech, ellipsis and tags. You are given guidance on how to prepare your own transcripts for analysis. Letters written in institutional contexts provide the data in Unit C2. We take you through the steps necessary to conduct a move analysis (see Unit A4) of the different letter samples and then look at typical grammatical choices within the moves. Unit C3 focuses on academic writing and uses samples of concordance lines and comparative frequency data to examine grammatical patterns associated with *seem* and *hope*, verbs associated with hedging the claims and judgements of academic writers. Unit C4 looks at electronic (instant) messaging via computer. Features such as ellipsis, abbreviation, graphic representation of intonation and the importance of interpersonal interaction are explored. Instant messaging and text messaging could also be explored as examples of 'little texts', which is the focus for Unit C5. The grammar of small advertisements offering services and newspaper headlines highlights a variety of characteristic omissions such as articles, auxiliary verbs, and subjects and verbs which help to condense these messages. In Unit C6 we explore the relationships between grammatical complexity and developments over time in the written work of one child collected between the ages of six and ten years. Second-language acquisition contexts are the focus of Unit C7. Spoken and written data from Singaporean and Malaysian students are used to investigate tense choices and word classes more generally. Spoken data from classroom interactions by groups of boys and girls is used to explore the relationship between grammar and gender in Unit C8. Analysis relating to communicative functions is introduced and then the grammatical patterns associated with these functions are compared for the boys and the girls. The final unit in this section, Unit C9, explores differences between the grammar of 'Standard English' and first a British regional dialect from Birmingham and then an international variety, Indian English.

Each unit ends with *Ideas for further research* either on the topic under consideration or alternatively on other topics but using the research methods demonstrated in the unit. As well as ideas for research you will also find suggestions about where to find or how to collect relevant data for analysis. Your own explorations may result in findings that do not fit the relationships between grammar and context that you have read about or that we have presented. We hope this will cause you to reflect on and reconsider the ideas and methods that we have talked about here. Investigating the connections between grammar and context is an area of study in its infancy, and there is much still to be discovered.

# Unit C1
# Exploring grammar in conversation

## INTRODUCTION AND BACKGROUND TO DATA

Traditionally, grammars have described the written language, with unplanned speech often considered to be an ill-formed variant of writing. However, analysis of audio-recorded and transcribed speech, and more recently studies of large corpora of speech, have led to this view of grammars and what is grammatical being challenged. The tasks in this unit encourage you to explore spoken data for yourselves. In particular, we explore the characteristics of the grammar of conversation and how these are different from the grammar of writing. We go on to consider the context for conversation and how this affects grammatical features.

Aspects of the grammar of spoken language have been examined in both Sections A and B. Before working on this unit you should remind yourself particularly of Unit B1 and also Text B8.2 from the paper by Stephen Levey on *like*.

The data in this unit (from Cullen 1996) is taken from a conversation between three adults; one female, Alex (A), and two males, Paul (P) and Neil (N). They are all members of the same family, and the conversation takes place in the family home.

 **Task C1.1**

*Focus*

> This activity focuses on difficulties in transferring our usual methods of analysing the grammar of written text to speech, and the context for conversation.

➤ Give reasons why it is difficult to mark sentence divisions in the following extract.

➤ The word classes of traditional grammar are noun, verb, adjective and adverb. Into which category would you put 'like' in this extract?

➤ What is it about the context in which this and most other conversations are created that result in it having different grammatical features from those found in written texts?

## Data

In this extract, Paul is talking about a visit to his hairdresser, Nev. '. . .' indicates a pause of longer than one second. A comma indicates a restart, where Paul repeats or recasts what he was saying.

> he's a funny old stick Nev is . . . he says you see that dog he's got a lit–, there's a little terrier dog mooching round and it's a nice little dog actually it's about this big . . . belongs to his daughter Jackie . . . so he says see that dog down there and I said yeah . . . I couldn't see it like i'm sitting there having me hair cut like doing . . . and he's, and he's standing there in front of me and he says you see that dog down there and I say yeah . . . and he said uh . . . you wouldn't think he could get his head in that cup would you . . . he's got a mug, a tea mug on the thing . . . and I looked at the mug and you know it's an ordinary mug and I said . . . no he said he can't . . . he said all that hair he said sticks out he said when it's smoothed back and he says . . . his, his head's narrow he said

## Commentary

■ Some of the difficulties in marking sentence divisions relate to false starts and incomplete clauses (e.g. *he's got a lit–, there's a little terrier dog mooching round . . .; i'm sitting there having me hair cut like doing . . . and he's, and he's standing there in front of me . . .*). We might also identify problems associated with the repeated use of 'and', used to link a series of 'sentences' together. A further difficulty is the way in which the conversation has been transcribed: we have no evidence of intonation or of paralinguistic features such as gesture which might function in the same way as punctuation in writing and help us divide speech into units. (For information on approaches to transcription, see pages 222–223.)

■ Because *like* in *I couldn't see it like i'm sitting there having me hair cut like . . . doing* is clearly not a noun, verb or adjective, we might choose to label it by default as adverb. But if we define an adverb as something that describes or gives more information about a verb, adjective, adverb or phrase, there are clearly difficulties in saying very precisely what 'like' is describing or giving information about and what additional information is being provided. Some of the explanations concerning the use of 'like' as a discourse marker in Unit B8 may provide a better starting point.

■ Perhaps the most obvious difference in the context for conversation and most written text is that conversation typically takes place in real time; that is, planning what to say and saying it happen almost simultaneously, even though the speaker may have thought about what they are saying (and, indeed, may have said something similar) many times before. At each moment there is a need for speakers to move the conversation forward; to avoid silences and to contribute to the discourse as it unfolds. In writing, in contrast, there is a longer thinking time before committing words to paper or screen, and there is often an opportunity to redraft. Grammatical consequences of this in conversation are such things as incomplete cohesive units of meaning, hesitations, filled pauses, and rephrasing as we modify and add to things said previously.

A second major difference is that conversation takes place between two or more people who may know one another well, and usually in a face-to-face setting in which interactants cooperate in developing the discourse. In contrast, written texts are often produced for an impersonal audience (we may know the kind of person who will be reading the text or their purpose for reading, but not the individuals themselves), to be read at some distance from the time and location of its production. One consequence for the grammar of conversation is that we can often afford to be imprecise; we can use vague language (e.g. *that kind of stuff*) or even omit elements that we would include in writing, and still be understood. Further, conversation is typically peppered with items which do not themselves constitute full clauses, which speakers use to indicate how their message is to be interpreted (e.g. *you know, I mean*) and to indicate understanding (e.g. *uh-huh, yeah*).

 **Task C1.2**

*Focus*

Here we will explore in more detail some of the characteristic features of conversation as they are represented in the extract in Task C1.1 above. Some additional extracts from other parts of the conversation are given as further data for you to examine. Use these extracts to respond to the points below.

➤ Note two things about the way speech is reported.

➤ What do you observe about the tense use in the narrative? Why do you think these tenses are chosen?

➤ The additional data below gives examples (underlined) of *tags* used in the conversation. Can you find a further tag near the beginning of the extract in Task C1.1? What is the purpose of this tag and those in the additional data below?

➤ In conversation, speakers leave out elements that would normally be included in well-formed written English. This omission of parts of the structure, usually recoverable from the context more generally, is known as *ellipsis*. Look again at the extract in Task C1.1 and identify any examples of ellipsis in it. The additional data below gives extracts in which there is ellipsis. Consider in each case what was elided (left out).

### Additional data

*Tags*

    a.  *P*:  and he set off <u>this chap</u>
    b.  *N*:  is it a one man show <u>this uh barber's</u>
    c.  *A*:  it's the way he starts off these little accounts <u>isn't it</u>
    d.  *A*:  you know who carries the gene for that <u>don't you</u>
    e.  *P*:  it's won the Chelt–, Cheltenham Gold Cup <u>or something</u>
    f.  *A*:  he said i think he's from Wales or Scotland <u>or somewhere like that</u>
    g.  *P*:  duck and geese <u>and that</u>

*Ellipsis*

    a.  *P*:  he must have some flaming freezer, deep freezer
        *A*:  must be like a shop one
    b.  *P*:  this French family had two kids . . . you know boy the same age as me and a little girl younger
    c.  *P*:  so they sent him on a course, you know a rehabilitation course about a fortnight and he came back as hairdresser he's o—, he's okay you know short back and sides
    d.  *N*:  why did he buy them in the first place
        *A*:  because they were cheap
    e.  *P*:  it was about the America that we, we know
        *A*:  nobody every sees
    f.  *P*:  you don't know what the devil day it is do you
        *A*:  don't know don't care

### Commentary

■  Paul gives an account of the conversation in the hairdresser's in direct speech; that is, as if the words he is reporting are exactly those used at the time, even though it would need an extraordinary feat of recall actually to do this. As he begins sections of direct speech he signals this with *I said* or *he says/ said*. The verb 'go' is also commonly used for this purpose in conversation. These are both common features of narrative in conversation. Notice that Paul does not feel obliged, say for reasons of stylistic variation as we might find in written text, to vary the reporting verb used in the reporting clauses.

■  The tenses in the reporting clause alternate between present simple (*he says, I say*) and past simple (*he said, I said*), and the tenses in the narrative are predominantly present simple and present continuous (*there's a little terrier dog, I'm sitting there . . . and he's standing there*). Present tenses are commonly used in conversational narratives to produce a more immediate account, as if the events were taking place at the time of the narrative.

■ An example of a tag in the extract in Task C1.1 is *he's a funny old stick Nev is*. We noted in the commentary in Task C1.1 that one of the consequences of conversation being produced in real time is that speakers will often modify something they have just said, adding to or changing it. In the extract in Task C1.1 and extracts a and b in the additional data on tags, speakers provide a referent for the pronoun ('Nev' is 'he', 'this chap' is 'he', 'this barber's' is 'it') perhaps because, after the event, they decide they need to clarify exactly who or what it is they are talking about. Extracts c and d include question tags intended to elicit agreement or answers from the other participants. In extracts e–g, the tags seem to convey the meaning that what has just been said should not be taken to be exact or complete. In reporting that Nev talked about the 'Cheltenham Gold Cup or something' Paul suggests that this may not be the horse race that Nev mentioned, but could have been some other. 'Wales or Scotland or somewhere like that' is rather more difficult to interpret: what other places are like Wales or Scotland? Perhaps the intention is to indicate 'somewhere in Britain outside England'. 'Duck and geese and that' suggests that duck and geese are just examples of a more complete list of, in this context, edible birds, that could have been mentioned.

■ One example of ellipsis in the data in Task C1.1 is the omission of the subject pronoun *it* in the underlined part of *it's a nice little dog actually it's about this big . . . belongs to his daughter Jackie*. In written text, ellipsis is frequent and normally used to avoid unnecessary repetition (e.g. He started working the factory at the age of fourteen and for the next ten years (he) knew nothing else.). Ellipsis is also very common in conversation, particularly of subject pronouns, as above and in a in the additional data on ellipsis (*[it] must be like a shop one*). However, there is a much wider range of elements omitted in conversation than in most forms of writing. In b, an article is omitted before 'boy' and 'who was' after 'girl', and in c 'for' is omitted before 'about'. Sometimes it is difficult to say precisely what is omitted, and therefore what the speaker's exact meaning was. Also in extract c, Paul says, '*he's okay you know short back and sides*'. Clearly something is omitted around 'short back and sides', but we can't know whether this was 'He's okay you know [he's good at] short back and sides' or 'He's okay you know [he's okay at] short back and sides [but nothing else]', or some other possibility. But even without this knowledge, the conversation goes on after this without either of the other speakers indicating that they haven't understood.

In extracts d, e and f we find ellipsis at the beginning of speaker responses. We would probably not expect Alex in d to say 'He bought them in the first place because they were cheap' unless she wanted to make a particular point in doing so, as the repetition would be redundant. In f there seems to be an omission of 'The America (that) . . .', entirely recoverable from Paul's previous turn. In f, as we saw in c, what exactly is omitted in Alex's response is unclear. Paul's use of 'you' in '. . . *you don't know what the devil day . . . it is do you*' refers to people in general, rather than to either Alex or Neil. So it may be that Alex is omitting a similar reference ('We (= people in general) don't know and we don't care'), or a reference to herself ('I don't know and I don't care'), or even a combination

('We don't know, and I don't care'). Again, though, any ambiguity is not sufficient for either of the other participants in the conversation to call for clarification. In ellipsis, words are omitted that have low informational value. Of course, the assessment of 'low informational value' is made by the speaker in the context of the conversation, and a request for clarification from another speaker after ellipsis would, in effect, be saying that the speaker has made a mis-judgement. In the give and take of conversation between friends and family, even when there may not be full understanding, such challenges are usually avoided.

## Task C1.3

### Focus

Here is a data extract from later in the same conversation. They are talking about accents, and Alex begins to recount her experience when her family moved to Nottingham.

➤ What do you observe about reporting speech, tags, and ellipsis?

➤ What other features can you observe that are different in this conversation from what you would expect to find in well-formed written text?

➤ Using this analysis and what you have read about grammar in speech, make a list of the points you might highlight in arguing that a traditional grammatical description is insufficient as a description of grammar in conversation.

### Data

A: so weird . . . and a lot of, you know people that we were meeting for the first time in Nottingham you know friends and relatives that we haven't really met before .. you know they would listen to the children and say ooh no they haven't really got, you know they haven't picked up the accent at all really have they

P: mmm

A: and I'd think oh yes they have but they're just not using it

P: yeah yeah

A: because they've been back three days you know

P: yeah I know wh-, when I went in the army there was a boy there and he, he actually came from Pembroke in Wales you see so he had

N: oh that's where me mum comes from

P: he had that accent, that Welsh

N: mmm

P: accent . . . and when I heard him talk I didn't know he was Welsh from Wales but . . . I'd grown up . . . of, as a kid with, next door to us was a

French family who, they'd come over, the father worked for the Michelin tyre company which had just been built in

N: mmm

P: Stoke-on-Trent . . . and, and uh this French family had two kids you know boy the same age as me and a little girl younger and he, he played with the rest of us you see and he very quickly picked up English

N: mmm

P: but . . . oddly enough he, although he picked it all up he still had a French accent if you know what I mean

## RESEARCH NOTE

Look back at the transcriptions of speech in Unit B1. You will notice that while in Text B1.2 Biber *et al.* use punctuation such as question marks, dashes, commas, etc. in their transcription, Carter and McCarthy in Text B1.1 do not. Look at the examples below from Joan Swann (2001) and Suzanne Eggins and Diane Slade (1997):

*Table C1.1* Transcription of student–teacher talk

| Transcription | | | Notes |
|---|---|---|---|
| 1 | T: | You [student's name] have you got | |
| 2 | | many toy animals at home | |
| 3 | S1: | Yes I have {(.) I have a got | |
| 4 | T: | {mmh | |
| 5 | S1: | many toy animals at home | |
| 6 | T: | That's good that's right what toy | |
| 7 | | animals have you got at home (.) | |
| 8 | | what name for animals (.) | low voice |
| 9 | | [student's name] what toy animals | |
| 10 | | have you got at home (.) I'm like a tiger | |
| 11 | Ss: | <laughter> | |
| 12 | T: | What yes | |
| 13 | S2: | I have {I have got {(.) I | T nods; lowers S2's |
| 14 | T: | {mmh {mmh a (.) | hand and places on |
| 15 | | or maybe two or {maybe three | desk |
| 16 | S2: | {I have got a many | |
| 17 | | toy animals | |
| 18 | T: | mmh I have got {many toy animals | |
| 19 | S2: | {many toy animals | |

**Key**

| | |
|---|---|
| T | = Teacher |
| S | = Student (S1 = Student 1 etc.) |
| student's name | underlining indicates any feature you wish to comment on |
| (.) | brief pause |
| (1sec) | timed pause |
| {maybe | brackets indicate the start of overlapping speech |
| {I have got | |
| <laughter> | transcription of a sound etc that forms part of the utterance |

Source: Swann 2001: 331

*Table C1.2* Transcription of casual conversation

| 11b | S4 | [to S3] That's nothing to do with it. |
| | | [turns to S1] Where's the cigarettes, [name]? |
| 12b | S1 | Sorry, [name]. I've cut you off. You said you'd had the last |
| | | one. You promised me the last one was the last one. |
| 13b | S4 | Well I want to have one more. |
| 14b | S1 | Cost you a buck. |
| 15b | S4 | Oh, give me a break, [name]! |

Source: Eggins and Slade 1997: 9

These researchers have used different transcription conventions. Of particular value in Swann's is the column for 'notes'. These enable the researcher to give contextual information that can help make sense of the utterances. Swann was transcribing video recorded data, but the same system is useful if the researcher is present at the speech event and made notes at the time or remembered some of the activity taking place. In their book on conversation, Eggins and Slade make careful use of transcription conventions which will convey information to the reader who is not familiar with some of the very detailed and complex systems used by some conversational analysts. Here is the key to their use of punctuation symbols (1997: 2):

a) **Full stops.** These mark termination (whether grammatically complete or not), or certainty, which is usually realised by falling intonation. By implication, the absence of any turn-final punctuation indicates speaker incompletion, either through interruption or trailing off.

b) **Commas,** These signal speaker parcellings of non-final talk. Thus, commas are used to make long utterances readable, and usually correspond to silent beats in the rhythm (but not breaks or pauses, which are marked with . . .).

c) **Question marks?** These are used to indicate questions or to mark uncertainty (typically corresponding to rising intonation or WH-questions).

d) **Exclamation marks!** These mark the expression of counter-expectation (e.g. surprise, shock, amazement etc.). Typically corresponding to tone 5 in Halliday's (1994) system of intonation analysis.

e) **Words in capital letters WOW** These are used conservatively to show emphatic symbols.

f) **Quotation marks " "** These capture the marked change in voice quality that occurs when speakers directly quote (or repeat) another's speech.

A number of research ideas are suggested below, many of which will require you to collect and transcribe your own data before undertaking grammatical analysis. This brief discussion of different approaches to transcription should help you to make decisions on what information you might indicate in your own transcription and conventions for doing so.

## IDEAS FOR FURTHER RESEARCH

Here are some suggestions on further research that you carry out in the area of grammar and conversation.

- Find some informants who are happy to record some of their conversations. The data we have explored in this unit comes from friends and relatives sitting around a table having a meal. There are many advantages in recording in this situation: the speakers are close together and don't move around much; and people who are comfortable with each other are less likely to be distracted by being recorded. Here are some possible grammatical areas that you could focus on: prefaces, tags, ellipsis, indirect speech, *this/ that/ these/ those*, or negation.

- If you are not able to record spontaneous conversation of this type, you could try recording radio phone-in programmes. The callers on this kind of programme are not usually practised broadcasters and have not prepared their contributions in detail, so their speech shows more of the features of conversation than, say, scripted radio or TV drama.

- If you teach English as a second or foreign language, find examples in teaching materials of written conversations. (There may be recordings to go with them.) Discover whether the grammatical features of conversation that you have identified in this unit also occur in this material. If not, what are the implications for teaching, and what improvements would you suggest?

- If you have access to groups of native and non-native English speakers, record them talking about a topic you have given them. If you give the same topic, this makes comparison easier to some extent. What grammatical features of conversation do you find similar or different in the two recordings? Consider why there should be differences and (if this is of interest to you) what implications there are for teaching.

- Take the script of a play or look at the direct speech in a novel. In what ways is this written speech similar to or different from authentic conversation? If it is different, should this affect how you evaluate the play or novel?

# Unit C2
# Exploring grammar in institutional contexts

## INTRODUCTION AND BACKGROUND TO DATA

In Unit A4 we considered the particular patterns of interaction that occur in institutional settings such as hospitals, businesses and universities, and how these are reflected in the spoken and written genres that are produced. Although there may be local variations, genres have broadly similar characteristics across institutions within a sector. In this unit, we will look at two examples of genres where affective features such as evaluation, politeness, and hedging are influenced by the institutional setting. The first is the letter of recommendation, with samples from an academic context, and the second letter responding to client concerns or complaints, with samples from a business context. The analytical approach we take here is a 'move analysis', which, as we suggested in Unit A4, offers a productive way of exploring the relationship between context, text organisation, and lexical and grammatical choices.

The letter of recommendation is an important document in the process of granting and gaining access to an institution in the form of a job or a place on a course. It provides evidence of the suitability of the applicant to supplement evidence gained in other ways, such as letters of application, curricula vitae, interviews and tests. Traditionally, it has been a confidential document seen only by the writer and the representatives of the institution. However, the recent trend is for receiving institutions to permit applicants to see letters of recommendation after the selection process is complete and, indeed, in some countries legislation now makes this a right of applicants. This change in the confidential status of letters of recommendation may well have an impact on the language used in them, in particular making writers less inclined to offer criticism, or at least offering criticism only where there is substantial evidence to support it. This, in turn, may eventually come to have an impact on its perceived value in the selection process. The letters of recommendation in the first part of this unit (from Collins 1999) come from an academic institutional context. The letters were written by Canadian academics for students applying for jobs or places on postgraduate programmes (referred to as 'graduate' programmes in the letters).

The data in the second part of the unit are letters written by a member of staff of a computer software company to clients who have previously expressed concern about its planned merger with a larger company.[22]

Our aim here is to identify the stages or moves in these letters, and what purpose these moves have in the communication between writer and institution or institution and client. We will go on to explore the grammatical choices made in some of these moves and consider why these choices are made.

Before working on this unit you should have read Unit B2, and it may also be useful to reread Unit A4.

 **Task C2.1**

*Focus*

The first two letters of recommendation are broadly supportive of the applicant. (Sentence numbers have been added to the main part of the letter for ease of reference.)

➤ Identify the moves in these letters and discuss the purpose of each move. The beginning of a table giving a move analysis is provided here as a guide.

| Move | Location (letter/sentence) | Purpose |
|---|---|---|
| 1 Statement of reason for writing | A (1) B (1) | Orientates the reader, providing a link between the letter, the applicant and the relevant job or course. |
| 2 Initial indication of the writer's position | A included in (1); '. . . in support of . . .' B (2) | Provides the reader with a preliminary indication that the recommendation will be positive. |

*Data*

*Letter A*

Dear Sir/ Madam

(1) I am writing in support of the application of *[name]*. (2) He was a student in three of my courses (Human Relations and Policy and Strategic Management), thus I am able to comment not only on his academic skills, but also on his ability to work in groups.

(3) I believe that his transcript is a true reflection of his ability and initiative. (4) The grades he received in my courses fall right in line with his overall evaluation.

(5) *[Name]* has demonstrated the ability to work in groups and is often looked to for leadership. (6) He has indicated to me a career path which would be enhanced by graduate study. (7) The business experience he has gained since graduation has added to his overall level of maturity.

(8) For the above reasons, I would recommend him as a candidate for your graduate program.

Sincerely yours,

*Letter B*

Re: *[Name]*

(1) *[Name]* is applying to the degree program of journalism and has asked me to provide a letter of reference. (2) I am pleased to do so.

(3) I have known *[name]* for the past six years. (4) I have found him to be a very good student, intelligent, well spoken and enthusiastic. (5) He was always well prepared, was prompt with his assignments and was active in class participation.

(6) *[Name]* is somewhat distinguished from the majority of our students in that he has a particular artistic flair. (7) He is a lover of music in all of its many aspects. (8) His senior project was the development of a record label which was very well done; the public presentation was unique and effective. (9) I have a sense that this side of his personality will be quite helpful to him in his journalism studies and at the same time make him an interesting student to have in the program.

(10) I have no hesitation in recommending him for acceptance.

Yours truly,

## Commentary

You may have identified the following moves in these letters:

*Table C2.1* Identification of moves in letters

| Move | Location (letter/ sentence) | Purpose |
|---|---|---|
| 1 Statement of reason for writing | A (1) B (1) | Orientates the reader, providing a link between the letter, the applicant and the relevant job or course. |
| 2 Initial indication of the writer's position | A included in (1); '. . . in support of . . .' B (2) | Provides the reader with a preliminary indication that the recommendation will be positive. |
| 3 Indication of relationship between writer and applicant | A (2) B (3) | Provides the reader with information about the basis on which the writer is able to make their judgement of the applicant. |
| 4 Factual information about what the applicant has achieved | A (4) | Factual information provides a basis for the more subjective evaluation of the applicant, which usually follows. A report of factual information in a letter of recommendation may be used by the institution to confirm what the applicant has said in a letter or CV. |
| 5 Evaluation of the applicant's abilities in general | A (3, 5–7) B (4–8) | 5 and 6 are perhaps the core of the letter of recommendation. The institution wishes to have a personal judgement from the writer of the applicant's abilities or suitability for the job or course as an indicator of whether the applicant is likely to succeed. |
| 6 Evaluation of the applicant's abilities as they relate to the job or course applied for | B (9) | |
| 7 Summary statement of the writer's judgement of the applicant's suitability for the job or course applied for | A (8) B (10) | An explicit statement (or restatement) of the writer's position removes any possible ambiguity. An indication is given of the level of support ('I have no hesitation in recommending him . . .' seems to offer stronger support than '. . . I would recommend him . . .'). |

Of course, not all letters will include all of these moves, nor will all follow them in this order.

## Task C2.2

### Focus

Here are two further letters of recommendation. However, these are much less supportive than the first two.

➤ Do a move analysis in the form of a table as in the Commentary on p. 228.

➤ Which of the moves you identified in letters A and B are also found in letters C and D?

➤ Decide whether any are missing.

➤ Decide whether any different moves are used.

➤ Consider why moves are left out or new moves included.

### Data

*Letter C*

To whom it may concern:
(1) *[Name]* is a reasonably bright young woman, who is now starting to show some of her potential. (2) She entered university with a rather mediocre high school record, and it was not until her third year that she became a serious student.

(3) She has extremely good interpersonal skills, communicates effectively and has developed a good work ethic. (4) She has yet to demonstrate solid quantitative abilities, and I feel that she will have to work extremely hard in this area if she is to be successful in graduate work.

(5) If she enters an MBA program, she is likely to be successful in the foundation courses provided she applies herself with the same vigour she has displayed in the last three semesters. (6) I feel that she could perform at an above average level were she to concentrate in the behavioural areas in her second year.

(7) I trust the above will be helpful to you.

*Letter D*

Dear *[Name]*:

(1) *[Name]* is applying for this position and has asked me to write on his behalf. (2) He is aware that I have serious concerns about his background and experience for the position but would like me to make reference to his character and abilities.

(3) *[Name]* has an exceptional talent for getting along well with people. (4) He is very popular, meets people extremely well, and is a genuinely likeable person. (5) He gives the impression of being concerned for the welfare of those he works with and is considered to be a real team player.

Yours truly,

### *Commentary*

Letter C has only two of the moves identified in the more supportive letters analysed above:

5.  Evaluation of the applicant's abilities in general (Sentences 1, 2 [although the first part could be taken to be a factual statement rather than evaluation], 3 and 4 [first part])
6.  Evaluation of the applicant's abilities as they relate to the job or course applied for (Sentences 4 [second part], 5 and 6)

Note that there is no orientation, indication of relationship, initial indication of support, or summary statement. Based on the evaluation offered, only a negative summary statement could be made. The writer avoids this option by choosing the more neutral option in sentence 7 (which seems to be a different kind of move, which we might label simply 'Closing').

Letter D has the following moves:

1.  Statement of reason for writing (sentences 1 and 2 [from '. . . but would like me to . . .'])
2.  Initial indication of the writer's position (sentence 2 [first part])
5.  Evaluation of the applicant's abilities in general (sentences 3–5)

As in letter C, there is no indication of relationship and no summary statement. The given reason for writing in this case is that the applicant has requested the writer to do so, although they would clearly prefer not to. In more supportive letters, writers may, as in letter B, state not only their willingness but their pleasure in being able to support the applicant. The initial indication of the writer's position explicitly fails

230

to offer support and, as in letter C, there is no negative summary statement. The evidence of these four letters suggests that while explicit summary statements are found in supportive letters, the writers of critical letters prefer to leave it up to the reader to infer their position on the applicant from what is said in moves 5 and 6.

## Task C2.3

### *Focus*

We noted above (and in Unit A4) that particular lexical or grammatical features are often characteristic of moves within a particular genre. Before going back to the four letters above to explore what grammatical features are found in each move, we need to note a limitation of this activity. Because we are dealing with only a small amount of data in this unit, we cannot with any certainty say either that the moves we have identified will be found in most letters of recommendation, or that grammatical features we observe within the moves of these sample letters are commonly found in these moves in others. With this limitation in mind, any observations we make here must be treated as preliminary, eventually to be tested against further data of this kind.

All the letters have one of moves 5 and 6, or both, so we will focus attention on these.

➤ What do you notice about grammatical choices in these moves in the four letters?

➤ How do these contribute to the evaluative purpose of these moves?

### *Commentary*

Writers are dealing here with personal opinions, and generally would not wish to make stronger claims for the applicant's abilities or suitability for the job or course than they have evidence for. Consequently, writers use a number of techniques for hedging their support, stepping back from making this support unqualified. One is to make explicit that what follows is an opinion by using an initial 'I' followed by a noun or verb related to belief or experience as in:

'*I believe* that his transcript is a true reflection of his ability and initiative.' (rather than 'His transcript is a true reflection . . .')

'*I have found him to be* a very good student . . .'

'*I have a sense that* this side of his personality will be quite helpful to him . . .'

Another is to use an adjective expressing a degree of certainty:

> 'If she enters an MBA program, she is *likely* to be successful . . . provided..'
> (rather than '. . . she will be successful . . .')

or a modifying adverb:

> '*[Name]* is a *reasonably* bright young woman . . .' (rather than '*[Name]* is a bright young woman . . .')

The writer of letter D uses a further technique, an agentless passive form to distance themselves from a supportive statement in:

> 'and *is considered to be* a real team player'

The alternatives '(he) is a real team player', the hedged 'I consider him to be a real team player', or even a passive with agent included, as in '(he) is considered by his colleagues to be a real team player' would have offered degrees of stronger support. The agentless passive, however, presents the claim almost as hearsay, as if the writer doesn't know whether it is true or not. The same writer goes even further in withholding support in:

> '*He gives the impression of being concerned* for the welfare of those he works with . . .'

Not only does this hedge support more than would 'He is concerned for the welfare of those he works with . . .'; it suggests that the applicant is not actually concerned with their welfare but wishes to be seen as such. Of course, whether this is a deliberate strategy or just an unfortunate wording can only be known by the writer.

In move 6 of letter C we find a series of conditional clauses using *if*, *provided*, and *were (she) to*:

> '*she will* have to work hard *if she is to* be successful in graduate work'

> '*If she enters* an MBA program, she is likely to be successful in the foundation courses *provided* she applies herself. . . .'

> 'she *could* perform at an above average level *were she to* concentrate in . . .'

The writer offers support for the applicant, saying that she has the potential to succeed. This support is qualified, however, by indicating that, in their view, success would be dependent on a number of circumstances. Not only does this use of conditional clauses convey the writer's reservations, it also allows the writer to protect themselves from future blame or criticism should the applicant be offered a place on the course but eventually fail.

A further feature of moves 5 and 6 is the coordination of two or more noun phrases or clauses, as in:

'*[Name]* has demonstrated the ability to work in groups and is often looked to for leadership.'

'I have found him to be a very good student, intelligent, well-spoken and enthusiastic.'

'He was always well prepared, was prompt with his assignments and was active in class participation.'

'She has extremely good interpersonal skills, communicates effectively and has developed a good work ethic.'

'He is very popular, meets people extremely well, and is a genuinely likeable person.'

This allows the writer to list applicants' attributes within a sentence in an efficient way, without necessarily elaborating on them. Comparable lists of criticism seem less likely, as the writer would probably feel it necessary to offer justification for them.

## Task C2.4

### *Focus*

Here are two letters written as part of a business communication. They are both written in response to concerns raised by company clients.

➤ Following the procedure we have illustrated above, identify moves in the letters and consider their communicative purpose.

➤ Decide whether there are any moves common to both.

➤ Try to identify any grammatical choices that seem to be related to purpose.

## Data

*Letter E*

Dear *[Name]*

I would like to respond to your concerns that you raised during our telephone conversation yesterday. You had some legitimate questions regarding the recent merger between *[Company X]* and *[Company Y]*. You are a valued customer of *[Company X]* and it is very important that you know all of the facts.

The Executive Board of *[Company X]* has recommended to all of its shareholders that we merge with *[Company Y]*. Subject to shareholder approval, the deal should be signed by December. This means that *[Company X]* will be a wholly owned subsidiary of *[Company Y]*. *[Company Y]* does not have any competing products to the current suite of tools. Therefore, the investment you have made in *[Company X]* products will not be affected. In fact, the additional resources that *[Company Y]* will provide to *[Company X]* will only improve the already high quality of products and support that you have come to expect from our company.

This merger is a positive step for *[Company X]* and especially for its clients. Should you have any additional questions or concerns regarding this merger, please contact me. I am also available to meet with you anytime this week.

Sincerely,

*Letter F*

Re: *[Company Y]*'s acquisition of *[Company X]*

Dear *[Name]*

Following our conversation, please find below a summary of our discussion.

Your initial reaction is quite normal; there have been a lot of mixed feelings from the market following the announcement of the merger. However, this move is very positive for both organisations.

First, our technologies complement each other. *[Company Y]*'s core products are connectivity software between PC's and UNIX servers, which means that *[Company X]* will greatly gain from the added technology and will be able to offer its customers a broader range of options.

In addition, *[Company Y]* has confirmed their commitment to move into the Data Warehousing market through a series of acquisitions. This commitment means that *[Company X]* will then benefit from added stability and influx of funds and be part of a group worth over US$100m.

What does this mean to you, as a customer?

The additional funds will allow us to increase our range of services and support schemes and expand their accessibility. But more so importantly *[sic]*, we will be able to invest more in Research and Development, which means even more product enhancements and features to respond to your future requirements.

This is where, *[sic]* you, as a key customer, get a unique opportunity. Your feedback in the past has always been of great value to us, and now you have an even greater influence into our future product developments as well as new services.

I trust you now can see this merger with a more positive outlook, and by all means, should you have any doubt left or any further queries, please fell *[sic]* free to contact me. You can reach me at any time on my mobile *[number]*.

Thank you again for your support on *[sic]* our products and services.

Yours sincerely,

## IDEAS FOR FURTHER RESEARCH

Here are some suggestions on further research that you could do in the area of the grammar of communication in institutional contexts.

■  One of the difficulties in researching communication in institutional contexts is that, due to concerns about confidentiality, data can be hard to obtain or to obtain in sufficient quantity. If you do have access to an institution where these difficulties can be overcome, then there are many kinds of text that could usefully be analysed using the approach we have outlined above. For example, in a business you might look at various kinds of internal documents (reports, memos, business or strategy plans, proposals, technical instructions, contracts, emails) or external documents (product information, contracts, letters, faxes or emails). However, other business documents are not subject to such restrictions, and are freely available, often on company websites. Examples include mission statements (see also Unit A4), company accounts and annual reports, press releases, and advertising material. Public documents such as these are often intended to persuade readers to buy products or to convince the reader of the value of investing in the company, and your analysis could concentrate on grammatical elements of how this persuasion is effected. Other kinds of institution also produce publicly available 'persuasive' texts. Universities, for example, often have prospectuses, mission statements, and academic programme descriptions intended to market the institution or its programmes, or to convince the reader of its integrity.

It is not, of course, necessary to analyse the complete text of long documents, but instead you could focus on just one part. For example, university prospectuses often begin with a 'welcome' statement (sometimes in the form of a letter) from its head, and company annual reports similarly may begin with a letter from the managing director.

The general procedure in a move/ grammatical analysis would be as we have illustrated in the activities in this unit. That is:

1.  Begin by identifying moves in one or two texts in the corpus to produce a preliminary model;
2.  Analyse further texts using the model, and adapt and refine it as necessary until you have a general model that represents the organisation of most, if not all, of the texts;
3.  Try to identify recurring grammatical features in each of the moves;
4.  Consider how these are related to the purpose of the move and of the texts more generally in the context in which they are written.

■ Although we have focused here on move analysis, it is of course possible to undertake different kinds of investigation of texts in order to explore patterns of interaction in institutional contexts. For example, it would be valuable to look more generally at modality and the use of personal pronouns in any of the documents we have noted so far.

■ Other institutional texts may not lend themselves to the kind of move analysis that we have outlined here. For example, legal documents such as wills or terms and conditions are perhaps less interesting for their organisation than the particular language associated with them. Wills have to be worded in such a way as to leave no doubt about a person's intentions. As a consequence of this, the content of the will (that is, specification of the actions that the person wants taken after their death) takes up a relatively small proportion of the text, with the bulk of it consisting of language intended to ensure that there is no ambiguity in its interpretation. The complexity of coordination and sub-ordination in legal texts has been noted and would be an interesting area for further investigation. (The website in note 2 on p. 319 is a good source of wills.)

■ In this unit we have focused particularly on written communication in institutional contexts. Of course, spoken communication in educational, medical, business or other workplace settings can also provide valuable information about context. For example, explorations of the use of personal pronouns, hedging (see also Unit C3), modality, and indications of politeness in spoken interaction can shed light on the roles of participants and their relative status. While it can be more difficult to gain access to spoken data in such contexts, some spoken data is freely available. A good source is the transcribed speeches of senior managers that are often posted on the websites of large companies. While these may well be 'tidied up', so that some of the features of speech (false starts, grammatical infelicities and so on) that may have appeared in the original are removed, these often are obviously written representations of spoken events rather than carefully prepared written texts. As such speeches have been made public they are often intended to represent the company in a positive light, and analysis of grammatical components of this perspective are an interesting area of investigation. For example, you could focus on adjective or adverbial usage, or on how reports of weaknesses in the company performance are hedged.

■ In Unit A4 we looked at national differences in communication. If you have access to comparable institutional texts in two languages or from two different English-speaking countries, this can be a fruitful area of investigation. You could explore how cultural differences are reflected in and constructed through text organisation and grammatical realisations in particular elements of the text.

# Unit C3
# Exploring grammar in academic writing

## INTRODUCTION AND BACKGROUND TO DATA

We saw in Unit B3 that a considerable amount of research has been carried out into the characteristics of academic writing. In that unit we looked in detail at some of the grammatical features that are typical of science writing in general, and then went on to explore how different academic disciplines make use of different grammatical resources. One of the major determinants of language choice is how detached and impersonal academic writers feel they need to be. Although a common perception of academic text is that its main purpose is to present information in an objective and impersonal way, it also forms part of an ongoing scholarly debate in which writers try to persuade readers of the validity of the positions they are adopting. One aspect of this, as we will see below, is that opinions, evaluations and criticisms tend to be phrased in a cautious manner. Strong positions can conventionally only be held and expressed with convincing evidence; otherwise, writers expose themselves to criticism from their colleagues in the academic community.

To explore how academic caution manifests itself grammatically, we focus in this unit on the grammatical patterns associated with the verb *seem*. This verb plays an important part in 'hedging' a writer's full commitment to a proposition: saying that something 'is' the case presents a stronger claim than saying that something 'seems to be' the case, where the proposition is presented as a judgement rather than fact. To highlight the particular characteristics of *seem* in academic text, and identify any differences between its use in this context and in others, we will compare and contrast its use in academic text with that in a corpus of spoken discourse.

The investigative method we will demonstrate in this unit is that of analysis of concordance lines extracted from two electronic corpora, one of written academic English and the other of spoken English. (See Unit A9 for more information about corpora in investigations of grammar and context.). Both are samples from the much larger British National Corpus. Our corpus of academic written English totals 1,077,966 words and comprises extracts from texts such as academic journals and books. It is referred to as the 'academic corpus' below. Our corpus of spoken English totals 1,108,195 words, and includes extracts from unscripted informal conversation and speech recorded in other contexts, such as radio shows and phone-ins. It is referred to as the 'spoken corpus' below. We have taken fifty randomly selected concordance lines from each for the key words *seem*, *seems* and *seemed*. We refer below to this set of key words as the key term *seem**, and these two fifty-line samples are referred to as the 'academic corpus sample' and the 'spoken corpus sample'.

## RESEARCH NOTE

Corpus analysis of grammatical patterns gives us detailed information about the text surrounding a particular key word. This kind of investigation is ideally done sitting in front of a computer terminal, exploring large numbers of concordance lines. However, we are limited here to using small samples generated from these two corpora. Consequently, we need to keep in mind that what we are undertaking is very much a preliminary study of a sample from a larger corpus. Any observations we make may or may not reflect what we would find in the larger corpus. Our work, therefore, should be viewed as generating questions for further investigation rather than seeking to provide definitive answers. Published work that you may read using corpus data is generally based on much larger samples. Suggestions are given in *Ideas for further research* at the end of this unit for other corpora already available for you to explore, or for how you might build your own.

Before working on this unit you should have read Unit B3.

## Task C3.1

### *Focus*

To begin, we briefly consider how far the samples are representative of the two corpora more generally, and go on to explore grammatical patterns associated with *seem** that come after the key term.

➤ Table C3.1 below gives the number of occurrences of *seem*, *seems* and *seemed* in the two corpora and in the samples, and expresses these as percentages of the total corpus or sample. From this information, how representative do the two corpus samples appear to be of the two larger corpora?

➤ Look at the academic corpus sample. Try to classify the grammatical patterns that <u>follow</u> the key term *seem** and count the number of each (e.g. noun phrase, *not* + *to* + infinitive etc.).

➤ Now look at the spoken corpus sample and do the same. Compare the numbers you have calculated for the two corpora and the concordance lines in each category. What similarities and differences do you observe between the corpora?

## Data

Table C3.1 Frequency of occurrence of *seem** in the two corpora and the two corpus samples

| | Academic corpus | Academic corpus sample | Spoken corpus | Spoken corpus sample |
|---|---|---|---|---|
| seem | 255 (35%) | 12 (24%) | 106 (42%) | 7 (14%) |
| seems | 371 (51%) | 28 (56%) | 103 (40.5%) | 27 (54%) |
| seemed | 103 (14%) | 10 (20%) | 45 (17.5%) | 16 (32%) |
| Total | 729 (100%) | 50 (100%) | 254 (100%) | 50 (100%) |

| | | | |
|---|---|---|---|
| 1 | . . . remarked what a long way it | seemed. | We were early and stood in the. . . |
| 2 | . . . had been about power, it | seems | almost equally possible that his. . . |
| 3 | . . . the environmental cause | seems | as strong as ever. Thus, The Times. . . |
| 4 | . . . respect, this approach | seems | curiously narrow and may be. . . |
| 5 | . . . style of writing (which now | seems | dated) too often obscured the probity. . . |
| 6 | . . . part of him or her, and they | seem | discrepant with an everyday or normal. . . |
| 7 | . . . time about Balbinder. She | seemed | distressed, 'I mean Balbinder, he. . . |
| 8 | . . . of bottom-living habits | seems | eminently reasonable for them. But. . . |
| 9 | . . . Radiologists Working Party | seems | flawed. Using an uncontrolled study. . . |
| 10 | . . . 1990b). More than that, it | seems | highly likely that the social science. . . |
| 11 | . . . that would otherwise have | seemed | incompatible. Apart from the. . . |
| 12 | . . . the ones which at present | seem | indisputable. At this point the. . . |
| 13 | . . . First World War period we | seem | little nearer to finding the. . . |
| 14 | . . . The woman's killing the man | seems | metaphorical only, but it fits the. . . |
| 15 | . . . some tannins): alkaloids | seem | not to be a deterrent as many can. . . |
| 16 | . . . as a category | seems | not to imply such a perspective. This. . . |
| 17 | . . . coffee made there. It | seems | quite reasonable to assume that, when. . . |
| 18 | . . . transformation.It therefore | seemed | reasonable that other colliding wave. . . |
| 19 | . . . suffers no damage. It might | seem | self-evident that the commission of a. . . |
| 20 | . . . no defence at all, so it | seems | strange and unnecessary that a. . . |
| 21 | . . . controlled conditions. It | seemed | that it might be possible to relate. . . |
| 22 | . . . system. However it does | seem | that mental models can be developed in. . . |
| 23 | . . . so great a difference? It | seems | that problems of proof loom large here. . . |
| 24 | . . . were taking were inert. It | seems | that the symbolic giving of. . . |
| 25 | . . . soon frustrated by what | seemed | the weakness of their leaders in. . . |
| 26 | . . . or sixty years. 9. There | seems | to be a memory for elaborate patterns. . . |
| 27 | . . . effective, administering it | seems | to be a one way bet at. . . |
| 28 | . . . amounts to a crime, and it | seems | to be assumed that players do, and. . . |
| 29 | . . . classical studies,which may | seem | to be at the other extreme of the. . . |
| 30 | . . . analysis of rRNA genes) | seem | to be circulating. Toxin. . . |
| 31 | . . . of 'topic', a notion which | seems | to be essential to concepts such as. . . |
| 32 | . . . between 1982 and 1985 | seems | to be evident, within the current .. |
| 33 | . . . we had got it right. This | seemed | to be further corroborated when we. . . |
| 34 | . . . molluscs, like the bivalves | seemed | to be immune. The group persisted. . . |
| 35 | . . . truth anyway then there | seems | to be little need for dialectical. . . |
| 36 | . . . Within many genera, there | seemed | to be little variation, but, within. . . |
| 37 | . . . debates. Science, somehow, | seems | to be scarcely relevant to the most. . . |
| 38 | . . . behind this proposal | seems | to be that the two parties are adult. . . |
| 39 | . . . instruction Be relevant | seems | to cover all the other instructions.. . . |
| 40 | . . . causing this redistribution | seems | to have been a massive increase in. . . |
| 41 | . . . risk in negligence | seems | to have been recognised by MacKenna. . . |
| 42 | . . . came in 1952. Gironella | seems | to have been very confident about. . . |

| 43 | . . . sauropod dinosaurs they | seem | to have got bigger and bigger during. . . |
| 44 | . . . humans in the Philippines | seem | to have lived in the savannas, so. . . |
| 45 | . . . as anomalous and unjust | seems | to mistake present values as well as. . . |
| 46 | . . . Employers in the main | seem | to see little direct relevance of. . . |
| 47 | . . . once or twice but did not | seem | to set much store by it. She. . . |
| 48 | . . . of particular species | seems | to show elaborate systems for. . . |
| 49 | . . . of either would not have | seemed | to signify a great change. Moreover. . . |
| 50 | . . . 1960) (as quoted above) | seems | to take almost as axiomatic, and. . . |

*Figure C3.1* Academic corpus sample for key term *seem**

| 1 | . . . a bit of a nerve isn't it?, | seems | a bit of a nerve asking us to . . . |
| 2 | . . . are they any more? Yeah. It | seems | a pity but it's not for very . . . |
| 3 | . . . can be used, still. Mhm. But | seems | a pity doesn't it? Mm. On . . . |
| 4 | . . . a good think for sponsor. It | seems | a funny day though. Yeah well she . . . |
| 5 | . . . what. It doesn't really | seem | all that long since our lads . . . |
| 6 | . . . would be. It's quite a, it | seems | at least quite a pleasant hospital . . . |
| 7 | . . . me switch this thing off, it | seems | I've done it now . . . |
| 8 | . . . people you know, they all | seem | jolly. Oh dear. extra half hour . . . |
| 9 | . . . Was he? Aye! It doesn't | seem | long since, looking like Chris . . . |
| 10 | . . . to you somehow the upstairs | seemed | much better. Yeah. Cos it's . . . |
| 11 | . . . yet though we got. She, he | seems | quite er er from the place . . . |
| 12 | . . . What an awful man! She | seems | quite nice really. Mm mm. A . . . |
| 13 | . . . the other hand i, it does | seem, | seem well you've been occupied . . . |
| 14 | . . . four. Mm. When I qualify. | seems | sensible to start as soon as . . . |
| 15 | . . . You know, yeah. She doesn't | seem | the type that would be a school . . . |
| 16 | . . . t must do. The sides always | seem | thinner and shorter than the back . . . |
| 17 | . . . out of this office. There | seems | to be an awful lot of us going . . . |
| 18 | . . . working up by er Well they | seem | to be anyway. they'd gone past . . . |
| 19 | . . . busy yesterday and, and it | seemed | to be a really busy week, but a . . . |
| 20 | . . . that other one nan No, it | seems | to be filling Were they filling? . . . |
| 21 | . . . Because just everything | seems | to be going to pot! Yeah. Mummy . . . |
| 22 | . . . mine I'll make a move. | seems | to be making up a bit. You . . . |
| 23 | . . . ready for anything! Yeah he | seems | to be. Mummy, my head hurts! Your . . . |
| 24 | . . . three letters. Doesn't | seem | to be on. Ya I've seen . . . |
| 25 | . . . like doing that don't you? | seems | to be our general general start . . . |
| 26 | . . . in the night really. He | seemed | to be over it much quicker. And . . . |
| 27 | . . . bit, the walk into college | seems | to be, that bit. Yeah. Cos . . . |
| 28 | . . . of it you know Bit of a | seems | to be wide awake could of got up . . . |
| 29 | . . . still there too? And she | seemed | to call her, she was known as Mrs . . . |
| 30 | . . . Oh yes but I mean they they | seem | to concentrate pretty well round . . . |
| 31 | . . . how many he got, he didn't | seem | to do too badly, but he said Alex . . . |
| 32 | . . . if you think about it. He | seems | to enjoy the job doesn't he? . . . |
| 33 | . . . time at all. Mm. But we | seem | to er where we live erm at the . . . |
| 34 | . . . the problem. Yeah, he always | seems | to fiddle. Well I mean the Sugar . . . |
| 35 | . . . has he? Really? No. He never | seems | to have any homework to do though . . . |
| 36 | . . . half past ten, but eh, it | seems | to have cured the problem we had . . . |
| 37 | . . . going to support. Yeah. They | seem | to have got it together a bit more . . . |
| 38 | . . . good jollop well she Yes. | seemed | to have Well yes, but I mean it . . . |
| 39 | . . . for a. At the start it | seemed | to improve the matches but it . . . |
| 40 | . . . not completely sure. He | seems | to know me cos he erm when we . . . |
| 41 | . . . be working on that now it | seems | to me. Er in principle. Yes . . . |
| 42 | . . . dried up quite well, they | seemed | to of [=have] dried up we'll see . . . |
| 43 | . . . he's on crutches but he | seems | to quite nicely. So how do you . . . |
| 44 | . . . Why, what happened? Well I | seem | to recall that we were in the . . . |
| 45 | . . . think it was in this one. I | seem | to remember looking at it in the . . . |

continued

| 46 | . . . we Andy and Michelle? I | seem | to remember she says she's gonna . . . |
| 47 | . . . Hold your breath and push | seems | to work on me. stand on your . . . |
| 48 | . . . when we lose but it doesn't | seem | to work work. Any ideas ? Well yeah . . . |
| 49 | . . . Times may be tough but it | seems | we're taking less care of our . . . |
| 50 | . . . in. I know, but that one | seems | worse than anywhere, isn't it . . . |

*Figure C3.2* Spoken corpus sample for key term *seem**

## Commentary

■ We can see from these figures that both corpus samples under-represent *seem*, but over-represent both *seems* and *seemed*. The most substantial discrepancy is the under-representation of *seem* in the spoken corpus sample. It is worth bearing this information in mind as you explore the two corpus samples.

■ Here is a possible classification of grammatical patterns that follow *seem** in the academic corpus sample.

| Grammatical pattern | Examples | Number |
|---|---|---|
| seem* + [adj phrase]+ to + infinitive | (17)  . . . seems quite reasonable to assume . . . | 28 |
| seem* + [not] + to + infinitive | (26)  . . . seems to be a memory . . . | |
| | (16)  . . . seems not to imply . . . | |
| seem* + [adj phrase] + that-clause | (10)  . . . seems highly likely that . . . | 9 |
| | (21)  . . . seemed that it might be possible . . . | |
| seem* + [adv] + adj phrase | (4)  . . . seems curiously narrow . . . | 11 |
| | (5)  . . . seems dated . . . | |
| seem* + noun phrase[1] | (25)  . . . seemed the weakness . . . | 1 |
| Other | (1)  . . . seemed. We . . . | 1 |

*Note*:

Example 25 could, alternatively, be classified as a *seem** + to + *infinitive* + *noun phrase* with *to* + *infinitive* omitted: 'seemed [to be] the weakness of their leaders . . .'.

Here is a similar classification for the spoken corpus sample.

| Grammatical pattern | Examples | Number |
| --- | --- | --- |
| seem* + [adj phrase]+ to [+ infinitive][1] | (14) ... seems sensible to start ... | 31 |
| | (17) ... seems to be an awful ... | |
| | (43) ... seems to quite nicely ... | |
| seem* + [noun phrase] + *that*-clause | (15) ... seem the type that ... | 3 |
| *and* seem* + [that]-clause[2] | (7) ... seems I've done it now ... | |
| seem* + [adv] + adj phrase | (12) ... seems quite nice ... | 6 |
| | (8) ... seem jolly ... | |
| seem* + [adv phrase] + noun phrase | (6) ... seems at least quite a pleasant hospital | 5 |
| | (1) ... seems a bit of a nerve ... | |
| Other[3] | (11) ... seems quite er er ... | 4 |

*Notes:*

1 In one case, (43), the infinitive is recoverable from the wider context and omitted after *to*: 'seems to [be walking around] quite nicely . . .'.
2 We have classified 7 and 49 as having *that*-clauses with *that* omitted: 'seems [that] I've done it now . . .'; '. . . seems [that] we're taking less care . . .'.
3 In three cases, 11, 13 and 33, clauses are incomplete. 41 includes a pattern that occurs only once.

Here are some observations that you might have made in comparing the figures and the sample concordance lines:

- The pattern *seem + adj phrase/not + to + infinitive* is the most frequent in both samples, with similar numbers in each. The two occurrences of *seems not to* in the academic sample, compared with none in the spoken sample may indicate that this is a pattern preferred in academic writing. If we look to the left of the keyword, we find three examples of negation of *seem* with *doesn't* in the spoken sample (24, 31, 48), but only one in the academic sample (47: *did not*), and it may be that this is the preferred form in speech.

When we looked at the larger academic and spoken corpora we found the following number of occurrences (and frequency per 10,000 words) of these and related patterns. Do they support our observations from analysis of the samples? What else do they suggest?

| Pattern | Academic corpus | Spoken corpus |
|---|---|---|
| *seem\* not to* + infinitive | 5    (0.05) | 0    (0) |
| *doesn't/don't seem to* + infinitive | 4    (0.04) | 39    (0.35) |
| auxiliary *(do/does/did/may/ would etc.)* + *not seem* | 21    (0.2) | 1    (0.01) |
| Total | 30    (0.28) | 40    (0.36) |

Returning to the corpus samples, the most common infinitive in this pattern is *be*, with similar numbers in each. However, looking to the right of *be* suggests differences. In the academic sample it is commonly followed by an adjective, with or without a preceding adverb – *essential, evident, immune, scarcely relevant* – while in the spoken sample the only example is *wide awake*. Also present in the academic sample, but missing from the spoken sample are *be* + *past participle* (*assumed, corroborated*) and the pattern *seem\* to be little* + *noun phrase* (*need, variation*). A more likely alternative to this last pattern in speech might be *doesn't/didn't seem to be much.*

- The pattern *seem\** + *[noun phrase]* + *that-clause* is considerably more frequent in the academic than in the spoken sample. Further, in only one of the three examples of this pattern in the spoken sample is *that* included. The evidence suggests, then, that in academic writing the preference is to include *that* where it is grammatically possible to omit it ('seems that mental modes can be developed' rather than 'seems mental modes can be developed'), but in speech to omit it ('seems we're taking less care' rather than 'seems that we're taking less care'). We return to *that*-clauses in Activity 3 below. (You might also look back at the work of Greenbaum *et al.* reported in Unit A9.2 at this point.)
- The pattern *seem\** + *[adverb]* + *adjective* is more common in the academic sample. In most examples in both samples, the writer or speaker is giving their opinion on something they have previously mentioned ('this approach seems curiously dated', 'they all seem jolly').
- While there are six examples of the pattern *seem+ [adverb phrase]* + *noun phrase* in the spoken sample, there is only one in the academic sample. Noun phrases found in the spoken sample, such as 'a bit of a nerve' and 'a pity', are more appropriate for informal contexts, and the evidence suggests that this pattern is not a common way of expressing opinion in academic writing.

In all six cases in the spoken sample, 'to be' could have been inserted after *seem\**: e.g. 'seems [to be] a bit of a nerve'. There is one example in the academic sample of *seem\** + *to be* + *noun phrase* where 'to be' could have been omitted: 'seems [to be] a one way bet'. However, there is also an example where it is omitted but could have been included: 'seemed the weakness of their leaders'. While the evidence suggests that the preference is to omit 'to be' in speech, where there is a choice, it is not clear from this sample whether the preference in writing is to include or omit it. We would need to look further at the corpus to investigate this.

## Task C3.2

### Focus

We will now look to the left of the keyword. As the concordances lines printed above are sorted alphabetically according to the word <u>after</u> the keyword, it is more difficult to identify patterns that come before. Here, then, we will focus only on one feature: the word *it* as the subject of the verb *seem*\*. Note that this may come immediately before *seem* or there may be words between the subject and verb.

➤ How many occurrences of *it* as the subject of *seem*\* are there in the two corpus samples?

➤ Can you classify them according to their meaning?

➤ What differences do you observe between the uses of *it* in the two samples? (Having identified the relevant concordance lines, it may help to look for patterns to the right of the keyword.)

### Commentary

It might be that you have identified just two categories: *it* referring to a person or thing (e.g. Sp (3): At the start *it* seemed to improve the matches . . .), and *it* having another function (e.g. Ac (28) . . . *it* seems to be assumed that players do . . .). In the table below we have also made this division, but have gone on to make a finer distinction within the 'other function' category, between *it* functioning as an introductory subject and *it* functioning as an empty subject.

As an introductory subject (sometimes also called 'anticipatory *it*'), *it* anticipates a clause. For example, in

   . . . *it* seems to be assumed that players do . . .

*it* anticipates the following *that*-clause, and is understood to mean something like

   'that players do seems to be assumed'.

As an empty subject, *it* is used were there is no participant to go into the subject slot in the clause, as in

   . . . *it* seemed to be a really busy week . . .

| Meaning | Academic sample: number | Examples | Spoken sample: number | Examples |
|---|---|---|---|---|
| Referring to a thing | 2 | (1) . . . what a long way it seemed. (27) . . .administering it seems to be . . .[1] | 6 | (3) . . . It seems a funny day though . . . (36) . . . it seems to have cured the problem . . . |
| Introductory subject | 11 | (2) . . . it seems almost equally possible that . . . (17) It seems quite reasonable to assume that . . . | 6[2] | (2) . . . It seems a pity . . . (49) . . . it seems we're taking less care . . . |
| Empty subject | 0 | | 2 | (7) . . . it seems I've done it now . . . (19) . . . it seemed to be a really busy week . . . |
| Total | 13 | | 14 | |

*Notes*:

1  Here 'it' is part of the subject 'administering it'.
2  It could be argued that 1 and 2 are also in this category but 'it' is omitted.

We need to be very cautious when interpreting these figures, as we are dealing with very small numbers of examples. However, we might note that the reference function of *it* is more common in the spoken than the written sample. It would be unsurprising if this did not represent a more general tendency, given that in speech we are more likely to refer to things in the immediate physical environment than we are in academic writing, where the only 'physical' entity is the text itself. Second, the figures suggest that the empty subject is less common in the academic corpus than in the spoken corpus.

We can observe a clearer distinction if we look at the kinds of clauses that follow an introductory *it*. In all eleven examples in the academic sample, introductory *it* anticipates a *that*-clause. For example:

2.   it seems almost equally possible *that*. . . .
10.   it seems highly likely *that* . . .

We noted in the *Introduction and Background to Data* that academic writers typically hedge their claims when reporting results, interpretations, conclusions, and so on, and that choice of the verb *seem* is one way of doing this. Further, the pattern *it* + *seem\** + *that*-clause provides a 'slot' between the verb and the *that*-clause where the writer can indicate the extent of their commitment to a proposition in the *that*-clause, as in:

10.   it seems *highly likely* that . . .

or in some other way add a comment or opinion on the proposition:

> 28. it seems *to be assumed* that players do . . .
> 20. it seems *strange and unnecessary* that . . .

The evidence suggests, then, that this is a frequent pattern in academic writing which is found less commonly in speech.

Before going on, consider what you have learnt from your explorations in Tasks C3.1 and C3.2 of the grammatical patterns associated with *seem\**. What differences have you observed in the academic and spoken corpus samples, and how do these differences reflect the contexts in which the two sets of data were produced?

## Task C3.3

### *Focus*

Here are four more sets of concordance lines for you to explore. Samples 1*a* and 1*b* below are from the academic writing corpus, and samples 2*a* and *b* are from the spoken corpus, with the key term *hope\** (the keywords *hope, hopes* and *hoped*). The *a* samples are sorted alphabetically according to the word to the right of the key term and the *b* samples are sorted alphabetically according to the word to the left of the key term.

The table below gives some preliminary information about the number of occurrences of *hope, hopes,* and *hoped*. The figures in brackets give the number of occurrences of each per 10,000 words.

|  | Academic corpus | Spoken corpus |
|---|---|---|
| hope (noun) | 22 (0.2) | 6 (0.05) |
| hope (verb) | 32 (0.3) | 199 (1.8) |
| hopes (noun) | 8 (0.07) | 6 (0.05) |
| hope (verb) | 1 (0.01) | 2 (0.02) |
| hoped | 14 (0.13) | 6 (0.05) |

➤ Explore the sets of samples. What observations can you make from these about the grammar of *hope\** in the two corpora?

247

## Data

| | | |
|---|---|---|
| 1 | . . . it now, it spells out a lot of | hope'. Yet she felt little had been . . . |
| 2 | . . . for Balbinder that we had | hoped. There were complaints about his . . . |
| 3 | . . . original language' as Foucault | hopes. The problem for Foucault is that . . . |
| 4 | . . . and though you will consider my | hope a baseless one I still entertain . . . |
| 5 | . . . to make reality out of pious | hopes, and it recognized the propaganda . . . |
| 6 | . . . over many years and whose | hopes and aspirations are at one with . . . |
| 7 | . . . end remains to be seen, but I | hope at the very least I have been able . . . |
| 8 | . . . had said, wistfully, 'I do | hope Balbinder learn so quickly he will . . . |
| 9 | . . . such schemes rarely have the | hoped for success because the . . . |
| 10 | . . . structure, investing their | hopes for greater happiness in the . . . |
| 11 | . . . yet to be released. The only | hope for a pessimist like Law was to . . . |
| 12 | . . . conceding all that could be | hoped for from Ulster's resistance, but . . . |
| 13 | . . . state of mind, undermined | hopes for their social progress. The . . . |
| 14 | . . . known as 'normal'. However, I | hope I am not so complacent that I am . . . |
| 15 | . . . inertia, there is also, we | hope, little shirking of awkward issues . . . |
| 16 | . . . benefit system which it is | hoped may provide more flexible support . . . |
| 17 | . . . Sartre at last abandons all | hope of proving History as a . . . |
| 18 | . . . grounds for assisting it, in | hopes of booty or even territorial gain . . . |
| 19 | . . . responses with any reasonable | hope of reliability let alone validity . . . |
| 20 | . . . pursued the government in the | hope of catching them out in a snap . . . |
| 21 | . . . in the Labour movement in the | hope of carrying them over into . . . |
| 22 | . . . the Empire and the last | hope of reversing the drift into class . . . |
| 23 | . . . carried with it the last | hope of consolidating the Empire and . . . |
| 24 | . . . questionnaire too long in the | hope of getting just that little bit . . . |
| 25 | . . . in opening up this area. I | hope other historians will now follow . . . |
| 26 | . . . rather than France. Again this | hope seems set against the tides of . . . |
| 27 | . . . his pension scheme with the | hope that the sufferings, the . . . |
| 28 | . . . It was explained that it was | hoped that they would 'befriend' a . . . |
| 29 | . . . acceptable. If nothing else we | hope that by attending college the . . . |
| 30 | . . . can lead to effectiveness. We | hope that improved methodology will . . . |
| 31 | . . . forever. We might perhaps | hope that one species lingered on . . . |
| 32 | . . . It will seem obvious, I | hope, that a rule for learning or for . . . |
| 33 | . . . Disaster Reduction. Let us | hope that G1S can, in some small way . . . |
| 34 | . . . even earlier history, and we | hope that the crucial steps did not . . . |
| 35 | . . . reflex generated vain | hopes that psychology, and in . . . |
| 36 | . . . 1951). At the time it was | hoped that eventually it would be . . . |
| 37 | . . . my life over again I wish and | hope that everything happens the same . . . |
| 38 | . . . all this to Mrs Singh and | hoped that I would be able to explain . . . |
| 39 | . . . still to be gone through and | hoped that they would soon hear whether . . . |
| 40 | . . . a feminist perspective. We | hope this will be of value to both . . . |
| 41 | . . . so the intellectual can best | hope to be specific rather than . . . |
| 42 | . . . abroad. By this means we | hope to place at the disposal of our . . . |
| 43 | . . . control, from Cluny, which | hoped to reabsorb the abbey into its . . . |
| 44 | . . . I am sure that we cannot | hope to do this rethinking while still . . . |
| 45 | . . . of Western metaphysics, I | hope to make her work more accessible . . . |
| 46 | . . . several years' service, might | hope to be rewarded with fiefs. Others . . . |
| 47 | . . . life and death in a sward and | hope ultimately to be able to collect . . . |
| 48 | . . . funding arrangements, which I | hope will not add to the difficulties . . . |
| 49 | . . . Mr Asquith this session. I | hope you will understand. In later . . . |
| 50 | . . . Manchester Dispatch: I | hope you will continue this form of . . . |

*Figure C3.3* Academic corpus sample for key term *hope** (right word sorted)

| 1 | . . . Sartre at last abandons all | hope | of proving History as a . . . |
| 2 | . . . my life over again I wish and | hope | that everything happens the same . . . |
| 3 | . . . life and death in a sward and | hope | ultimately to be able to collect . . . |
| 4 | . . . still to be gone through and | hoped | that they would soon hear whether . . . |
| 5 | . . . all this to Mrs Singh and | hoped | that I would be able to explain . . . |
| 6 | . . . conceding all that could be | hoped | for from Ulster's resistance, but . . . |
| 7 | . . . so the intellectual can best | hope | to be specific rather than . . . |
| 8 | . . . had said, wistfully, 'I do | hope | Balbinder learn so quickly he will . . . |
| 9 | . . . original language' as Foucault | hopes. | The problem for Foucault is that . . . |
| 10 | . . . for Balbinder that we had | hoped. | There were complaints about his . . . |
| 11 | . . . end remains to be seen, but I | hope | at the very least I have been able . . . |
| 12 | . . . known as 'normal'. However,I | hope | I am not so complacent that I am . . . |
| 13 | . . . in opening up this area. I | hope | other historians will now follow . . . |
| 14 | . . . funding arrangements, which I | hope | will not add to the difficulties of . . . |
| 15 | . . . It will seem obvious, I | hope, | that a rule for learning or for . . . |
| 16 | . . . of Western metaphysics, I | hope | to make her work more accessible . . . |
| 17 | . . . Mr Asquith this session. I | hope | you will understand. In later . . . |
| 18 | . . . Manchester Dispatch: I | hope | you will continue this form of . . . |
| 19 | . . . grounds for assisting it, in | hopes | of booty or even territorial gains . . . |
| 20 | . . . benefit system which it is | hoped | may provide more flexible support . . . |
| 21 | . . . carried with it the last | hope | of consolidating the Empire and . . . |
| 22 | . . . the Empire and the last | hope | of reversing the drift into class . . . |
| 23 | . . . several years' service, might | hope | to be rewarded with fiefs. Others . . . |
| 24 | . . . although you will consider my | hope | a baseless one I still entertain . . . |
| 25 | . . . I am sure that we cannot | hope | to do this rethinking while still . . . |
| 26 | . . . now, it spells out a lot of | hope'. | Yet she felt little had been . . . |
| 27 | . . . yet to be released. The only | hope | for a pessimist like Law was to . . . |
| 28 | . . . forever. We might perhaps | hope | that one species lingered on, like . . . |
| 29 | . . . to make reality out of pious | hopes, | and it recognized the propaganda . . . |
| 30 | . . . responses with any reasonable | hope | of reliability let alone validity . . . |
| 31 | . . . such schemes rarely have the | hoped | for success because the difficulty . . . |
| 32 | . . . questionnaire too long in the | hope | of getting just that little bit . . . |
| 33 | . . . his pension scheme with the | hope | that the sufferings, the sacrifices . . . |
| 34 | . . . in the Labour movement in the | hope | of carrying them over into . . . |
| 35 | . . . pursued the government in the | hope | of catching them out in a snap . . . |
| 36 | . . . structure, investing their | hopes | for greater happiness in the power . . . |
| 37 | . . . rather than France. Again this | hope | seems set against the tides of . . . |
| 38 | . . . state of mind, undermined | hopes | for their social progress. The . . . |
| 39 | . . . Disaster Reduction. Let us | hope | that G1S can, in some small way . . . |
| 40 | . . . reflex generated vain | hopes | that psychology, and in particular . . . |
| 41 | . . . It was explained that it was | hoped | that they would 'befriend' a life . . . |
| 42 | . . . 1951. At the time it was | hoped | that eventually it would be . . . |
| 43 | . . . can lead to effectiveness. We | hope | that improved methodology will . . . |
| 44 | . . . even earlier history, and we | hope | that the crucial steps did not all . . . |
| 45 | . . . a feminist perspective. We | hope | this will be of value to both . . . |
| 46 | . . . If nothing else we | hope | that by attending college the . . . |
| 47 | . . . inertia, there is also, we | hope, | little shirking of awkward issues . . . |
| 48 | . . . abroad. By this means we | hope | to place at the disposal of our . . . |
| 49 | . . . control, from Cluny, which | hoped | to reabsorb the abbey into its . . . |
| 50 | . . . over many years and whose | hopes | and aspirations are at one with . . . |

*Figure C3.4* Academic corpus sample for key term *hope** (left word sorted)

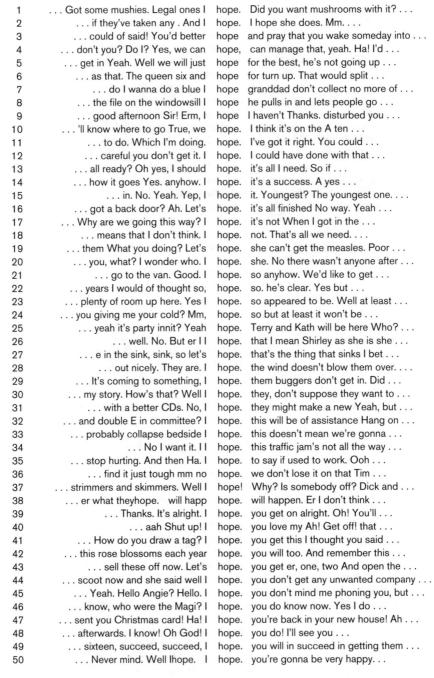

| | | | |
|---|---|---|---|
| 1 | . . . Got some mushies. Legal ones I | hope. | Did you want mushrooms with it? . . . |
| 2 | . . . if they've taken any . And I | hope. | I hope she does. Mm. . . . |
| 3 | . . . could of said! You'd better | hope | and pray that you wake someday into . . . |
| 4 | . . . don't you? Do I? Yes, we can | hope, | can manage that, yeah. Ha! I'd . . . |
| 5 | . . . get in Yeah. Well we will just | hope | for the best, he's not going up . . . |
| 6 | . . . as that. The queen six and | hope | for turn up. That would split . . . |
| 7 | . . . do I wanna do a blue I | hope | granddad don't collect no more of . . . |
| 8 | . . . the file on the windowsill I | hope | he pulls in and lets people go . . . |
| 9 | . . . good afternoon Sir! Erm, I | hope | I haven't Thanks. disturbed you . . . |
| 10 | . . . 'll know where to go True, we | hope. | I think it's on the A ten . . . |
| 11 | . . . to do. Which I'm doing. | hope. | I've got it right. You could . . . |
| 12 | . . . careful you don't get it. I | hope. | I could have done with that . . . |
| 13 | . . . all ready? Oh yes, I should | hope. | it's all I need. So if . . . |
| 14 | . . . how it goes Yes. anyhow. I | hope. | it's a success. A yes . . . |
| 15 | . . . in. No. Yeah. Yep, I | hope. | it. Youngest? The youngest one. . . . |
| 16 | . . . got a back door? Ah. Let's | hope. | it's all finished No way. Yeah . . . |
| 17 | . . . Why are we going this way? I | hope. | it's not When I got in the . . . |
| 18 | . . . means that I don't think. I | hope. | not. That's all we need. . . . |
| 19 | . . . them What you doing? Let's | hope. | she can't get the measles. Poor . . . |
| 20 | . . . you, what? I wonder who. I | hope. | she. No there wasn't anyone after . . . |
| 21 | . . . go to the van. Good. I | hope. | so anyhow. We'd like to get . . . |
| 22 | . . . years I would of thought so, | hope. | so. he's clear. Yes but . . . |
| 23 | . . . plenty of room up here. Yes I | hope. | so appeared to be. Well at least . . . |
| 24 | . . . you giving me your cold? Mm, | hope. | so but at least it won't be . . . |
| 25 | . . . yeah it's party innit? Yeah | hope. | Terry and Kath will be here Who? . . . |
| 26 | . . . well. No. But er I I | hope. | that I mean Shirley as she is she . . . |
| 27 | . . . e in the sink, sink, so let's | hope. | that's the thing that sinks I bet . . . |
| 28 | . . . out nicely. They are. I | hope. | the wind doesn't blow them over. . . . |
| 29 | . . . It's coming to something, I | hope. | them buggers don't get in. Did . . . |
| 30 | . . . my story. How's that? Well I | hope. | they, don't suppose they want to . . . |
| 31 | . . . with a better CDs. No, I | hope. | they might make a new Yeah, but . . . |
| 32 | . . . and double E in committee? I | hope. | this will be of assistance Hang on . . . |
| 33 | . . . probably collapse bedside I | hope. | this doesn't mean we're gonna . . . |
| 34 | . . . No I want it. I I | hope. | this traffic jam's not all the way . . . |
| 35 | . . . stop hurting. And then Ha. I | hope. | to say if used to work. Ooh . . . |
| 36 | . . . find it just tough mm no | hope. | we don't lose it on that Tim . . . |
| 37 | . . . strimmers and skimmers. Well I | hope! | Why? Is somebody off? Dick and . . . |
| 38 | . . . er what theyhope.   will happ | hope. | will happen. Er I don't think . . . |
| 39 | . . . Thanks. It's alright. I | hope. | you get on alright. Oh! You'll . . . |
| 40 | . . . aah Shut up! I | hope. | you love my Ah! Get off! that . . . |
| 41 | . . . How do you draw a tag? I | hope. | you get this I thought you said . . . |
| 42 | . . . this rose blossoms each year | hope. | you will too. And remember this . . . |
| 43 | . . . sell these off now. Let's | hope. | you get er, one, two And open the . . . |
| 44 | . . . scoot now and she said well I | hope. | you don't get any unwanted company . . . |
| 45 | . . . Yeah. Hello Angie? Hello. I | hope. | you don't mind me phoning you, but . . . |
| 46 | . . . know, who were the Magi? I | hope. | you do know now. Yes I do . . . |
| 47 | . . . sent you Christmas card! Ha! I | hope. | you're back in your new house! Ah . . . |
| 48 | . . . afterwards. I know! Oh God! I | hope. | you do! I'll see you . . . |
| 49 | . . . sixteen, succeed, succeed, I | hope. | you will in succeed in getting them . . . |
| 50 | . . . Never mind. Well Ihope.   I | hope. | you're gonna be very happy. . . . |

*Figure C3.5* Spoken corpus sample for key term *hope** (right word sorted)

| 1 | . . . to do. Which I'm doing. | Hope | I've got it right. You could . . . |
|---|---|---|---|
| 2 | . . . as that. The queen six and | hope | for turn up. That would split . . . |
| 3 | . . . could of said! You'd better | hope | and pray that you wake someday into . . . |
| 4 | . . . don't you? Do I? Yes, we can | hope, | can manage that, yeah. Ha! I'd . . . |
| 5 | . . . what they hope will happ | hope | will happen. Er I don't think . . . |
| 6 | . . . my story. How's that? Well I | hope | they, don't suppose they want to . . . |
| 7 | . . . stop hurting. And then Ha. I | hope | to say if used to work. Ooh . . . |
| 8 | . . . well. No. But er I I | hope | that I mean Shirley as she is she . . . |
| 9 | . . . if they've taken any. And I | hope. | I hope she does. Mm. . . . |
| 10 | . . . good afternoon Sir! Erm, I | hope | I haven't Thanks. disturbed you but . . . |
| 11 | . . . sixteen, succeed, succeed, I | hope | you will in succeed in getting them . . . |
| 12 | . . . careful you don't get it. I | hope | I could have done with that . . . |
| 13 | . . . plenty of room up here. Yes I | hope | so appeared to be. Well at least . . . |
| 14 | . . . you Christmas card! Ha! I | hope | you're back in your new house! Ah . . . |
| 15 | . . . Why are we going this way? I | hope | it's not When I got in the . . . |
| 16 | . . . know, who were the Magi? I | hope | you do know now. Yes I do . . . |
| 17 | . . . out nicely. They are. I | hope | the wind doesn't blow them over. . . . |
| 18 | . . . probably collapse bedside I | hope | this doesn't mean we're gonna . . . |
| 19 | . . . afterwards. I know! Oh God! I | hope | you do! I'll see you anyway. . . . |
| 20 | . . . Never mind. Well I | hope | I hope you're gonna be very happy. . . . |
| 21 | . . . how it goes Yes. anyhow. I | hope | it's a success. A yes . . . . |
| 22 | . . . go to the van. Good. I | hope | so anyhow. We'd like to get . . . |
| 23 | . . . and skimmers. Well I | hope! | Why? Is somebody off? Dick and . . . |
| 24 | . . . aah Shut up! I | hope | you love my Ah! Get off! that . . . |
| 25 | . . . you, what? I wonder who. I | hope | she. No there wasn't anyone after . . . |
| 26 | . . . in. No. Yeah. Yep, I | hope | it. Youngest? The youngest one. Ah . . . |
| 27 | . . . means that I don't think. I | hope | not. That's all we need . . . |
| 28 | . . . No I want it. I I | hope | this traffic jam's not all the way . . . |
| 29 | . . . Thanks. It's alright. I | hope | you get on alright? Oh! You'll . . . |
| 30 | . . . How do you draw a tag? I | hope | you get this I thought you said . . . |
| 31 | . . . do I wanna do a blue I | hope | granddad don't collect no more of . . . |
| 32 | . . . some mushies. Legal ones I | hope. | Did you want mushrooms with it? Yes . . . |
| 33 | . . . the file on the windowsill I | hope | he pulls in and lets people go past . . . |
| 34 | . . . Yeah. Hello Angie? Hello. I | hope | you don't mind me phoning you, but . . . |
| 35 | . . . scoot now and she said well I | hope | you don't get any unwanted company . . . |
| 36 | . . . It's coming to something, I | hope | them buggers don't get in. Did . . . |
| 37 | . . . double E in committee? I | hope | this will be of assistance Hang on . . . |
| 38 | . . . with a better CDs. No, I | hope | they might make a new Yeah, but C . . . |
| 39 | . . . in Yeah. Well we will just | hope | for the best, he's not going up . . . |
| 40 | . . . got a back door? Ah. Let's | hope | it's all finished No way. Yeah . . . |
| 41 | . . . in the sink, sink, so let's | hope | that's the thing that sinks I bet . . . |
| 42 | . . . sell these off now. Let's | hope | you get er, one, two And open the . . . |
| 43 | . . . them What you doing? Let's | hope | she can't get the measles . . . |
| 44 | . . . you giving me your cold? Mm, | hope | so but at least it won't be . . . |
| 45 | . . . find it just tough mm no | hope | we don't lose it on that Tim . . . |
| 46 | . . . all ready? Oh yes, I should | hope | it's all I need. So if . . . |
| 47 | . . . years I would of thought so, | hope | so. he's clear. Yes but . . . |
| 48 | . . . know where to go True, we | hope | I think it's on the A ten . . . |
| 49 | . . . yeah it's party innit? Yeah | hope | Terry and Kath will be here Who? . . . |
| 50 | . . . this rose blossoms each year | hope | you will too. And remember this day . . . |

*Figure C3.6* Spoken corpus sample for key term *hope** (left word sorted)

## IDEAS FOR FURTHER RESEARCH

In this unit we have investigated a commercially available corpus of academic text. Details of this and other corpora, and links to further information on topics such as concordancing software can be found at http://www.natcorp.ox.ac.uk. The alternative is to build your own corpus of academic text, either by scanning paper versions of academic text or by downloading texts from the Internet. If you plan to do this, there are questions of copyright to consider, and it is sensible to obtain permission from publishers before adding text to a corpus on your own computer. Lynn Bowker and Jennifer Pearson's book *Working with Specialized Language* (2002) has many helpful suggestions on building corpora and obtaining permissions. In most of the suggestions that follow on further research that you could do in the area of the grammar of academic writing we assume that you can build your own corpora with the necessary permissions to do so. Always, however, keep in mind that your corpus will be relatively small, so may not be as representative as a much larger corpus. This will influence your interpretation of your findings.

Here are some ideas on types of corpora you could build and comparisons you could undertake in order to explore the contexts in which written texts are produced:

- Compare particular genres across academic disciplines. For example, you could compare journal articles in different disciplines, or you could take particular sections of a genre (such as abstracts within research articles) across disciplines.
- Compare different genres within the same discipline. For example, you could compare undergraduate textbooks with journal articles, or school textbooks with undergraduate textbooks.
- Compare a student corpus of writing with published writing in the same discipline. As students are sometimes told explicitly that the style of writing that they should aim for at university should be that represented in journal articles, this would make a valid comparison.
- If you have access to students who are non-native speakers of English, build a learner corpus of their academic writing and compare it with a corpus of published writing from the discipline in which they work.
- If you have access to both native and non-native speakers of English following the same course of study, build a corpus of similar academic writing (such as essays) from each group, and compare the two.

Here are a few grammatical features that you could possibly explore in any of the comparisons suggested above and which lend themselves to corpus analysis. Some of these are explained in more detail in texts presented in Section B of this book:

- Directives. Ken Hyland (2002; see also B3) studies the following directive forms. Imperatives *Add, Allow, Analyse, Apply, Arrange, Assess, Assume, Calculate, Choose, Classify, Compare, Connect, Consider, Consult, Contrast, Define, Demonstrate, Determine, Do not, Develop, Employ, Ensure, Estimate, Evaluate, Find, Follow, Go, Imagine, Increase, Input, Insert, Integrate, Key, Let A = B, Let's,*

*Look at/etc., Mark, Measure, Mount, Note, Notice, Observe, Order, Pay, Picture, Prepare, Recall, Recover, Refer, Regard, Remember, Remove, See, Select, Set, Show, Suppose, State, Think about, Think of, Turn, Use;* Necessity modals *Should, Ought, Need to, Needs to, Have to, Has to, Must; It is . . . It is critical to do, It is crucial to, It is essential to, It is imperative to, It is important to, It is imperative to, It is indispensable to, It is necessary to, It is obligatory to, It is required to, It is significant to, It is vital to.*

- Personal pronouns and other 'informal' elements such as sentence initial *and, but, so, or,* and *however* (see also Yu-Ying Chang and John Swales 1999, and B3)

- Conjunctions. For example, those expressing: condition, either directly (*if, unless*) or indirectly (*in the event of/that, provided/providing(that), assuming (that), suppose/supposing (that)*; or concession (*although, though, even though, while, whilst, whereas*).

- Grammatical components of 'hedging'. For example, the verbs *indicate, would (not), may (not), suggest, could, appear, might (not), should, seem.*

While the exploration of an electronic corpus of text using specialised software allows large quantities of data to be analysed speedily, of course not all work on academic writing needs to use this technique. You could undertake any of the research we have suggested above using paper texts, although it is likely that the amount of data that you can work with will be considerably less. Indeed, some grammatical analyses will probably be better conducted in this way. For example, nominalisation and grammatical metaphor (see Michael Halliday's paper in Unit B3) would be difficult to analyse thoroughly using only key word searches and concordance lines.

Although our focus in this unit is on academic writing, there is a ready-made corpus of speech produced in academic contexts available at http://www.hti.umich.edu/m/micase/. The Michigan Corpus of Academic Spoken English (MICASE) is a collection of transcribed speech events from the University of Michigan in the United States, including lectures, meetings, seminars, and so on. Online you can search the corpus for words or phrases in specified contexts and receive up to 500 concordance lines with information about the speech event each line occurred in, together with links to the full transcripts. As a starting point, you could look for the search terms *seem** or *hope**, comparing your findings in this unit with what you discover in the MICASE.

You can find other ideas for further research in Tony McEnery, Richard Xiao and Yukio Tono's *Corpus Based Language Studies: An advanced resource book* (2005).

## Unit C4
## Exploring grammar in computer-mediated communication: instant messaging

### INTRODUCTION AND BACKGROUND TO DATA

The speed of change in how we communicate by electronic means has been so rapid since the 1990s that it is difficult to predict with any certainty what will be the commonplace form of electronic communication by the time you are reading this. If we had been writing in 1990, an account of text messaging on mobile phones would have seemed almost futuristic. However, at the time of writing it is commonplace within parts of society in many countries.

In this unit we will explore the relationships between context and grammar in a form of written communication that is becoming popular at the present time: sending electronic messages using software such as MSN Messenger – instant messaging. The features of instant messaging are that, like email, written messages are sent between computers but, unlike most uses of email, responses are intended to be more or less instantaneous, with sender(s) and receiver(s) simultaneously logged on to their computers, so that a conversation-like discourse is built up between participants. Recent reductions in the cost of long Internet connection, and the introduction of Broadband technology allowing the user to be permanently on line, are making instant messaging viable for home computer users, particularly – in our experience – young people.

The data in this unit is a sample of instant messaging between, Mark, aged 15, and Linda, 14, in Activity 1 and between Mark and Angela, 14, in Activity 2. (All names have been changed.)

Before working on this unit you should have read Unit B4, focusing particularly on the differences between electronic and face-to-face communication noted by David Crystal.

**Task C4.1**

*Focus*

Linda (L) begins a conversation with Mark (M), and makes the first contribution 'hi' and the second, 'im a frend of kt's [I'm a friend of Katie's]'. After a contribution is sent, Messenger indicates whether the recipient is composing a response, allowing overlap between contributions to be avoided, but not preventing more than one contribution per turn. Difficulties arising from turns overlapping in their composition can occur, particularly where more than two participants are involved, but in the sample we look at here this appears not to be a problem. In Messenger interaction, the participant's screen 'name' precedes each contribution. However, as these can be long (Mark's is twenty-six words long and Linda's ten!), they are omitted here.

➤ Look at the extract and consider what differences there are between its grammar and that of standard written grammar, and why these differences might occur.

➤ Consider also how Mark and Linda simulate features of face-to-face spoken interaction in their messages.

Notes are added to clarify some parts of the interaction.

*Data*

1   L   hi

2   L   im a frend of kt's

> An expression of pleasure, but probably intended to be ironic.

3   M   joy, which friend?

4   L   linda

5   M   linda . . . ???

6   L   smith

7   M   and which kt by da way?

> lol – 'laughs out loud'

8   M   lol

9   L   brown or jones#

> The Katie they are referring to uses two surnames, Brown or Jones, because her parents are separated.

10   M   oh rite, its just my sis is kt 2, I was just makin sure, lol

11   L   how r u anyway

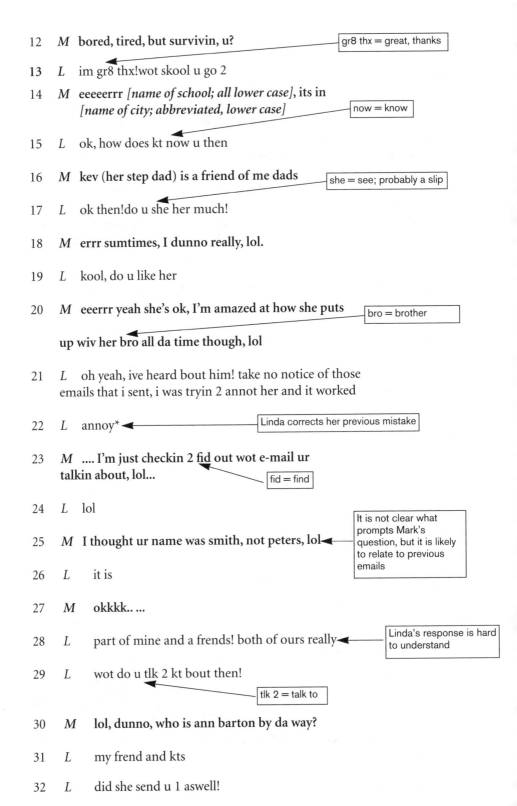

12  *M*  bored, tired, but survivin, u?

>  gr8 thx = great, thanks

13  *L*  im gr8 thx!wot skool u go 2

14  *M*  eeeeerrr *[name of school; all lower case]*, its in
        *[name of city; abbreviated, lower case]*

>  now = know

15  *L*  ok, how does kt now u then

16  *M*  kev (her step dad) is a friend of me dads

>  she = see; probably a slip

17  *L*  ok then!do u she her much!

18  *M*  errr sumtimes, I dunno really, lol.

19  *L*  kool, do u like her

20  *M*  eeerrr yeah she's ok, I'm amazed at how she puts

>  bro = brother

    up wiv her bro all da time though, lol

21  *L*  oh yeah, ive heard bout him! take no notice of those
        emails that i sent, i was tryin 2 annot her and it worked

22  *L*  annoy*

>  Linda corrects her previous mistake

23  *M*  .... I'm just checkin 2 fid out wot e-mail ur
        talkin about, lol...

>  fid = find

24  *L*  lol

>  It is not clear what prompts Mark's question, but it is likely to relate to previous emails

25  *M*  I thought ur name was smith, not peters, lol

26  *L*  it is

27  *M*  okkkk.. ...

>  Linda's response is hard to understand

28  *L*  part of mine and a frends! both of ours really

29  *L*  wot do u tlk 2 kt bout then!

>  tlk 2 = talk to

30  *M*  lol, dunno, who is ann barton by da way?

31  *L*  my frend and kts

32  *L*  did she send u 1 aswell!

33    *M*    yup, lol. I'm startin 2 feel popular, lol

34    *L*    u feel popular den! lol

35    *M*    I will!


## Commentary

The context for messaging shares some of the features of most conversational contexts: there is more than one participant, participants take turns, interchange is informal, the participants have some members of their social circles in common, the participants work cooperatively in producing the conversation, and the interaction takes place in real time (although with delays for written turn composition). The obvious differences, however, are that messaging does not make use of the spoken medium, is not face to face, and – a caveat to what we said above – it does not <u>quite</u> take place in real time. Aspects of the context necessitate that turns should be short and speedily produced: if the response is delayed too long, the conversation may move on to another topic before a response to the previous message has been sent. Consequently, methods are devised to make contributions as concise as possible while maintaining their communicative effectiveness.

One obvious manifestation of this economy of communicative effort is in punctuation. Full stops and capital letters are rarely used, and apostrophes usually omitted (*im, ive*). Commas, however, are frequently used, both in conventional positions (*bored, tired, but survivin . . .*), but also to replace full stops (*eeerrr yeah she's ok, I'm amazed at how . . .*), and as a more general marker of division before a 'spoken' contribution and 'lol' (*. . . I was just makin sure, lol*). Question marks are sometimes used conventionally (*and which kt by da way?*), but also to reproduce features of pronunciation and delivery (see below). Exclamation marks are relatively frequent, both for conventional purposes (*I will!*) where there is an indication that a word would be spoken loudly for some purpose of affect or emphasis, but also, it appears, as a substitute for a full stop (*im gr8 thx!wot skool u go 2*). Spaces are sometimes omitted after punctuation marks where they are considered unnecessary.

A second feature of economy is the abbreviation of language, both lexical and grammatical. Lexical abbreviation is very frequent and takes a number of forms, including deletion of letters in word initial, medial and final positions (*bout* for *about*, *frends* for *friends*, *sis* for *sister*), spelling simplifications (*wot* for *what*, *rite* for *right*, *sumtimes* for *sometimes*, *u* for *you*), and the use of numbers as word and part-word replacements (*2* for *to(o)*, *gr8* for *great*). We might also note the use of non-standard spoken forms (*me* for *my*, *wiv* for *with*, *da* for *the*, *den* for *then*) whose influence may be regional dialect or Black Englishes. Instant messaging allows participants to manipulate their identities. For example, the non-standard forms used here by Mark are not part of his usual spoken repertoire. You might also have noticed that Mark uses more non-standard forms than Linda, which may be related to gender (see Unit B8).

Ellipsis in this message is very similar to that found in conversation (see the papers by Douglas Biber *et al.* and by Ronald Carter and Michael McCarthy in Unit B1). For example:

> *L*   how r u anyway
> *M*   **[I'm] bored, tired, but survivin, [and] u?**
>
> *M*   **I thought ur name was smith, not peters, lol**
> *L*   it is [smith]

Other ellipsis occurs that would be considered non-standard in speech. An example is the omission of the auxiliary in

> *L*   . . . wot skool [do] u go 2

although whether this is a slip or a deliberate choice is unclear as elsewhere the same participant includes auxiliaries:

> *L*   do u she [=see] her much!

While economy of time and space is important in creating the need for and determining the form of abbreviation, participation in the creation of a new variety of English, specific to instant messaging (although sharing some of the characteristics of mobile phone text messaging) is clearly an important factor here. New participants learn the language from others by taking part in instant messaging, but there is scope even for novices to introduce new language forms. Creating the language of instant messaging, and being part of the community that shares it, are among the attractions of being an active 'messenger'.

Some features of face-to-face conversation are simulated in instant messaging using the resources of written text. Intonational features are simulated with punctuation. For example, . . . ??? is used in

> *M*   *linda . . . ???*

to represent the lengthening, level tone and pause that would be used in speech to invite completion. Lengthening is more overtly indicated in *eeeeerrr* and in Mark's second turn in

> *M*   **I thought ur name was smith, not peters, lol**
> *L*   it is
> *M*   **okkkk. . . .**

which in conversation might be said with a lengthened rising or falling-rising tone, indicating some reservation about understanding ('I <u>think</u> I understand, but . . .'). Similarly, features of connected speech are indicated with deletions – *makin, tryin, survivin, checkin, talkin* – and other more conventional representations – *dunno.*

**Task C4.2**

*Focus*

Here is an extract from the middle of a different instant messaging event between Mark and Angela. Although instant messaging often consists of inconsequential banter, as we saw in the data in C4.1, more serious discussion also takes place, and this is well illustrated in the data below.

➤ Consider what features this extract and the one we looked at above have in common, and what differences you can observe.

*Data*

. . .

1  A  im so confused

2  M  y?

3  A  cos i am

4  A  about anythin an evrythin

5  **M lol**

6  **M fair enuf**

7  A  i dunno who i am anymore

8  A  i keep changin

9  A  evrythin about me keeps changing

10  **M cool**

11  A  no not kool

12  A  see?                          no1=no-one

13  A  no1 understands me

14  A  this is wot i woz on about the other nite

15  A  i talk about me an evry1s jus like "rite, ok" or " "        " " = 'silent'

16  **M lol**

17  **M its cos ur very negatively self analytical, lol**

18  A  rite

19　A　im not

20　A　i jus tell it how it is

21　**M　ur still bein negative!**

22　A　i ent　◄──────────  ent = 'ain't' = am not

23　A　im bin truthful
　　　　　　◄──────  im bin = I'm being

24　A　if the truth is negative i cant help that

25　**M　u can help da way u express it though**

26　A　i express it how it is

27　A　how i like

28　A　interpret it how u like

29　**M　the only reason 4 expression is to direct the interpretation, lol**

30　A　not necessarily

31　A　things can b expressed in an open way

32　*A*　open 2 different interpretations　　　　　ur = you are

33　*M* **but da point is that ur expressin them in a linear – negative way, lol**

34　*M* **if it were openly then it wudn't be so bad!**

35　*A*　i was expressin them as i wanted 2

36　*A*　if u had an open mind u could interpret them how u like

37　*A*　if u looked beneath the words an phrasin

38　*M* **in this medium dats all there is to go on, besides possibly timing which is very vague in the circumstances**

39　*A*　its not

40　*A*　u can use my words an wot i sed an interpret them in ur own way usin ur own mind

41   *A*   u dont need 2 necessarily know anythin else

42   *M* but u r limited to pre-learned definitions of the vocabulary used, which, not including double entendre, is extremely linear!!!! wiv few interpretations!

43   *A*   u rnt ◄————————— | u rnt = you aren't |

44   *A*   look at wot i sed

45   *A*   take out the negative parts

46   *A*   use wots left

47   *A*   interpret it in ur way that is not necessarily negative

48   *A*   wot i sed cud b interpreted as very positive

49   *A*   i jus expressed it in my own way, negatively

50   *M* if u intend 4 other ppl 2 ignore da negative bits:

     1) y include them?                        | ppl = people |

     2) y delay telling them (or me) till now?

51   A   i dont intend them 2 ignore them

52   A   they can if they want 2 interpret the words differently

53   A   an i included them cos that woz my individual way of expressin the way i felt
     . . .

## IDEAS FOR FURTHER RESEARCH

■   Instant messaging is, of course, only one of the growing number of forms of electronic communication that we could have looked at in this unit. The language produced in text messaging, email, Internet chat rooms, bulletin boards, discussion groups and virtual worlds are all possible data sources for further research. Collection of some of these data sources (such as text messaging or instant messaging) can present challenges, and in all cases, it is probably easier to collect data if you are one of the participants. The disadvantage of this is that your language might be influenced by the focus of the investigation that you are conducting. It is probably more satisfactory if you can identify reliable informants who are willing to save and share their communications with you (as we did with the data collected for this unit). However, other data is relatively easy to gather, including archives of messages that have been posted to discussion lists.

■ Whatever source of data you look at, the linguistic focus of your investigation is likely to be the ways in which the grammar of electronic texts is similar to and different from conversation and more traditional modes of writing. Your observations can help you to explore the communication possibilities and constraints of the medium, and also the relationship between writer and reader(s) in these kinds of interaction. Suggestions on the grammatical features you might investigate have been given in this unit and further possibilities can be found in Text B4.2 by Collot and Belmore. Alternatively, you could take a work which describes the grammar of conversation as your reference point; for example, Biber *et al.* (1999: ch. 14) or Carter and McCarthy (forthcoming).

■ Comparative studies of electronic communication in different social and linguistic contexts provide further potential areas of research. For example, you might compare grammatical features of 'social' emails and 'work' emails, or compare the language of texting or instant messaging in different international varieties of English.

# Unit C5
# Exploring grammar in 'little texts'

## INTRODUCTION AND BACKGROUND TO DATA

In Unit C4 we investigated the language of instant messaging, a form of communication in which contributions need to be short in order to allow the discourse to progress turn by turn. Long contributions, which take time to prepare, run the risk of missing their place in the developing interchange in much the same way that the moment can be lost for saying something in a conversation if we take too long to think about what to say. Aspects of the context, then, constrain what can be written. We saw also in Unit B5 how time constraints influence language choice in sports commentaries.

In this unit we look at other types of written text – 'small ads' and newspaper headlines – that are constrained, not here by the need to produce them rapidly, but by the need to achieve their purpose in a very limited space. As a consequence of this restriction these 'little texts' (as we will call them) tend to have a grammar which differs from that of other registers which don't face such restrictions. While many little texts share features because of the constraint of length, because each type has its own purposes and is produced in a particular context, differences will be found across types.

The first set of data we look at is a collection of 'small ads' offering services, taken from the staff magazines of a number of British universities. These magazines appear both in paper form and are also posted on the universities' websites, from which they were taken. Names have been changed and contact details removed. The small ads have a number of purposes. They need, of course, to describe the service that is being offered. They also need to persuade the reader either that the service offered matches their need or, in one or two cases here, to create a need in the reader that they may not have realised they had! Further, they must emphasise that the service is efficient, reasonable value, and conducted in a professional manner. And all of this has to be achieved in the space of just a few words. Unlike in many newspapers, charges are not per word. Instead the instructions for placing small ads give a price for placing an ad of a particular length (for example, '£5.50 for 30 words') with the implication that advertisers should work within this limit or be charged extra. In Task 2 we go on to look at a further little text, newspaper headlines.

Before working on this unit you should have read Unit B5, particularly extract 5(b) in which the analysis of another little text, the dating advertisement, is reported.

 **Task C5.1**

### Focus

This activity focuses on the grammar of small ads offering services. The most obvious thing to notice about the 12 examples is that they are a reduced version of the form they would take if they were 'translated' into more general English.

➤ Identify and make a list of recurring patterns in how these reductions are made (and also note when reductions are not made), and any other characteristic features of their grammar.

### Data

a. Typing service, accurate and fast, by experienced secretary. Tape transcriptions from all types of tape, plus usual word processing software. Reliable service, anything tackled. Tel *[first name + surname]* on *[tel no]*, mobile *[tel no]* or email *[email]*.

b. If you can write it, I can type it! Fast, accurate, reliable service, essays, dissertations, CVs, anything undertaken, reasonable rates. Please contact *[first name]* on *[tel no]*.

c. Coleman Independent Secretarial Services. Accurate, fast, word processing £10 per 5,000 words straight copy. *[email]*. Voicemail *[tel no]*.

d. Painters, decorators and property maintenance. Free estimates. Can work evenings and weekends. Tel *[first name]* on *[tel no]* or *[tel no]*.

e. Clifton-Modern Jive Classes. Every Monday night, The Park House, New St beginners welcome every week. Great fun for all ages. No partner required. Call *[first name]* on tel *[tel no]* or go to *[website address]*.

f. Send a balloon-in-a-box gift anywhere in the UK. A great alternative to flowers! *[website address]* tel *[tel no]*. Go on – make someone smile!

g. Photography by William K. Martin ampa, family portraits, weddings, children and pets. The ideal gift idea. Digital and film imaging. Contact *[first name + surname]* on *[tel. no]* evenings or *[tel. no]* mobile. Email *[email address]*. Student discounts given.

h. Piano lessons. Experienced and enthusiastic musician offers piano lessons for children and adults. All levels welcome. Please contact *[first name + surname]* BS Hons (Music) on *[tel. no]*. (Member of the Incorporated Society of Musicians).

i. Need help with your French GCSE, AS or A level? Contact Alliance Française de Oxford. We are French nationals and experienced trained teachers. Tel. *[tel no]*. Email *[email address]*.

j.   Professional woman, mid 50's, available to house and pet sit in or near Newtown. References available. Contact *[first name]*, tel: *[tel no]* or email: *[email address]*.

k.   Builder: Currently studying, available for carpentry, landscaping, minor plumbing, project management etc. Refs available. Email *[email address]*, tel. *[tel no]* or *[tel no]*.

l.   Feeling stressed? Stress massage, reflexology and aromatherapy available Wednesdays 9.30–7 at The Austen Clinic Tel. *[tel no]* *[website address]*.


## Commentary

Here are some of the things that you might have observed:

- Articles are usually omitted, as in: a *by [an] experienced secretary, plus [the] usual word processing software*; h *[An] Experienced and enthusiastic musician.* However, they are included in some cases. The definite article is kept where it is part of a fixed expression in place and organisation names. e *The Park House*, f *the UK*, h *the Incorporated Society of Musicians and* l *The Austen Clinic*.

   If the article had been left out in g *The ideal gift idea*, there would have been ambiguity over whether the intention was 'The ideal . . .' (i.e. exactly the right one) or 'An ideal . . .' (i.e. just one of a number). Including the definite article here allows the writer to explicitly highlight the uniqueness of the present. Only in f is the indefinite article included: *a balloon-in-a-box gift . . . A great alternative.* In both cases it could have been omitted without affecting the clarity of the ad, and it may simply be that, in a particularly short small ad, leaving out 'a' was an economy of space that was simply unnecessary.

- The auxiliary elements of verb phrases are usually omitted, as in: e *No partner [is] required*; h *All levels [are] welcome*; j *References [are] available*; l *Stress massage, reflexology and aromatherapy [are] available.* Sometimes it is difficult to reconstruct the omitted part of the verb phrase and this can leave the message open to interpretation. For example, in g, *Student discounts given* might be interpreted are 'are given' (i.e. always) or 'can be given' (i.e. it is discretionary).
- In many cases, both subject and verb are omitted, with only a noun phrase remaining (usually the object of a 'translated' version), although the exact subject and verb intended may be difficult to reconstruct: a *[I offer/can do] Tape transcriptions from all types of tape*; e *[It is] Great fun for all ages.* In other cases, only part of the verb phrase is omitted: d *[I] Can work evenings and weekends*; k *[I am] currently studying.* This occurs in both of the questions in the data: i *[Do you] Need help with your French GCSE?*; l *[Are you] Feeling stressed?*

   Less frequently, subject and verb are included. They are included, for example, in: i *We are French nationals and experienced trained teachers.* Here omission of 'We are' would leave the ad potentially ambiguous: does 'French nationals and experienced trained teachers' refer to who is offering the service or who may take it up. Clearly, with only a little thought the former is intended, but perhaps the advertisers decided that for complete clarity the omission should not be made.

- In two cases, the relevant characteristics of the advertiser are specified in the subject of the sentence, a pattern not usually found in grammar more generally: h *Experienced and enthusiastic musician offers piano lessons for children and adults* (rather than 'I am an experienced and enthusiastic musician. I offer . . .'); j *Professional woman, mid 50's, available to house and pet sit.* (rather than 'I am a professional woman in my mid 50's. I am available . . .').
- Many of the ads include noun phrases which are not attached to other sentence elements. For example: c *Coleman Independent Secretarial Services*; d *Free estimates*; f *A great alternative to flowers*; h *Piano lessons*; k *Builder*.
- The use of lists is characteristic of many of the ads. A series of two or more adjectives or nouns is found in a variety of positions within phrases and functioning in different sentence elements. For example:

  - as modifiers before the head noun: b *Fast, accurate, reliable service*; c *Accurate, fast, word processing*; or after the head noun: a *Typing service accurate and fast*;
  - as unattached noun phrases: d *Painters, decorators and property maintenance*; g *family portraits, weddings, children and pets*;
  - as part of a prepositional phrase: k *available for carpentry, landscaping, minor plumbing, project management, etc.*;
  - as a noun phrase acting as subject: l *Stress massage, reflexology and aromatherapy available.*

 **Task C5.2**

*Focus*

➤ Try to identify recurring grammatical patterns in the following set of little texts. They are headlines, in the 'National' sections, taken from the online versions of three newspapers on 6 October 2003: *The New Straits Times* from Malaysia, *The Age* from Melbourne, Australia, and *The New York Times*. Look first for characteristics of the grammar of the headlines in general and make a list as you did in Task C5.1, and then see if you can identify any variation across the three newspapers. It may help first to look back at the discussion of newspaper texts in Unit A6.

## Data

Table C5.1  Headlines from three newspapers

| The New Straits Times | The Age | The New York Times |
| --- | --- | --- |
| 1  Kobena members urged to make project a success [Kobena = National Youth Co-operative] | 1  PM clears cash boost for Medicare [Medicare = health insurance scheme] | 1  Medicare Plan Lifts Premiums for the Affluent [Medicare = health insurance scheme] |
| 2  KL seeking ways to revitalise the OIC [KL = Kuala Lumpur; OIC = Organisation of the Islamic Conference] | 2  Job market defies rate rise talk [rate = interest rate] | 2  Recall Voters Face an Intricate Ballot, and, Indeed, Chads [Chads = small circles removed from a ballot card to indicate voting preference] |
| 3  Tiger attack copter option for army [Tiger attack copter = the Eurocopter Tiger attack helicopter] | 3  Beazley a relic, says Latham [Beazley and Latham = Australian politicians] | 3  Supreme Court's Docket Includes 48 New Cases [Docket = list of cases to be dealt with in court] |
| 4  Banks criticised for being uncooperative | 4  Former court heads attack ministers | 4  Pastor and 2 Others Are Killed in Shooting at Atlanta Church |
| 5  Get ready to move out, says Abdullah | 5  Megawati will not join PM [Megawati = Indonesian President Megawati Soekarnoputri; PM = Prime Minister John Howard] | 5  Striking Trash Haulers in Chicago Reject a Raise Offer |
| 6  Revised fees for Socso panel doctors [Socso = The Social Security Organisation] | 6  Cormo Express delayed in Kuwait [Cormo Express = name of ship] | 6  No. 2 State Dept. Official Visits Afghan Region of New Attacks |
| 7  Police probe RM5m cheque scam report [RM = Malaysian Ringgit (Dollar)] | 7  New tune for Napster [Napster = Internet company offering music downloads] | 7  US Avoids Criticism of Raid, but Urges Caution on Israel |
| 8  30 JPs to be appointed second class magistrates [JPs = Justices of the Peace] | 8  Ruling threatens state coffers | 8  White House to Overhaul Iraq and Afghan Missions |
| 9  Be active in PTAs, parents advised [PTA = Parent-Teachers Associations] | 9  Police chief seeks global hotline to fight terror | 9  G.O.P. Novice Reaches Runoff for Governor of Louisiana [G.O.P. = Grand Old Party; the Republican Party] |
| 10  'Probe destination of dredged sand' [Probe = verb] | 10  Pioneering skydiver killed | 10  Jacuzzi U.? A Battle of Perks to Lure Students [U = University] |
| 11  RM30m more to house the poor in Terengganu [Terengganu = northern state of Malaysia] | 11  Archbishops clash on the issue of homosexuals | 11  Accused Graduates Remain in Military |

continued

Table C5.1 Headlines from three newspapers

| The New Straits Times | The Age | The New York Times |
| --- | --- | --- |
| 12 MAS aircraft veers off runway after landing at Changi [Changi = airport in Singapore] | 12 Land costs soaring on city's fringe | 12 24 Win MacArthur 'Genius Awards' of $500,000 |
| 13 Fifty Selangor Govt workers get the sack this year [Selangor = central state of Malaysia] | 13 Airport fire close to disaster: police | 13 A Missing Statistic: US Jobs That Went Overseas |
| 14 Six Vietnamese charged with rioting | 14 Rolls-Royce lifestyle on unemployment benefits | 14 2 Disclaim Leaking Name of Operative |
| 15 Non-Muslims urged not to regard aggression as distant issue | 15 Labor revolt over education job cuts | 15 Officials See Nile Virus Taking Aim at California [Nile virus = disease carried by mosquitoes] |
| 16 Asean Summit: Leaders expected to sign Asean Concord II [ASEAN = Association of South East Asian Nations] | 16 Council bid to avert Carlton parking crisis [Carlton = area in Melbourne] | 16 Stewart Lawsuit Dismissed [Stewart = a person's family name] |
| 17 Former Padungan assemblyman dies [Padungan = Malaysian region] | 17 Tests show how Victorian pupils are shaping up [Victorian = from the state of Victoria] | 17 Hospital Apologizes for Barring Black Workers |
| 18 Measures to protect shipping lanes from terrorism | 18 'No witnesses' to shooting at dockers' function | 18 Onstage Attack Casts Pall Over Las Vegas Strip [Strip = street with businesses, shops etc.] |

## RESEARCH NOTE

In this kind of investigation, you should gather as large a collection of texts as possible (bearing in mind, of course, the scale of your research and the time you have available) and try to identify recurring features of their grammar. The larger the collection, the more representative a sample you are likely to have. Once you have gathered your data, you can narrow the scope of your analysis by looking in detail at a small number of texts. The findings of this detailed small-scale analysis can be used to generate research questions or hypotheses to be tested on your larger collection of data. You can then see how far what you have observed in the sample occurs in the data more generally, and go on to consider how the grammatical patterns you have identified are influenced by the context in which the texts are produced.

## IDEAS FOR FURTHER RESEARCH

There are many other kinds of 'little text' whose grammatical characteristics you could explore. Some suggestions are:

- product labels
- instructions (e.g. recipes, for flat-pack furniture assembly, for use of medicines)
- public notices (e.g. signs giving warnings or restrictions)
- graffiti
- house advertisements
- book or DVD blurbs.

You might also want to take into account how much information is conveyed by the surrounding printed context in diagrams, pictures, use of different colours and typefaces and so on.

Spoken little texts might also be investigated. For example, you could look at public announcements (e.g. in railway stations or airports, or on trains or planes) or jokes.

If you have access to this kind of data, it would be interesting to gather similar little texts from different countries in order to look at cross-cultural and/ or cross-linguistic differences (see, for example, Text B10.2). An example of what might be done is in our exploration of headlines from newspapers from different countries in Task C5.2.

# Unit C6
# Exploring grammar in the language of children

## INTRODUCTION AND BACKGROUND TO DATA

This unit looks at grammar in the language of children, how it differs from that of mature language users, and how it changes as children get older. It follows on from the discussion of developing language in Unit B6. We focus on written language, particularly that of non-fiction, with the data being taken from the writing of a British male child, David, at various ages. It is important to recognise that the language of one child may not be representative of all children in a language group. To build up a more general picture, studies of much larger numbers of children are necessary. However, small scale explorations of the type you will conduct here are a useful starting point. They can also give a fascinating insight into the development of an individual child or form the basis for further comparative work.

The data in this unit are three complete narratives written during primary school. The first gives an account of an event during the previous weekend written when David was aged six years, six months. (The 'what I did at the weekend diary' is a familiar Monday morning activity in British primary schools.) The second and third were written after school trips; the first to a local railway museum (at age nine years, three months), and the second to a local historical building, Blakesley Hall (at age ten years, eleven months). The tasks are all quite similar, recounting actual events, so that the variations present can more safely be attributed to developing maturity as a writer rather than the effect of different types of writing.

Before working on this unit you should have read Unit B6.

 **Task C6.1**

*Focus*

Read the first sample of David's writing below.

➤ What do you observe about the grammar used there?

➤ How does it differ from the grammar of a mature writer?

➤ What signs of a more mature writer do you find in this extract?

## Data

'What I did at the weekend', written at six years, six months.

> yesterday I went to my mummy and daddy's Friends house. and they war
> calld David and Marjorie. and we went to a big and very old house and in
> the house thar was a instrument callad a claviola and it sounds like a organ.

## Commentary

Here are some of the things you might have observed:

- Perhaps the most obvious feature of grammar to note is that the text's 'sentences' are rather different from those found in mature writing. While David shows some understanding that his writing needs to be divided into sentences using full stops, he does not use capital letters at the beginning of sentences, and begins sentences with unnecessary 'and's. The function of 'and' in each case appears to be simply to keep the discourse moving forward, a characteristic of narrative in speech.

- The only tenses used are simple: past and present. The interesting shift to present tense in the last clause may have been a consequence of David not having heard the claviola played during the visit; he was told by a guide that this was what it sounded like. Using a past simple would suggest that he had heard it played.

- There is only one relative clause, in 'an instrument called a claviola', and only one attempt to produce a complex noun phrase, in 'my mummy and daddy's Friends house'. This last example might be more characteristic of speech than writing, where a mature writer is more likely to 'unpack' the phrase than produce a complex possessive of this type.

- David attempts to make even this short text cohesive by linking the theme elements (see Unit A5.4) of main clauses with the rheme elements in the previous clause in:

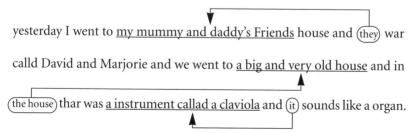

**Task C6.2**

*Focus*

> Read the next sample of David's writing below. (Corrections given in brackets
> have been added to make the text easier to understand.)

➤ What do you observe about the grammar of the sample below?

➤ What differences do you note between this and the first sample?

➤ How does it differ from the grammar of a mature writer?

➤ What signs of a more mature writer do you find in this extract?

*Data*

'The railway museum', written at nine years, three months:

> We got of the coach and put are *[our]* bags in a train that was about 45
> years old. Then we whent to the visitors center and the guides told us a
> story about how they bult *[built]* railways and then then one of the guides
> took are *[our]* group to look around the museum.
>
> First we went to a gards caradge *[guard's carriage]* and it had a big fire in
> the middle and the guide talked about the gards job. Then we whent in a
> 95 year old tram. After that craig *[moved]* a 1 ton wheel by pushing a bit
> sticing *[sticking]* out of the axle. Then we whent on the train robbed by
> the great train robbers. Then we whent to the train workshop were *[where]*
> they made and repared trains and then we whent back to the train and had
> lunch on the train and then the guide showed us round the signal box and
> then he took us back to the visitors center and showed us some things he
> had got then we whent back to school.

*Commentary*

Here are some of the things you might have observed.

■ The writing now has sentences. Although there are still examples of 'and'
   functioning simply to move the discourse forward:

> First we went to a gards caradge and it had a big fire in the middle . . .

most uses seem more clearly to be indicating chronological sequence with a
meaning similar to 'then':

then we whent back to the train and had lunch on the train . . .

David appears to have a greater range of ways of indicating time sequence, using 'First', 'then' and 'after that' in addition to 'and'. However, the last sentence closely resembles the text in the data in Task C6.1, with a series of clauses connected by 'and then' rather than 'and'.

- Past simple is the only tense used. David may, of course, have control of a greater variety of tenses but does not need to use them to achieve his purposes in this text.
- Perhaps the most striking difference is the greater number and type of subordinate clauses used. (See extract 6(b), Unit B6, for more on this.) In this short text he demonstrates that he can use a variety of relative clauses:

> a train that was about 45 years old (non-defining)

> the train workshop were they made and repared trains (defining)

> on the train robbed by the great train robbers (a 'reduced' relative equivalent to 'the train which was robbed')

nominal (or noun) clauses:

> a story about how they bult railways

and adverbial clauses:

> craig moved a 1 ton wheel by pushing a bit sticing out of the axle

- There is evidence of more complex noun phrases as in:

> a 95 year old tram    a 1 ton wheel

- There is further evidence of cohesion produced in the text with, for example:

> First we went to a gards caradge and it had a big fire in the middle

However, this is not always unproblematic. In both:

> Then we whent to the visitors center and the guides told us a story about how they bult railways

and

> and then we whent back to <u>the train</u>

the meaning of the underlined words is ambiguous. 'they' is presumably intended to mean something like 'people 45 years ago', but could refer to 'the guides'. The closest referent to 'the train' is 'the train robbed by the great train robbers'; however, the reference is presumably to the '45 years old' train mentioned in the first line of the text.

■ We might also note the preference for repetition rather than pronominal reference in:

and then we whent back to the train and had lunch on the train

where a mature writer might use

and then we whent back to the train and had lunch there

 **Task C6.3**

### Focus

Read this, the third text from David, written about one year and eight months after the previous one.

➤ Explore the text using the questions given before the previous text as a guide. Focus on the grammatical features highlighted in the two commentaries you have read so far, but note any other features of interest.

### Data

'A visit to Blakesley Hall', written at ten years, eleven months:

On Friday, we whent to Blakesly Hall. Blakesly Hall is a Tudor house. When we got there, we went into a big barn. The barn had a very strange smell. After that, we went on a guided tour.

We started by going into a very small outdoor porch. It had the initials of the person who lived there. They where RS. That stood for Richard Smallbrook. Then, we walked into the great hall. The great hall is the room where everyone ate, including the servants (Richard was very rich), and that was also where they welcomed there *[their]* guests. Richard liked to show how rich he was by having very decrotive *[decorative]* furniture. He also had his initials carved on furniture like that. He had a cubord *[cupboard]* in the great hall to show that there was also a big fire that they used to heat the room. Servants would have to get up the chimney and clean it out (a petty horreble job)! After we had looked at the great hall, we went into the family palour *[parlour]*.

The palour was the room where Richard and his familly would go after their meal. it was probably the room that they had spent the most on. It has very ornate degsigns *[designs]* over the fireplace but they also had glass windows (the rest of the house also had glass windows). Some people took their windows out when they went on a journy. They took the glass with them because glass was rare and expensive.

Then, we whent up the stairs to the top of the house. The stairs went in the pattern of ₍bottom₎ ⌒ ᵗᵒᵖ. They lead onto a long hall called the long gallery. The long gallery was a hall that, on a rainy day, they would walk up and down to get some exercise. Houses with a long gallery would also mean that they woudn't have to walk from bedroom to bedroom just to get to another bedroom! At one end there was a big box for spring sheets and linen. Next to it was a box for storing money and valuebals *[valuables]*. This was called an armada box (I have no idea why). The long gallery had a sloping floor. It's shape was ⌐ / . It was sloping because of old age and because when Richard died, his daughter bult *[built]* an extention and that had pulled it. (Dont forget this house is nearly five-hundred years old)! Before we whent to the long gallery, we went to Richard's bedroom, also upstairs. It was also called "The Painted Chamber" because it has very ornate degsins *[designs]* on the wall. After the long gallery we *[end; the writing was incomplete]*

## RESEARCH NOTE

Gathering data on children or vulnerable adults, as discussed below, needs to be undertaken with due care. If you are collecting spoken or written data from children, other than your own, you should ask permission from parents or guardians, and if you are collecting data in a school or other institutional setting, the head or principal should be consulted first. Similarly, when working with adults, it is good practice to tell them about the research and ask if they are willing to participate. For some types of research this can be problematic. If, for example, people are aware that they are being recorded or their writing will be analysed, they may change their behaviour. This phenomenon is so common that it has been given the name the 'observer's paradox'. You can get round the problem to some extent by giving only a vague explanation of why you are collecting data and then showing an example of the analysis later when it cannot affect behaviour. In writing up the results of research it is perfectly acceptable to acknowledge that the informants may have been influenced by the presence of the researcher, microphone etc.

## IDEAS FOR FURTHER RESEARCH

Here are some suggestions on further research that you could do in the area of the grammar of children's developing language, and sources of information. We have focused on change over time in the writing of just one child. If you have access to child informants, here are some other investigations you could conduct:

- Gather samples of writing in response to the same task from groups of children of different ages. Compare grammar across the age groups.
- Gather samples of writing in response to the same task from groups of children of the same age but different levels of writing ability. (You may need help from a knowledgeable class teacher for this.) Compare grammar across the ability groups.
- At one particular stage of development, a child may display different degrees of maturity in writing different text types or genres. You could gather samples of different genres written by a small group of children: for example, you could compare fiction (such as a short story) with non-fiction (such as an account of a visit, or a letter to a penfriend).

In this unit we have been concerned only with children's written language. If you are interested in exploring children's *spoken* language, a useful starting point for ideas, data and references is the website of the Child Language Data Exchange System (CHILDES): http://childes.psy.cmu.edu. The CHILDES project, directed from Harvard University by Brian MacWhinney with Catherine Snow provides an international database of child language for the study of first and second language acquisition. The website allows you to investigate a database of transcribed child language stored in text files, some with audio, using a set of computer software tools for searching and manipulate the database.

Although our interest here is in the language of children, you will have read in Unit B6 a brief report about research on language change in old age. Interesting work can be done on the grammatical characteristics of this change, particularly in those who are suffering from forms of dementia, in whom language change is most pronounced. If you have access to such informants, you could, for example, encourage them to give an oral history of some part of their lives. Your explorations could focus on how their language differs from that of mature, mentally unimpaired adults.

# Unit C7
# Exploring grammar in second-language learning

## INTRODUCTION AND BACKGROUND TO DATA

For most learners of a second or foreign language, the classroom is an important site for gaining exposure to the target language and practising it. Indeed, for many learners it may be the only place where they have an opportunity to use it. Consequently, study of the kind of interaction that takes place in the classroom context is important in a very practical way in order to optimise its value in the second-language learning process. Early work in the 1960s focused especially on the amount and type of teacher language used in the classroom (the number of questions, instructions etc. used), while more recent investigation has concentrated on learner language. In particular, there has been growing interest in the relationship between activity type and interaction between learners and teacher, and among groups of learners. The assumption is that different kinds of classroom organisation will result in different patterns of interaction and language production and these, in turn, will offer better or worse preparation for communication outside the classroom. In addition, it is now widely accepted that if learners are engaged in activities where they have to use their linguistic resources to negotiate an understanding between themselves and others, rather than, for example, producing language to order in drills, this provides a better learning opportunity.

Of course, it is not only activity type that influences the language that learners produce. When we speak a second or foreign language (or even our first language) we are aware that if we have time to plan and reflect on what we want to say or write, we can produce more accurate language than in circumstances where we are under pressure or where our attention to language is distracted by what is going on around us. Variability in the language produced will, then, be partly determined by how much attention to what we say and write is permitted by the context.

In this unit we will explore the variability in the speech and writing of learners of English as a second language from Singapore and Malaysia. In particular, we will focus on grammatical aspects of the language produced in instructional contexts where the activities and other factors are deliberately varied. By carrying out this kind of investigation, we hope to identify aspects of teaching which are more helpful or less helpful to students.

The first set of data (from Cheah 1992) provides samples of the written and spoken language of two female Singaporean university students whose first language is Chinese. The written texts are a response to the question 'Write an essay expressing your opinion about the value of matchmaking' (that is, arranging marriage partners for others, a practice widely found in traditional Chinese society). Students were asked to write 300–500 words (although we have taken just the first 200 or so words) and given three hours, although they completed well within the time allowed. The spoken texts are interviews with an older native speaker of Singaporean English whom the students had not met before. With a tape recorder in full view, the context was designed to introduce some anxiety in the students. Comparing the written and spoken data, we may be able to find evidence of variation in the language resulting from the different degrees of attention to and monitoring of the students' own language in the two contexts.

In the second set of data (from Warren 1985) Malaysian secondary school children aged 14 or 15 are engaged in classroom tasks and games. In 'Hangman', five boys try to guess a word selected by one of the students. In 'Maps', two students are separated by a screen. Each has a map of an island, but on one of these key features are missing. The student with the full map has to tell the other where these features are, and the second student draws them on their map. The teacher was present in these activities, but did not participate. In 'Fashion Photographs', photographs from a magazine aimed at teenagers were spread out on a table in front of five girls. The women in the photographs had clothes and hairstyles very different from those that would normally be worn by the girls. They were not given any guidance on what should be said, except that everything should be in English. In 'Nazri's Story', seven boys were asked to read an unfinished story about a boy called Nazri. Two questions were asked at the end of the story: 'What do you think Nazri saw?' and 'What do you think happened next?' The teacher was not present in these last two activities.

'Hangman' and 'Maps' are typical of those activities adopted in communicative language teaching in which speakers are expected to transfer information in order to complete a particular task. The proponents of 'communicative activities' such as these reject traditional methods of language teaching in which the aim is to provide knowledge of the language system. Warren contrasts communicative activities with what he calls 'discourse activities', such as 'Fashion photographs' and 'Nazri's story', in which there is less control over the language produced by the constraints of the task. He argues that the resulting language is more 'natural' in that it has charac-teristics closer to discourse produced outside the classroom. Through discourse activities, therefore, students are better prepared to participate in 'real-world' communication. Comparing these two types data, we may be able to find evidence of variation in the language resulting from the different activity types.

We need, of course, to add our usual note of caution at this point. We are dealing here with tiny samples of data, and for a systematic study of the relationship between language and instructional context we would need to extend the investigation to a much larger body of data. This exploration is, then, very much a starting point.

Before working on this unit you should have read Unit B7.

**Task C7.1**

*Focus*

Although we could explore many different aspects of grammar in these samples, we will focus here only on verb tense and aspect. This is an area of English grammar that is particularly problematic for learners, and, as verb tense and aspect have to be selected in every clause with a finite verb, provides a reasonable number of instances for us to examine even in small samples of data.

Look at the first two samples, the essay and the interview, for Student 1. (Ignore the contributions by the interviewer for this analysis.)

➤ Identify the finite verbs and classify them according to 'tense' (including aspect and voice) under such headings as present simple active, past simple active, present simple passive etc. Include a separate category for verb phrases with a modal verb (e.g. 'may find').

➤ Note whether each verb tense is correct or not and, if it is incorrect, decide what verb form should probably have been used. You may find it helpful to record your answers in a table such as the following:

| Tense | No. correct | No. incorrect | Total |
|---|---|---|---|
| Present perfect continuous (active) | | | |
| Present simple (active) | | | |

➤ For each tense category, count the number of choices made by the student, and also the number of 'target' choices. By target choices we mean both the correct choices made by the student and the correct choices made where the student got it wrong.

➤ With these findings, go on to compare:

the total percentages of correct and incorrect tense choices in the essay and the interview;

the number of occurrences in each of the tense categories in the essay and the interview;

the number of actual tense choices (that is, made by the student) with the target choices in the essay and in the interview.

## Data

*Essay: Student 1*

For many centuries, matchmaking has been playing an important role in the societies helping people to get a marriage. The strict traditional form of matchmaking, however, creates many tragedies. In the past, parents usually have the authority to decide the marriages for their children through matchmaking. In such a scheme, a pair of couple don't have any opportunity to know each other well before they get married, they may find difficultie in getting along with the life partners. This type of matchmaking is not encouraged and thus was replaced by a modern way of matchmaking as time passes.

Modern form of matchmaking, such as computer dating and the creation of Social Developing Unit (SDU), which is a modern matchmaking agency are now more widely practised. I think these modern types of match-making should be encouraged and were necessary. Now, Singapore is facing a problem that arising number of Singaporeans were single. Matchmaking could be a remedy to it. Marriage, was a means by which people maintained racial homogeneity, social power, economic security and social status. With the help of matchmaking, people have more chance to find their marriage mate. In this modern way of matchmaking, people have their own choice and right to choose their life partner, not compelling by their parents, their previous tragedies can be avoided. . . .

*Interview: Student 1*

The student is asked to talk about her work experience from her last vacation. Keep this in mind as you judge whether the student's tense choices are correct.

*Int.:*  tell me about your work experience
*S1.:*  actually I'm a staff clerk . sometimes I deal with salesperson . then is regarding door ah sales of doors and I have to ???
*Int.:*  door? d-o-o-r-s?
*S1.:*  d-o-o-r
*Int.:*  oh I see I thought dogs
*S1.:*  and it's quite a good experience for me because previously I didn't involve in any work . except operator . and then . I face many kind of people]
*Int.:*  problem

> *S1.:* problem also because I'm not very socialise
> *Int.:* you look okay
> *S1.:* then I have to mix around with my colleagues . they are all very . they are much older than me . we have a communication breakdown . them um those salesmen . I think they are very cunning . sometimes then I don't know how to
> *Int.:* take advantage of you
> *S1.:* ya . and I have to face my boss he's very close to me so I felt very pressurized. because he examine . my work and all that lah

## Commentary

First, here is our own analysis of these data samples. In square brackets after each choice are the tense choices made by the student and (if we judge it to be incorrect) a suggested correction.

### Essay: Student 1

For many centuries, matchmaking (1) has been playing ✗ *[present perfect continuous; has played]* an important role in the societies helping people to get a marriage. The strict traditional form of matchmaking, however, (2) creates ✗ *[present simple; created]* many tragedies. In the past, parents usually (3) have ✗ *[present simple; had]* the authority to decide the marriages for their children through matchmaking. In such a scheme, a pair of couple (4) don't have ✗ *[present simple; didn't have]* any opportunity to know each other well before they (5) get ✗ *[present simple; got]* married, they (6) may find ✗ *[modal verb phrase; may have found]* difficultie in getting along with the life partners. This type of matchmaking (7) is not encouraged ✗ *[present simple passive; was not encouraged]* and thus (8) was replaced ✓ *[past simple passive]* by a modern way of matchmaking as time (9) passes ✗ *[present simple; passed]*.

Modern form of matchmaking, such as computer dating and the creation of Social Developing Unit (SDU), which (10) is ✓ *[present simple]* a modern matchmaking agency (11) are now more widely practised ✓ *present simple passive]*. I (12) think ✓ *[present simple]* these modern types of matchmaking (13) should be encouraged ✓ *[modal verb phrase]* and (14) were ✗ *[past simple; are]* necessary. Now, Singapore (15) is facing ✓ *[present continuous]* a problem that arising number of Singaporeans (16) were ✗ *[past simple; are]* single. Matchmaking (17) could be ✓ *[modal verb phrase]* a remedy to it. Marriage, (18) was ✓ (?) *[past simple]* a means by which people maintained racial homogeneity, social power, economic security and social status. With the help of matchmaking, people (19) have ✓ *[present simple]* more chance to find their marriage mate. In this modern way of matchmaking, people (20) have ✓ *[present simple]* their own choice and right to choose their life partner, not compelling by their parents, their previous tragedies (21) can be avoided ✓ *[modal verb phrase]* . . .

In the table below we give the number of correct and incorrect tense choices made by the student for each category.

*Tense choices made by Student 1: essay*

| Tense | No. correct | No. incorrect | Total |
|---|---|---|---|
| Present perfect continuous (active) | | 1 | 1 |
| Present simple (active) | 4 | 5 | 9 |
| Present simple (passive) | 1 | 1 | 2 |
| Past simple (active) | 1 | 2 | 3 |

| Tense | No. correct | No. incorrect | Total |
|---|---|---|---|
| Past simple (passive) | 1 | | 1 |
| Present continuous (active) | 1 | | 1 |
| Modal verb phrase | 2 | 2 | 4 |
| | | | |

In the next table we give the target tense choices.

*Target tense choices: essay*

| Target tense | Number |
|---|---|
| Present perfect (active)[1] | 1 |
| Present simple (active) | 6 |
| Present simple (passive) | 1 |
| Past simple (active) | 6 |
| Past simple (passive) | 2 |
| Present continuous (active) | 1 |
| Modal verb phrase | 4 |

*Note*:

1 Although we have suggested that the present perfect is the most likely choice in item 1 ('has played'), the past simple would also be a possibility here.

*Interview: Student 1*

*Int.:* tell me about your work experience

*S1.:* actually (1) I'm ✗ *[present simple; was]* a staff clerk . sometimes I (2) <u>deal</u> ✗ *[present simple; dealt]* with salesperson . then (3) <u>is</u> ✗ *[present simple; was ?]* regarding door ah sales of doors and I (4) <u>have</u> ✗ *[present simple; had]* to ???

*Int.:* door? d-o-o-r-s?

*S1.:* d-o-o-r

*Int.:* oh I see I thought dogs

*S1.:* and (5) it'<u>s</u> ✗ *[present simple; was]* quite a good experience for me because previously I (6) <u>didn't involve</u> ✗ *[past simple; wasn't involved]* in any work . except operator . and then . I (7) <u>face</u> ✗ *[present simple; faced]* many kind of people]

*Int.:* problem

*S1.:* problem also because (8) I'<u>m</u> ✓ *[present simple]* not very socialise

*Int.:* you look okay

*S1.:* then I (9) <u>have</u> ✗ *[present simple; had]* to mix around with my colleagues . they (10) <u>are</u> ✗ *[present simple; were]* all very . they (11) <u>are</u> ✗ *[present simple; were]* much older than me . we (12) <u>have</u> ✗ *[present simple; had]* a communication breakdown . them um those salesmen . I (13) <u>think</u> ✓ *[present simple]* they (14) <u>are</u> ✓ *[present simple]* very cunning . sometimes then I (15) <u>don't know</u> ✗ *[present simple; didn't know]* how to

*Int.:* take advantage of you

*S1.:* ya . and I (16) <u>have to</u> ✗ *[present simple; had to]* face my boss (17) he'<u>s</u> ✗ *[present simple; was]* very close to me so I (18) <u>felt</u> ✓ *[past simple]* very pressurized. because he (19) <u>examine</u> ✗ *[present simple; examined]* . my work and all that lah

*Tense choices made by Student 1: interview*

| Tense | No. correct | No. incorrect | Total |
|---|---|---|---|
| Present simple active | 3 | 14 | 17 |
| Past simple active | 1 | 1 | 2 |

*Target tense choices: interview*

| Tense | Number |
|---|---|
| Present simple active | 3 |
| Past simple active | 16 |

In the essay, 10 out of the 21 choices were correct (48%) and 11 incorrect (52%). In the interview, four out of 19 were correct (21%) and 15 incorrect (79%). This seems to give a good indication that in writing, where there is more thinking time and perhaps less pressure, the student is able to make a higher proportion of correct choices. If we go on to compare actual and target tense choices, we can see that in both data samples the student overuses the present simple but under uses the past simple. However, in the interview this tendency is much more marked.

We might also note the greater variety of tenses (both actual and target) in the essay. While this may suggest that in contexts where it is more difficult to pay attention to language the range of tense choices is relatively limited, it may simply reflect the fact that fewer tense choices were needed in the interview to convey the intended meanings. However, this might be something to be explored further.

 **Task C7.2**

*Focus*

Here are two more similar pieces of data from a different student.

➤ Do the same kind of analysis as in Task C7.1.

➤ Do you observe the same tendencies?

*Data*

*Essay: Student 2*

In the older day, girl women did not socialise with the men, thus when there came the age of marriage the couple was always matched by a matchmaker.

Nowadays people mention about matchmaking again because more and more women are getting unmarried. The government is especially worry about this problem because of the shrinked in the population. Thus they established SDU (Social Developing Unit) in 1984 to help people between 25 and 35.

In fact people do conduct matchmaking here and there in an invisible manner when new friends with opposite sex being introducinged to each other. Many organisations such as community youth groups, clans and other private societies or associations etc do organise various kinds of activities or courses in which boys and girls are mixed around when they are participated in these activities. Therefore all these organisations are just acting like a matching centre in which people can choose their partners freely.

For the case of SDU it has organised the similar kind of activities in order to bring boy and girl come together. However, the response may not be good because it has done the things purposely and stated its aim clearly which make people feel unnatural to take part in its activities . . .

*Interview: Student 2*

(The student has been asked to say what she did during the break the previous week. Keep this in mind as you judge whether the student's tense choices are correct.)

*S2*: last week ? stay at home
*Int.*: I know stay at home but
*S2*: ya catch up some of the work for example we got a lot of things we got a lot of um extra not really not really homework lah for example we have to read up some text because sometime we can't catch up you see so we have to spend this within this times we are able to read up some and then do some tutorial . um just catch up lah I mean I didn't spend I didn't spend extra time for outing
*Int.*: so you spend a lot of your time actually
*S2*: no I didn't say a lot of time spend most of the time
*Int.*: I see how many hours do you actually . . . on on studying
*S2*: per day?
*Int.*: per day
*S2*: at least . I think . depend because depend if we got attend any activity then say let say I don't have anything tonight by the time I reach my house it'll be roughly evening time so roughly 5 hours . should be more than that including Saturday and Sunday roughly 5 hours
*Int.*: I see before you came to university you must have some expectation of a a university life
*S2*: not really I just like I enter here because I got to enter here that's all
*Int.*: you mean you didn't want to come or your parents asked you to come
*S2*: I didn't mean I don't want to come just a process of education you see just you got out you carry on and on until you cannot go further that's all

## Task C7.3

### *Focus*

We now turn to samples of speech from a Malaysian secondary school class-room. While they could be compared and evaluated on a variety of dimensions (e.g. the amount of talk generated, turn-taking behaviour), here we will consider only grammatical features of the discourse generated by these 'com-municative' and 'discourse' activities. Rather than focus on one area of grammar as we did in Tasks 1 and 2 above, we will look more generally at word classes.

We have provided a sample of ten turns from each of the four activities. (As one of the turns in 'Hangman' is in Malay, the sample comprises eleven turns in total.)

➤ Analyse each sample by listing every occurrence of the word classes given in Table C7.1. In the 'main verb' column, also give an indication of tense and aspect (e.g. present simple, past continuous, base [form]). An analysis of the 'Hangman' sample is done for you:

*Table C7.1* Word class analysis of 'Hangman' data sample

| Nouns | Adjectives | Adverbs | Main verbs | Auxiliary verbs |
|---|---|---|---|---|
| words<br>U (x2)<br>S (x3)<br>B (x2) | | there (x5)<br>no (x3)<br>notIn't (x2) | is [pres simple]<br>(x4)<br>wait [base] (x3)<br>relax [base] | |

| Determiners | Pronouns | Prepositions | Conjunctions | Exclamations |
|---|---|---|---|---|
| what<br>a (x3) | it (x3) | in (x3) | | er<br>OK<br>ah |

➤ On the basis of your findings (but bearing in mind that we are working with a very limited sample), how far do you agree with Warren's contention that 'discourse activities' produce language that better reflects the relative un-predictability and open-endedness of natural discourse than do 'communicative activities'?

## Data

*Hangman*

> *S1*: What words?
> *S2*: Is there a U in it?
> *S3*: U? er, no
> *S4*: [comment in Malay]
> *S5*: Wait, wait
> *S4*: Is there a S in it?
> *S3*: S, S no there isn't
> *S2*: OK, relax! Ah!
> *S1*: Is there a B in it?
> *S3*: B no there isn't
> *S5*: Wait!

*Maps*

S1: The coconut trees under the Kampong Kelantan. [pause] Right?
S2: Right.
S1: The volcano under the jungle. [pause]
S2: Under the jungle?
S1: Yes.
S2: OK Roslan OK.
S1: The road from Jason Bay to Desaru Bay. [pause]
S2: OK.
S1: The town behind the Desaru Bay and Jason Bay. [pause] Finish?
S2: Relax. [pause] Finish.

*Fashion photographs*

S1: Who likes this one?
S2: Aah, I like this.
S3: I like this pink pattern jump suit.
S1: I like jeans. [laughter]
S2: Oh you —
S4: I like satin.
S2: You must be a very, very bad.
S1: Trousers – lah. [laughter] Jeans or Levis.
S3: Now Malaysian girls also wearing, what.
S2: They also not so good, lah. Modern!

*Nazri's story*

S1: Maybe Nazri kicked the [inaudible]
S2: Only Nazri maybe or maybe a secrantus [?] or like that.
S1: I think maybe Nazri kicked the table.
S3: Nazri ran – can't open the door –
S2: I don't think so because just because – the little you know.
S3: Because he didn't find the door handle. Why be can go out from the house and the villagers.
S4: The robbers must have stolen Nazri then.
S5: But we cannot say the robbers was catched the Nazri but the we don't know what the happened to the Nazri at the end of the story.
S2: Maybe.
S1: I think Nazri locked the door – and ran away.

What we have done is just one kind of grammatical analysis allowing us to compare grammar across texts. What limitations do you think it has?

## IDEAS FOR FURTHER RESEARCH

Here are some suggestions on further research that you could do in the area of grammar in second-language learning.

■ Developing the activities in this unit, you could explore the effect that variability in task has on the language produced by a particular group of students. We have focused here on spoken language, contrasting speech and writing, but you could also explore the effect of different degrees of planning on grammar in writing. For example, you could give students an unprepared writing task, setting a limit of, say, thirty minutes for the task of describing major changes that have taken place in their home town in the last ten years and planned changes for the future. (This would encourage a range of tenses, which could be the focus of your investigation.) Some time later, give the same students thirty minutes or more to prepare for a similar writing task. (For example, you could ask them to write about their past and current leisure interests, and what interests they hope to develop in the future.)

■ Longitudinal studies similar to that exemplified in Unit C6 can be carried out on particular students or groups of students to provide very valuable findings in this area, allowing investigation of changes in second language over time. For example, a student's written or spoken language could be sampled, by collecting the same kind of data, weekly or monthly over a period of study. Analysis can focus on particular grammatical features, such as tenses, articles, conjunction, or subordination, and changes in this area can be traced through the study period. However, if you are doing a project with a short time in which to gather data, this kind of study may not be feasible.

An alternative is to take comparable samples of data from similar groups of students at different stages in second language learning. For example, you could collect data from students writing and/or talking about a particular topic (their interests or family, or giving an opinion on a current event) at elementary, intermediate and advanced levels.

■ If you are familiar with the first language of a group of students learning English as a second or foreign language, explore its influence on their written or spoken language (or 'interlanguage'; see Text B7.2). Again, it can be interesting to look at how this influences changes at different stages of language learning.

■ Interlanguage is also an area that can be explored using the methods of corpus analysis, as you practised in Unit C3. A number of websites provide information useful to investigations in this area of grammar and context. Information about the International Corpus of Learner English (ICLE), a corpus of student writing from a wide variety of first language backgrounds, and the Lindsei (Louvain International Database of Spoken English Interlanguage) database of spoken learner English from French mother-tongue learners, is available at http://www.fltr.ucl.ac.be/fltr/germ/etan/cecl/cecl.html

The site tells you how to contribute to and gain access to the data, and links can be found to some sites where you can access concordance lines from the data from particular groups of learners.

# Unit C8
# Exploring grammar and gender

## INTRODUCTION AND BACKGROUND TO DATA

A growing area of study in recent years has been the characteristic use of language by males and females, and evidence has started to be gathered which suggests that the genders tend to use language in different ways (see Unit B8). A concern of much of this work has been not only to identify these differences, but also to consider how language is used to construct gender identities: in other words, how language both projects and creates the features of the group. Sex-based differences have been identified in, for example, intonation, the amount of interruption that occurs, and the use of politeness strategies. Here, however, we will focus on grammatical differences.

In Text B8.1 you read part of a report on a study conducted in Sydney, Australia, into how language is influenced by gender, age and social class. The focus was on non-standard grammatical forms and the contextual variables that influence their use by girls and boys of different ages. Age and gender were also found to be significant in the different discoursal functions of the word 'like'. In both these studies, grammatical choices were seen to be part of the way in which girls and boys constructed or represented their developing identities. In this unit we demonstrate another approach to data analysis which allows the relationship between gender and language to be explored, although other contextual factors could also be investigated using a similar approach. You might like to bear in mind our discussion in Unit A2 on the dynamism of context when conducting the analysis. The identities that the boys and girls in the data construct shift during the course of their interaction although, as we will see, there is a general preference for particular grammatical choices which appear to reflect behavioural differences between the boys and the girls as distinct social groups.

The analysis we will undertake is based on an approach devised by Sinclair and Coulthard (1975), and developed by Francis and Hunston (1992) and Sauntson (2001). In this approach, discourse is categorised into a hierarchy of structural levels. At the lowest level are *acts*, which combine into *moves*, which in turn combine into *exchanges*. Here is a short sample analysis from Sauntson (2001: 569) in which three boys are talking in a classroom.

| Speaker | Dialogue | Act | Move | Exchange |
|---------|----------|-----|------|----------|
| A | Shaggy | starter | | |
| | have you finished yours | neutral proposal | eliciting | Elicit |
| B | yeah | informative | informing | |
| A | show me | directive | directing | Direct |
| C | is it good | neutral proposal | eliciting | Elicit |
| B | it's all right | informative | informing | |

Here we will be concerned only with the level of *move*. Our focus will be an analysis of *informing, eliciting* and *directing* moves which represent the three fundamental communicative behaviours: giving information, asking for information, and getting people to do things. Typically, the main part of these moves are realised grammatically as follows:

- *informing moves* are realised by declarative clauses (e.g. *It's this way*)
- *eliciting moves* are realised by interrogative clauses (e.g. *Which way is it?*)
- *directing moves* are realised by imperative clauses (e.g. *Walk this way*)

However, as we will see below, this correspondence is not always found. We will try to show how an exploration of these moves and their grammatical realisation in the data can help us identify differences in how girls and boys organise their discourse in the classroom, and how this is a reflection of attitudes to power and status within groups.

Before working on this unit you should have read Unit B8.

## Task C8.1

### *Focus*

The data samples in this unit (from Sauntson, 2001) are from transcripts of a group of girls and a group of boys, all aged around twelve, speaking in Design and Technology lessons in the first year of secondary school. In the first data sample, three boys are involved in group work.

➤ Classify each of the moves according to their function; that is, whether they are:

*informing* (that is, they supply information), *eliciting* (that is, they elicit information, a decision or agreement) or *directing* (that is, they request an action).

Some of these are already done; try to complete the rest. To help, the main part of each informing, eliciting and directing move is underlined, and you should focus attention on these.

(Note that other move types are left out of consideration here, and these are indicated with a '–' in the 'Move' column.)

### Data

*Table C8.1* Move types: a

|  |  |  | Move |
|---|---|---|---|
| 1 | M2 | <u>draw it</u> draw the spatula | directing |
| 2 | M1 | yeah you do | – |
| 3 | M3 | <u>draw the spatula</u> | directing |
| 4 | M2 | I can't see it all the way over there | – |
| 5 | M3 | look <u>it's got a hole in it</u> {laughter} | informing |
| 6 |  | boys boys Alex look <u>it's got one there</u> | informing |
| 7 | M1 | Alistair <u>get on with it</u> | ............. |
| 8 | M2 | I can't draw | – |
| 9 | M3 | Alex <u>stop being rude</u> | ............. |
| 10 | M2 | look at that little {inaudible} | – |
| 11 | M1 | oh <u>we have one of them</u> | ............. |
| 12 | M3 | a little {inaudible} | – |
| 13 | M2 | <u>look that that charity bin</u> let me put 20p in | ............. |
| 14 | M1 | oy | – |
| 15 | M3 | <u>I'm going to put a pound in</u> | ............. |
| 16 | M2 | come on then come on | – |
| 17 | M1 | <u>what's it used for</u> | eliciting |
| 18 | M3 | <u>to make pancakes</u> | ............. |
| 19 | M1 | no | – |
| 20 | M3 | <u>to throw the pancakes in the air</u> | ............. |
| 21 | M1 | and what's that go in two er two er throw pancakes {aside} | eliciting |
| 22 | M3 | <u>there's no Y in throw</u> | ............. |
| 23 | M2 | yeah there is | – |
| 24 | M1 | to throw pancakes {aside} | – |
| 25 | M2 | cakes in the {aside} | – |
| 26 | M3 | God man <u>we've only done three</u> | ............. |
| 27 | M2 | <u>he's run out of space</u> | ............. |
| 28 |  | <u>ow that hurt</u> | ............. |
| 29 |  | <u>that's to cut cheese that is</u> | ............. |
| 30 | M3 | I know how to cut cheese <u>that's to make it bigger that's to make is smaller</u> | ............. |
| 31 | M1 | <u>what's that used for</u> | ............. |
| 32 | M3 | yeah yeah <u>what about the yeah in the end what's it used for</u> | ............. |
| 33 | M2 | <u>pancakes</u> ] | ............. |
| 34 | M1 | <u>pancake mix</u> ] to make pancakes | ............. |
| 35 | M3 | <u>I'm a dickhead</u> I'm writing in blue | ............. |
| 36 | M2 | oh Alistair <u>why did you swear</u> | ............. |

Here are Sauntson's suggested codings for the other moves:

7 directing, 9 directing, 11 informing, 13 directing, 15 informing, 18 informing, 20 informing, 22 informing, 26 informing, 27 informing, 28 informing, 29 informing, 30 informing, 31 eliciting, 32 eliciting, 33 informing, 34, informing, 35 informing, 36 eliciting.

➤ Now look at the grammatical form of the directing, the eliciting and the informing moves. What general patterns do you observe?

### Commentary

The boys' directing moves all include at least one imperative verb form: *draw, get, stop*, and *look*. Their eliciting moves are all *wh*-questions with *what* or *why*. Their informing moves all include declaratives (statements) – *it's got a hole in it, it's got one there, we have one of them* – some of which have the subject and perhaps other items elided (left out) – *[It's] to make pancakes, [It's for] pancakes*.

### Task C8.2

### Focus

➤ Do the same for the following data sample in which three girls are engaged in group work. Again, some moves are coded for you. The girls start talking about characters – Po and Tinky Winky – from the television programme *Teletubbies*. (If you haven't seen the programme, it will be helpful for you to know that the characters have television screens on their stomachs!)

### Data

*Table C8.2*  Move types: b

|  |  |  | Move |
|---|---|---|---|
| 1 | F1 | right <u>I was thinking we could do em a round cake yeah like them small cakes we made</u> | eliciting |
| 2 | F2 | <u>yeah</u> | informing |
| 3 | F1 | <u>a round cake right?</u> | ............. |
| 4 | F2 | <u>yeah</u> | ............. |
| 5 | F1 | <u>and then you cooked it so it's nice and then em and then you put a teletubby in the middle</u> | eliciting |
| 6 | F2 | <u>a little one like Po</u> | ............. |
| 7 | F1 | <u>Po Po can be with a girl</u> | ............. |
| 8 | F2 | <u>no do Tinky Winky if it's a boy</u> | ............. |
| 9 | F1 | <u>and then em pink icing around the outside so then it's a girl's and a boy's</u> | ............. |
| 10 | F2 | <u>yeah ]</u> | ............. |

| 11 | F1 | that's it ] | .............. |
| 12 | | we just need the crayons | directing |
| 13 | F2 | yeah so just put right put this picture of a cake {inaudible} | – |
| 14 | F1 | have you got any crayons | .............. |
| 15 | F3 | yeah | .............. |
| 16 | F1 | put the picture picture of the cakes | .............. |
| 17 | F2 | two cakes? | .............. |
| 18 | F1 | no you're only doing one a girl and a boy | .............. |
| 19 | | yeah both together so if you draw something like a round circle shape | .............. |
| 20 | F3 | the picture of the cakes {inaudible} | – |
| 21 | F1 | so shall we put and then you draw some wiggly icing | .............. |
| 22 | F3 | okay | .............. |
| 23 | F1 | then draw a teletubby | .............. |
| 24 | F3 | I'm good at drawing teletubbies | .............. |
| 25 | F2 | are you | .............. |
| 26 | F3 | well as long as we have a registered trademark you know it's illegal to draw cakes without it | .............. |
| 27 | F2 | who are we having Tinky Winky? | .............. |
| 28 | F3 | yeah | .............. |
| 29 | | how did you know? | .............. |
| 30 | F2 | she told me | .............. |
| | | {laughter} | |
| 31 | F3 | please don't sing | .............. |
| 32 | F2 | sorry | – |
| 33 | | have you seen Jane's | .............. |
| 34 | | mine's a bit fat anyway | .............. |
| 35 | F3 | well teletubbies are meant to be fat | – |
| 36 | F1 | cos they've got a big stomach | .............. |
| 37 | F31 | for a television | – |
| 38 | F1 | right let's colour it in | .............. |
| 39 | F3 | okay | – |

Here are Sauntson's suggested codings for the other moves:

3 eliciting, 4 informing, 6 eliciting, 7 informing, 8 eliciting, 9 eliciting, 10 informing, 11 informing, 14 eliciting, 15 informing, 16 eliciting, 17 eliciting, 18 informing, 19 eliciting, 21 eliciting, 22 informing, 23 directing, 24 informing, 25 eliciting, 26 informing, 27 eliciting, 28 informing, 29 eliciting, 30 informing, 31 directing, 33 eliciting, 34 informing, 36 informing, 38 directing

## *Commentary*

■ The girls' directing moves, although small in number, show a wider variety of forms than those produced by the boys. Three have an imperative form – *draw, don't sing, let's* – although the last two of these at least could be said to be less 'commanding' than the boys': *don't sing* is preceded by *please*, and the use of *let's* turns the directive into something closer to an inclusive suggestion than a command (compare the more forceful *Colour it in*).

■ Considerably more variety is also shown in the girls' eliciting moves. While all five of the boys' eliciting moves were *wh-* questions, only two of the girls' were of this form (*who are we having Tinky Winky; how did you know?*) and only three others were interrogatives eliciting 'yes' or 'no' answers *(have you got any crayons; are you; have you seen Jane's).* The majority include statements which function as suggestions to which agreement is elicited: *right I was thinking we could do em a round cake yeah like them small cakes we made . . . and then you cooked it so it's nice and then em and then you put a teletubby in the middle . . . and then em pink icing around the outside so then it's a girl's and a boy's; put the picture picture of the cakes; yeah both together so if you draw something like a round circle shape; so shall we put and then you draw some wiggly icing.* Notice that some of the suggestions include grammatical choices which make the suggestions tentative, including: past continuous verb form (*I was thinking . . .*), past simple verbs (*you cooked it . . . and then you put . . .*), an *if*-clause (*so if you draw something like . . .*), and *shall we . . .* Other elicitations take the form of noun phrases, sometimes with a questioning intonation, which serve either to make a suggestion or to check understanding (*a round cake right?; a little one like Po; two cakes?*).

■ While eight of the girls' fourteen informing moves, like the boys', include declaratives (e.g. *Po Po can be with a girl; no you're only doing one a girl and a boy*) the remaining six are short affirmatives (*yeah, that's it, okay*) which concur with or confirm what has been said previously.

## Task C8.3

### *Focus*

So far we have identified quantitative differences in the proportion of eliciting, informing and directing moves in these samples of data from the girls and the boys, and qualitative differences in the grammatical forms of the utterances that realise these move types. Two further questions now arise:

➤ How representative are these samples of Sauntson's wider data?

➤ What might these linguistic differences tell us about the way groups of girls and groups of boys interact?

To help us consider the first of these, Table C8.3, provides information about the number and percentage of these moves in all of Sauntson's data and in the two samples you have looked at.

➤ Study the figures and spend some time thinking about the two questions posed above.

Table C8.3 Move type distribution of girls' and boys' discourse

| Move type | All data | | | | Data samples | | | |
| | Girls | | Boys | | Girls | | Boys | |
| | No. of moves | % of all moves | No. of moves | % of all moves | No. of moves | % of moves in sample | No. of moves | % of moves in sample |
| --- | --- | --- | --- | --- | --- | --- | --- | --- |
| Eliciting | 358 | 31.6 | 556 | 29.5 | 15 | 40.5 | 5 | 16 |
| Informing | 476 | 42.1 | 870 | 46.1 | 14 | 37.8 | 15 | 48.4 |
| Directing | 60 | 5.3 | 193 | 10.2 | 4 | 10.8 | 5 | 16 |
| Others | 238 | 21 | 267 | 14.2 | 4 | 10.8 | 6 | 19.4 |
| Total | 1132 | 100 | 1886 | 100 | 37 | 99.9 | 31 | 99.8 |

Figures for 'All data' from Sauntson 2001: 212

## *Commentary*

- In terms of the number and relative frequency of occurrence of eliciting, informing and directing moves, the samples seem only moderately representative of the data as a whole. In the whole data, informing moves are most frequent, eliciting some way behind, and directing moves relatively infrequent. The boys produce proportionately more informing and directing moves, but the frequency of eliciting moves is similar. In the samples, eliciting moves are most frequent in the boys' data, but eliciting moves seem to be somewhat underrepresented. In the girls' data sample, on the other hand, eliciting moves would seem to be overrepresented. Directing moves are relatively more frequent in both the boys' and girls' sample data. From these figures, of course, we have no way of knowing whether qualitatively the samples are representative of the larger data body. What we must take from this, then, is that we need to frame any findings from our analysis of the samples as research question or hypotheses for further explorations.

With this caution in mind, here are some comments on what our findings suggest about the way groups of girls and groups of boys interact:

- The girls used proportionately fewer directing moves in the data as a whole, and the evidence from the sample suggests that these may be realised differently to some extent. Fewer directing moves may indicate less concern with controlling the interaction (on the basis that the person who 'commands' is in control), and modifying imperatives or using structures other than imperatives to request a non-verbal response may suggest a wish to avoid the role of being the person who seeks to take control in this way. The evidence from the boys, on the other hand, suggests that control of the group is of more importance, and one way this is achieved is through unmodified imperative forms.
- If the boys are concerned with controlling the interaction, we might anticipate that they would produce fewer eliciting moves: an elicitation represents an admission that the speaker lacks some information. While the data samples would offer support for this, the figures from all of Sauntson's data show that the girls produce slightly more eliciting moves. It may be, however, that we can find differences in the *function* of eliciting moves from the boys and girls. The evidence from the samples suggests that, while the boys' elicitations are information-seeking *wh*-questions, the girls' elicitations are more usually concerned with eliciting confirmation or information checking. Rather than projecting, as the boys do, a relationship between members of the group as simply 'seekers' and 'providers' of information, the girls seem to construct the group as negotiators of information, collaborating to share information in a non-confrontational way.
- Similarly, we might expect that, as the boys are more concerned with control, they will produce more informing moves than the girls: in 'telling' they are providing information that others don't have and so are in a more powerful position. The figures for both the data samples and the data as a whole seem to

support this, although the difference between the percentage figures for girls and boys in all the data (42.1% as opposed to 46.1%) is not substantial. Again, though, the function of the informing moves may be different. The evidence from the data samples suggests that the girls' informing moves are more likely to be concerned with confirming what others have said rather than telling information that may or may not have been elicited.

In general, then, the grammatical evidence that we have gathered from our data samples (supplemented by the figures in Table C8.3) suggests the boys show more concern with power and status in their interaction than do the girls. The girls, on the other hand, show more evidence of co-operation and avoidance of confrontation.

## IDEAS FOR FURTHER RESEARCH

Here are some suggestions on further research that you could undertake in the area of grammar and gender.

- We have focused here on groups of girls and groups of boys. Similar analysis could be done in mixed groups of young people or adults.
- While we have looked only at groups working in the classroom, similar analysis of eliciting, informing and directing moves could be done in, for example, seminars, tutorials or other kinds of meeting (staff meetings in schools and colleges or business meetings in companies.)
- The informants in the data we have explored were British. If you have access to similar groups in other countries, you could compare what you have observed here with the interaction in a cross-linguistic or cross-cultural study.
- We have looked only at clause type in this analysis, but other grammatical features might be explored. For example, previous research has noted that males are more inclined to use non-standard forms than females (see Text B8.1). While much of this research looks at pronunciation and vocabulary, analysis of non-standard grammatical features, for example in verb phrases, would be worth investigating (see also Trudgill's work reported in Unit A8 for information and ideas).

We need to remember, however, that any differences that we find in this kind of analysis may not be directly related to gender identity. Other factors such as age, social class and ethnic group may be equally, if not more, significant influences on language, and only when we have a considerable body of research relevant to language and gender will the relationship between these two begin to become more apparent.

# Unit C9
# Exploring grammar in varieties of English

## INTRODUCTION AND BACKGROUND TO DATA

In earlier parts of the book, particularly in Units A8, B9 and B10, we have seen that the notion of 'variety' in language can be looked at in a number of different ways. For example, we have discussed sociolinguistic variety, comparing features of the English typically used by working-class and middle-class groups, and also geographical variety, noting that differences in English occur both across the regions of a country and from one country to another where the language is used. An important related – though controversial – concept is that of 'Standard English' against which a variety might be compared. This is controversial because it is sometimes claimed (either explicitly or implicitly) that the 'standard' has a higher status than a variation from it. While we will be asking you in this unit to compare language samples with your own perception of 'Standard English', we would encourage you to do this in a non-judgemental way, so that what you observe is accepted simply as differences between varieties rather than considering non-standard to be inferior. We can observe differences between British and North American English without judging one to be 'better' than the other; similarly, we can identify differences between, say, Southern British English (SBE), and other regional and international varieties without claiming that these varieties are 'incorrect'.

With this in mind, we explore grammatical features in small samples of two varieties of English. The first sample consists of extracts taken from interviews with people from Birmingham, England (from Thorne 2003). They are illustrative, therefore, of the Birmingham dialect. The second sample consists of a series of short extracts from a corpus of 'Indian English' (The Indian Component of the International Corpus of English[23]). Although for convenience we refer here to Indian English (IE), it is perhaps more accurate to think of this as 'Indian varieties of English' as contact between English and the many native languages of India has produced considerable regional varieties in the country.

The aim is to identify differences between grammar in these samples and in a 'standard' variety of English with which you are familiar. Because we are dealing here with very small samples from just a few users, we need to treat any differences observed as indicative of what might be wider characteristics of the variety. Think of your observations as generating hypotheses or research questions about the varieties that you could go on to test in much larger bodies of data.

Before working on this unit you should have read Units B9 and B10.

 **Task C9.1**

*Focus*

All the people interviewed and interviewing in the data extracts in Tasks C9.1 and C9.2 were working-class people from Birmingham who had lived in the city for most if not all of their lives. The interviews took place in a relaxed setting, and the informants were asked to talk about their memories of bygone Birmingham.

Transcription conventions for these extracts are given below:

(.)      Brief pause
(2.0)   Longer pause to the nearest 0.5 of a second.
( )      Unintelligible section
?        Rising intonation
" "      Quotation of another person's speech or thoughts
'        Omitted sounds or syllables

Some words are written to represent how they were pronounced (e.g 'ya' = you)

➤ Study the first extract and try to identify any features of grammar that you would consider to be 'non-standard' forms.

*Data*

*Interview with Albert Fletcher (86 years of age, recorded 19 June 1989)*

1. *AF*: I met Rosie in erm in erm (.) I met 'er in Studley Street
2. *I*: did ya?
3. *AF*: yes 'cause they lived in Ombersley Road
4. *I*: yeah
5. *AF*: the Archers
6. *I*: yeah
7. *AF*: and erm 'er said to me d— "would you like to marry me?" I said "I don't want to marry nobody, I'm stickin' to me bleedin' self" she said "oh" she said "I know you like a drop to drink, you know, but" she said "I don't drink" she said "it don't worry me"
8. *I*: yeah

## Commentary

Three features of non-standard grammar can be seen in turn 7 of this extract:

■  . . . 'er said to me . . .

A standard form would be 'She said to me'. Using the object pronoun *her* (with initial /h/ omitted) instead of the subject pronoun *she* is a fairly typical feature of Birmingham dialect. No other subject–object substitutions are made; for example, 'Them said . . .' and 'Him said. . .' are not used for 'They said. . .' and 'He said. . .'.

■  I **don't** want to marry **nobody** . . .

A standard form would be 'I don't want to marry anybody . . .'. The use of two negative forms in this way is typical of Birmingham and other urban working-class dialects in British cities such as London and Liverpool.

■  it **don't** worry me

A standard form would be 'It doesn't worry me'. The use of 'don't' instead of 'doesn't' is common in many non-standard dialects, including Birmingham.

## Task C9.2

### Focus

Read three more data extracts and answer the questions below:

➤  Are the three features we noted above repeated in any of them?

➤  What additional 'non-standard' grammatical features do you observe?

### Data

*Interview with Gladys Davidson (87 years of age, recorded 14 August 1987)*

1.  *GD*:  'e was what we called very very good we couldn't never understand why (.) 'e was so good to p– (.) 'e was so good to p– (.) 'e- you did- you did get them people in them days who was good to what they called the poor
2.  *I*:  yeah
3.  *GD*:  you know
4.  *I*:  yeah
5.  *GD*:  erm to us– erm (.) a day out to the Lickey 'ills was our 'olidays in them days, it was five pence on the tram

6. *I:*    yeah
7. *GD:*    and erm it w– that– that– was regular (.) a tram to the Lickey 'ills and back for the day (.) that was what we called 'olidays (.) apart from Blackpool Illuminations

*Notes:*

The Lickey Hills are a park and woodland area on the outskirts of Birmingham.

The Blackpool Illuminations are an annual event in the northern seaside resort of Blackpool when the town is decorated with colourful lights.

*Interview with Nelly Mason (81 years of age, recorded 19 August 1991)*

1. *NM:*    well let's face it (.) the war broke out (.) and we was up Warstock— up erm Warstock, that was it (.) and we come back twelve month after (.) we left in the April and we come back that followin' April (2.0) and erm (1.5) no there was more (.) more compact
2. *I:*    compact yeah
3. *NM:*    they was (.) there to 'elp one another
4. *I:*    yeah
5. *NM:*    erm (.) the bombin's an' all that (.) it med 'em all the more tighter mixed
6. *I:*    yeah
7. *NM:*    and erm (.) 'course the chaps gooin' orff to the army and- (.) and then (.) then they got bombed out they (.) they moved further afield and
8. *I:*    yeah
9. *NM:*    then they all dispersed ( ) I mean there was (.) Edie Carey at St Pauls Road (2.0) that was erm
10. *X:*    Mac's—
11. *NM:*    Mac's wife
12. *X:*    she got blowed up dain't 'er?
13. *NM:*    yes (.) she got blowed up savin' er babbies (.) and there was Nellie- 'cause Nellie was married and away (.) but there was Eileen the daughter (2.0) you see what it was (.) they all used to meet down the shelter in – on Moseley Road

*Notes:*

Participant X in this extract was a friend or relative of the interviewee who was present at the interview but who wished to remain anonymous.

'med' (turn 5) = 'made'
'gooin' orff' (turn 7) = 'going off'
'dain't er' (turn 12) = 'didn't she'
'babbies' (turn 13) = 'babies, or children more generally'
'the shelter' (turn 13) = 'air-raid shelter'

*Interview with Ted and Alice Stokes (80 and 82 years of age, recorded 7 July 1993)*

1. *AS:* 'ow long was yer out of work for when you was on ( ) Street?
2. *TS:* four years
3. *I:* four years
4. *TS:* an' I used ter pass a place (.) in Wallace Road (.) I used ter every- goo down there every day 'cause that was one o' the main races
5. *I:* yeah
6. *TS:* them was- after work them days (.) an' I kep' lookin' up at it so this day I went there an' I thought "oh I'll 'ave a walk down 'ere" (.) walks down an' it was ( ) works (.) you don't – you don't remember that do you?
7. *I:* no
8. *AS:* no
9. *TS* it was down a big drive- opposite ( ) works (.) I mean that was there =
10. *I:* yeah an' that's just by the Green ennit?
11. *TS:* that's it
12. *AS:* that's it yes
13. *TS:* well I started there on nights
14. *I:* yeah
15. *AS:* I come um with erm
16. *I:* I bet you was well pleased worn't yer?
17. *TS:* gawd blimey yeah
18. *AS:* I come um with Dor with Doreen in a pram (.) I'd bin walkin' all day fed up an' erm (.) 'is aunt stopped me (.) Edie Stokes lived in erm (.) bottom o' Brunswick Road (.) she went "where 'ave you bin?" I sez "walkin" she said "Edward's gone to work" I said "work?" she sez "yes, 'e's got a job (.) borrowed tuppence off me this morning" eh-heh-heh

*Notes*:

'goo' (turn 4) = 'go'
'ennit' (turn 10) = 'isn't it'
'on nights' (turn 13) = 'working at night'
'I come um' (turn 15) = 'I came home'
'gawd blimey' (turn 17) = an exclamation or expression of surprise

## Task C9.3

### *Focus*

The extracts below come from a corpus of spoken and written Indian English. An indication is given at the end of each extract of whether it is speech or writing, and the type of communication it comes from.

> Try to identify grammatical features of the extracts that you consider are different from SBE or another Standard English with which you are familiar. The extracts are grouped into sets of five, which share features that are different from SBE.

### Data

*Set 1*

a. Since a long time people have tried to extract pure haemoglobin from other animals and use it in man. *[Writing: non-academic]*
b. They have been postponing his uh promotion right since eleven years. *[Speech: conversation]*
c. I am enjoying overdraft facility with your Branch since last five years and I am very much thankful for the financial assistance given by the Bank. *[Writing: business letter]*
d. I'm residing at above said address since my birth. *[Speech: conversation]*
e. I am now in a new place since one year. *[Writing: social letter]*

*Set 2*

a. What exactly he wants to do? *[Speech: business transaction]*
b. What he does every morning? *[Speech: unscripted monologue]*
c. What kind of jewels you have? *[Speech: conversation]*
d. What kind of *mangalsutra* you want to buy? *[Speech: conversation]*
e. Now what you are going to do about them? *[Speech: unscripted commentary]*

*Note*:

A *mangalsutra* is a necklace worn by married women as a symbol of their marriage.

### Commentary

■ In Set 1, there are differences between SBE use of *since* as a time adverb and its use in IE as represented in these extracts. In SBE *since* refers to a particular point in the past. In IE (in examples a, b, c and e it is used in the way that *for* would be used in SBE, with reference to a period of time. We might also note the use of the present continuous ('I am enjoying' [c], 'I'm residing' [d]) with *since* in IE, where in SBE the present perfect or present perfect continuous would be more likely ('I have enjoyed' or 'I have been enjoying', 'I've resided' or 'I have been residing').

■ Looking at Set 2, in IE, 'what-questions' are formed without the subject-verb inversion and introduction of auxiliary *do* that would be used in SBE (*a–d*):

'What exactly he wants ... ?' rather than 'What exactly does he want ... ?', and so on. Similarly, in e there is no subject-auxiliary inversion in IE: '... what you are going to do ... ?' rather than '... what are you going to do ... ?'

## Task C9.4

### *Focus*

➤ Now do the same with the following sets of extracts from the same corpus.

### *Data*

*Set 3*

    a.  I am having two roommates. *[Speech: conversation]*
    b.  The society is having 1,500 members working in its eight branches. *[Writing: student essay]*
    c.  How many years prior to the incident you had been knowing Chandrahas Chipre? *[Speech: legal cross-examination]*
    d.  So I think Shammi must be knowing her sister. *[Speech: conversation]*
    e.  ... I was not belonging to a particular community. *[Speech: conversation]*

*Set 4*

    a.  He told that that fort it was actually build by the Rastrakutas ... *[Speech: conversation]*
    b.  Shri Suvarna informed that at present the managing committee has not worked out any pl- uh plan or estimate about the conversion ... *[Speech: business transaction]*
    c.  Mr Chougule reported me that you and honourable madam have proposed to stay in Kolhapur for the purpose of completion of the ICE project. *[Writing: social letter]*
    d.  I assure that my services will be commensurate with expectations of all the concerned. *[Writing: business letter]*
    e.  So he wants that we should relate the concept of intelligibility to the concepts of appropriateness and effectiveness in a speech situation. *[Speech: unscripted monologue]*

*Set 5*

a. It has exported over one thousand heavy equipments and earned the country foreign exchange of two hundred and twenty crore rupees. *[Speech: scripted broadcast news]*

b. Researches have also been on to find a PFC that is more soluble and to make most of the already available PFCs. *[Writing: non-academic writing]*

c. The Grapevine can carry only a few type of informations like . . . *[Writing: examination script]*

d. Not I want to prove the insistent inconsistency with the piece of evidences . . . *[Speech: unscripted legal presentation]*

e. These comprise countless different materials: Dust, food wastes, packing in the form of paper, metals, glass, wornout clothings and furnitures . . . *[Writing: academic]*

## IDEAS FOR FURTHER RESEARCH

Here are some suggestions on further research that you could undertake in the area of grammar in varieties of English.

■ In this unit we have explored examples of Indian English from the International Corpus of English. You can find details of this and other corpora at http://www.ucl.ac.uk/english-usage/ice/. At the time of writing, corpora of East African, British, Indian, New Zealand, Philippines and Singapore English were available. If you have access to concordancing software (see also Unit C3) you can produce concordance lines from these corpora to explore grammatical features. Alternatively, you can make use of the 'Find' facility in a word processor to conduct investigations.

■ A number of publications list the grammatical features of regional or international varieties of English which are different from those found in SBE (or another standard English). See, for example, Gramley and Pätzold (2004). There is also a list of common non-standard features given in Unit A8. You could explore these features in a corpus and consider, where the corpus permits, whether they are found in both spoken and written contexts, and whether you observe variety in them in different communicative events.

■ Rather than using a ready-made corpus of language, you could build your own more specialised (and probably smaller) corpora for exploring international varieties. For example, you could identify a particular text type written in English (e.g. newspaper sports reports, wills, company reports, tourist information), find examples of these on the Internet from the countries you are interested in, and compare language in them. If the sample is small, grammatical analysis is likely to be part of a wider lexical and grammatical investigation. You could again use already published research on differences as a guide to what you might find, but anticipate finding others.

■ If you are in a position to gather spoken data from informants who use a regional variety of English, you might follow the procedures that were used to gather the data from Birmingham speakers explored above. Older working-class people who may have spent much of their lives in a particular area often make particularly good informants for interview data, both because their language is likely to provide good evidence of a regional variety and also because they may be readily willing to share their time to talk about their past experiences. If you are able to compare this kind of data with that produced by younger informants, you may also be able to identify possible change over time in the variety.

# Some final thoughts

By the time you read this page we hope that we will have interested you in taking your study of grammar and context further. If you have worked through this book you should be in a good position to do this. You will have an understanding of key grammatical concepts; you will have read and thought about the complex relationships between grammar and context; you will have read some of the most important published texts on the subject; and you will have conducted a number of small-scale grammatical analyses of authentic data taken from a wide variety of sources.

We have given a number of ideas for research topics that will allow you to contribute to what is known about grammar and context. You might, of course, have to adapt these so that they are practical for your own local situation. You might also have your own ideas for research. If you want further information about new relevant reading as it appears, and more suggestions for research please look at the following website: http://routledge.tandf.co.uk/textbooks/0415310814. This will be updated regularly and we hope it will provide a valuable additional resource for you.

# Glossary of grammatical terms

| | |
|---|---|
| ACTOR | (see AGENT) |
| ADJECTIVE | A word that describes a noun (e.g. a *stunning* view) or a pronoun (e.g. a *large* one). |
| ADJECTIVE PHRASE | An element of a clause in which the main word is an adjective (e.g. It's *rather good.*) |
| ADJUNCT | A word or group of words in a clause that give information about time, place or manner. Sometimes used as another word for ADVERBIAL. |
| ADVERB | A word that gives more information (where, when etc.) about a verb (e.g. She walked *quietly*), adjective (e.g. a *surprisingly* good film), another adverb (e.g. He asked *very* politely), or a phrase (e.g. She's *rarely* in a hurry). |
| ADVERBIAL | A word or group of words that says where, when, etc. something happens. It may be an adverb, an ADVERBIAL PHRASE, a PREPOSITIONAL PHRASE, a NOUN PHRASE, or an ADVERBIAL CLAUSE (e.g. *After I got home*, I went to straight to bed.) (See also ADJUNCT.) |
| ADVERBIAL CLAUSE | A clause that functions as an ADVERBIAL within a main clause. |
| ADVERBIAL PHRASE | An element of a clause that says when, how, where, etc. something happens (e.g. *with a lot of effort, over a month ago*). |
| AGENT (or ACTOR) | The person or thing that performs the action described in a verb. It is usually the subject in an ACTIVE clause and follows 'by' in a PASSIVE clause. |
| AGREEMENT | (see CONCORD) |
| ANTECEDENT | An expression which a PRONOUN refers to. It usually comes before the pronoun. |
| ANTICIPATORY 'IT' (or **extraposed** 'it') | This occurs in a sentence in which the subject is placed at the end and it is inserted in the normal subject position (e.g. *It must be emphasised that the* |

*results are provisional*). Also referred to as a sentence with an EXTRAPOSED SUBJECT.

| | |
|---|---|
| APPOSITION | A term which usually refers to placing a NOUN PHRASE or clause after another name when both refer to the same thing (e.g. *the Prime Minister, Mr Blair*; He faced *the risk/ that he would fall*). |
| ARTICLE | The words *the* (the **definite article**) and *a/ an* (the **indefinite article**). |
| ASPECT | A term used in the grammatical description of verbs indicating the way that duration or time is marked by the verb. The usual distinction is between **continuous** (or **progressive**) aspect and **perfect** aspect. |
| ATTRIBUTE | A term used mainly in systemic functional linguistics. Some RELATIONAL PROCESS clauses link a CARRIER with its attribute. For example, in the clause *The exam seemed quite easy* the verb *seemed* is relational process linking the attribute *quite easy* with the carrier *The exam*. That is, the carrier *The exam* is said to have the attribute that it is *quite easy*. |
| AUXILIARY VERBS | The verbs *be, have* and *do* when they are used with a main verb to form questions, negatives, tenses, passive forms, etc. MODAL VERBS are also auxiliary verbs. |
| BENEFICIARY | A term mainly used in systemic functional linguistics. In a MATERIAL PROCESS clause a participant which benefits from the process in some way is the beneficiary. For example, in the clause *She gave some flowers to her teacher*, 'her teacher' is the beneficiary. |
| CARRIER | (see ATTRIBUTE) |
| CLAUSE | A group of words containing a verb, which may be a complete sentence or part of a sentence. A **main** (or **independent**) clause can exist as a separate sentence, while a SUBORDINATE (or **dependent** clause) cannot. Types of subordinate clause include **relative clauses** (e.g. My brother, *who lives in London*, is an architect), **conditional clauses** (e.g. *If you work hard*, you'll pass your exams), ADVERBIAL CLAUSES and NOUN CLAUSES. |
| CLAUSAL UNIT | A term used by Biber *et al.* (1999) to refer to a structure consisting of an independent clause together with any dependent clause EMBEDDED within it. Language that falls outside clausal units is referred to as **non-clausal material**. |
| CLAUSE COMPLEX | A term used mainly in systemic functional linguistics to refer to two or more clauses linked by |

COORDINATION and/ or by SUBORDINATION to form a larger grammatical unit.

CLIENT
A term used mainly in systemic functional linguistics to refer to a BENEFICIARY **for** whom something is done. For example in *I'll carry it for you*, 'you' is the beneficiary. (Compare RECIPIENT.)

COHESION
The various relations between grammatical structures and lexical items that combine to form a text. PRONOUNS and CONJUNCTIONS have particular importance in cohesion. **Lexical cohesion** can take the form of repetition or choosing words that are in some way related to previous ones.

COMPLEMENT
A term which usually refers to a phrase or clause (a **complement clause**) which follows the verb *be* (or similar verbs such as *appear, become, feel* and *seem*) and describes the subject (e.g. Gary is *a solicitor*) or object (e.g. It seems the parcel *had been sent to me*).

CONCORD (or AGREEMENT)
A relationship between elements of language in which one form of a word requires a corresponding form of another word. The most important type of concord in English is between subject and verb: a singular subject is followed by a singular verb and a plural subject is followed by a plural verb.

CONDITIONAL CLAUSE
(see CLAUSE)

CONJUNCTION
A word that links two words, phrases or clauses. **Coordinating conjunctions**, including *and, but* and *or*, link elements of equal status. **Subordinating conjunctions**, including *whereas, if* and *because*, link elements of different status, where one element is dependent on the other.

COORDINATION
Linking two words, phrases or clauses together of equal status. (See also CONJUNCTION.)

COPULA
The name given to the verb *be* and sometimes also verbs such as *appear, seem, become, feel* which link a subject to its COMPLEMENT. Also called **link** or **linking verbs**.

DEICTIC
Words which 'point to' what they refer to. They include the DEMONSTRATIVES and the adverbs *now, then, here, there*.

DEMONSTRATIVE
The words *this, that, these* and *those*, which are used before a noun (e.g. *These* cakes) or as a pronoun (e.g. *That* sounds good).

DETERMINER
A word used at the beginning of a NOUN PHRASE, including the articles (*the, a, an*), *some, any, my, your, this, that*, etc.

311

| | |
|---|---|
| DISCOURSE MARKER | A word or phrase used in speech that marks a transition point in discourse and signals to the listener how they are to understand what follows (e.g. *You see, Mind you*). |
| ELLIPSIS | Leaving out words which can be reconstructed from elsewhere in the discourse or from the wider context (sometimes referred to as **situational ellipsis**). |
| EMBEDDING | Including one unit as part of another unit of the same type. For example, in *on the other side of the street, of the street* is embedded. SUBORDINATE CLAUSES are also sometimes said to be embedded in a MAIN CLAUSE. Also referred to as **nesting**. |
| ERGATIVE | A verb which can be TRANSITIVE or INTRANSITIVE, and which allows the same noun as object when it is transitive as subject when it is intransitive (e.g. *I closed the door* [transitive], *The door closed* [intransitive]). |
| EXPERIENTIAL | (See METAFUNCTION) |
| EXTRAPOSED 'IT' | (See ANTICIPATORY 'IT') |
| FILLED PAUSE | A pause filled with a sound like *er* or *erm*. |
| FINITE VERB | A verb form which can vary for present and past tense (e.g. *wait – waits – waited*) in contrast to a **non-finite** form which cannot (e.g. *Waiting* for over two hours, he began to feel annoyed). |
| GOAL | The person or thing affected by the action of the verb (e.g. The dog ate *the bone*). Also referred to as **patient** or **recipient**. |
| HEAD | The main word in a PHRASE. The head of a noun phrase is usually a noun or pronoun; the head of an adjective phrase is an adjective; and so on. |
| INTERPERSONAL | (see METAFUNCTION) |
| LEXICAL COHESION | (see COHESION) |
| MATERIAL PROCESS | (see PROCESS) |
| METAFUNCTION | Systemic functional linguistics usually recognises three broad metafunctions of language: the **experiental**, the **interpersonal**, and the **textual**. In general terms: **experiental** meanings are to do with how we describe our experience of the world; **interpersonal** meanings are to do with how we use language to interact with others; and **textual** meanings are to do with how messages are organised. |
| MAIN CLAUSE | (see CLAUSE) |
| MATERIAL PROCESS | (see PROCESS) |

| | |
|---|---|
| MENTAL PROCESS | (see PROCESS) |
| MODALITY | The expression of the attitude of the speaker towards the factual content of what is being said. It is therefore to do with such notions as uncertainty, possibility, probability, and necessity. The MODAL VERBS are an important means of expressing modality. Two types of modality (or **modal meaning**) are traditionally recognised. **Epistemic modality** is to do with the speaker's judgement of the truth of a proposition. **Deontic modality** is to do with some kind of human control over the proposition, such as ability, permission or obligation. |
| MODAL VERBS | A group of verbs (*can, could, dare, may, might, must, need, ought to, shall, should, will, would, used to*) that give information about possibility, necessity, obligation, etc. (See also AUXILIARY VERBS.) |
| MOOD | Clauses are often classified into those having **imperative mood** (e.g. *Wait here*), **declarative mood** (e.g. *I'm waiting*), and **interrogative mood** (e.g. *Have you been waiting long?*). Together, declarative and interrogative are referred to as the **indicative mood**. |
| NOMINAL CLAUSE | (see NOUN CLAUSE) |
| NOMINAL GROUP | (see PHRASE) |
| NOMINALIZATION | The process of forming a noun from some other word class (e.g. He *proposed* changes; His *proposal* was ignored). |
| NON-FINITE | (see FINITE) |
| NOUN | A word that refers to a person, place, thing, or abstract idea such as a feeling or quality. |
| NOUN CLAUSE (or **nominal** clause) | A type of SUBORDINATE CLAUSE that functions as a NOUN PHRASE (e.g. I've no idea *where she's gone*). |
| NOUN PHRASE | An element of a clause in which the main word is a noun. |
| OBJECT | The person or thing affected by the action of the verb or that is involved in the result of the action (e.g. I ate *some cheese*). (Compare SUBJECT.) |
| PARTICIPANT | A term used mainly in systemic functional linguistics to refer to the people or thing involved in a PROCESS. |
| PHRASE | A grammatical unit (also called a **group**) made up of one or more words, which is a constituent of a CLAUSE. For example, a **noun phrase** (or **noun group** or **nominal group**) is a phrase in which the main word is a noun (e.g. I was talking to *the woman who* |

*lives next door*). Other main phrase types – **verb phrase**, **prepositional phrase**, **adjective phrase** and **adverb phrase** – are named after the word class of the main word in the phrase.

| | |
|---|---|
| PREDICATE | The part of the clause that follows the subject (e.g. The train *left an hour late*). |
| PREPOSITION | A word such as *in*, *on*, or *by* that comes before a noun, pronoun, noun phrase or -ing form (e.g. *in* January, *on* the table, *by* working hard). |
| PREPOSITIONAL PHRASE | A group of words that consists of a PREPOSITION and its **prepositional object** (a noun, pronoun, noun phrase, or -ing form) (e.g. *in front of our car*). |
| PROCESS | In systemic functional linguistics the process is usually expressed by the verb phrase. A division is made between: **material processes**, which involve physical action (e.g. *eating, walking*); **mental processes** (e.g. *thinking, imagining*); and **relational processes**, which often relate a PARTICIPANT to a quality (e.g. He *felt* ill). |
| PRONOUN | A word that is used instead of a noun or noun phrase. |
| RECIPIENT | A term used mainly in systemic functional linguistics to refer to a BENEFICIARY to whom something is given. For example, in *An award was given to my daughter*, 'my daughter' is the recipient. (Compare CLIENT.) |
| REFERENCE | Grammatical devices which allow the speaker or writer to indicate whether something is new to the text or discourse or whether it is something that has already been introduced. These include third person personal pronouns (*he, it* etc.) and DEMONSTRATIVES. |
| REFERENT | The person or thing referred to by a noun phrase. |
| RELATIONAL PROCESS | (see PROCESS) |
| RELATIVE CLAUSE | (see CLAUSE) |
| REPORTING VERB | A verb used in a clause that describes what people say or think (e.g. He *asked* . . ., . . . she *agreed*). |
| RHEME | A term used in systemic functional linguistics to refer to the part of a clause that follows the THEME. |
| SUASIVE VERBS | Verbs such as *arrange, order, request*, and *suggest*, which imply an intention to bring about some change in the future. |
| SUBJECT | The person or thing that does the action of the verb (e.g. *Suzanne* came home). (Compare OBJECT.) |

| | |
|---|---|
| SUBORDINATE CLAUSE | (see CLAUSE.) |
| SUBORDINATION | Linking two clauses together so that one clause is dependent on the other. (See also CONJUNCTION). |
| SUBSTITUTION | The use of words instead of repeating the original words (e.g. I asked them to keep quiet and they *did*). |
| TEXTUAL | (see METAFUNCTION) |
| THEME | A term used in systemic functional linguistics to refer to the first element of a clause, which comes before the RHEME. |
| TRANSITIVE | A **transitive verb** takes an object (e.g. He was carrying *some books*), while an **intransitive verb** does not (e.g. It *disappeared*). |
| VERB | A **finite verb** has a tense (e.g. She *sat down*; She *is sitting down*). **Non-finite** verb forms are infinitives (e.g. We went to *hear* them) and participle forms (e.g. *Looking* carefully, I was able to see the scratches; *Built* in 1800, the concert hall is still used today). |
| VERB PHRASE | A group of words consisting of one or more verbs (e.g. *takes, is taking, may have been taking*). |
| VOICE | A verb can have either **active voice** (e.g. The police *have arrested* a man) or **passive voice** (e.g. A man *has been arrested* (by the police)). |

# Further reading

## UNIT A1   GRAMMAR, GRAMMARS AND GRAMMATICALITY

Crystal (1997, ch. 16) gives a wide-ranging discussion of **grammar** and **grammars**. McCarthy (2001, ch.3) on problems with the **sentence** as a unit of grammatical analysis. Lerner (1991) and McCarthy and Carter (2001) on **grammar in conversation**.

## UNIT A2   CONTEXT: SOME PRELIMINARIES

Giles and Coupland (1991, ch. 1) for a wide-ranging discussion of the relationship between **context and language** in general (not only grammar). Brown and Yule (1983, ch. 2) on the role of **context in interpretation**. Holmes (2001, ch. 10) on **context and register**. Hoey (2001, ch. 3) on **intertextuality**. Halliday (1999) on **context in language education**.

## UNIT A3   THE LOCAL SITUATION CONTEXT

Eggins (1994: 52–80) for more on **field, tenor** and **mode** and their relationship with **register** (see also Unit A4). Bell (2001) on how and why people adjust their language **style** (including grammar) depending on audience. Coupland, Coupland and Giles (1991) on language used by and to elderly people.

## UNIT A4  THE WIDER SOCIO-CULTURAL CONTEXT

Swales (1990, ch. 2) on **discourse communities**, Lave and Wenger (1991) and Meyherhoff (2002) on **communities of practice**, and Johns (1997, ch.4) on both of these topics. Hyon (1996) on approaches to the notion of **genre**, Swales (2004) on academic **research genres** and Candlin and Hyland (1999) and Candlin (2002) on **academic and professional contexts**. For detailed investigations of grammar choices in **academic contexts** see Cutting (2000, ch. 4), Hewings (2001), Hyland (2000) and Schlepegrell (2001).

## UNIT A5  CONTEXT IN APPROACHES TO GRAMMAR

Malmkjaer (2004) gives very useful brief summaries on the main **approaches to grammar**. Bloor and Bloor (2004), Eggins (1994) and Thompson (2004)) provide introductions to **systemic functional linguistics**. Hunston and Francis (1999, ch. 9) and Willis (2004) on **implications of pattern grammar for teaching** English.

## UNIT A6  PRESENTING A VIEW OF THE WORLD THROUGH GRAMMATICAL CHOICES

Thompson (2004, ch. 5) on **transitivity** and Fairclough (2001, ch. 5) on both **transitivity** (dealt with mainly under the heading 'agency') and **nominalisation**. Text B3.1 deals with nominalisation in some detail.

## UNIT A7  EXPRESSING INTERPERSONAL RELATIONS THROUGH GRAMMAR

Holmes (2001, ch. 1) or Mesthrie *et al.* (1999) for an overview of **sociolinguistic categorisations of context and interpersonal relations**. Facchinetti, Krug and Palmer (2003) for a collection of papers on **modality**. Palmer's paper in this volume provides an introduction to the topic. Hyland (2001) for a detailed analysis of first person **personal pronoun** use in the context of academic writing and Poncini (2004, ch. IV) for a study of personal pronouns and identity in a business meeting. Thompson (1994) on **reporting verbs**. Fairclough (2001) deals with a variety of aspects of **interpersonal positioning** in different written and spoken contexts, and in Fairclough (2000) he deals specifically with grammatical choices in political speeches and writings.

## UNIT A8  STANDARDS AND VARIETIES

Various papers in Bex and Watts (1999) on **Standard English**. Gramley and Pätzold (2004) on **national and international varieties** of English. Holmes (2001, ch. 4) on **lingua francas, pidgins** and **creoles**. Foley *et al.* (1998) on **Singapore English**, and Foley and Thompson (2003) on **language learning in multilingual settings**.

## UNIT A9  CORPUS APPROACHES TO THE STUDY OF GRAMMAR

Hunston (2002) and Bowker and Pearson (2002) on the design and applications of **language corpora**. Coffin, Hewings and O'Halloran (2004) for a collection on papers combining **corpus and functional approaches to grammar**. Carter and McCarthy

(1997) and Carter, Hughes and McCarthy (2000) on the analysis of corpora for **English language teaching**. Granger (1998) on **learner corpora**. Sinclair (1991, ch. 6) on the links between **grammar and lexis**. Sinclair (2004) for a collection of papers on **corpus investigations of language**.

# Notes

1 In the 1960s survey the informants ranked the sentences in the following order of acceptability. By averaging the four situation-responses a percentage acceptance rate was worked out for each, and these are given in brackets. 1 (i.e. most acceptable) g (50%), 2 b (47%), 3 i (46%), 4 h (45%), 5 c (43%), 6 a (42%), 7 j (42%), 8 d (35%), 9 c (27%), 10 f (11%)

2 Source: The Will of Diana, Princess of Wales. Available online at http://www.courttv. com/legaldocs/newsmakers/wills/diana/part1.html (accessed 9 March 2004)

3 Source: Eggins, S. (1994). *An introduction to systemic functional linguistics*. London: Pinter, p. 25.

4 Source: *Gibbons Stamp Monthly*, July 2000, p. 54. (Supplement to *Stanley Gibbons Great Britain Specialised Catalogue*, volume 4 (eighth edition).)

5 These and many of the other examples in this section come from a British national newspaper report on the events surrounding a meeting of world leaders on the French/ Swiss border: Miller, S. (2003) Carnival turns to confrontation. *Guardian Online*, Monday 2 June 2003, accessed 2 June 2003. Others are taken from the British National Corpus (BNC), or other sources indicated.

6 Chris Tryhorn (Tuesday 5 August 2003). Cuts continue as *Mirror* axes reporters. *Guardian*.

7 *Socialist Worker Online* (accessed 7 October 2003). *13 toxic ships have the rules waived* http://www.socialistworker.co.uk/1871/sw187106.htm)

8 Littlejohn, R. 2003. 'Truth behind Gordon's gobbledygook'. *Sun* 10 June 2003, p. 11.

9 Lands' End Direct Merchants June 2003 catalogue, p.26.

10 Rea-Dickins, P. and Germaine, K. (1992). *Evaluation*. Oxford: Oxford University Press. Section reprinted as 'Purposes for evaluation'. In Hall, D. and Hewings, A. (eds.) (2001). *Innovation in English Language Teaching* (pp. 253–262). London: Routledge.

11 Koul, P.A., Bhat, F.A., Wahid, A., and Shaban, M. (accessed 15 October 2003). Haemostasis in rheumatoid arthritis without vasculitis. *Medicine On-Line*. http:// www.priory.com/med.htm.

12 An edited version of the Chancellor Gordon Brown's speech made on 9 June 2003 from *Daily Telegraph* 10 June 2003, p. 11.

13 Barn, R. (1990). Black children in local authority care: admission patterns. *New Community*, 16, 2, 229–246. Reproduced in Thompson, G. (1994). *Reporting. Collins COBUILD English Guides 5* (pp. 180–181). London: HarperCollins.

14 http://www.ncaction.org.uk/subjects/english/levels.htm, accessed on 28 October 2003.

15 The most recent style guide is available online at http://www.guardian.co.uk/styleguide, and constantly updated. A facsimile of the 1928 style guide in pdf format is available at the same site.

16 Johnston, J. (2003). Teachers call for urgent action as pupils write essays in text-speak. *Sunday Herald*, 2 March 2003. Accessed online at http://www.sundayherald.com/print31826 on 21 October 2003.

17 http://www.nus.edu.sg/prose/singlish.htm, accessed on 22 October 2003.

18 The software used to produce these concordance lines is *Monoconc Pro 2.2* (Barlow 2002) and the corpus from which they are taken is a sample of the British National Corpus (see Unit C3 for more details).

19 McEwan, I. 2002. *Atonement* p. 20. London: Vintage.

20 Sorry, can't talk, wasn't meant to be on the computer. *Lord of the Rings* was amazing. I love Legolas. His elephant thing was great! Did you enjoy it? What else have you been up to? The spider was terrifying and I'm scared of spiders anyway. Text back.

21 Soulmates. *Guardian*, 4 November 2003, G2, p.18.

22 We would like to thank Louise Ravelli for providing this data.

23 The Indian Corpus was compiled by Professor S. V. Shastri and Professor Dr Gerhard Leitner and forms part of the International Corpus of English held at the Department of English Language and Literature, University College London.

# References

Aijmer, K. (1989) 'Themes and tails: the discourse function of dislocated elements', *Nordic Journal of Linguistics*, 12, 2: 137–54.

Allison, P., Beard, R. and Willcocks, J. (2002) 'Subordination in Children's Writing', *Language and Education*, 16, 2: 97–111.

Anderson, G. (1997) '"They like wanna see like how we talk and all that": The use of *like* as a discourse marker in London teenage speech', in Ljung, M. (ed.) *Papers from the 17th International Conference on English Language Research on Computerized Corpora*, ICAME, 17: 37–48.

Baker, C.L. (1995) 'Contrast, discourse prominence and intensification, with special reference to locally-free reflexives in British English', *Language*, 71, 63–101.

Barlow, M. (2002) *MonoConc Pro 2.2*, Houston, TX: Athelstan Publications, available from www.athel.com.

Bazerman, C. (1988) *Shaping Written Knowledge*. Madison: University of Wisconsin Press.

Becher, T. (1989) *Academic Tribes and Territories: intellectual inquiry and the cultures of disciplines*. Milton Keynes: The Society for Research into Higher Education and Open University Press.

Bell, A. (1991) *The Language of the News Media*. Oxford: Blackwell.

—— (2001) 'Back in style: reworking audience design', in Eckert, P. and Rickford, J.R. (eds) *Style and Sociolinguistic Variation*. Cambridge: Cambridge University Press.

Bernstein, B. (1959) 'A public language: some sociological implications of a linguistic form', *British Journal of Sociology*, X: 311–26; reprinted in *Class, Codes and Control, Volume 1 Theoretical Studies towards a Sociology of Language* (1971). London: Routledge & Kegan Paul.

—— (1971) *Class, Codes and Control, Volume 1 Theoretical Studies towards a Sociology of Language*. London: Routledge & Kegan Paul.

Bex, T. and Watts, R.J. (eds) (1999) *Standard English: the widening debate*. London: Routledge.

Biber, D. (1988) *Variation Across Speech and Writing*. Cambridge: Cambridge University Press.

Biber, D., Johansson, S., Leech, G., Conrad, S. and Finegan, E. (1999) *Longman Grammar of Spoken and Written English*. Harlow: Longman.

Bizzell, P. (1992) *Academic Discourse and Critical Consciousness*. Pittsburgh, PA: University of Pittsburgh Press.

Bloor, T. (1996) 'Three hypothetical strategies in philosophical writing', in Ventola, E. and Mauranen, A. (eds) *Academic Writing: intercultural and textual issues*. Amsterdam: John Benjamins.

Bloor, T. and Bloor, M. (2004) *The Functional Analysis of English*, second edn. London: Hodder Arnold.

Bowker, L. and Pearson, J. (2002) *Working with Specialized Language*. London: Routledge.

Britain, D. (1998) 'High rising terminals in New Zealand English: who uses them, when and why?' *Essex Research Reports in Linguistics*, 21: 33–56.

Brown, G. and Yule, G. (1983) *Discourse Analysis*. Cambridge: Cambridge University Press.

Bruyn, A. (1995) 'Relative clauses in early Sranan', in Arends, J. (ed.) *The Early Stages of Creolization*. Amsterdam: Benjamins.

Candlin, C.N. (ed.) (2002) *Research and Practice in Professional Discourse*. Hong Kong: City of Hong Kong Press.

Candlin, C.N. and Hyland, K. (1999) *Writing: texts, process and practices*. Harlow, UK: Addison Wesley Longman.

Carter, R., Hughes, R. and McCarthy, M. (2000) *Exploring Grammar in Context*. Cambridge: Cambridge University Press.

Carter, R. and McCarthy, M. (1995) 'Grammar and the spoken language', *Applied Linguistics*, 16, 2: 141–158.

—— (1997) *Exploring Spoken English*. Cambridge: Cambridge University Press.

—— (forthcoming) *The Cambridge Advanced Learners' Grammar of the English Language*. Cambridge: Cambridge University Press.

Carterette, E.C. and Jones, M.H. (1974) *Informal Speech: alphabetic and phonemic texts with statistical analyses and tables*. Berkeley: University of California Press.

Celce-Murcia, M. and Larsen-Freeman, D. (1983) *The Grammar Book*. Rowley, MA: Newbury House.

Chafe, W. (1982) 'Integration and involvement in speaking, writing, and oral literature', in Tannen, D. (ed.) *Spoken and Written Language*. Norwood, NJ: Ablex.

Chang, Y.-Y. (1997) 'Elements of informality in English scholarly writing: Prescriptivism vs. Practices', unpublished qualifying research paper, University of Michigan.

Chang, Y.-Y. and Swales, J.M. (1999) 'Informal elements in English academic writing: threats or opportunities for advanced non-native speakers?' in Candlin, C.N. and Hyland, K. (eds) *Writing: texts, processes and practices*. London: Longman.

Cheah, D.S.L. (1992) 'Interlanguage variability in verb tense/aspect', unpublished Ph.D. thesis, University of Aston, United Kingdom.

Cheshire, J. (1999) 'Spoken Standard English', in Bex, T. and Watts, R.J. (eds) *Standard English: the widening debate*. London: Routledge.

Cheshire, J. and Williams, A. (2002) 'Information structure in male and female adolescent talk', *Journal of English Linguistics*, 30: 217–38.

Chomsky, N. (1957) *Syntactic Structures*. The Hague: Mouton.

Coates, J. (1987) 'Epistemic modality and spoken discourse', *Transactions of the Philological Society*, 85: 110–31.

—— (1998) *Language and Gender: A Reader*. Oxford: Blackwell.

Coffin, C., Hewings, A. and O'Halloran, K.A. (2004) *Applying English Grammar*. London: Arnold.

Collins, K. (1999) 'In reference to reference letters: an analysis of moves and politeness strategies in reference letters', unpublished MA dissertation, Centre for English Language Studies, University of Birmingham, United Kingdom.

Collinson, D., Kirkup, G., Kyd, R., and Slocombe, L. (1992) *Plain English*, second edn. Buckingham, UK: Open University Press.

Collot, M. and Belmore, N. (1996) 'Electronic language: a new variety of English' in Herring, S. (ed.) *Computer-Mediated Communications: linguistic, social and cultural perspectives*. Amsterdam: John Benjamins.

Coupland, J. (1996) 'Dating advertisements: discourses of the commodified self', *Discourse & Society*, 7, 2: 187–207.

Coupland, N., Coupland, J. and Giles, H. (1991) *Language, Society and the Elderly: discourse, identity and ageing.* London: Blackwell.

Crystal, D. (1987) *The Cambridge Encyclopedia of Language.* Cambridge: Cambridge University Press.

—— (1997) *The Cambridge Encyclopedia of Language,* second edn. Cambridge: Cambridge University Press.

—— (2001) *Language and the Internet.* Cambridge: Cambridge University Press.

Crystal, D. and Varley, R. (1993) *Introduction to Language Pathology,* third edition. London: Whurr.

Cullen, J. (1996) 'The negotiation of instantial meaning', unpublished Ph.D. thesis, University of Birmingham, United Kingdom.

Cutting, J. (2000) *Analysing the Language of Discourse Communities.* Oxford: Elsevier Science.

Dailey-O'Cain, J. (2000) 'The sociolingistic distribution of and attitudes toward focuser *like* and quotative *like*', *Journal of Sociolinguistics,* 4: 60–80.

Danet, B. (2002) *Brenda Danet on why Internet is so playful,* available http://130.238.50.3/ilmh/Ren/digital-idanet-playful.htm#top (accessed 23 December 2003).

Dijkstra, K., Bourgeois, M., Petrie, G., Burgio, L. and Allen-Burge, R. (2002) 'My recaller is on vacation: discourse analysis of nursing-home residents with dementia', *Discourse Processes,* 33, 1: 53–76.

Dik, S.C. (1978) *Functional Grammar.* Oxford: North Holland Publishing Co.

Dodd, W. (2000), *Working with German Corpora.* Birmingham, UK: Birmingham University Press.

Drew, P. and Heritage, J. (1992) 'Analyzing talk at work: in introduction' in Drew, P. and Heritage, J. (eds) *Talk at Work: interaction in institutional settings.* Cambridge: Cambridge University Press.

Eckert, P. (1997) 'Gender, race and class in the preadolescent marketplace of identities', paper presented at the Annual Meeting of the American Anthropological Association, Washington DC.

Eggins, S. (1994) *An Introduction to Systemic Functional Linguistics.* London: Pinter.

Eggins, S. and Slade, D. (1997) *Analysing Casual Conversation.* London: Cassell.

Ellis, R. (1985) *Understanding Second Language Acquisition.* Oxford: Oxford University Press.

Ellis, R. (1986) 'The effects of linguistic environment on the second language acquisition of grammatical rules', paper presented at the British Association of Applied Linguistics Conference, 1986.

Ellis, R. and Roberts, C. (1987) 'Two approaches for investigating second language acquisition', in Ellis, R. (ed.) *Second Language Acquisition in Context.* Englewood Cliffs, NJ: Prentice Hall International.

Eisikovits, E. (1981) 'Inner-Sydney English: An investigation of grammatical variation in adolescent speech', unpublished Ph.D. thesis, University of Sydney.

—— (1998) 'Girl-talk/Boy-talk: sex differences in adolescent speech', in Coates, J. (ed.) *Language and Gender: a reader.* Oxford: Blackwell.

Facchinetti, R., Krug, M. and Palmer, F. (2003) *Modality in Contemporary English.* Berlin: Mouton de Gruyter.

Fairbanks, K. (1983) 'Variability in interlanguage', unpublished manuscript, ESL Program, University of Minnesota.

Fairclough, N. (2000) *New Labour, New Language?* London and New York: Routledge.

—— (2001) *Language and Power,* second edn. Harlow: Longman.

Ferguson, C.A. (1977) 'Baby talk as a simplified register', in Snow, C.E. and Ferguson, C.A. (eds) *Talking to Children.* Cambridge: Cambridge University Press.

Ferguson, G. (2001) 'If you pop over there: a corpus-based study of conditionals in medical discourse', *English for Specific Purposes*, 20: 61–82.

Ferguson, L., MacLulich, C. and Ravelli, L. (1995) *Meanings and Messages: Language Guidelines for Museum Exhibitions*. Sydney: Australian Museum.

Fetzer, A. and Akman, V. (2002) 'Contexts of social action: guest editors' introduction', *Language and Communication*, 22, 4: 391–402.

Firth, J.R. (1957) *Papers in Linguistics 1934–51*. London: Oxford University Press.

Flowerdew, J. and Dudley-Evans, T. (2002) 'Genre analysis of editorial letters to international journal contributors', *Applied Linguistics*, 23, 4: 463–489.

Foley, J.A., Kandiah. T., Zhiming, B., Gupta, A.E., Alsagoff, L., Chee Lick, H., Wee, L., Talib, I.S. and Bokhorst-Heng, W. (1998) *English in New Cultural Contexts: reflections from Singapore*. London: Oxford University Press.

Foley, J. and Thompson, L. (2003) *Language Learning: a lifelong process*. London: Arnold.

Francis, G. and Hunston, S. (1992) 'Analysing everyday conversation', in Coulthard, M. (ed.) *Advances in Spoken Discourse Analysis*. London: Routledge.

Francis, G., Hunston, S., and Manning, E. (1996) *Collins COBUILD Grammar Patterns 1: Verb*. London: HarperCollins.

—— (1998). *Collins COBUILD Grammar Patterns 2: Nouns and Adjectives*. London: HarperCollins.

Fraser, B. (1980) 'Conversational mitigation', *Journal of Pragmatics*, 4: 341–50.

Garfinkel, H. (1967) *Studies in Ethnomethodology*. Englewood Cliffs, NJ: Prentice Hall.

Gatbonton, E. (1978) 'Patterned phonetic variability in second language speech: a gradual diffusion model', *Canadian Modern Language Review*, 34, 3: 335–47.

Geluykens, R. (1992) *Discourse Process to Grammatical Construction: on left-dislocation in English*. Amsterdam: John Benjamins.

Giles, H. and Coupland, N. (1984) *Communication and the Elderly: an interdisciplinary approach*, research programme submitted to ESRC, London; reported in Ryan, E.B., Giles, H., Bartolucci, G. and Kenwood, K. (1986) 'Psycholinguistic and social psychological components of communication by and with the elderly', *Language and Communication*, 6, 1/2: 1–24.

Giles, H. and Coupland, N. (1991) *Language: contexts and consequences*. Milton Keynes, UK: Open University Press.

Gledhill, C. (2002) 'The discourse function of collocation in research article introductions', *English for Specific Purposes*, 19: 115–35.

Gramley, S. and Pätzold, K.-M. (2004) *A Survey of Modern English*, second edn. London: Routledge.

Granger, S. (ed.) (1998) *Learner English on Computer*. London: Longman.

Greenbaum, S. (1996) *The Oxford English Grammar*. Oxford: Oxford University Press.

Greenbaum, S., Nelson, G. and Weitzman, M. (1996) 'Complement clauses in English' in Thomas, J. and Short, M. (eds) *Using Corpora for Language Research*. Harlow, UK: Longman.

Gumperz, J. (1982) *Discourse Strategies*. Cambridge: Cambridge University Press.

Halliday, M.A.K. (1973) *Explorations in the Functions of Language*. London: Edward Arnold.

—— (1975) *Learning How to Mean*. London: Edward Arnold.

—— (1978) *Language as Social Semiotic*. London: Edward Arnold.

—— (1981) 'Three aspects of children's language development: learning language, learning through language, learning about language', in Goodman, Y.K., Haussler, M.M and Strickland, D.S. (eds) *Oral and Written Language Development: impact on schools: proceedings from the 1979 and 1980 IMPACT conferences*, International Reading Association and National Council of Teachers of English.

—— (1993) 'Some grammatical problems in scientific English' in Halliday, M.A.K. and Martin, J.R. (eds) *Writing Science: literacy and discursive power*. London: Falmer Press.

—— (1994) *An Introduction to Functional Grammar*, second edn. London: Edward Arnold.

—— (1999) 'The notion of "context" in language education', in Ghadessy, M. (ed.) *Text and Context in Functional Linguistics*. Amsterdam: John Benjamins.

Halliday, M.A.K. and Hasan, R. (1976) *Cohesion in English*. London: Longman.

Halliday, M.A.K. and Matthiessen, C. (2004) *An Introduction to Functional Grammar*, third edn. London: Hodder Arnold.

Harpin, W. (1976) *The Second 'R': writing development in the junior school*. London: Allen & Unwin.

Hasan, R. (1985) 'Meaning, context and text – fifty years after Malinowski' in Benson, J.D. and Greaves, W.S. (eds) *Systemic Perspectives on Discourse Vol. 1 Selected Theoretical Papers from the 9th International Systemic Workshop*, (Advances in discourse processes vol. 15). Norwood, NJ: Ablex.

Hasan, R. (1989) 'The identity of the text', in Halliday, M.A.K. and Hasan, R. *Language, Context, and Text: aspects of language in a social-semiotic perspective*, second edn. Oxford: Oxford University Press.

Haslam, D. (2003) *Guardian* 26 August, *G2*, p. 9.

Hatch, E., Shapira, R. and Gough, J. (1978) 'Foreigner-talk discourse', *ITL: Review of Applied Linguistics*, 39–40: 39–60.

Herzberg, B. (1986) 'The politics of discourse communities', paper presented at the CCC Convention New Orleans, LA, March, 1986.

Hewings, A. and Coffin, C. (2004) 'Grammar in the construction of on-line discussion messages' in Coffin, C., Hewings, A. and O'Halloran, K.A. (eds) *Applying English Grammar*. London: Arnold.

Hewings, M. (2001) *Academic Writing in Context: implications and applications*. Birmingham, UK: University of Birmingham Press.

Hewings, M. and Hewings, A. (2002) '"It is interesting to note that . . .": a comparative study of anticipatory "it" in student and published writing', *English for Specific Purposes*, 21: 367–383.

Hoey, M. (2001) *Textual Interaction: an introduction to written discourse analysis*. London: Routledge.

Holmes. J. (1986) 'Function of *you know* in women's and men's speech' in *Language in Society*, 15: 1–21.

—— (1990) 'Politeness strategies in New Zealand women's speech' in Bell, A. and Holmes, J. (eds) *New Zealand Ways of Speaking English*. Clevedon, UK: Multilingual Matters.

—— (2001) *An Introduction to Sociolinguistics*, second edn. Harlow, UK: Longman.

Hopper, P.J. (1998) 'Emergent Grammar', in Tomasello, M. (ed.) *The New Psychology of Language: cognitive and functional approaches to language structure*. Mahwah, NJ: Lawrence Erlbaum.

Huddleston, R. and Pullum, G.K. (2002) *The Cambridge Grammar of the English Language*. Cambridge: Cambridge University Press.

Hunston, S. (2002) *Corpora in Applied Linguistics*. Cambridge: Cambridge University Press.

Hunston, S. and Francis, G. (1999) *Pattern Grammar*. Amsterdam: John Benjamins.

Hunston, S. and Sinclair, J. (2000) 'A local grammar of evaluation', in Hunston, S. and Thompson, G. (eds) *Evaluation in Text*. Oxford: Oxford University Press.

Hyland, K. (1999) 'Disciplinary discourses: writer stance in research articles' in Candlin, C.N. and Hyland, K. (eds) *Writing: texts, processes and practices*. London: Longman.

—— (2000) *Disciplinary Discourses: social interactions in academic writing*. London: Longman.

—— (2001) 'Humble servants of the discipline? Self-mention in research articles', *English for Specific Purposes*, 20, 3: 207–226.

—— (2002) 'Directives: Argument and engagement in academic writing', *Applied Linguistics*, 23, 2: 215–239.

Hymes, D.H. (1962/74) *The Ethnography of Speaking*, in Blount, B.G. (ed.) *Language, Culture and Society*. Cambridge, MA: Winthrop.

—— (1964/72) Towards ethnographies of communication: the analysis of communicative events"', in Giglioli, P.P. (ed.) *Language and Social Context*. Harmondsworth: Penguin.

—— (1974) *Foundations in Sociolinguistics*. Philadelphia, PA: University of Pennsylvania Press.

Hyon, S. (1996) 'Genre in three traditions: implications for ESL', *TESOL Quarterly*, 30: 693–722.

Jespersen, O. (1909–1949) *A Modern English Grammar on Historical Principles*, (7 volumes). London: Allen & Unwin.

Johansson, S., Atwell, E., Garside, R. and Leech, G. (1986) *The Tagged LOB Corpus Users' Manual*. Bergen, Norway: Norwegian Computing Centre for the Humanities.

Johansson, S., Leech, G. and Goodluck, H. (1978) *Manual of Information to Accompany Lancaster-Oslo/Bergen Corpus of British English, for Use with Digital Computers*, Department of English, University of Oslo.

Johns, A. (1997) *Text, Role, and Context*. Cambridge: Cambridge University Press.

Johns, T. (1994) 'From printout to handout: grammar and vocabulary teaching in the context of data-driven learning' in Odlin, T. (ed.) *Perspectives on Pedagogical Grammar*. Cambridge: Cambridge University Press.

Johnstone, B. (1987) '"He says . . . so I said": Verb tense alternation and narrative depictions of authority in American English', *Linguistics*, 25, 1: 33–52.

Kenner, H. (1987) *The Mechanical Muse*. New York: Oxford University Press.

Kenning, M.-M. (1998) 'Parallel concordancing and French personal pronouns', *Languages in Contrast*, 1, 1, 1–21.

Krashen, S. (1981) *Second Language Acquisition and Second Language Learning*. Oxford: Pergamon Press.

Labov, W. (1964) 'Stages in the acquisition of Standard English', in Shuy, R. (ed.) *Social Dialects and Language Learning*. Champaign, IL: National Council of Teachers of English.

—— (1966) *The Social Stratification of English in New York City*. Washington, DC: Centre for Applied Linguistics.

—— (1970) 'The study of language in its social context', *Studium Generale*, 23: 30–87.

—— (1972) *Language in the Inner-city: Studies in the Black English Vernacular*. Philadelphia: University of Pennsylvania Press.

—— (1984) 'Intensity' in Schiffrin, D. (ed.) *Meaning, Form, and Use in Context: linguistic applications*. Washington, DC: Georgetown University Press.

Lakoff, R. (1975) *Language and Woman's Place*. New York: Harper Colophon.

Lave, J. and Wenger, E. (1991) *Situated Learning: legitimate peripheral participation*. Cambridge: Cambridge University Press.

Leech, G. (2003) 'Modality on the move: The English modal auxiliaries 1961–1992' in Facchinetti, R., Krug, M. and Palmer, F. (eds.) *Modality in Contemporary English*, Berlin: Mouton de Gruyter.

Lerner, G.H. (1991) 'On the syntax of sentences in progress', *Language in Society*, 20: 441–58.

Levey, S. (2001) 'Relative clauses and register expansion in Tok Pisin', *World Englishes*, 20, 3: 251–67.

—— (2003) 'He's like "Do it now!" and I'm like "No!" Some innovative quotative usage among young people in London', *English Today*, 73, 19, 1: 24–32.

Levi, J.N. (1994) 'Language as evidence: the linguist as expert witness in North American courts', *Forensic Linguistics*, 1, 1: 1–26.

Levinson, S. (1983) *Pragmatics*. Cambridge: Cambridge University Press.

Lewis, M. (1993) *The Lexical Approach: the state of ELT and a way forward*, Hove, UK: Language Teaching Publications.

Lock, G. (1996) *Functional English Grammar*. Cambridge: Cambridge University Press.

Long, M.H. (1983) 'Does second language instruction make a difference? A review of the research', *TESOL Quarterly*, 17, 3: 359–82.

Louw, B. (1993) 'Irony in the text or insincerity in the writer? The diagnostic potential of semantic prosodies', in Baker, M., Francis, G. and Tognini-Bonelli, E. (eds) *Text and Technology: In Honour of John Sinclair*. Amsterdam: John Benjamins.

Lowth, R. (1762) *A Short History of English Grammar*, second edn, republished 1995 in London: Routledge/Thoemmes Press.

Luzon Marco, M.J. (2000) 'Collocational frameworks in medical research papers: a genre-based study', *English for Specific Purposes*, 19, 1: 63–86.

Macaulay, R.K.S. (1991) *Locating Dialect in Discourse: the language of honest men and bonnie lasses in Ayr*. New York: Oxford University Press.

Macaulay, R.K.S. (1995) 'The adverbs of authority', *English World-Wide* 16: 37–60.

Macaulay, R.K.S. (2002) 'Extremely interesting, very interesting, or only quite interesting? Adverbs and social class', *Journal of Sociolinguistics*, 6, 3: 398–417.

McCarthy, M.J. (1992) 'English idioms in use', *Revista Canaria de Estudios Ingleses*, 25: 55–65.

—— (1994) 'It, this and that', in Coulthard, M. (ed.) *Advances in Written Text Analysis*. London: Routledge.

—— (1998) *Spoken Language and Applied Linguistics*. Cambridge: Cambridge University Press.

—— (2001) *Issues in Applied Linguistics*. Cambridge: Cambridge University Press.

McCarthy, M. and Carter, R. (1994) *Language as Discourse: perspectives for language teaching*. Harlow: Longman.

—— (2001) 'Ten criteria for a spoken grammar', in Hinkel, E. and Fotos, S. (eds) *New Perspectives on Grammar Teaching in Second Language Classrooms*. Nahwah, NJ: Lawrence Erlbaum Associates.

McEnery, T., Xiao., R. and Tono, Y. (2005) *Corpus-Based Language Studies: an advanced resource book*. London: Routledge.

Macnamara, J. (1982) *Names for Things*. Cambridge, MA: MIT Press.

Malcolm, I. (2001) 'Aboriginal English: adopted code of a surviving culture' in Blair, D. and Collins, P. (eds.) *English in Australia*. Amsterdam/Philadelphia: John Benjamins.

Malinowski, B. (1923) 'The problem of meaning in primitive languages' in Ogden, C.K. and Richards, I.A. *The Meaning of Meaning*. London: Routledge & Kegan Paul; reprinted edited version in Maybin, J. (ed.) (1994) *Language and Literacy in Social Practice*. Clevedon, UK: Multilingual Matters.

Malmkjaer, K. (2004) *The Linguistics Encyclopedia*, second edn. London: Routledge.

Markevitch, M., Vikhlinin, A., Forman, W.R., and Sarazin, C.L. (1999) 'Mass profiles of the typical related galaxy clusters A2199 and A496', *The Astrophysical Journal*, 527: 545–553.

Marley, C. (2002) 'Popping the question: questions and modality in written dating advertisements', *Discourse Studies*, 4, 1: 79–83.

Master, P. (1994) 'The effect of systematic instruction on learning the English article system', in Odlin, T. (ed.) *Perspectives on Pedagogical Grammar*. Cambridge: Cambridge University Press.

Mesthrie, R., Swann, J., Deumert, A. and Leap, W. (1999) *Introducing Sociolinguistics*. Edinburgh: Edinburgh University Press.

Meyherhoff, M. (2002) 'Communities of practice', in Chambers, J.K., Trudgill, P. and

Schilling-Estes, N. (eds) *The Handbook of Language Variation and Change*. Oxford: Blackwell.

Miller, J. and Weinert, R. (1995) 'The function of *LIKE* in spoken language', *Journal of Pragmatics*, 23: 365–93.

Mittins, W.H., Salu, M., Edminson, M. and Coyne, S. (1970) *Attitudes to English Usage*. Oxford: Oxford University Press.

*Multiconcord* developed by David Woolls (see http://web.bham.ac.uk/johnstf/paracon.htm).

Nattinger, J. R. and DeCarrico, J.S. (1992) *Lexical Phrases and Language Teaching*. Oxford: Oxford University Press.

Newbrook, M. (1998) 'Which way? That way? Variation and ongoing changes in the English relative clause', *World Englishes*, 17, 1: 53–59.

Nickerson, C. (2000) 'Playing the corporate language game', *Utrecht Studies in Language and Communication*, 15. Amsterdam: Rodopi.

Nordberg, B. (1984) 'Om ungdomars samstalsstil. Några preliminara iakttagelser', *Nysvenska Studier*, 64: 5–27.

Ochs, E. (2002) 'Becoming a speaker of culture', in Kramsch, C. (ed.) *Language Acquisition and Language Socialization: ecological perspectives*. London: Continuum.

Ouhalla, J. (1994/1999) *Introducing Transformational Grammar*. London: Edward Arnold.

Overstreet, M. (1999) *Whales, Candlelight and Stuff Like That: general extenders in English discourse*. Oxford: Oxford University Press.

Painter, C. (1984) *Into the Mother Tongue*. London: Pinter.

Painter, C. (2004) 'The development of language as a resource for learning', in Coffin, C., Hewings, A. and O'Halloran, K.A. (eds) *Applying English Grammar*, London: Arnold.

Palmer, F. (2003) 'Modality in English: theoretical, descriptive and typological issues' in Facchinetti, R., Krug, M. and Palmer, F. (eds) *Modality in Contemporary English*. Berlin: Mouton de Gruyter.

*Paraconc* developed by Michael Barlow (see http://www.ruf.rice.edu/~barlow/pc.html).

Partington, A. (1998) *Patterns and Meanings*. Amsterdam: John Benjamins.

Perera, K. (1984) *Children's Writing and Reading: analysing classroom language*. London: Blackwell.

Poncini, G. (2004) *Discursive Strategies in Multicultural Business Meetings*. Bern: Peter Lang.

Powell, M.J. (1992) 'The systematic development of correlated interpersonal and metalinguistic uses in stance adverbs', *Cognitive Linguistics*, 3: 75–110.

Quirk, R., Greenbaum, S., Leech, G. and Svartvik, J. (1985) *A Comprehensive Grammar of the English Language*. London: Longman.

Roberts, C. and Sarangi, S. (2003) 'Uptake of discourse research in interprofessional settings: reporting from medical consultancy', *Applied Linguistics*, 24, 3: 338–59.

Rogerson-Revell, P. (1998) 'Interactive style and power at work: an analysis of discourse in intercultural business meetings', unpublished Ph.D. thesis, University of Birmingham, United Kingdom.

Romaine, S. (1999) *Communicating Gender*. Mahwah, NJ: Lawrence Erlbaum.

Ronowicz, E. and Yallop, C. (1999) 'Australia – the Great South Land', in Ronowicz, E. and Yallop, C. (eds) *English: One Language, Different Cultures*. London: Cassell.

Rorty, R. (1979) *Philosophy and the Mirror of Nature*. Princeton, NJ: Princeton University Press.

Rust, S.W., Kumar, P., Burgoon, D.A. Niemuth, N.A. and Schulz, B.D. (1999) 'Influence of bone-lead stores on the observed effectiveness of lead hazard intervention', *Environmental Research Section A*, 81: 175–184.

Sarangi, S. and Roberts, C. (eds) (1999), *Talk, Work and Institutional Order: discourse in medical, mediation and management settings*. Berlin: Mouton de Gruyter.

Sauntson, H.V. (2001) 'Girls, boys and discourse performances: pupil interaction and construction of gender in the Key Stage 3 Technology classroom', unpublished Ph.D. thesis, University of Birmingham, UK.

Schiffrin, D. (1987) *Discourse Markers*. Cambridge: Cambridge University Press.

Schleppegrell, M.J. (2001) 'Linguistic features of the language of schooling', *Linguistics and Education*, 12, 4: 431–459.

Schumann, J. (1978) *The Pidginization Process: a Model for Second Language Acquisition*. Rowley, MA: Newbury House.

Scollon, R. and Scollon, S.W. (1995) *Intercultural Communication*. Oxford: Blackwell.

Sealey, A. (2000) *Childly Language: children, language and the social world*. Harlow, UK: Pearson.

Shalom, C. (1997) 'That great supermarket of desire: attributes of the desired other in personal advertisements', in Harvey, K. and Shalom, C. (eds) *Language and Desire*. London: Routledge.

Shuy, R., Wolfram, W. and Riley, W. (1966) *A Study of Social Dialects in Detroit*, Final report, Project 7-1347. Washington, DC: US Office of Education, Department of Health, Education and Welfare.

Simpson, P. (1993) *Language, Ideology and Point of View*. London and New York: Routledge.

Sinclair, J. (1990) *Collins COBUILD English Grammar*. London: Collins.

—— (1991) *Corpus, Concordance, Collocation*. Oxford: Oxford University Press.

—— (2004) *Trust the Text: language, corpus and discourse* (papers edited by R. Carter). London: Routledge.

Sinclair, J.McH. and Coulthard, R.M. (1975) *Towards an Analysis of Discourse*. London: Oxford University Press.

Smith, P. (1985) *Languages, the Sexes and Society*, Language in Society, 8. Oxford: Blackwell.

Stubbs, M. (1996) *Text and Corpus Analysis*. Oxford: Blackwell.

Svarvik, J. (ed.) (1990) *The London–Lund Corpus of Spoken English*. Lund, Sweden: Lund University Press.

Swales, J.M. (1990) *Genre Analysis: English in academic and research setting*. Cambridge: Cambridge University Press.

—— (2001) 'Issues of genre: purposes, parodies and pedagogies' in Moreno, A.I. and Colwell, V. (eds) *Recent Perspectives on Discourse*, León: Asociación Española de Lingüística Aplicada/ Universidad de León.

—— (2004) *Research Genres: explorations and applications*. Cambridge: Cambridge University Press.

Swales, J., Ahmad, U., Chang, Y.-Y., Chavez, D., Dressen, D. and Seymour, R. (1998) 'Consider this: the role of imperatives in scholarly writing', *Applied Linguistics*, 19, 1: 97–121.

Swales, J.M. and Rogers, P.S. (1995) 'Discourse and the projection of corporate culture: the mission statement', *Discourse and Society*, 6: 223–242.

Swann, J. (2001) 'Recording and transcribing talk in educational settings', in Candlin, C. and Mercer, N. (eds) *English Language Teaching in its Social Context*. London: Routledge.

Sweet, H. (1892) *A New English Grammar. Part I: Introduction. Phonology and Accidence*. Oxford: Clarendon.

—— (1898). *A New English Grammar. Part II: Syntax*. Oxford: Clarendon.

Tannen, D. (1989) *Talking Voices: repetition, dialogue and imagery in conversational discourse*. Cambridge: Cambridge University Press.

Tannen, D. and Wallat, C. (1987) 'Interactive frames and knowledge schemas in interaction: examples from a medical examination/ interview', *Social Psychology Quarterly*, 50: 205–16.

Tarone, E. (1982) 'Sysematicity and attention in interlanguage', *Language Learning*, 32, 1: 69–84.

Thompson, G. (1994) *Reporting: Collins COBUILD English Guides 5*. London: Harper Collins.

—— (2004) *Introducing Functional Grammar*, second edn. London: Arnold.

Thompson, G. and Thetela, P. (1995) 'The sound of one hand clapping: the management of interaction in written discourse', *Text*, 15, 1: 103–27.

Thornborrow, J. (2002) *Power Talk: language and interaction in institutional discourse*. Harlow, UK: Longman.

Thorne, S. (2003) 'Birmingham English: a sociolinguistic study', unpublished Ph.D. thesis, University of Birmingham, UK.

Tottie, G. (1991) *Negation in English Speech and Writing: a study in variation*. London: Academic Press, Inc.

Trudgill, P. (1972) 'Sex, covert prestige and linguistic change in the urban British English of Norwich', *English in Society*, 1: 179–95.

—— (1999) 'Standard English: What it isn't', in Bex, T. and Watts, R.J. (eds) *Standard English: the widening debate*. London: Routledge.

van Valin, D. (2001) *An Introduction to Syntax*. Cambridge: Cambridge University Press.

Warren, M. (1985) 'Discourse analysis and English language teaching: a contrastive study of discourse based on communicative activities', unpublished MA thesis, University of Birmingham, UK.

Whitley, R. (1984) *The Intellectual and Social Organisation of the Sciences*. Oxford: Clarendon Press.

Widdowson, H. (1988) 'Grammar, nonsense, and learning', in Rutherford, W. and Sharwood Smith, M. (eds) *Grammar and Second Language Teaching*. New York: Newbury House.

Willis, D. (2004) *Rules, Patterns and Words: grammar and lexis in English language teaching*. Cambridge: Cambridge University Press.

Willis, D.D. (1977) 'Participant deixis in English and baby talk', in Snow, C.E. and Ferguson, C.A. (eds) *Talking to Children*. Cambridge: Cambridge University Press.

Witte, S. (1992) 'Context, text and intertext: toward a constructionist semiotic of writing', *Written Communication*, 9: 237–308.

Wolfram, W. (1969) *A Sociolinguistic Description of Detroit Negro Speech*, Urban Language Series 5, Washington, DC: Center for Applied Linguistics.

Wouk, F. (1998) 'Solidarity in Indonesian conversation: the discourse marker *kan*', *Multilingua*, 17, 4: 379–406.

Yamada, H. (1997) 'Organisation in American and Japanese meetings: task versus relationship' in Bargiela-Chiappini, F. and Harris, S. (eds) *The Language of Business: an International Perspective*. Edinburgh: Edinburgh University Press.

Zribi-Hertz, A. (1989) 'A-type binding and narrative point of view', *Language*, 65: 695–727.

# Index

co-text *see* local linguistic context; textual context
Coffin, C. 150
cohesive text 271, 273
*Collins COBUILD English Grammar* (Sinclair) 82
Collot, M. 142–9
command 8
communication: computer mediated 254–62; difficult areas 112; disability 16; economy of 135; electronic and face to face 254–62; importance of context 26; in institutional contexts 216–24; interpersonal dimension 63; patterns of 34; real world 278; recurring 36; routines and formulas 153; starting point of grammar 51–3; type of 303–6
communicative language teaching 278
communicative purpose 39–42; grammatical features 42; moves 40–1; steps 40–1
communities of practice 38
complement 6
component clauses 82–3
computational linguistics 15, 94
computer mediated communication 254–62
computers 138
concordance lines 81, 84, 88, 89–90, 238–53
concordances, parallel 86
concordancing software 252, 306
conditional clauses 232
conditional subordination 148
conditionals 112, 113; function 113–16; hypothetical 113–14
congruent form 119
conjunctions 5, 120, 207; use of 193
constraints: processing 106; production 106
context 8–9, 13, 17–25, 96; adversative 13; adverts 263–6; and approaches to grammar (Unit A5) 46–55; 'bucket' view 23; characterisation of 19–23; classroom learning 277–89; constraints 263–9, 277; dynamism 23–4, 290; educational 191; and grammatical choices 44, 225–37; importance in communication 26; inferred 18–19; instant messaging 257; interviews and written texts 278–84; irrelevant features 22; and lexical choices 44, 225–37; linguistic components 173; multifaceted 19–23; neglect of 48; new 19; newspaper headlines 263; patterns of interaction and language production 277–89; problematic 13; projection of 65;

shaped by utterances 23; situational components 173; social 23, 28; study through language 22–3; and text organisation 225–37; *see also* local linguistic context; local situational context; wider linguistic context; wider socio-cultural context
contextual clues, in history 36
contextual factors 18, 27, 29, 42–3; influence on communication 142
contextualisation cue 22–3
contractions 144, 146
conversation 8; casual 94, 95–6, 100; exploring grammar (unit C1) 216–24; face to face 140–1; further research 224; and grammar (Unit B1) 94–108; participation in 186; power and status 291; in real time 217–18, 220, 257; restricted (Unit B5) 151–9; speaker involvement 106–7; transcribed 217; and written text 216–24
conversation-like discourse 254–62
conversational interaction 189
conversational mitigation 107
conversational strategies 186
copular verb 95
corporate culture 42–4
corpus 13, 49, 208; academic 238–53; build your own 252; comparison across 83–4; computer readable 144; and grammar in context 82–90; and language study 81–2; parallel 86–7; spoken 84–5, 239–53, 303; use in language teaching 88; written 303; *see also* electronic corpora
corpus analysis 13, 94, 112–16, 239, 288; lexical and grammatical meaning 89–90
corpus linguistics 53
correctness 9–11
Coupland, N. 31
creole 78, 204, 206–12; continuum from pidgin 206; as a primary language 206
criticism 238
Crystal, D. 138–41
cultural background 189

Danet, B. 138
declaratives 8, 63–4
deixis 20
dementia 160, 169–72; grammatical characteristics 276; language change 276
demonstratives 149
denials 106–7
deontic modality 66

linguistic context 173; and interlanguage
    development 175–8
linguistic features: communicative function
    144; of a genre 42–3
linguistic form: analysis of 18; descriptive and
    analytical 194
lists 266
literature (Unit B4) 135–50; role of
    language 135–8; traditional writing 135,
    141
local linguistic context 20–1, 94
local situational context (Unit A3) 22, 26–33;
    and language 26–8
Lock, G. 46
*Longman Grammar of Spoken and Written
    English (LGSWE)* (Biber) 8, 11, 12, 82
*Louvain International Database of Spoken
    English Interlanguage (Lindsei)* 288
Lowth, R. 9

Macaulay, R. 197–202
McCarthy, M. 13, 59, 84, 94–101
main clauses 5
Malcolm, I. 78–9
Malinowski, B. 26
Marley, C. 154–8
Master, P. 178–80
material processes 57, 138
meaning potential 160, 163–4
mediation 109–10
medical discourse 112–16
mental processes 58, 60, 138
mental verbs 107
*Michigan Corpus of Academic Spoken English
    (MICASE)* 253
Miller, J. 187
mission statements 44–5, 235–6
modal verbs 66
modality 56, 63, 66–8; *see also* deontic
    modality; epistemic modality;
    semi-modals
modality markers 67–8
modals 128–9; frequency of 86; of obligation
    123; prediction & necessity 148
mode 28
modes of expression 122
mood 7, 50, 56, 63–4, 131
motherese *see* baby talk
moves 40–1, 226, 290; analysis 225; frequency
    295–7; and gender 293–5; identification of
    228–31; level of 291
MSN Messenger 254

naming 161–2
narratives 94, 95–6, 98, 100, 137, 270
national culture 42–4; and grammar 34–6;
    and language 34–6
Nattinger, J.R. 96
naturalistic learners 175
negatives 31, 106–7; multiple 182
nesting *see* embedding
Netspeak 138–41; evolution of 139; as a third
    medium 141; and traditional writing 141
Newbrook, M. 209–12
Nickerson, C. 42
node *see* keyword
nominal clauses 273
nominalisation 60–2, 118, 121, 253; and
    compressing information 61
non-clausal units 8, 101–4
non-contrastive focusing device 187–8
Nordberg, B. 188
noun phrases 5, 6, 265–6, 273; coordination
    of 233; tags 105
nouns 5, 120, 207; common noun-proper
    noun distinction 179

object 6, 57
object participant 58
observer's paradox 275
occupational groups: and grammar 36–42;
    and language 36–42
Ochs, E. 23
opinions 238
orthographic word 103
overtures 101, 103–4

Painter, C. 160–5
paralinguistic features 217
parallel concordances 86
parallel corpora 86–7
participants 27, 29, 57; mood choice 64;
    multiple roles 24; role relations 58–60, 64;
    roles 58, 109–10, 163
passive: agentless 148; *get* 13
past continuous 99–100
past participal clauses 148
past simple 100
past tense 147; non-standard 182
pattern grammar 53–4
Pätzold, M. 204–9, 306
Pearson, J. 252
pedagogical grammars 9–10
perfective aspect 147
personal pronouns 56, 64–5, 207; and

Widdowson, H. 180
wider linguistic context 21–2
wider socio-cultural context (Unit A4) 22,
    34–45, 79, 111
Willis, D. 29
Wolfram, W. 183
word classes 5, 285–7
word order inversions 151

Worldwide Web 139–41
Wouk, F. 189
written corpus 303
written text, and conversation 216–24

Yallop, C. 34
Yamada, H. 44